GUIDE TO
HOTELS
AND
COUNTRY INNS
OF CHARACTER

IN FRANCE

CW00369994

GUIDE TO
HOTELS AND COUNTRY INNS
OF CHARACTER AND CHARM
IN FRANCE

Founding editors Michelle Gastaut,
Jean de Beaumont, Martin Wolff,
Bruno Guiblet, Pascal de Peyrelongue

Editorial director Michelle Gastaut

RIVAGES

© Copyright 1993 by Editions Rivages
106 Boulevard St Germain, 75006 Paris
10 Rue Fortia, 13001 Marseille

English translation by Marie Elise Palmier Chatelaine,
Edmund Swinglehurst and Christina Thistlethwayte

Editions Rivages is represented in the UK by
Bay View Books Ltd, Bideford, EX39 2QE

ISBN 1 870979 36 2
Printed in Italy

INTRODUCTION

This guide contains 491 addresses, all selected for their charm, quality of welcome, food and good hotelkeeping. The establishments included range from the comparatively simple to the luxurious, and the text will be your guide to what category any of the hotels falls into.

Before making your reservation, remember that you cannot expect as much of a room costing 200F as you can of one costing 400F or more. Please also note that the prices given were quoted to us at the end of 1992 and may of course be revised by the hoteliers during the year.

We recommend that when you make your reservation you ask for the exact prices for half board (*demi-pension*) and full board (*pension*) as they can vary depending on the number in your party and the length of the stay.

Two other things to take note of: firstly, that half board is often obligatory; and secondly that rooms are generally held only until 6 or 7pm, so if you are going to be late, let the hotel know.

STAR RATING

The classification of a hotel – the number of stars – is something the hotelier has to ask for. If he does, an official body assigns stars, from 1 to 4. This classification takes account of the comfort of the hotel, above all the number of bathrooms and toilets in relation to the number of rooms. This star rating has nothing at all to do with 'subjective' criteria such as charm or quality of welcome, which we do take into account. Some of the hotels in this guide have no stars – and that is because the hoteliers have never asked for them.

HOW TO USE THE GUIDE

We have listed the hotels by regions, and within each region in alphabetical order of *départements* and districts. The number of the page on which a hotel is described is the number appearing on the flag on the road map to show its position, and is also used in the contents list and index.

PLEASE LET US KNOW...

If you are impressed by a small hotel or inn not featured here which you think ought to be included, let us know so that we can visit it.

Please also tell us if you are disappointed by one of our choices. Write to our UK office: Rivages Guides, c/o Bay View Books Ltd, 13a Bridgeland Street, Bideford, EX39 2QE.

CONTENTS LIST

CONTENTS

P A R I S

A Q U I T A I N E

B O U R G O G N E

B R E T A G N E

C E N T R E

C H A M P A G N E - P I C A R D I E

C   O   R   S   E

F R A N C H E - C O M T É

I L E - D E - F R A N C E

L A N G U E D O C - R O U S S I L L O N

NORD - PAS - DE - CALAIS

P A Y S   D E   L A   L O I R E

P O I T O U - C H A R E N T E S

P R O V E N C E - C O T E   D ' A Z U R

R H O N E - A L P E S

Prices shown in brackets are prices for a double room, sometimes with half board. For precise details, go to the page mentioned.

KEY TO THE MAPS

Scale: 1:1,000,000
Maps 30 & 31: scale: 1:1,180,000

MOTORWAYS

❶ Interchange
❷ Half-interchange
❸ Toll-barrier

Kilometre-distance
❶ in total
❷ partial

Motorway
❶ under construction
❷ projected

ROAD CLASSIFICATION

Dual-carriageways

High traffic road

Trunk road

Other road

Road ❶ under construction
❷ projected

TOWNS CLASSIFICATION

❶ by the population

— less than 10.000 inhabitants
— from 10.000 to 30.000
— from 30.000 to 50.000
— from 50.000 to 100.000
— more than 100.000
— towns with over 50.000 inh.

❷ Administrative
— Chief-town of department

TARBES

— Main subdivision of department

CARPENTRAS

— Districts

Combeaufontaine

— Commune, hamlet

Andrézieux-Bouthéon

ROAD WIDTH

4 carriageways

3 lane or
2 wide lane
2 lane

Narrow road
Kilometre-distance
❶ in total
❷ partial

BOUNDARIES

National boundary

County boundary

TOURISM

Picturesque locality

Chenonceaux

Very picturesque locality

Amboise∗

Interesting site or natural curiosity

Roches de Ham

Historic castle
Ruins of outstanding beauty
Abbey
National park

DIVERS

Civil Airport
Dam

Canal
Car-ferries

Motorail

Pass
1045

Summit
▲ 2392

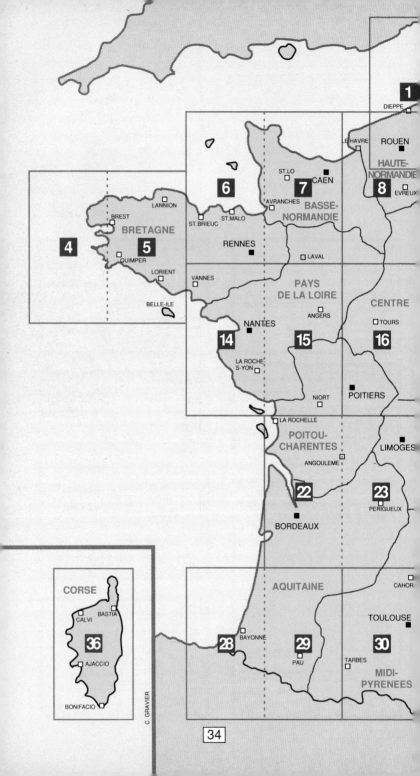

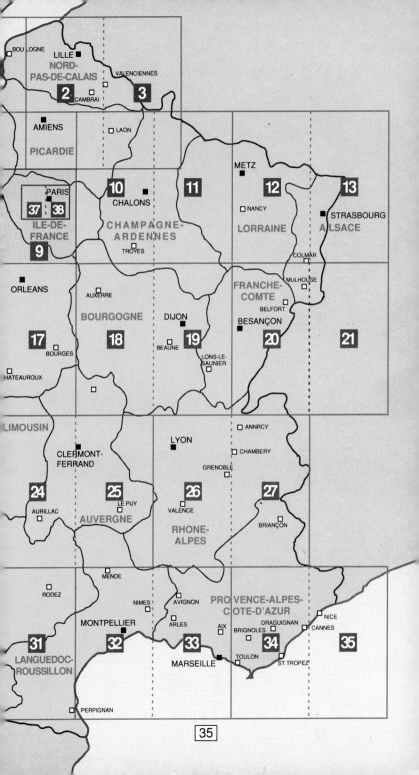

BOULOGNE

LILLE
**NORD-
PAS-DE-CALAIS**

2

CAMBRAI

VALENCIENNES

3

AMIENS

LAON

PICARDIE

METZ

10

11

12

STRASBOURG

13

PARIS

37 **38**

CHALONS

NANCY

**ILE-DE-
FRANCE**

9

**CHAMPAGNE-
ARDENNES**

LORRAINE

ALSACE

TROYES

COLMAR

ORLEANS

AUXERRE

**FRANCHE-
COMTE**

MULHOUSE

BOURGOGNE

DIJON

BELFORT

BESANÇON

17

18

19

20

21

BOURGES

BEAUNE

LONS-LE-
SAUNIER

CHATEAUROUX

LIMOUSIN

ANNRCY

LYON

CHAMBERY

CLERMONT-
FERRAND

GRENOBLE

24

25

26

27

AURILLAC

LE PUY

AUVERGNE

VALENCE

BRIANÇON

**RHONE-
ALPES**

MENDE

RODEZ

PROVENCE-ALPES-
COTE-D'AZUR

NIMES

AVIGNON

NICE

MONTPELLIER

ARLES

AIX

DRAGUIGNAN

CANNES

BRIGNOLES

31

32

33

34

35

**LANGUEDOC-
ROUSSILLON**

MARSEILLE

TOULON

ST.TROPEZ

PERPIGNAN

35

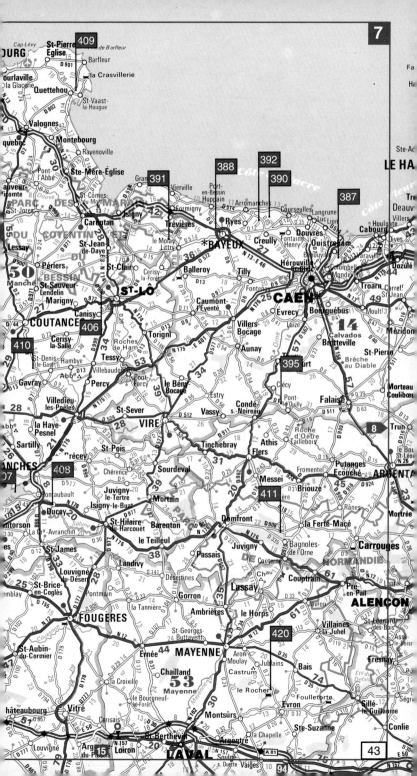

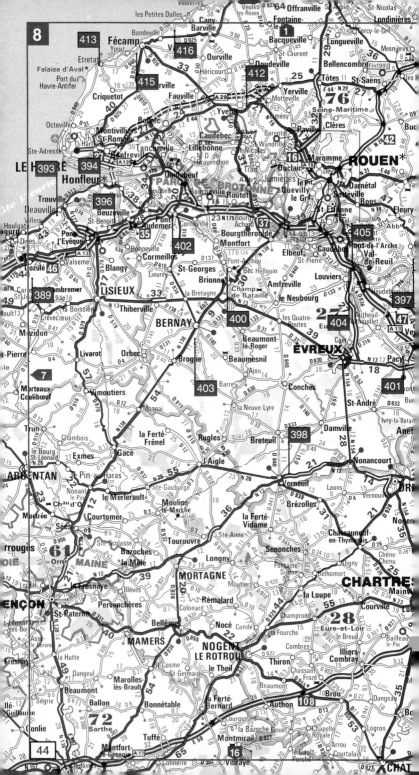

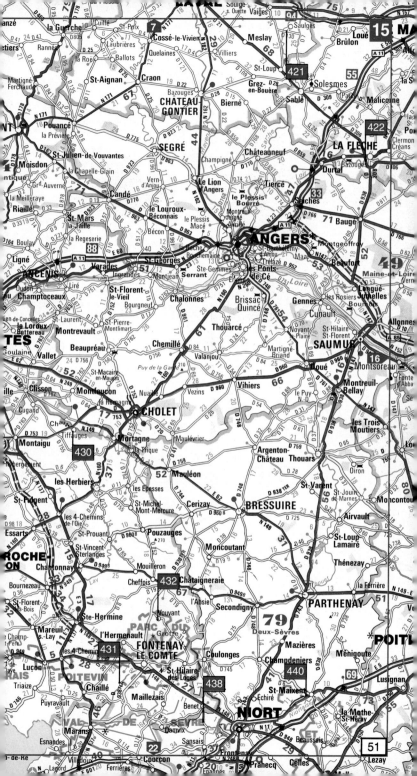

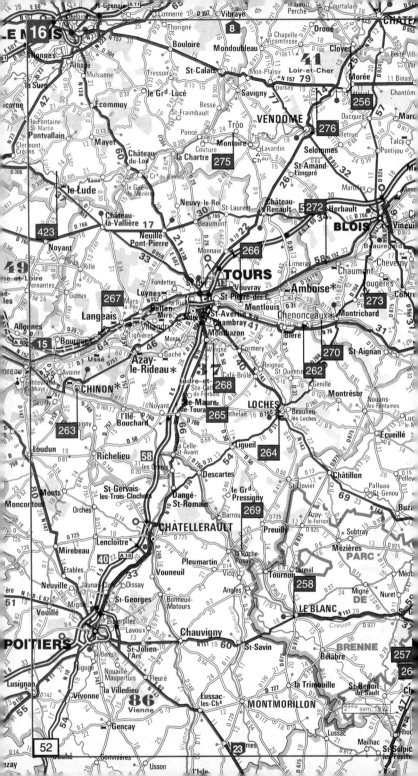

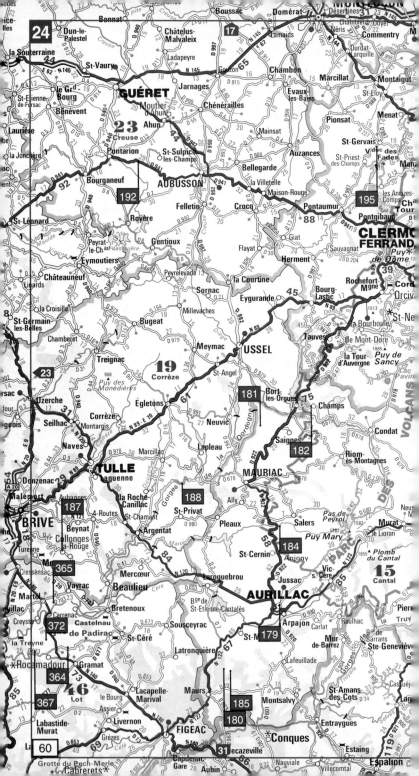

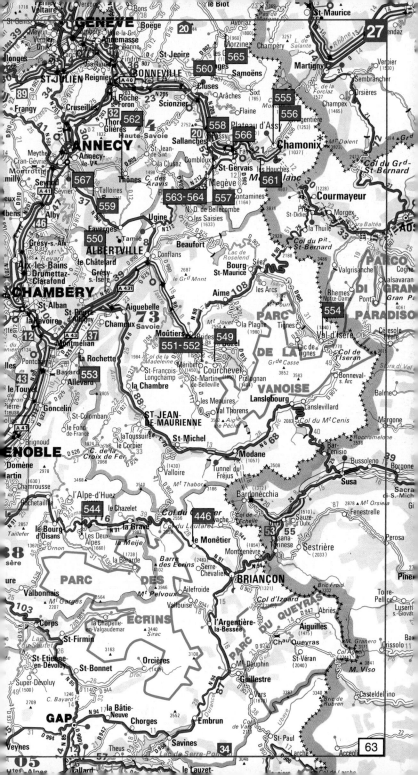

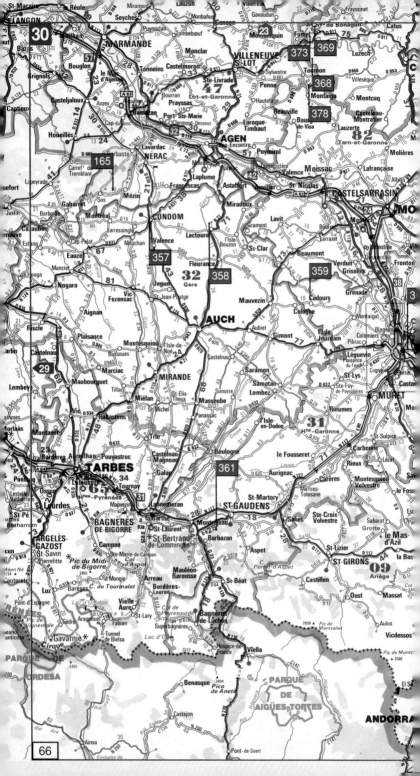

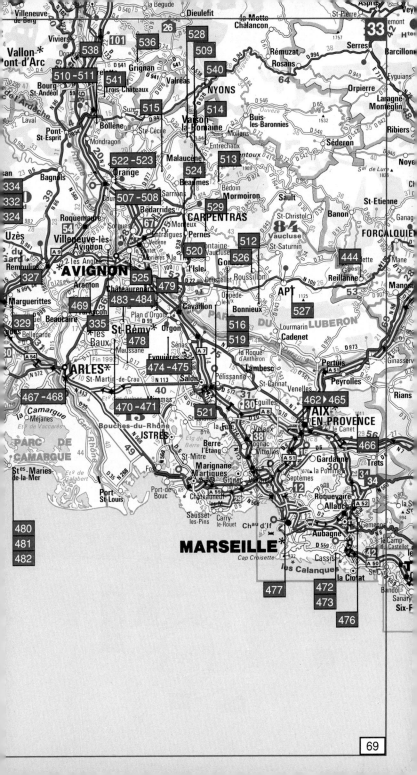

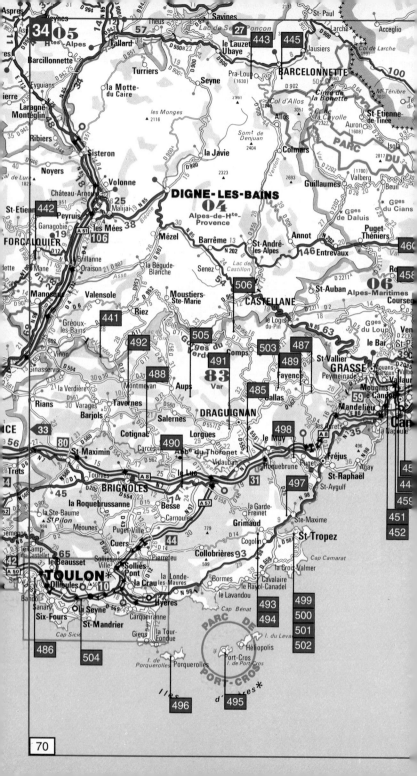

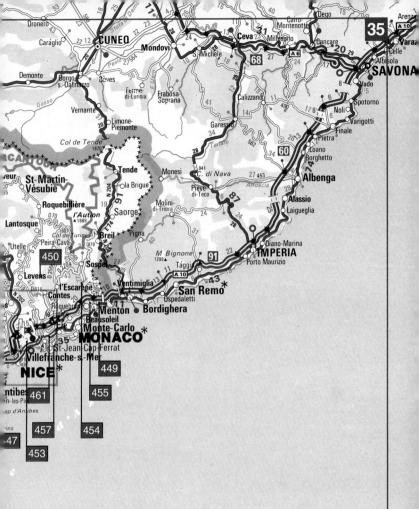

Cap Corse

Ile de la Giraglia

302

Rogliano

Pino · Sta-Sévera
Luri · D 180

Canari · D 80

Nonza · Bran · Erbalunga

303

San-Martino-di-Lota

BASTIA

Désert des Agriates

St-Florent · Oletta

Santo-Pietro-di-Tenda

Ste-Michele

l'Ile-Rousse · N 197

297-298-299

301

CALVI

Algajola

St-Antonino · Belgodère

Lama · Murato · Borgo · la Canonica

Campitello · Casamozza

Olmi-Cappella · Castifao

Calenzana · Vescovato

300

Asco · Ponte · Folelli

Gorges · Leccia · Pero-Casevecchie

Popolasca · Campile · la Porta · D 506

Muro · Aregno · D 71

Olivi

M¹ Cinto · Francardo

2707

Morosaglia · Piedicroce · San-Nicolao

San-Lorenzo · Cervione

293 **296**

Girolata

Calacuccia · Omessa · Valle-d'Alesani · Pietra-di-Verde

292

Porto* · CORTE · Sermano

Col de Vergio · Casamaccioli · Moïta

1464 · Piedicorte

Piana · Evisa

Venaco · Vezzani

Soccia · D 16

294 · Vico · Guagno-les-Bains · Vivario · Ghisoni · Aleria

Cargèse · Salice · M¹ d'Oro · 2391

Sagone · Vizzavona

85 · Bocognano

Sari-d'Orcino · Mᵗᵉ Renoso · Prunelli-di-Fiumorbo

Carbuccia · 2351

Carrola-Carcopino · **2A** · Bastelica

la Punta · **CORSE - DU - SUD**

AJACCIO

Iles Sanguin

295

288

Cauro · Frasseto · Zicavo · Solenzara

Chiavari · Bicchisano · Petreto · *Col de Bavella* · 1243

Acqua Doria · Aullène

Filitosa · Serra-di-Scopamène · Zonza

Porto-Pollo · Olmeto · Levie · San-Gavino-di-Garbini

Propriano · Ste-Lucie-de-Tallano

291

Campomoro · **SARTÈNE**

Cauria · N 196 · Porto-Vecchio

Iles Cerbicale

Figari · N 198

recta foldex

Copyright RECTA FOLDEX

Bonifacio · Ile de Cavallo

289-290 · Ile de Lavezzi

S. Teresa · Gallura

C. Testa · la Maddalena

CARTES
RECTA FOLDEX
POUR VOYAGER
EN FRANCE ET DANS
LE MONDE ENTIER

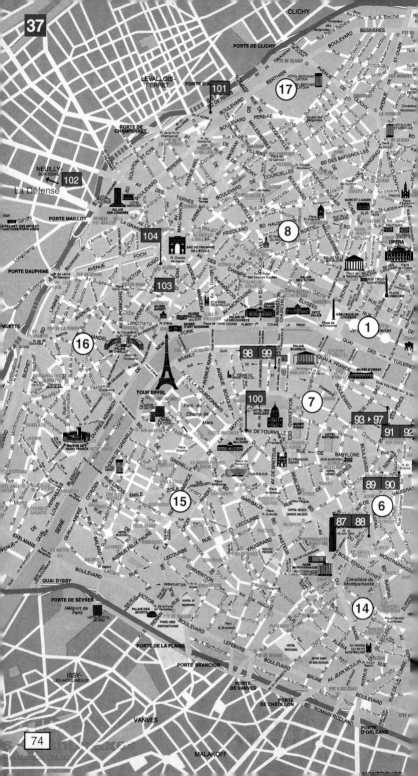

Hôtel de Notre-Dame★★★

19, rue Maître-Albert – 75005 Paris
Tel. (1) 43.26.79.00 – Fax (1) 46.33.50.11
M. Fouhety

Open all year. **Rooms** 34 with bath or shower and WC, soundproofing, telephone, cable TV, hairdryer, minibar. **Price** double 650-790F. **Meals** breakfast 40F with orange juice, no restaurant. **Credit cards** not accepted. **Pets** no dogs allowed. **Parking** at 1 Rue Lagrange. **Services** bookings, laundry, dry cleaning.

You will have no difficulty in spotting the Hôtel de Notre-Dame, in a small street typical of this old quarter of Paris: its wide frontage was once the window of a shop on the ground floor of the building. In the hotel, which has recently been refurbished, partition walls have been put up without spoiling the original beamed ceilings. Louis XIII-style furniture, antiques, and a fine tapestry lend a strong period atmosphere to the reception, bar and sitting areas. The bedrooms are attractively furnished and have all the modern comforts and facilities, including spacious bathrooms. Its position close to Notre-Dame, and the quais of the Seine, with their barges and second-hand booksellers, adds to the hotel's many charms.

How to get there (Map 38): Metro Saint-Michel, RER Cluny-Saint-Michel, Bus 21, 24, 27, 38, 47, 85, 96.

Hôtel Esmeralda★★

4, rue Saint-Julien-le-Pauvre - 75005 Paris
Tel. (1) 43.54.19.20 - Fax (1) 40. 51. 00. 68
Mme Bruel

Open all year. **Rooms** 19 with bath or shower or basin and WC, telephone. No lift.
Price double 320-480F, suite 520-620F. **Meals** breakfast 45F (in rooms, no breakfast
room), no restaurant. **Credit cards** not accepted. **Pets** dogs allowed. **Parking** at 1
Rue Lagrange, Maubert and Notre-Dame. **Services** bookings.

Many a passer-by must wonder, on walking through the
cloisters of the tiny church of Saint-Julien-le-Pauvre, what
the subdued lighting and the air of privacy of this house conceal:
a private dwelling or an antique shop? Indeed it could be both,
were it not for the fact that Mme Bruel receives guests. Throughout
the hotel, flowery wall-papers, hexagonal floor-tiles and waxed
wood floors, period furniture and curios, create a charmingly old-
fashioned atmosphere. You will want to book one of the bedrooms
with a view of Notre-Dame, which, incidentally, are also the most
comfortable (some can even accommodate a family of four). But
the rooms overlooking the courtyard are just as charming, and even
more reasonably price. This is a truly delightful hotel.

How to get there *(Map 38): Metro Saint-Michel, RER Cluny-Saint-Michel,
Bus 21, 24, 27, 38, 47, 85, 96.*

Hôtel des Deux Iles★★★

59, rue Saint-Louis-en-l'Ile - 75004 Paris
Tel. (1) 43. 26. 13. 35 - Fax (1) 43. 29. 60. 25
Mme Buffat

Open all year. **Rooms** 17 with bath or shower and WC, soundproofing, telephone, TV, hairdryer. **Price** single 650F, double 750F. **Meals** breakfast 37F, snacks available. **Credit cards** not accepted. **Pets** dogs not allowed. **Parking** at 2 Rue Geoffroy-l'Asnier and square in front of Notre-Dame. **Services** bookings, laundry, dry cleaning.

Monsieur and Mme Buffat have converted two buildings into charming hotels between a former archbishop's palace, the Church of Saint-Louis-en-l'Ile, and Bertillot, famous as makers of the best ice creams in Paris. We have chosen this one for its atmosphere, English with a tinge of exoticism: flowery fabrics and painted cane and bamboo furniture are the main features of the decor, which is predominantly yellow and blue. The bedrooms are not very large, but delightful. Provençal fabrics replace the chintzes used in the lounge, and the en-suite bathrooms are lined with warm blue tiles. Everything here is comfortable and cosy, including the fine vaulted breakfast room. This hotel has a faithful following with foreign guests, and often there are no vacancies. If this is the case, you might be able to book a room in the Hôtel de Lutèce just next door, which is an attractive place too.

How to get there *(Map 38): Metro Pont-Marie, Bus 24, 63, 67, 86, 87.*

Hôtel de Nesle★
7, rue de Nesle – 75006 Paris
Tel. (1) 43. 54. 62. 41
Mme Busillet

Open all year. **Rooms** 20 with shower or basin and WC. **Price** single and double 190-360F. **Meals** breakfast incl., no restaurant. **Credit cards** not accepted. **Pets** dogs allowed. **Parking** at 27 Rue Mazarine. **Services** laundry.

It is hard to find better prices than at this small hotel, which is very popular with foreign guests. A room here, in the middle of the Quartier Latin, with its own shower room, will cost you less than 300 francs! The hotel is very simple, but each bedroom has been individually decorated by Mme Busille. For a small extra charge you can treat yourself to the 'Arabe', 'Egyptienne' or 'Molière' bedrooms: they are larger, and have impeccable bathrooms. On the first floor, there is a little garden for guests. A friendly and informal atmosphere prevails.

How to get there *(Map 38): Metro Odéon, RER Cluny-Saint-Michel, Bus 24, 27, 58, 63, 70, 86, 87, 96.*

Hôtel des Grandes Ecoles★★

75, rue du Cardinal-Lemoine - 75005 Paris
Tel. (1) 43.26.79.23 - Fax (1) 43.25.28.15
Mme Le Floch

Open all year. **Rooms** 48 with bath or shower or basin and WC, telephone. **Price** single 300-350F, double 450-600F. **Meals** breakfast 35F, no restaurant. **Credit cards** Visa. **Pets** dogs allowed. **Parking** at 20 Rue Soufflot and Place du Panthéon. **Facilities** garden. **Services** bookings.

This family-run hotel certainly owes some of its charm to its garden, a patch of countryside in the Quartier Latin. Only two of the three houses which originally stood on the site remain, and they are being gradually refurbished. Although the comfort of the larger bedrooms has been improved, and all now have en-suite bathrooms, the smaller ones, which have retained their ancient 'toile de Jouy' fabrics and 19th-century furniture, have far more character (but only closets with a wash-basin). Breakfast is served in the rustic style dining-room in the main building, and in the garden as soon as the weather is fine enough.

How to get there *(Map 38): Metro Cardinal-Lemoine and Monge, RER Luxembourg, Bus 47, 84, 89.*

Hôtel des Grands Hommes★★★

17, place du Panthéon - 75005 Paris
Tel. (1) 46.34.19.60 - Fax (1) 43.26.67.32
Mlle Brethous

Open all year. **Rooms** 32 with bath and WC, telephone, cable TV, hairdryer, minibar. **Price** single 600F, double 730F. **Meals** breakfast 35F with orange juice, no restaurant. **Credit cards** accepted. **Pets** dogs allowed. **Parking** at 20 Rue Soufflot and Place du Panthéon. **Services** bookings, laundry, dry cleaning.

The Hôtel des Grands Hommes draws its name from those great men of the French nation who, starting with Mirabeau, Voltaire and Victor Hugo, have been buried in the Panthéon. The reception area, with its ornate mouldings, 1930s armchairs and subtle orange pink colour scheme, sets the style for the entire building, which has recently been renovated. The atmosphere is both classic and refined. Delicate colour tones have also been used in the bedrooms, which have brass beds and bathrooms tiled in beige. The most charming rooms are those located on the top floor of the building, with sloping ceilings and balconies looking out onto the Place du Panthéon. The Hôtel du Panthéon just next door is run by the same family and is also a good hotel. Although more traditional in style, it is just as welcoming.

How to get there *(Map 38): Metro Cardinal-Lemoine, RER Luxembourg, Bus 21, 27, 38, 82, 84, 85, 89.*

Hôtel des Trois Collèges★★

16, rue Cujas - 75005 Paris
Tel. (1) 43.54.67.30 - Fax (1) 46.34.02.99

Open all year. **Rooms** 44 with bath or shower and WC, sound-proofing, telephone, hairdryer. **Price** single 350-490F, double 420-590F, suite 750F. **Meals** breakfast 40F with orange juice, no restaurant. **Credit cards** Amex, Diners, Visa. **Pets** dogs not allowed. **Parking** at 20 Rue Soufflot. **Services** bookings, laundry, dry cleaning.

The most famous seat of learning on the Montagne-Sainte-Geneviève is La Sorbonne, founded in the 13th century. The Collège Saint-Barbe, created in the 15th century, is the most ancient private school in France. As for the Collège de France, it has the most prestigious professorial chairs in the land. In the shadow of these illustrious and historic buildings stands the small and discreet Hôtel des Trois Collèges. Simplicity is the key-word: the decoration is deliberately sober in style, and white is the dominant colour. The bedrooms are comfortable and fully equipped, with pretty bathrooms or shower rooms. The largest rooms are on the top floor and overlook the Sorbonne and the Panthéon. Breakfast here is delicious and includes home-made jams. It is served in a pleasant little dining-room where an old well has been preserved.

How to get there *(Map 38): Metro Saint-Michel, RER Luxembourg and Cluny-Saint-Michel, Bus 21, 27, 38, 63, 82, 84, 86, 87.*

Hôtel Résidence Henri IV★★★

50, rue des Bernardins - 75005 Paris
Tel. (1) 44. 41.31.81 – Fax (1) 46.33.93.22
Famille Brethous

Open all year. **Rooms** 14 (of which 5 are apartments) with bath and WC, telephone, cable TV, hairdryer and minibar. **Price** double 900F, apartment 1200F. **Meals** breakfast 40F, no restaurant. **Credit cards** accepted. **Pets** dogs allowed. **Parking** at 1 Rue Lagrange. **Services** bookings, laundry, dry cleaning.

This quiet hotel in a shady square turns its back on the hustle and bustle of the Boulevard Saint-Michel. Its 19th-century facade is rather ornate but lends it character. The hotel has just been refurbished and the new management is extremely efficient. The bedrooms have been designed mainly for long stays, or to accommodate families: some of them can be turned into apartments, and all have a kitchenette. The decoration is classic in style and shows attention to detail. The stuccoed ceilings and marble chimneypieces have been preserved, and the mouldings, painted to match the dominant colour in the rooms, stand out against white walls. The type of accommodation the hotel offers is well worth considering, all the more so as there are special reduced rates for week-long stays.

How to get there *(Map 38): Metro Cardinal-Lemoine and Maubert-Mutualité, RER Cluny-Saint-Michel, Bus 47, 63, 86, 87.*

Résidence des Gobelins★★

9, rue des Gobelins – 75013 Paris
Tel. (1) 47.07.26.90 – Fax (1) 43.31.44.05
M. and Mme Poirier

Open all year. **Rooms** 32 with bath or shower and WC, telephone, TV. **Price** single 350F, double 390-420F. **Meals** breakfast 35F with orange juice, no restaurant. **Credit cards** accepted. **Pets** dogs allowed. **Parking** at 60 Boulevard Saint-Marcel and 1 Rue Lagrange. **Facilities** patio. **Services** bookings.

Close to the 'Manufacture Royale des Gobelins' after which it is named, this hotel is a haven of peace in a busy, colourful neighbourhood. The Rue Mouffetard and its popular, bustling market are within short walking distance, as well as the souks, hammams, cafés and restaurants surrounding the Mosquée de Paris (the city's oldest and most important mosque). The decoration of the hotel is bright and pleasant. In the bedrooms bamboo furniture sets the style and imposes the colour scheme. Some of the rooms on the upper floors command pretty views of the courtyard and of a garden, and those on the top floor have sloping ceilings. The breakfast room leads out into a flowery patio with teak furniture. A friendly welcome.

How to get there (Map 38): Metro Gobelins, RER Port-Royal, Bus 27, 47, 83, 91.

Hôtel du Parc Montsouris★★

4, rue du Parc-Montsouris - 75014 Paris
Tel. (1) 45.89.09.72 - Fax (1) 45.80.92.72
M. Grand and Mme Piguet

Open all year. **Rooms** 35 with bath or shower and WC, telephone, TV, minibar. **Price** single and double 310-420F, suite 470F. **Meals** breakfast 35F with orange juice, snacks available. **Credit cards** Amex, Diners, Visa. **Pets** dogs tolerated. **Parking** in private road. **Facilities** conference room. **Services** laundry, bookings.

A stay in this part of the 14th arrondissement will show you a new side of Paris, with its quiet cul-de-sacs, and 1930s villas, among them some interesting creations by Sauvage, Le Corbusier and Lurçat. But the 14th arrondissement also boasts two big parks: the one surrounding the international student residence, and the Parc Montsouris. The Hôtel du Parc Montsouris has been set up in one of those villas, near the park. It has been fully renovated, and its columns and Art Deco paintings convey something of the original atmosphere of the house. The decoration is classic in style, and the bedrooms and bathrooms are comfortably fitted. The neighbourhood is quiet, which is an advantage in Paris.

How to get there *(Map 37): Metro Porte d'Orléans, RER Cité Universitaire. Bus for Orly from Porte d'Orléans. Bus PC, 27, 47.*

Hôtel Danemark★★★

21, rue Vavin – 75006 Paris
Tel. (1) 43.26.93.78 – Fax (1) 46.34.66.06
M. and Mme Nurit

Open all year. **Rooms** 15 with bath and WC, sound-proofing, telephone, TV, hairdryer and minibar. **Price** single and double 660-760F. **Meals** breakfast 40F with orange juice and cheese, snacks available. **Credit cards** Amex, Diners, Visa. **Pets** dogs allowed. **Parking** at 116 Boulevard de Montparnasse. **Facilities** possibility of jacuzzi, small conference room. **Services** bookings, laundry, dry cleaning.

The Hôtel Danemark stands just opposite the remarkable 'maison à gradins sportive' (house with a tiered facade) which is covered in white ceramic tiling and was built in 1912 by Sauvage. Maybe as a tribute to that building, or simply as a reminder of Danish enthusiasm for contemporary design, the decoration of this hotel is resolutely modern in style. Bright and strongly contrasting colours have been chosen for the reception and sitting area. A more subdued colour scheme prevails in the bedrooms, to match 1930s furniture. There are few rooms, all extremely comfortable and well soundproofed. You will find a friendly and attentive welcome.

How to get there *(Map 37): Metro Vavin and Notre-Dame-des-Champs, RER Port-Royal, Bus 58, 68, 75, 82, 83, 91.*

Hôtel Ferrandi★★★

92, rue du Cherche-Midi - 75006 Paris
Tel. (1) 42.22.97.40 - Fax (1) 45.44.89.97
Mme Lafond

Open all year. **Rooms** 41 and 1 suite, with bath or shower and WC, soundproofing, telephone, TV, hairdryer. **Price** double 440-920F, suite 950-1200F. **Meals** breakfast 60F with fresh fruit juices and traditional jams, light meals available. **Credit cards** Amex, Diners, Visa. **Pets** dogs allowed. **Parking** garage at hotel (110F per day) and at Bon Marché. **Services** bookings, laundry, dry cleaning.

As soon as you walk through the door of this hotel you will be charmed by the welcome, even before you can take in all its other qualities. The reception rooms are vast and decorated in Restoration style, with mahogany furniture and lavishly draped hangings. The bedrooms are also spacious, and no two of them are alike. In each one, a different bed has provided the style and colour scheme for the decor. The bathrooms are perfect. The Hôtel Ferrandi stands just opposite the delightful hôtel de Montmorency, which now houses the works of the 19th-century French artist Ernest Hébert. You might take the opportunity to discover him...

How to get there (Map 37): Metro Saint-Placide and Sèvres-Babylone, Bus 39, 48, 84, 89, 94, 95, 96.

Hôtel de l'Abbaye Saint-Germain★★★

10, rue Cassette – 75006 Paris
Tel. (1) 45.44.38.11 – Fax (1) 45.48.07.86
M. Lafortune

Open all year. **Rooms** 42 and 4 suites (duplex with terrace and minibar) with bath, WC and telephone. TV in larger rooms and suites. **Price** standard room 800-900F, large room 1500F, duplex or apartment 660-1900F. **Meals** breakfast incl., snacks available. **Credit cards** Amex, Diners, Visa. **Pets** dogs not allowed. **Parking** at Place Saint-Sulpice. **Facilities** patio, bar. **Services** bookings, laundry, dry cleaning.

The latest refurbishment of the Hôtel de l'Abbaye has further enhanced its charm and character. The ground floor has been restructured to make the best of the view onto the patio and the elaborate green lattice-work covering its walls. It is full of flowers, and breakfast and drinks can be served there, weather permitting. In the new lounge, deep sofas tempt one to relax by the fireplace. The decoration of the bedrooms, in subtle shades, is elegant and refined. The rooms vary in size: the larger ones are those at garden level, the duplexes with a terrace, and the most recently renovated ones. The location of the hotel, close to the Place Saint-Sulpice and the Jardin du Luxembourg, is another attractive feature.

How to get there *(Map 37): Metro Saint-Sulpice and Sèvres-Babylone, Bus 48, 63, 70, 84, 87, 95, 96.*

Hôtel de l'Odéon★★★

13, rue Saint-Sulpice - 75006 Paris
Tel. (1) 43.25.70.11 - Fax (1) 43.29.97.34
M. and Mme Pilfert

Open all year. **Rooms** 30 with bath or shower and WC, soundproofing, telephone, cable TV, hairdryer and safe. Air-conditioning in some rooms. **Price** single 580F, double 710-830F, suite 940F. **Meals** breakfast 42F, snacks available. **Credit cards** accepted. **Pets** dogs allowed. **Parking** at Place Saint-Sulpice and opposite 21 Rue de l'Ecole-de-Médecine. **Services** bookings, laundry, dry cleaning.

This fine 16th-century building accommodates a skilful blend of decorative styles. Thus, in the ground-floor lounges, Louis-Philippe period wing chairs and pedestal tables rub shoulders with a large church pew, and Persian rugs with a flowery English fitted carpet, creating a warm and cosy atmosphere. The bedrooms are all individually decorated and you can choose among stately rooms with four-poster beds, or romantic rooms with large brass beds or Sicilian painted iron twin beds. All have a sitting area. As this is the centre of Paris, the rooms overlooking the street are well soundproofed, and the more exposed ones have air-conditioning for the summer. Lavish amounts of care and attention have been devoted to creating a stunning decor.

How to get there *(Map 37): Metro Odéon, Saint-Sulpice and Saint-Germain-des-Prés, RER Cluny-Saint-Michel, Bus 58, 63, 70, 86, 87, 96.*

Hôtel Les Marronniers★★★

21, rue Jacob - 75006 Paris
Tel. (1) 43.25.30.60 - Fax (1) 40.46.83.56
M. Henneveux

Open all year. **Rooms** 37 with bath or shower and WC (of which 4 for 3/4 pers.). **Price** single and double 450-1170F. **Meals** breakfast 42F, no restaurant. **Credit cards** not accepted. **Pets** dogs not allowed. **Parking** opposite 169 Boulevard Saint-Germain and at Place Saint-Sulpice. **Services** bookings.

The Hôtel Les Marronniers is a truly delightful place, and its garden – a real garden in Paris! – is the height of luxury. An ornate Napoleon III verandah houses the lounge and breakfast room, its elegant decoration perfectly in tune with its character. The white cast iron garden furniture, flowery carpets and Austrian blinds in shades of pink and green would have met with Empress Eugénie's approval. The bedrooms and en-suite bathrooms are more conventional in style. To have a view of the garden your room has to be on at least the third floor and have a number ending in 1 or 2. The rooms on the fifth and sixth floors overlooking the courtyard also look out over the rooftops. Pleasant welcome.

How to get there (Map 37): Metro Saint-Germain-des-Prés, Bus 39, 48, 63, 68, 69, 86, 87, 95.

Hôtel d'Angleterre★★★

44, rue Jacob - 75006 Paris
Tel. (1) 42.60.34.72 - Fax (1) 42.60.16.93
Mme Soumier

Open all year. **Rooms** 29 with bath, WC, telephone, TV. **Price** single and double 850-1100F. **Meals** breakfast 45F with orange juice, no restaurant. **Credit cards** Amex, Diners, Visa. **Pets** dogs not allowed. **Parking** opposite 169 Boulevard Saint-Germain. **Services** bookings, laundry, dry cleaning.

This fine house has historic associations: the independence of the federated United States was acknowledged there. It is now a marvellous hotel, with high-ceilinged rooms, ornate panelling, ancient beams and antique furniture. The bedrooms are all individually decorated. In one of the most remarkable among them, a wall with exposed stonework provides a stunning backdrop for some beautiful items of 17th-century furniture, including a four-poster bed. It is worth noting that the largest rooms are those overlooking the garden. High standards of service prevail, and everything will be done to make your stay in Paris as pleasant as possible, including booking theatres and restaurants. An excellent address.

How to get there *(Map 37): Metro Saint-Germain des Prés, Bus 39, 48, 63, 70, 86, 87, 95, 96.*

Hôtel des Saints–Pères★★★

65, rue des Saints-Pères - 75006 Paris
Tel. (1) 45.44.50.00 - Fax (1) 45.44.90.83

Open all year. **Rooms** 37 rooms and suites with bath or shower and WC, soundproofing, telephone, TV, safe and minbar. **Price** single and double 450-1500F, suite 1500F. **Meals** breakfast 50F, snacks available. **Credit cards** Eurocard, MasterCard, Visa. **Pets** dogs not allowed. **Parking** opposite 169 Boulevard Saint-Germain. **Facilities** bar, patio. **Services** bookings, laundry, dry cleaning.

An atmosphere of elegance and comfort prevails in this fine establishment, a classic among Parisian hotels; not even the slightest details are overlooked by the staff and the attentive management. Simplicity and refinement are the key-words to the tasteful decoration of the spacious bedrooms and their bathrooms. Worthy of special note is the 'chambre à la fresque', which has retained its lovely period ceiling. Most of the rooms overlook the hotel patio, and the ground-floor reception rooms lead out into it: a delightful courtyard full of flowers, where comfortable cane chairs are set up in the shade in summer. The service is extremely efficient and professional.

How to get there *(Map 37): Metro Saint-Germain-des-Prés, Bus 39, 48, 63, 70, 84, 86, 87, 95.*

Hôtel de l'Université★★★

22, rue de l'Université - 75007 Paris
Tel. (1) 42.61.09.39 - Fax (1) 42.60.40.84
Mme Bergmann

Open all year. **Rooms** 27 with bath or shower and WC, telephone, TV and safe. **Price** single 600-650F, double 750-900F, apartment 1500F. **Meals** breakfast 45F, with fruit juice and cheese; snacks available. **Credit cards** not accepted. **Pets** dogs not allowed. **Parking** at 9 Rue de Montalembert and opposite 169 Boulevard Saint-Germain. **Facilities** bar. **Services** bookings, laundry, dry cleaning.

This is a fine hotel which owes its long-established and lasting reputation to an attentive and discriminating management committed to creating the atmosphere and charm of a family house rather than a hotel. The original vaulted ceilings, their oak supporting pillars, the staircase and the fireplaces have been preserved. A subtle ochre colour scheme has been chosen for the damasks and velvets covering the settees and antique chairs in the sitting rooms. The same colour scheme has been carried through to the bedrooms, which have period furniture and curios. Standards of service are high, and light meals can be served in the rooms.

How to get there *(Map 37): Metro Rue-du-Bac and Saint-Germain-des-Prés, RER Gare d'Orsay, Aérogare des Invalides, Bus 24, 27, 39, 48, 63, 68, 69, 70, 87, 95.*

Hôtel de Beaune★★

29, rue de Beaune – 75007 Paris
Tel. (1) 42.61.24.89 – Fax (1) 49.27.02.12
Mme Chelali

Open all year. **Rooms** 19 with bath or shower and WC, telephone. **Price** single and double 385-680F. **Meals** breakfast 35F, no restaurant. **Credit cards** Visa. **Pets** dogs allowed. **Parking** at 9 Rue Montalembert. **Facilities** bar. **Services** bookings, laundry, dry cleaning.

If you're looking for an inexpensive yet pleasant hotel in the Saint-Germain district, the Hôtel de Beaune is the place for you. Despite its apparent simplicity, the hotel is well-kept and tastefully decorated. The bedrooms are a little austere, with brass beds and bistro style tables and chairs, but quite pleasant. The bathrooms are small but fully equipped. Room 19 on the top floor has a lounge. Considering the quality of this hotel and its location, the prices are extremely reasonable.

How to get there *(Map 37): Metro Rue-du-Bac, RER Gare d'Orsay, Bus 24, 63, 68, 69, 83, 84, 94.*

Hôtel de l'Académie★★★

22, rue des Saints-Pères - 75007 Paris
Tel. (1) 45.48.36.22 - Fax (1) 45.44.75.24
M. Chekroun

Open all year. **Rooms** 34 with bath or shower and WC, telephone, satellite TV, hairdryer. **Price** single 580-670F, double 690-780F. **Meals** breakfast 45F, served 0700-1100; snacks available. **Credit cards** accepted. **Pets** dogs allowed. **Parking** opposite 169 Boulevard Saint-Germain. **Facilities** bar. **Services** bookings, laundry, dry cleaning.

Set in the heart of the Faubourg Saint Germain, just opposite the Medical Faculty in the Rue des Saints-Pères, the Hôtel de l'Académie is being handsomely refurbished. The Empire style motifs on the window boxes which stand out against the newly restored facade set the tone for the whole building. On the ground floor the layout of the rooms – reception and bar areas, a small lounge and a breakfast room – has been particularly well devised. There are fine items of 18th-century and Directoire style furniture, enhanced by original beams and ancient stonework, and perfectly matched by superb green and red fabrics. Pink and green are the dominant colours in the bedrooms, which all have fully equipped bathrooms. It is worth asking for a room overlooking the courtyard, as these are quieter. The only feature attracting criticism is the somewhat worn-out carpeting in the corridors, but this is bound to be changed soon. A car park is to be added to the hotel facilities: this certainly is an asset in Paris.

How to get there (Map 37): Metro Saint-Germain-des-Prés, Bus 34, 48, 63, 70, 84, 86, 87, 95.

Hôtel Bersoly's★★★

28, rue de Lille – 75007 Paris
Tel. (1) 42.60.73.79 – Fax (1) 49.27.05.55
Mme Carbonnaux

Open all year except 15-31 Aug. **Rooms** 16 with bath or shower and WC, soundproofing, telephone, cable TV, hairdryer, safe. **Price** single and double 550-650F. **Meals** breakfast 50F with fruit juice, snacks available. **Credit cards** Visa. **Pets** dogs allowed on reservation. **Parking** at 9 Rue de Montalembert and opposite 169 Boulevard Saint-Germain. **Facilities** bar. **Services** bookings, laundry, dry cleaning.

Bersoly's is a small hotel with an intimate atmosphere in an ancient building which still has its original stone floors. The Louis XIII furniture in the reception area is perfectly in tune with the rustic architecture of the house, the breakfast room in the vaulted cellars of the hotel is more exotic. The bedrooms are decorated in a charming, crisp, country style, and all have large fans which prove very useful in summer. The largest rooms are on the ground floor. You will find a warm and friendly welcome.

How to get there (Map 37): Metro Rue-du-Bac and Solférino, RER Gare d'Orsay. Aérogare des Invalides. Bus 24, 27, 39, 48, 63, 68, 69, 86, 87, 95.

Hôtel de la Tulipe★★

33, rue Malar – 75007 Paris
Tel. (1) 45.51.67.21 – Fax (1) 47.53.96.37
M. Fortuit

Open all year. **Rooms** 20 with bath or shower and WC, soundproofing, telephone, TV, minibar. **Price** single and double 478-528F. **Meals** breakfast 32F with cheese, no restaurant. **Credit cards** Amex, Eurocard, MasterCard, Visa. **Pets** dogs allowed. **Parking** at Esplanade des Invalides. **Facilities** patio. **Services** bookings, laundry, dry cleaning.

A delightful cobbled yard engulfed in greenery is all that remains of the convent that once was here. In keeping with the ancestry of the building, the decoration of this small hotel is rustic in style, with a beamed ceiling, Louis XIII style furniture and bunches of dried flowers in the reception area. The bedrooms, many of which have exposed stonework walls, are very quiet, owing to their position overlooking the courtyard, or to efficient soundproofing on the street side. The management is efficient and welcoming, and there is a friendly, informal atmosphere.

How to get there *(Map 37): Metro Latour-Maubourg and Invalides, RER Pont de l'Alma. Aérogare des Invalides. Bus 28, 49, 63, 69, 80, 83, 92.*

Hôtel Sainte-Dominique★★

62, rue Saint-Dominique - 75007 Paris
Tel. (1) 47.05.51.44 - Fax (1) 47.05.81.28
Mme Petit and M. Tible

Open all year. **Rooms** 34 with bath or shower and WC, telephone, TV, hairdryer, safe, minibar. **Price** single and double 470-500F, suite 600-700F. **Meals** breakfast 40F with orange juice and cheese, no restaurant. **Credit cards** accepted. **Pets** dogs allowed. **Parking** at Esplanade des Invalides. **Services** bookings, laundry, dry cleaning.

If the activity in the lobby is anything to go by, the Hôtel Saint-Dominique is in great demand. Its convenient location, recent renovation, and reasonable prices can certainly account for its success. There's an English flavour to the decor of the lobby, where the pale pine furniture blends with the soft colours of the walls and the pinkish beige fabrics. A charming country style has been chosen for the bedrooms, which have well equipped bathrooms. Some of the bedrooms are larger, with a sitting area, and most of them overlook patios full of flowers in summer. A place where life seems sweet.

How to get there *(Map 37): Metro Latour-Maubourg and Invalides, RER Pont de l'Alma. Aérogare des Invalides. Bus 28, 42, 49, 69, 80, 92.*

Splendid Hôtel★★★

29, av. de Tourville/1, av. Duquesne - 75007 Paris
Tel. (1) 47.51.24.77 - Telex 206879 - Fax (1) 44.18.94.60
Mme Bogacki

Open all year. **Rooms** 48 with bath or shower and WC, telephone, satellite TV, hairdryer, safe, minibar. **Price** single 490-520F, double 560-680F, suite 760F. **Meals** breakfast 42F, no restaurant. **Credit cards** accepted. **Pets** dogs allowed. **Parking** 40F. **Facilities** bar. **Services** bookings, laundry, dry cleaning.

Located in the posh residential area surrounding the Champ-de-Mars and the Invalides, the Splendid Hôtel has just been fully refurbished. The hotel entrance is in Rue de Tourville. The decoration of the ground floor, where the lobby and the bar are, is a mixture of 1930s and 40s, with a bold turquoise colour scheme: 1930s Art Deco for the chairs and frosted-glass tables, 1940s for the burr sycamore furniture specially designed for the hotel. Upstairs the decor is more subdued. The bedrooms and bathrooms are not very large for the most part, but all are comfortable and fully fitted. For more spacious accommodation you should ask for a double room with twin beds; or for one of the suites, which seem mainly intended for business men as they are equipped with sockets for fax and computer. Our favourite rooms, however, are the ones on the top floors of the building overlooking the Rue Duquesne, with views of the rooftops of the Ecole Militaire. Kind welcome.

How to get there *(Map 37): Metro Ecole Militaire. Aérogare des Invalides. Bus 28, 82, 92, 95.*

Hôtel de Banville★★★

166, boulevard Berthier -- 75017 Paris
Tel. (1) 42.67.70.16 - Fax (1) 44.40.42.77
Mme Lambert

Open all year. **Rooms** 39 with bath or shower and WC, telephone, TV, hairdryer. **Price** single 550-600F, double 700F. **Meals** breakfast 40F-70F, snacks available. **Credit cards** Amex, Eurocard, MasterCard, Visa. **Pets** dogs allowed. **Parking** at 10 Boulevard de l'Yser. **Facilities** bar. **Services** bookings, laundry, dry cleaning.

The Hôtel de Banville is a good establishment in the quarter around the Porte Maillot near the Palais des Congrès and the Etoile. The Rue Berthier is a quiet street lined with plane-trees, and the hotel is a small 1930s building. The ground floor has just been redecorated: the flowery chintzes have given way to a lavish striped Rubelli fabric which beautifully sets off the antique furniture in the lounge. A lift as old as the building leads to the upper floors. The bedrooms are bright and spacious and overlook the leafy boulevard. From the seventh floor up they have panoramic views. Breakfast here is no small matter. With the romantic trompe l'oeil decor as a setting, there are three breakfasts to choose from: the traditional 'continental' French breakfast, the 'diététique' or the 'pleine-forme'. A friendly welcome awaits guests. Cast in the image of its owner, the Hôtel de Banville is a hotel of taste.

How to get there *(Map 37): Metro Péreire and Porte-de-Champerret. Bus for Roissy-Charles-de-Gaulle at Porte Maillot. Bus 83, 84, 92, 93.*

Hôtel Marina George Sand★★★
18, avenue Marceau - 92400 Courbevoie-La Défense
Tel. (1) 43.33.57.04 - Fax (1) 47.88.59.38
Mme Teil

Open all year. **Rooms** 31 (of which 17 with bath and WC) with telephone, TV and minibar. **Price** single 395-450F, double 450-480F. **Meals** breakfast 37F, evening buffet available. **Credit cards** Amex, Visa, Diners. **Pets** dogs allowed. **Services** bookings, laundry, fax, photocopying.

We hesitated to include this hotel, as it is not in Paris itself but in the immediate suburbs, within easy walking distance (about 15 minutes) of the Arche de la Défense. But as a new business and office centre La Défense is an integral part of the capital, and is thus entitled to its 'hôtel de charme' too. This newly opened hotel is a veritable museum of the distinguished writer George Sand. The lounge and lobby have a romantic 19th-century decor with period furniture and souvenirs dating back to the writer's days, such as sculptures by David d'Angers and Jean-Baptiste Clesinger, a pastel of George Sand, some books and a letter which belonged to her, a portrait of Liszt, a bust of Chopin... The bedrooms are individually decorated and extremely comfortable. The look may be 19th century but all up-to-date facilities are on hand, including fax and photocopying (particularly convenient for business clientele). Particular attention has also been devoted to breakfast, served here as a buffet.

How to get there *(Map 37): Saint-Lazare station, Metro La Défense. Bus 175, 176.*

Hôtel Galileo★★★

54, rue Galilée - 75008 Paris
Tel. (1) 47.20.66.06. - Fax (1) 47.20.67.17
M. Mencaroni

Open all year. **Rooms** 27 with bath and WC, telephone, safe, minibar. Lift to all rooms. **Price** single 800F, double 950-980F. **Meals** breakfast 50F. **Credit cards** Amex, Visa. **Pets** dogs not allowed. **Parking** Georges V. Facilities bar. **Services** bookings, laundry, dry cleaning.

Monsieur and Mme Buffat formerly ran a hotel in the Ile Saint-Louis and have successfully turned this small Haussmann-style building into a truly charming hotel, conveniently located between the Champs Elysées and the Avenue Georges V. Refinement and modernity are the key words. Refinement is in evidence throughout the hotel: in the lounge, with its 18th-century chimneypiece and Aubusson tapestry, in the breakfast room with its subtle colour scheme and lighting, in the verandah with its fine vista of a small Italianate garden. The elegant bedrooms are luxuriously equipped: all have air-conditioning, reading lamps which really permit reading in bed, a work area with fax socket, and extremely comfortable bathrooms complete with radio. All rooms are equally well appointed but some are more spacious: the two ground-floor rooms, and the two fifth-floor ones with a lovely verandah, are our favourites.

How to get there *(Map 37): Metro and RER Charles-de-Gaulle-Etoile and Georges V. Bus 22, 30, 31, 52, 73.*

Hôtel du Bois★★

11, rue du Dôme - 75116 Paris
Tel. (1) 45.00.31.96 - Fax (1) 45.00.90.05
M. Byrne

Open all year. **Rooms** 41 with bath or shower and WC, soundproofing, telephone, cable TV, minibar. No lift. **Price** single 395-415F, double 475-575F. **Meals** breakfast 42F with orange juice, no restaurant. **Credit cards** Amex, Visa. **Pets** dogs allowed. **Parking** at 8 Avenue Foch and 2 Rue Lauriston. **Services** bookings.

The Hôtel du Bois is like Montmartre on the Champs Elysées, and England in Paris. Montmartre, because a steep stairway leads off the avenue Victor Hugo up to the narrow Rue du Dôme. England, because everything in the hotel – from Paisley-patterned draped curtains, the intimate atmosphere created by subdued lighting, the Impressionist posters in the corridors, the fresh and flowery decor in the bedrooms, down to the exquisite welcome – irresistibly evokes all the comfort and cosiness usually associated with an English interior. Needless to say, M. Byrne is English... And last but not least, the prices, extremely reasonable considering the exclusive neighbourhood, will make your mind up for you.

How to get there *(Map 37): Metro Kléber and Etoile, RER and bus for Roissy-Charles-de-Gaulle. Bus 22, 30, 31, 52, 73, 92.*

Hôtel de la Place du Louvre★★★

21, rue des Prêtres Saint-Germain-l'Auxerrois 75001 Paris
Tel. (1) 42.33.78.68 - Fax (1) 42.33.09.95

Open all year. **Rooms** 20 with bath and WC, telephone, TV, safe, hairdryer. **Price** single 480-600F, double 600-800F, suite 800F. **Meals** breakfast 40F, snacks available. **Credit cards** Amex, Diners, Visa, Eurocard, MasterCard. **Pets** dogs not allowed. **Parking** at Place du Louvre-Saint-Germain-l'Auxerrois. **Facilities** bar. **Services** bookings, laundry, dry cleaning.

A room with a view! And what a view! One of the most famous in the world: the Louvre colonnade. Just minutes away from the Museum, its gardens, and the Pont des Arts, and within easy walking distance of Beaubourg, the Ile de la Cité and the Châtelet, this hotel is a haven of peace. A few beautiful vestiges of this ancient building's past have been preserved: a medieval wall and a wooden column combined with high-tech windows and metal girders, or an 18th-century sculpture standing out against a modern pastel fresco. The black leather armchairs of the lounge and bar await guests in a conservatory, while breakfast is served in a fine vaulted cellar – the 'Salle des Mousquetaires' – which once communicated with the Louvre. The bright, sunny bedrooms have every modern comfort, and each one of them has been named after a painter. Service is friendly and efficient.

How to get there *(Map 37): Metro Louvre-Rivoli and Pont-Neuf, RER Châtelet-les-Halles, Bus 21, 24, 27, 67, 69, 74, 76, 81, 85.*

Hôtel Saint-Paul-Le Marais***

8, rue de Sévigné - 75004 Paris
Tel. (1) 48.04.97.27 - Fax (1) 48.87.37.04
Mmes Leguide and Marcovici

Open all year. **Rooms** 27 with bath and WC, soundproofing, telephone, cable TV, hairdryer. **Price** single 500F, double 620F. **Meals** breakfast 45F with fruit juice, cheese and fresh fruit, no restaurant. **Credit cards** Amex, Diners, Visa. **Pets** dogs not allowed. **Parking** at 2 Rue Geoffroy-l'Asnier and 16 Rue Saint-Antoine. **Facilities** bar, patio. **Services** bookings, laundry, dry cleaning.

This hotel is ideal for those who love the Marais quarter with its impressive private mansions and craftsmen's workshops side by side with boutiques and tea rooms, and the famous Place des Vosges. Set in the same street as the Hôtel Carnavalet, little remains of the old building and the decoration is modern in style. The reception area, with wide windows onto the street, is light and airy, furnished with black leather armchairs standing out against the pastel colour walls. The same gentle colour scheme has been carried through to the bedrooms, which have beamed ceilings and comfortable bathrooms. Although all have been soundproofed, it is better to ask for a room overlooking the courtyard. A delicious breakfast is served in a vaulted basement room. Prices are reasonable and the service is efficient and friendly.

How to get there *(Map 37): Metro Saint-Paul, Bus 29, 67, 69, 76, 96.*

Hôtel Marchal★★

12, rue Wittertalhof
67140 Le Hohwald (Bas-Rhin)
Tel. 88.08.31.04 - Fax 88.08.34.05 - M. Marchal

Open 10 March – 5 Nov and 10 Dec – 3 March. **Rooms** 16 with telephone, bath or shower (12 with WC). **Price** single 190F, double 180-250F. **Meals** breakfast 30F, served 0800-0930; half board 250F, full board 300F (per pers., 3 days min.) **Credit cards** Eurocard, Visa. **Pets** dogs allowed (+15F). **Facilities** sauna (35F), parking. **Nearby** Alsace wine route from Marlenheim to Thann, kirsch route from Andlau to Ville (Steige distillery), Neuntelstein rock (2 hours walk there and back). **Restaurant** service 1200-1300, 1900-2030 (closed Tuesday in low season); menus 90-170F, also à la carte; specialities: civet d'épaule de Chevreuil, sandre aux petits légumes.

The village of Hohwald is spread along a small green valley surrounded by beautiful fir and beech forests. A little higher up the valley one finds the Marchal, an attractive small hotel with a friendly and quiet atmosphere. The rooms are light, warm and simply decorated and all have a pretty view. Room 10 has three windows facing south and Room 6 a little balcony. With their low beamed ceilings, those on the second floor are the most charming. The dining room is very pleasant with fine views over the countryside; the flowers arranged on the tables are lovingly chosen by Mme Marchal, and M. Marchal serves good food there. It is a perfect little country hotel, just right for city dwellers seeking rural calm.

How to get there *(Map 12): 47km south west of Strasbourg via A35 and A352, Obernai exit; N422 to Barr, D62 to Andlau, and D425.*

Hôtel Arnold***

98, rue Principale
67140 Itterswiller (Bas-Rhin)
Tel. 88.85.50.58 – Telex 870 550 – Fax 88.85.55.54 – Mme Arnold

Open all year. **Rooms** 28 with telephone, bath or shower, WC, TV and minibar. **Price** double 450-545F. **Meals** breakfast 48F, served 0800-1000; half board and full board 450-550F (per pers., 3 days min.). **Credit cards** MasterCard, Visa. **Pets** dogs not allowed. **Facilities** parking. **Nearby** Alsace wine route from Marlenheim to Thann, church at Andlau, church of Ste-Marguerite d'Epfig. **Restaurant** service 1130-1430, 1930-2100 (closed Sunday evening and Monday); menus 95-365F, also à la carte; specialities: noisette de chevreuil, civet de sanglier, choucroute, baeckeotte, foie gras.

The Hôtel Arnold is in the heart of the Alsatian vineyards, at the foot of the Vosges mountains. It is made up of three buildings constructed in the most pure Alsatian style. The windows and balconies are overflowing with flowers. The interior decor has warmth and the recently renovated bedrooms all offer a high degree of comfort. Many have balconies overlooking the valley and the vineyards. The Arnold family, who are concerned about conserving Alsatian traditions, invite you to try the regional specialities in the restaurant or to take them away with you: a shop offers wines, foie gras and other products of the estate.

How to get there *(Map 12): 41km south of Strasbourg via A35, Obernai exit; then N422 to Epfig and turn right on D335 to Itterswiller.*

Hôtel Gilg★★

1, route du Vin
67140 Mittelbergheim (Bas-Rhin)
Tel. 88.08.91.37 - M. Gilg

Open 4 Feb–28 June and 16 July–10 Jan (closed Tuesday evening and Wednesday). **Rooms** 10 with telephone, bath and WC. **Price** single 185F, double 220-330F. **Meals** breakfast 30F, served 0730-1000. **Credit cards** accepted. **Pets** dogs allowed. **Facilities** parking. **Nearby** Barr, church at Andlau, church of Ste-Marguerite at Epfig, Mont Ste-Odile. **Restaurant** service 1200-1400, 1900-2100; menus 125-300F, also à la carte; specialities: feuilleté chaud du vigneron, sandre à la moutarde de Meaux, émincé d'agneau au curry, cyrano glacé au croquant.

The Hôtel Gilg is to be found in the angle of two little streets in a lovely village largely dominated by wine growing. The rooms here are quiet, warm and cosy with furniture that is a little old-fashioned, but not without charm. A special mention must be made, however, of the pink bedroom and its extraordinary bathroom... For breakfast or dinner, settle down in the great dining room with its handsome traditional decor. There you can taste excellent regional cooking. A pleasant welcome and the authenticity of this hotel make it a recommended stop in this area of vineyards and ancient Alsatian villages.

How to get there *(Map 12): 37km north of Colmar via N83 to Sélestat and N422 towards Barr.*

Hôtel Anthon★★

40, rue Principale
67510 Obersteinbach (Bas-Rhin)
Tel. 88.09.55.01 – Mme Flaig

Open Feb – end Dec (closed Tuesday and Wednesday in Jan and 16 – 26 Aug.) **Rooms** 9 with telephone, bath (1 with shower), WC (7 with minibar). **Price** double 220-250F. **Meals** breakfast 45F, served 0800-1000. **Credit cards** Visa, Eurocard, MasterCard. **Pets** dogs allowed. **Facilities** parking. **Nearby** lake at Hanau, châteaux of Lutzelhardt and Falkenstein, 18-hole golf course at Bitche. **Restaurant** service 1200-1400, 1830-2100; menus 240-300F (also 100F weekdays), also à la carte; specialities: foie gras frais de canard, game in season.

The hôtel-restaurant Anthon is situated at Obersteinbach, a small picturesque village in the heart of the Vosges du Nord park. It has seven pleasant, well-renovated bedrooms, all overlooking the surrounding countryside as far as the wooded slopes of the Vosges. The dining room is spacious; it is circular in shape and its large bay windows give the impression of dining in a garden full of flowers, perfect surroundings for the very high quality food that is served there. The hotel also has a lively bar and a quiet lounge. Outside, the hotel's extensive grounds assure its tranquillity.

How to get there *(Map 13): 66km north of Strasbourg via A4 and D44 to Haguenau, then D27 to Lembach, and D3 to Obersteinbach.*

Hostellerie des Châteaux★★★

11, rue des Châteaux
67530 Ottrott-le-Haut (Bas-Rhin)
Tel. 88.95.81.54 - Telex 870 439 - Fax 88.95.95.20
Mme Schaetzel

Open 1 March–31 Jan. **Rooms** 65 with telephone, bath, WC and TV. **Price** single 230-260F, double 390-660F, suite 900-1000F. **Meals** breakfast 60F, served 0715-1015; half board 400-700F, full board 500-800F (per pers., 3 days min.) **Credit cards** accepted. **Pets** dogs allowed (+40F). **Facilities** covered swimming pool, sauna (60F), parking. **Nearby** Place de Boersch at Obernai, Mont Ste-Odile, Alsace wine route from Marlenheim to Thann. **Restaurant** service 1200-1400, 1900-2100 (closed Sunday evening and Monday in low season); menus 260-450F, also à la carte; specialities: filet d'empereur au bouillon de légumes, escalope de saumon au rouge d'Ottrott, pintadeau au vinaigre de framboise.

The Hostellerie des Châteaux is an old village house that has been restored and extended. From its facade, abundantly adorned with flowers, to the comfort of the interior – not forgetting the food – all is successful; the decoration of the lounges and bedrooms is particularly stylish. It is the same in the dining room, where Ernest Schaetzel offers an updated version of traditional cuisine that is fine and light, accompanied by good Alsace wines. Well sited at the foot of Mont Sainte-Odile, the hotel is a good starting point for pleasant walks in the forest. As it has got bigger, the hotel has become less intimate, but the flavour remains and guests are treated as attentively as before.

How to get there *(Map 12): 37km south west of Strasbourg via A352, Obernau exit, then N422 towards Obernau and D426.*

Auberge d'Imsthal★★

Route forestière d'Imsthal
67290 La Petite-Pierre (Bas-Rhin)
Tel. 88.70.45.21 - Fax 88.70.40.26 - M. Michaely

Open all year. **Rooms** 23 (2 with sitting room), with telephone, bath or shower (20 with WC and TV). **Price** single 200-320F, double 280-600F. **Meals** breakfast (buffet) 48F, served 0800-1000; half board 300-460F, full board 380-540F (per pers., 3 days min.). **Credit cards** accepted. **Pets** dogs allowed (+30F). **Facilities** health centre, sauna (50F), parking. **Nearby** Vosges du Nord regional park, Neuwiller-les-Saverne, Bouxvillier, Lichtenberg, crystal and glass factory at Wingen-sur-Moder, 18-hole golf course at Bitche. **Restaurant** service 1200-1400, 1900-2100 (closed Monday evening and Tuesday and 20 Nov–20 Dec except for residents); menus 80-250F, also à la carte; specialities: regional cooking.

The Auberge d'Imsthal sits by a lake in an exceptional setting – the picturesque village of La Petite-Pierre and the forests of the Vosges du Nord. After a day enjoying the many activities that the region offers, for it is rich in attractions of all sorts, you will be ready to appreciate the comfort of this inn: the lounge with its piano and big fireplace with blazing fire; the dining room, which is made up of a number of small rooms each having its own style; the bedrooms, quiet and comfortable with country furnishings. The Auberge is a very pleasant place from which to enjoy the charms of the countryside

How to get there (Map 12): 59km north west of Strasbourg via A4, Saverne exit, N4, D122, D133 and D178 to the lake of Imsthal.

Hôtel Neuhauser★★

Les Quelles
67130 Schirmeck (Bas-Rhin)
Tel. 88.97.06.81 - Fax 88.97.14.29
M. Neuhauser

Open all year (closed Wednesday in low season). **Rooms** 14 with telephone, bath or shower, WC (6 with TV). **Price** single 200-300F, double 250-300F. **Meals** breakfast 30F, served 0800-1000; half board 250-300F, full board 300-350F (per pers., 3 days min.) **Credit cards** Visa. **Facilities** heated swimming pool, parking. **Restaurant** service 1200-1400, 1900-2100 (closed 10–31 January); menus 110-300F, also à la carte; specialities: foie gras maison, filet de lapereau farçi, noisette de chevreuil forestière.

This hotel, and the few small houses which make up the hamlet, are ringed on all sides by meadows and forests. This isolation guarantees absolute tranquillity. The hotel does not have many rooms, but they are comfortable, well kept up and tastefully decorated in a traditional style (country furniture, beams...) The food is varied and well prepared, and meals are served in a vast panoramic dining room decorated like a winter garden. The wine list is worth close attention, as is the list of liqueurs and eaux de vie. Reasonably priced, this hotel is well worth a visit and has just installed a covered swimming pool for use in the summer months.

How to get there (*Map 12*): *56km south west of Strasbourg via A35 and A352, then N420 or D392 to Schirmeck, then Les Quelles.*

Hôtel du Dragon★★★

2, rue de l'Ecarlate - 12, rue du Dragon
67000 Strasbourg (Bas-Rhin)
Tel. 88.35.79.80 - Telex 871 102 - Fax 88.25.78.95 - M. Iannarelli

Open all year. **Rooms** 32 with telephone, bath, WC and TV. **Price** single 420-550F, double 480-590F, suite 730-840F. **Meals** breakfast 52F, served 0645-1000. No restaurant. **Credit cards** Eurocard, MasterCard, Visa. **Pets** dogs not allowed. **Nearby** La Wantzenau, Alsace wine route, 18-hole golf courses at Illkirch-Graffenstaden and Plobsheim.

We tend to use the word 'charm' when describing the picturesque, yet the Hôtel du Dragon, whose proprietors have opted for a resolutely modern decor within the walls of this 17th-century house, does not lack charm. The grey tones used to decorate the interior, and the modern furniture, create a slightly chilly ambience, but the friendly and welcoming service quickly overcomes this. You will be comfortable in the bedrooms which face on to one of the quiet streets of the old quarter. There is no restaurant but a good breakfast is served on pretty china in the Café Coste.

How to get there *(Map 13): in the centre of Strasbourg via the Quai St-Nicolas and the Quai Ch. Frey.*

Parc Hôtel★★★

39, rue du Géneral-de-Gaulle
67710 Wangenbourg (Bas-Rhin)
Tel. 88.87.31.72 - Fax 88.87.38.00 - M. Gihr

Open 20 March–4 Nov, 22 Dec–2 Jan. **Rooms** 34 with telephone, bath or shower and WC. **Price** single 228-252F, double 316-372F. **Meals** breakfast 43F, served 0730-0930; half board 283-328F, full board 304-348F (per pers., 3 days min.) **Credit cards** Visa, MasterCard. **Pets** dogs not allowed. **Facilities** covered swimming pool, tennis, sauna (50F), parking. **Nearby** château de Wangenbourg, Haslach forest, château and waterfall at Nideck, château de Saverne, abbey of Marmoutier. **Restaurant** service 1200-1330, 1900-2030; menus 115-270F, also à la carte; specialities: Munster chaud sur canapé, magret de canard au miel de sapin et confit d'orange.

The hotel lies in the heart of the village and is made up of a number of houses of different periods. It has a lovely park with its own nature trail, and is most attractively decorated, the delightful lounge and the billiard room being particularly worth mentioning. All the bedrooms are large and well equipped, some having a balcony looking over the garden. With the enjoyment of their guests in mind, the owners (who represent the sixth generation) have provided facilities for sport and relaxation, including a very nice covered swimming pool giving on to the lawn. Those who want to go on excursions or sightseeing will find all the information they need at reception. Every Thursday evening in the restaurant food is grilled on an open fire and the atmosphere becomes very convivial. This is a family hotel to which many guests return every year.

How to get there *(Map 12): 46km west of Strasbourg via A4, Saverne exit, then N4 towards Wasselonne, D224 and D218.*

Le Moulin de La Wantzenau★★

27, route de Strasbourg
67610 La Wantzenau (Bas-Rhin)
Tel. 88.59.22.22 - Fax 88.59.22.00
Mmes Dametti and Wolff

Open 2 Jan – 24 Dec. **Rooms** 20 with telephone, bath or shower, WC and TV. **Price** single and double 290-390F, suite 510F. **Meals** breakfast 42F. **Credit cards** accepted. **Pets** dogs allowed (+40F). **Facilities** parking (+35F). **Nearby** Strasbourg, Alsace wine route, 18-hole golf course at La Wantzenau. **Restaurant** (independent but at the hotel) service 1215-1345, 1915-2115 (closed Wednesday, Sunday evening, national holidays in the evening); menus 145-240F.

Though close to Strasbourg, this hotel is in the countryside and far from all noise. The old mill has been well restored and is plainly and comfortably furnished. The bedrooms, with their pale wood furniture, are spacious and have excellent bathrooms. The services offered are first class – for instance, you get a local daily paper with your breakfast and the hotel will press your clothes for you. The lounge with its great fireplace and generous armchairs is very inviting, especially as it also contains a library (which includes children's books). The restaurant is not part of the hotel but is right opposite. The food is very good and you will get good advice on the right wines to accompany the local specialities. The staff are efficient and welcoming.

How to get there *(Map 13): 12km north of Strasbourg via A4, Reichstett exit, D63, and D301 towards Zone Industrielle La Wantzenau, then D468; it's 14.5km from La Wantzenau.*

Hostellerie Le Maréchal****

4-6, place des Six Montagnes Noires
68000 Colmar (Haut-Rhin)
Tel. 89.41.60.32 - Fax 89.24.59.40 - M. and Mme Bomo

Open all year. **Rooms** 30 with air-conditioning, telephone, bath or shower, WC and TV. **Price** single 350-450F, double 550-700F, suite 900-1400F. **Meals** breakfast 60F, served 0730-1000; half board 650F, full board 800F (per pers., 3 days min.) **Credit cards** accepted. **Pets** dogs allowed (+35F). **Facilities** parking (+27F). **Nearby** Issenheim altarpiece at the Unterlinden Museum at Colmar, Alsace wine route, Neuf-Brisach, Munster, Trois-Epis, 18-hole golf course at Ammerschwihr. **Restaurant** service 1200-1400, 1900-2200; menus 150-380F, also à la carte; specialities: soupe de grenouilles à la bière, selle de lapereau à la pistache et aux pignons de pin.

Well situated in the old quarter of Petite Venise (Little Venice) in Colmar, the Hostellerie Le Maréchal occupies four old houses on the edge of the canals. The interior is delightful. Beams and stone go well with the Louis XIII furniture in the lounge and dining room. Each bedroom has its own style, and you can choose between medieval or 18th-century styles. They are elegant, comfortable and well equipped, and though some are a bit small, this fits in perfectly with the cosy atmosphere of the hotel. Get a room on the canal side if you can. The candlelit dinners in the long dining room beside the Lauch, the specialities offered there, and the warm solicitous welcome make the Hostellerie Le Maréchal the best stop-over in Colmar

How to get there (Map 12): in the centre of old Colmar.

Hôtel Goldenmatt★★

Route des Crêtes
68760 Goldbach (Haut-Rhin)
Tel. 89.82.32.86 – M. and Mme Butterlin

Open Easter – 3 Nov. **Rooms** 12, and 1 chalet, with telephone, shower (1 with bath), WC. **Price** single 160F, double 350F, chalet 500F. **Meals** breakfast 50F, served 0800-1100; half board 270-380F (per pers., 3 days min.) **Credit cards** accepted. **Pets** dogs allowed. **Facilities** fishing in the lake, parking. **Nearby** route des Crêtes, Grand Ballon de Guebwiller (1424m), le Hohneck, col de la Schlucht. **Restaurant** service 1200-1400, 1900-2100 (closed Monday lunchtime); menus 115-280F, also à la carte; specialities: truite chaude fumée, foie gras de canard, poulet au riesling.

The Goldenmatt overlooks a magnificent landscape of mountains, forests and pastures far from all noise. From the big windows of the dining room on a clear day you can see the Jura and even Mont Blanc. There, in congenial and rustic surroundings, you can eat food that has been prepared with great care. The bedrooms are quite comfortable but are most appreciated for their quietness and fine views. You can also stay in the little chalet beside the hotel. In the mornings a large and delicious breakfast awaits you, with boiled eggs, kouglof, tart, toast and bread – enough to give you the energy you will need to undertake one of the many walks that this region offers.

How to get there *(Map 20): 35km north west of Mulhouse via N66 to Willer-sur-Thur, and right on D13bv1 and D431 towards Le Grand Ballon.*

Hôtel La Clairière★★★

50, route d'Illhaeusern
68970 Guémar - Illhaeusern (Haut-Rhin)
Tel. 89.71.80.80 - Fax 89.71.86.22 - M. Loux

Open 1 March – 31 Dec. **Rooms** 25, and 2 apartments, with telephone, bath, WC and TV. **Price** single 410F, double 520-800F, suite 1200-1500F. **Meals** breakfast 60F, served 0730-1000. No restaurant. **Credit cards** Visa, Eurocard, MasterCard. **Pets** dogs allowed. **Facilities** tennis, swimming pool, parking. **Nearby** Colmar, Alsace wine route from Marlenheim to Thann, 18-hole golf course at Ammerschwihr (25km).

A way from the main road and at the edge of the forest, the Hôtel La Clairière offers 25 bedrooms in country style, pretty, comfortable and mostly with a good view over the plain and the Vosges. Comfortable armchairs and a good fire make the lounge welcoming and restful. There is no restaurant in the hotel but nearby is the excellent Auberge de l'Ill, one of the great eating places of France, with prices to match. The hotel has its own private tennis court and is also the starting point for numerous walks and rambles. The owners give you a warm welcome.

How to get there (Map 12): 17km north of Colmar via N83 towards Sélestat; at Guémar D106 towards Marckolsheim.

Les Hirondelles★★

33, rue du 25 janvier
68970 Illhaeusern (Haut-Rhin)
Tel. 89.71.83.76 – Mme Muller

Open March – Jan. **Rooms** 14 with telephone, shower and WC. **Price** double 200-220F. **Meals** breakfast 27F, served 0800-1000; half board 200-220F (per pers., 3 days min.) **Credit cards** Visa, MasterCard, Eurocard. **Pets** small dogs allowed. **Facilities** parking. **Nearby** Colmar, Alsace wine route from Marlenheim to Thann, Haut-Koenigsbourg, 18-hole golf course at Ammerschwihr. **Restaurant** on reservation, service from 1930 (closed Sunday evening and 1 Nov-Easter); menu 90F; specialities: traditional country cooking, Alsatian specialities.

Illhaeusern means houses on the edge of the Ill and indeed, the river flows nonchalantly past this little Alsatian village. On the bridge, don't forget to say hello to the famous 'Auberge de l'Ill', the gastronomic stopover known all over the world, before coming, a hundred metres further on, to this ancient farm of vast dimensions. The welcome here is really charming and informal. The bedrooms are in a large outbuilding which has been entirely refurbished. Thoughtfully and comfortably fitted out, they all have multicoloured wooden wardrobes, new but typically Alsatian. You have the choice of rooms giving on to flowery balconies and the courtyard or a more rural view looking over a landscape of little vegetable plots. On the ground floor, a welcoming lounge with cane furniture awaits you; to the side there is a large dining room where breakfast is served and also good dinners based on regional and home cooking. An agreeable stop, not far from the vineyards, and offering very reasonable prices.

How to get there *(Map 12): 12km north of Colmar via RN83 in the Strasbourg direction.*

Hostellerie de L'Abbaye d'Alspach★★

2-4, rue Foch – Kientzheim
68240 Kaysersberg (Haut-Rhin)
Tel. 89.47.16.00 – Fax 89.78.29.73 – Mme Schwartz

Open all year. **Rooms** 30 with telephone, bath or shower, WC (13 with TV). **Price** single 220-300F, double 300-400F. **Meals** breakfast (buffet) 42F, served 0800-1000. **Credit cards** accepted. **Pets** dogs not allowed. **Facilities** parking. **Nearby** Issenheim altarpiece at the Unterlinden Museum at Colmar, Alsace wine route, Kayersberg, Riquewihr, 18-hole golf course at Ammerschwihr, **Restaurant** service 1800-2100 (closed Wednesday and Thursday); à la carte; specialities: Alsatian cooking.

The Alsatian notion of comfort finds its full expression inside this hotel. The predominance of wood, the comfortable furniture, the hunting trophies on the walls, all contribute to the warm atmosphere which strikes you as soon as you enter. The bedrooms have all been completely renovated and are very pleasant; they are reached via a splendid stone spiral staircase and a wooden footbridge identical to the one once used by the nuns of the order St Clare in the Middle Ages. In the evenings a light dinner based on Alsatian specialities is served.

How to get there *(Map 12): 10km north west of Colmar; at Kaysersberg take the Ribeauvillé road for 2km.*

Auberge Les Alisiers★★

5 Faude
68650 Lapoutroie (Haut-Rhin)
Tel. 89.47.52.82 – Fax 89.47.22.38 – M. and Mme Degouy

Open 1 Feb – 31 Dec. **Rooms** 10 with telephone, bath or shower and WC. **Price** single 190F, double 350F. **Meals** breakfast (buffet) 32F, served 0730-1000; half board 280-340F. **Credit cards** Visa, MasterCard, Eurocard. **Pets** dogs allowed. **Facilities** parking. **Nearby** Colmar, Alsace wine route from Marlenheim to Thann, 18-hole golf course at Ammerschwihr. **Restaurant** service 1200-1300, 1900-2100 (closed Monday evening, except for guests on half board, and Tuesday); menus 75-189F, also à la carte; specialities: presskopf de queue de bœuf, oreille de porc panée, truite saumonée rôtie, Munster fondue.

The Auberge Les Alisiers lies 700 metres up in the mountains; the view from it over the Hautes Vosges and the Béhine valley is stunning, and the hotel itself is very pleasant. The bedrooms, with their pale wood furniture, are all different, but are all cosy and comfortable. Some have been recently renovated and these have the best bathrooms. An attractive dining room offers panoramic views across the Vosges mountains. The cooking is varied and good (with an excellent sauerkraut). The intimate and relaxed atmosphere of the auberge owes much to the friendliness of its owners.

How to get there (Map 12): 19km north west of Colmar via N415; at Lapoutroie go left in front of the church and follow the signs for 3km.

Hôtel Le Clos Saint-Vincent★★★★

Route de Bergheim
68150 Ribeauvillé (Haut-Rhin)
Tel. 89.73.67.65 - Fax 89.73.32.20 - M. Chapotin

Open 15 March – 15 Nov. **Rooms** 11, and 3 apartments, with telephone, bath, WC, TV and minibar. **Price** single 600F, double 680-840F, suite 970-1150F. **Meals** breakfast incl., served 0815-1030. **Credit cards** Visa. **Pets** dogs allowed (+30F). **Facilities** covered swimming pool, parking. **Nearby** Hunawihr, stork breeding centre, château de St-Ulrich, Riquewihr, Alsace wine route from Marlenheim to Thann, 18-hole golf course at Ammerschwihr. **Restaurant** service 1200-1400, 1900-2030 (closed Tuesday and Wednesday); menus 250F, also à la carte.

The position of the Clos Saint-Vincent is magical: standing among Riesling-producing vines, it dominates the Alsatian plateau, while in the distance the Black Forest and, further to the the west the Alps, can be seen. The hotel has three floors. On the first floor are reception and the restaurant. This is a great success, with its harmonious decor and panoramic view. The bedrooms contain some magnificent fabrics and furniture in Charles X or Empire styles (sometimes of the country type). They are light, comfortable and very quiet. Monsieur Chapoton's cooking is renowned, and the Clos Saint-Vincent is to be thoroughly recommended.

How to get there *(Map 12): 19km north of Colmar via N83 and D106 towards Ribeauvillé, then D1b towards Bergheim (follow the signs).*

Hôtel de la Rochette★★

La Rochette
68910 Labaroche (Haut-Rhin)
Tel. 89.49.80.40 - M. Preiss

Open all year (closed Sunday evening and Wednesday). **Rooms** 7 with shower and WC. **Price** double 245F, suite 400F. **Meals** breakfast (buffet) 45F, served 0800-0930; half board 260-290F (child 190F). **Credit cards** Amex, Visa. **Pets** dogs not allowed. **Facilities** parking. **Nearby** Turckheim, Colmar, Alsace wine route from Marlenheim to Thann, 18-hole golf course at Ammerschwihr (5km). **Restaurant** service 1230-1330, 1930-2100; menus 85-185F, also à la carte; specialities: traditional Alsatian cooking, foie gras maison, bouillabaisse (Nov-April).

Standing on a plateau in the heart of the green forests of the Vosges, the Hôtel de la Rochette is to be found a little way from the village. It is difficult not to be charmed by this small house, a hotel for fifty years, with its antique furniture, polished floors, and collections of folk art and local pottery. The bedrooms reflect the spirit of the house: they are all comfortable and no. 8 is quite sweet, but some could do with new carpets. It should be explained that this is really a restaurant with rooms, which is why some of the communal areas are not very big, though there is a bar. The welcome here is warm. When the weather is good drinks and snacks are served on the terrace.

How to get there *(Map 12): 15km west of Colmar via D417 to Turckheim, then D11 towards Orbay.*

Hôtel Au Moulin★★

Sainte-Croix-en-Plaine
68127 Herrlisheim (Haut-Rhin)
Tel. 89.49.31.20 - M. and Mme Wœlffle

Open end March – 15 Nov. **Rooms** 17 with telephone, bath, WC (3 with TV). **Price** single and double 200-400F. **Meals** breakfast 40F, served 0730-1000. No restaurant. **Credit cards** Visa. **Pets** dogs allowed (+30F). **Facilities** parking. **Nearby** Colmar, Neuf-Brisach, Munster, Trois-Epis, Alsace wine route from Marlenheim to Thann, 18-hole golf course at Ammerschwihr.

This former flour mill stands beside the Thur, which is also called the canal of the twelve mills – two of which are still working. It was built in the 17th century by a colony of Mennonites (a protestant sect) and was converted into a hotel in 1982. It is a large white building with windows brightened by geraniums. The owners, the Wœlffle family, live in adjoining buildings, the ensemble forming a pretty courtyard, with banks of flowers surrounding an old stone well. Spread over three floors, the bedrooms face either east, towards the Vosges, or across the fields. Most are spacious and all have very well equipped bathrooms. There are no televisions as peace and quiet are the main concern. Finally, there are three further rooms in another building facing on to the courtyard, where breakfast can be enjoyed to the sound of running water. This is a hotel with a very friendly atmosphere and very attractive prices.

How to get there *(Map 12): 6km south of Colmar via N422, then D1 towards Sainte-Croix-en-Plaine.*

Auberge La Meunière★★

30, rue Sainte-Anne
68590 Thannenkirch (Haut-Rhin)
Tel. 89.73.10.47 – Fax 89.73.12.31 – M. Dumoulin

Open Easter – All Saints. **Rooms** 15 with telephone, shower, WC (6 with TV). **Price** double 260-310F, suite 650F. **Meals** breakfast 25F, served 0830-0930; half board 220-250F, full board 280-330F. **Credit cards** Visa, Amex, Eurocard. **Pets** dogs allowed (+10F). **Facilities** health centre (150F for 2 pers.), parking. **Nearby** Haut-Koenigsbourg, Ribeauvillé, Riquewihr, Kaysersberg, 18-hole golf course at Ammerschwihr. **Restaurant** service 1215-1400, 1915-2100; menus 95-190F, also à la carte; specialities: foie gras de canard au gewürztraminer, langue de bœuf à la crème de radis noir, Kouglof glacé.

The little village of Thannenkirch lies in the foothills of the Vosges. It is impossible not to notice the typically Alsatian facade of this lovely auberge beside the main street. You will find the same charm in the dining room, with its almond green table linen, low ceilings and the wooden partitions that create several little intimate corners. The bedrooms, some furnished with antiques and some in more modern style, all have the same cosy and comfortable feel. Instead of numbers, the bedroom doors have enamelled plaques inscribed with women's names. We particularly liked 'Sophie' and 'Josephine' with their glazed balconies looking over the countryside towards the fortress of Haut-Koenigsbourg in the distance. The view is superb and everyone can take advantage of it when sitting on the large terrace, where meals are also served.

How to get there *(Map 12): 25km north of Colmar via N83 to Guémar, N106 and D42.*

Les Violettes★★★

68500 Jungholtz-Thierenbach (Haut-Rhin)
Tel. 89.76.91.19 – Fax 89.74.29.12
M. Munsch

Open all year. **Rooms** 24 with telephone, bath or shower, WC (20 with TV, 12 with minibar). **Price** single 220F, double 540-740F. **Meals** breakfast 55F, served 0800-1000. **Credit cards** accepted. **Pets** dogs allowed (+40F). **Facilities** sauna (150F for 2 pers.), parking. **Nearby** walks, car museum at Mulhouse, Unterlinden Museum at Colmar, 18-hole golf course at Ammerschwihr. **Restaurant** service 1200-1400, 1900-2100 (closed Monday evening and Tuesday); menus 170-380F, also à la carte; specialities: brioche de foie gras, chartreuse de saumon et langouste.

Monsieur and Mme Munch have devoted much care and attention to their small hotel. It is quiet, on the edge of a forest and has a lovely view over the valley and the little village of Thierenbach which lies just below. Inside, antique furniture, fine carpets, paintings and objets d'art create a warm and cheerful ambience. In the dining room with its panoramic windows and floral fabrics you will enjoy M. Munch's excellent cooking. All the bedrooms, whether in the main building or the annexe, are prettily decorated, with fine fabrics, lace, pictures and white lacquered or natural wood furniture. Some have a terrace looking out on the great trees of the forest. This is a charming place to stay.

How to get there *(Map 20): 5km south of Guebwiller in the direction of Soultz, at Thierenbach go left of the basilica, then 300m to the edge of the forest.*

Château d'Adoménil***

Rehainviller
54300 Lunéville (Meurthe-et-Moselle)
Tel. 83.74.04.81 - Fax 83.74.21.78 - M. Million

Open all year except Feb (closed Monday). **Rooms** 8 with telephone, bath, WC, TV and minibar. **Price** single 400F, double 500-800F, suite 1200F. **Meals** breakfast 65F, served 0800-1100; half board 690F (per pers., 3 days min.) **Credit cards** Visa, Diners, Amex. **Pets** dogs allowed. **Facilities** parking. **Nearby** château de Lunéville, crystal glass museum at Baccarat, Place Stanislas, School of Nancy museum and Emile Gallé museum at Nancy, St-Etienne cathedral at Toul. **Restaurant** service 1200-1400, 1930-2130 (closed Sunday evening and Monday and Tuesday lunchtime 1 Nov-31 March, and Monday and Tuesday lunchtime 1 April-31 June); menus 200-410F, also à la carte; specialities: matelote de poissons de rivière, foie gras poêlé.

About ten years ago Monsieur Million left his restaurant in Lunéville and moved into this château. The success of the restaurant has led to five spacious bedrooms being built in the old stables with lovely tiled floors, modern Italian furniture and luxurious bathrooms – they are all very elegant and face the orchard. In the château itself there are three other charming bedrooms in a more classic style. The château boasts a park of some 18 acres, and the little railway branch line nearby only occasionally disturbs the calm. The food, served in the dining room on the first floor, fully deserves its reputation and the breakfasts, which include a number of Viennese specialities, are delicious.

How to get there (Map 12): *50km south east of Nancy via N4 to Lunéville; 3km south of Lunéville via D914.*

La Bergerie★★

15, rue des Vignes
57640 Rugy (Moselle)
Tel. 88.77.82.27 - Fax 87.77.87.07 - Mme Keichinger

Open all year. **Rooms** 42 with telephone, bath or shower, WC and TV. **Price** single 280F, double 350F. **Meals** breakfast 35F, served 0630-1030. **Credit cards** Visa, Eurocard. **Pets** dogs allowed. **Facilities** parking. **Nearby** St-Etienne cathedral at Metz, Waliby Park (Schtroumpf), 18-hole golf course at Metz. **Restaurant** service 1200-1345, 1900-2130; menus 120-150F, also à la carte; traditional cooking.

La Bergerie is conveniently placed for the autoroute but stands in a green and quiet spot. The hotel consists of several buildings, some of which are very old. The bedrooms are modern, airy and functional and are furnished with lovely country fabrics. We particularly recommend those which overlook the park. There are two large and prettily decorated dining rooms to choose between, but, weather permitting, you will probably prefer to sit under the shady trellis with its little white tables. Professional and attentive service and the charm of the place make this a very agreeable stop.

How to get there *(Map 12): 10km north of Metz via A4, Ennery exit.*

Auberge du Kiboki★★

Route du Donon (D993)
57560 Turquestein (Moselle)
Tel. 87.08.60.65 - Fax 87.08.65.26 - M. Schmitt

Open 1 March – 31 Jan (closed Tuesday). **Rooms** 15 with telephone, bath or shower,
WC and TV. **Price** double 300F, suite 550F. **Meals** breakfast 38F, served 0800-1000;
half board 300F (per pers., 3 days min.) **Credit cards** MasterCard, Visa. **Pets** dogs
not allowed. **Facilities** swimming pool, tennis, parking. **Nearby** Dabo rock, crystal
glass factories, potteries at Niderviller. **Restaurant** service 1200-1400, 1900-2100;
à la carte 130-180F; specialities: grenadin de biche Ducs de Lorraine, terrine de
gibier aux pistaches, suprême de sandre à la rhubarbe.

In the middle of the forest in the valley of the Turquestein-
Blancrupt lies the authentic and traditional Auberge du Kiboki.
A very cosy atmosphere is created by the rustic decor in this hotel.
The dining rooms are very appealing: one has a doll's-house quality,
with checked table linen and matching curtains and lampshades;
the other is more intimate, with a large dresser laden with local
pottery. The comfortably furnished bedrooms echo the same
mood: a harmony of beige and brown, a canopied bed, an antique
wardrobe. This authentic forest house is an ideal place for a peaceful
stay. Family cooking with home grown produce.

How to get there *(Map 12): 73km west of Strasbourg via A352 and D392
towards Saint-Dié; at Schirmeck D392 towards Donon and D993 towards
Turquestein-Blancrupt.*

Hostellerie des Bas-Rupts★★★

88400 Gérardmer (Vosges)
Les Bas-Rupts
Tel. 29.63.09.25 - Fax 29.63.00.40 - M. Philippe

Open all year. **Rooms** 32 with telephone, bath or shower, WC and TV. **Price** single 340F, double 340-650F, suite 800F. **Meals** breakfast 60F, served 0700-1000; half board 420-620F. **Credit cards** Amex, Visa. **Pets** dogs allowed (+50F). **Facilities** tennis, garage, parking. **Nearby** Les Cuves waterfall, Longemer lake, Retournemer lake, Epinal, 18-hole golf course at Epinal. **Restaurant** service 1200-1400, 1900-2130; menus 140-450F, also à la carte; specialities: tripes au riesling, aiguillettes de canard, andouille fumée sur choucroute.

Gérardmer was once a favoured resort where well-heeled visitors from Alsace and Lorraine came to pass the time and lose money in the casino. Almost completely destroyed at the end of the war, the town has lost its charm and its splendid hotels. Even the beauty of the lake and the surrounding forests fail to diminish the town's nostalgic air. Just outside the town are this hotel and its flower-bedecked chalet, a famous and justly rosetted restaurant. In fact, there are flowers everywhere: painted on the beams, on the doors and on the bed-heads, and in fresh or dried bouquets on the tables and the walls. They add much to the charm and great comfort of the bedrooms in the annexe, but in the hotel itself some of the bedrooms are more ordinary. The service is both professional and extremely courteous.

How to get there (Map 12): *56km west of Colmar via D417 and D486 towards La Bresse.*

Auberge du Spitzemberg★★

La Petite-Fosse
88490 Provenchères-sur-Fave (Vosges)
Tel. 29.51.20.46 - M. and Mme Duhem

Open all year (closed Tuesday). **Rooms** 11 with telephone, bath or shower, WC (5 with TV). **Price** double 250-260F, suite 290F. **Meals** breakfast 30F, served 0800-0900; half board 210F, full board 275F (per pers., 3 days min.) **Credit cards** accepted. **Pets** dogs allowed. **Facilities** parking. **Nearby** cathedral and cloisters of Saint-Dié. **Restaurant** service 1200-1400, 1900-2100; menus 65-135F (child 50F), 110-135F on Sundays and national holidays, also à la carte; specialities: escalope de veau aux morilles, filet de sole aux coquilles Saint-Jacques, noix de Saint-Jacques au champagne, noisette d'agneau à la Chartres.

In the middle of the forests of the Vosges, the Auberge du Spitzemberg is a former farmhouse transformed into a charming small hotel, from all parts of which there are exceptional views across the countryside. The bedrooms are plainly decorated but are all comfortably equipped. The dining room is very cheerful and one can enjoy good traditional cooking there. A miniature golf course in a large field in front of the hotel offers an agreeable way of spending an afternoon, or if you prefer you can explore the surrounding area.

How to get there *(Map 12): 63km north west of Colmar via N83 to Sélestat, then N59 to Ste-Marie-aux-Mines, N159 via the tunnel to Provenchères-sur-Faves, and D45 to La Petite-Fosse.*

Hôtel de la Fontaine-Stanislas★★

Fontaine-Stanislas
88370 Plombières-les-Bains (Vosges)
Tel. 29.66.01.53 – Fax 29.30.04.31 – Mme Lemercier

Open 1 April-30 Sept. **Rooms** 19 with telephone, of which 11 with bath, 3 with shower, 11 with WC, 5 with TV. **Price** single 125-185F, double 135-270F. **Meals** breakfast 30F, served 0730-0930; half board 200-250F, full board 250-330F (per pers., 3 days min.) **Credit cards** Amex, Visa. **Pets** dogs allowed (+25F). **Facilities** parking. **Nearby** Epinal, Augronne and Semouse valleys, Guéhand waterfall, la Feuillée Nouvelle, 18-hole golf course at Epinal. **Restaurant** service 1200-1330, 1900-2030; menus 85-250F, also à la carte; specialities: cassolette d'escargots aux cèpes, coupe plombières.

This hotel is sublimely situated in the heart of the woods, close to the fountain that bears the name of the king of Poland. Apart from the peace and charm of this lovely spot, one is taken by the old-fashioned flavour of the hotel with its 1950s furniture. The bedrooms have the same character. We particularly liked the two bedrooms in the annexe and numbers 2, 3 and 11, which have small terraces. The garden is ideally arranged for enjoying the surroundings: one can have a drink there or just relax and admire the view over the woods and the valley. The welcome is a warm one, and the four generations who have successively run the hotel since 1933 are a guarantee of the professionalism of this establishment.

How to get there *(Map 20): 30km south of Epinal via D434 to Xertigny, then D3, D63 and D20; at Granges-de-Plombières take the forest road on the left.*

Chalets des Ayes***

Chemin des Ayes
88160 Le Thillot (Vosges)
Tel. 29.25.00.09 - M. Marsot

Open all year. **Rooms** 2, and 14 chalets (4-10 pers.), with bath or shower, WC, TV. **Price** double 320-420F. **Meals** breakfast 38F, served 0800-1000. **Credit cards** Visa. **Pets** dogs not allowed. **Facilities** swimming pool, tennis (30F), parking. **Nearby** cross-country and piste skiing, horse-riding, off-road driving, walks. **Restaurant** open during the holidays, service 1200-1300, 1930-2100; menus 98-128F; specialities: cooking from Alsace and the Vosges.

The Vosges region has a wild and seductive beauty, but it does sometimes seem difficult to find somewhere to spend the night there, and one can be faced with an unattractive choice between establishments which look suspect and hotels too big to have retained any rural charm. The Chalets des Ayes calls itself a hotel, though it isn't really one. It does however provide a practical and agreeable solution to the problem of where to stay: two rooms are available on a bed-and-breakfast basis. These are bright and cheerful, and there are also five small chalets which are well-equipped and attractively presented. Strictly the chalets are let by the week but, like the bedrooms, they can be taken for a few nights subject to availability. There is a garden and a swimming pool and the valley is a cheerful place even in the most wretched weather.

How to get there *(Map 20): 51km west of Mulhouse via N66 towards Remiremont.*

Auberge du Val Joli★★

88230 Le Valtin (Vosges)
Tel. 29.60.91.37 – Fax 29.60.81.73
M. Laruelle

Open all year (closed Sunday evening and Monday outside the holidays). **Rooms** 12 with telephone, of which 2 with bath, 7 with shower, 8 with WC and TV. **Price** single 138F, double 260F. **Meals** breakfast 30F, served 0800-1000; half board 214-333F, full board 316-405F. **Credit cards** Visa, Eurocard. **Pets** dogs allowed (+20F). **Facilities** parking. **Nearby** St-Dié cathedral, Gérardmer lake, 18-hole golf course at Epinal. **Restaurant** service 1230-1400, 1930-2100; menus 57-230F, also à la carte; specialities: truite fumée maison, pâté lorrain, tarte aux myrtilles.

The little village of Valtin has only 99 inhabitants, and the mayor is also the owner of this auberge lying at the bottom of one of the prettiest valleys of the Vosges. You only have to open the door to feel its character: low ceilings, stone beams, flagstones and fireplace create a completely authentic atmosphere. The dining room is very attractive, with its many small windows and particularly its carved wood ceiling, the work of an Alsatian carpenter. The comfort of the bedrooms and their bathroom facilities is rather variable. The best are those that have been renovated. Even though the hotel is on the road, there is not much noise; if in doubt reserve a room overlooking the mountain, such as numbers 16, 5, or 4. A place without pretensions in an unspoilt village.

How to get there (Map 12): 40km west of Colmar via D417 (by the Schlucht pass) to le Collet, then right on D23 to Le Valtin.

Château de Lalande★★★

24430 Annesse et Beaulieu (Dordogne)
Tel. 53.54.52.30 – Fax 53.07.46.67
M. and Mme Sicard

Open 15 March – 15 Nov. **Rooms** 22 with telephone, bath or shower, WC (TV on request). **Price** double 245-400F, suite 350F. **Meals** breakfast 37F, served 0800-0930; half board 275-360F, full board 345-430F (per pers.) **Credit cards** accepted. **Pets** dogs allowed. **Facilities** swimming pool, parking. **Nearby** Périgueux, Echourgnac and forest of la Double, Chancelade abbey, Saltgourde estate, Marsac, 18-hole golf course at Périgueux. **Restaurant** service 1200-1330, 1900-2100 (closed Wednesday lunchtime in low season); menus 95-295F (child 45F), also à la carte; specialities: croustade de pigeonneau aux truffes, foie frais maison, magret de canard en croûte.

This 19th-century château is in countryside not far from Périgueux. Nothing stiff and starchy here; the atmosphere is homely and relaxed. The sitting room is in Louis–Philippe style, the dining room has a high ceiling and is decorated in shades of brown. The bedrooms are simple but pleasant, with an old-fashioned charm; they all face towards the grounds. On the second floor the attic bedrooms are smaller but delightful. The lawn, with tables and sun loungers, looks over the countryside. In summer you can lunch and dine here in the shade of a large lime tree. An award winner for his sauces, M. Sicard prepares delicious Périgourdine specialities; equally noteworthy are the pastries and cakes.

***How to get there** (Map 23): 12km south west of Périgueux via N89, Montaceix exit, Razac-sur-l'Isle.*

Le Chatenet

Le Chatenet
24310 Brantôme (Dordogne)
Tel. 53.05.81.08 – Fax 53.05.85.52 – M. and Mme Laxton

Open all year. **Rooms** 10 with telephone, bath or shower, WC (3 with TV). **Price** double 380-580F, suite 780F. **Meals** breakfast 55F, served 0830-1000. No restaurant. **Credit cards** Access, MasterCard, Eurocard, Visa. **Pets** dogs allowed. **Facilities** heated swimming pool, tennis (40F), parking. **Nearby** bell tower of the abbey church at Brantôme, 'Peiro-Levado' dolmen, châteaux of Hierce, Puymarteau and St-Jean-de-Côle, Chancelade abbey, Saltgourde estate, Marsac, 18-hole golf course at Périgueux.

Le Chatenet, which owner Philippe Laxton describes as 'a family house open to friends and to friends of friends' is in the pretty countryside of Brantôme, a very pleasant place to stay. It is composed of two buildings built in local style. One accommodates the comfortable and spacious bedrooms as well as a dining-room and a lounge, and the other acts as a club-house, with bar and billiards. This family home has a most congenial atmosphere. Because the Laxtons opened Le Chatenet to provide a service for their restaurant owning friends, there is no restaurant. However, an ample breakfast is served on the patio whenever you like.

How to get there (Map 23): 27km north of Périgueux, 1.5km from Brantôme via D78 towards Bourdeilles.

Hôtel du Manoir de Bellerive★★★
Route de Siorac
24480 Le Buisson de Cadouin (Dordogne)
Tel. 53.27.16.19 - Fax 53.22.09.05 - Mme Huin

Open Easter – All Saints. **Rooms** 16 with telephone, bath or shower, WC, TV and minibar. **Price** single 390F, double 680F. **Meals** breakfast 50F, served 0800-1100. No restaurant. **Credit cards** accepted. **Pets** dogs not allowed. **Facilities** swimming pool, tennis, sauna (80F), parking. **Nearby** Le Bugue, cave of Bara-Bahau and Proumeyssac chasm, Limeuil, National Museum of Prehistory at Les Eyzies, 18-hole golf course at la-Croix-de-Mortemart.

Situated off the road in beautiful English parklike grounds, this 19th-century manor borders the Dordogne. It has been delightfully converted by two interior decorators. On the ground floor, the sitting room, bar and dining room open off a vast central colonnaded hall, from which a double staircase sweeps up to the first floor bedrooms. The pervading atmosphere of aestheticism and refinement has been created by a sensitive and masterly combination of colours, fabrics and trompe l'oeil marble. There are also antiques, fine carpets, engravings... Among the very comfortable bedrooms you have the choice of those with a view over the park or those overlooking the river. The bathrooms are luxurious. In good weather breakfast is served on the terrace, which overlooks the Dordogne. A real success and the most hospitable of welcomes.

How to get there (Map 23): 47km south east of Périgueux via N89 to Niversac, D710 to Le Bugue, and D31.

L'Eau à la Bouche★★

Moulin de Porteil
24260 Campagne-Le Bugue (Dordogne)
Tel. 53.07.16.88 - M. and Mme Laporte

Open May – Oct. **Rooms** 8 with telephone, bath or shower, WC and minibar. **Price** double 250-350F. **Meals** breakfast 30F; half board 270F. **Credit cards** Visa. **Pets** dogs allowed (+25F). **Facilities** swimming pool, parking. **Nearby** Le Bugue, cave of Bara-Bahau and Proumeyssac chasm, Limeuil, National Museum of Prehistory at Les Eyzies, 18-hole la-Croix de Mortemart golf course. **Restaurant** service at all times; menus 90-170F, also à la carte.

One would imagine that the nearness of the road would make this old mill a noisy place, but this is not so as buildings and screening trees keep the noise levels well down. The little bridge straddling one of the channels which once fed the mill machinery gives access to the garden and a wisteria covered pergola. From here you enter the lounge-bar-dining room. Decorated in 1930s style, it reflects the taste of M. Laporte, architect, and Mme Laporte, antique dealer. The bedrooms, decorated in pale green and white, are pleasant, comfortable and restful. Some pieces of old furniture add character. The best bedrooms (nearly all) have the use of a nice sheltered terrace which gives on to the garden and swimming pool. You will be impressed by the cooking. A warm and friendly welcome.

How to get there *(Map 23): 40km south east of Périgueux via N89 to Niversac, D710 to Le Bugue, and D703.*

Moulin du Roc★★★★

24530 Champagnac-de-Bélair (Dordogne)
Tel. 53.54.80.36 – Fax 53.54.21.31
M. Gardillon

Open all year except 15 Nov – 15 Dec and 15 Jan – 15 Feb. **Rooms** 14 with telephone, bath, WC, TV and minibar. **Price** single 380F, double 500-650F, suite 700F. **Meals** breakfast 55F, served 0800-1000; half board 750F. **Credit cards** accepted. **Pets** dogs allowed. **Facilities** swimming pool, tennis, parking. **Nearby** bell tower of the abbey church at Brantôme, 'Peiro-Levado' dolmen, châteaux of Hierce, Puymarteau and St-Jean-de-Côle, abbey of Chancelade, Saltgourde estate, Marsac, 18-hole golf course at Périgueux. **Restaurant** service 1200-1400, 1930-2100; menus 200-350F, also à la carte; specialities: chou farçi au foie gras, carré d'agneau aux noix.

Situated in the heart of Périgord, this old mill stands on the banks of the river Dronne and looks like a picture postcard, with a little bridge astride the stream which runs through the property, and a two-hectare garden with flowers and large trees. In summer all meals are served on a terrace looking out on to the garden and the river. There are two dining-rooms, a large sitting room in the old mill, and a small sitting room with a fireplace and an open fire in the winter; the decor is warm but a bit overdone. The bedrooms are all in different styles, with floral fabrics, and some have canopied beds. Superb breakfast with freshly squeezed orange juice, eggs and croissants. Cuisine gastronomique and a menu-pension which changes every day. Kindly and professional welcome.

How to get there (Map 23): 33km north of Périgueux via D939; 6km north east of Brantôme.

Manoir d'Hautegente★★★

Coly
24120 Terrasson (Dordogne)
Tel. 53.51.68.03 – Fax 53.50.38.52 – Mme Hamelin

Open 1 April – 11 Nov. **Rooms** 10 with telephone, bath, WC, TV and minibar. **Price** double 500-850F. **Meals** breakfast 50F, served 0830-1000; half board 490-700F (per pers.) **Credit cards** Visa, MasterCard, Eurocard. **Pets** dogs allowed. **Facilities** swimming pool, fishing, parking. **Nearby** Lascaux caves, abbey of Aubazines, Argentat, Collonges-la-Rouge. **Restaurant** service from 2000; menus 180-230F, also à la carte; specialities: terrine de foie gras frais de canard, magret à l'orange, confit à la purée d'oignons.

In a beautiful valley lined with walnut and oak trees stands the Manoir d'Hautegente. Former mill and forge of the abbey of Saint-Amand du Coly, it has been the property of the Hamelin family for nearly three centuries, and for several years it has been a lovely place to stay. The river sings sweetly to itself as it winds and flows in front of the manor. Ducks and geese strolling along the river banks will end up as confits (potted goose) or foie gras, for sale at reception. The bedrooms, as well as the series of reception rooms, are enhanced by old family furniture. Everything has been decorated with good taste; elegance and comfort are perfectly combined. The 'liserons' bedroom is a good size and has a private balcony.

How to get there *(Map 23): 30km south west of Brive-la-Gaillarde via N89 towards Périgueux to Le Lardin-Saint-Lazare, then D62.*

Hôtel Cro-Magnon***

24620 Les Eyzies-de-Tayac (Dordogne)
Tel. 53.06.97.06 - Fax 53.06.95.45
M. and Mme Leyssales

Open end April – 15 Oct. **Rooms** 20, and 4 apartments, with telephone, bath or shower, WC (10 with TV). **Price** double 350-550F, suite 600-800F. **Meals** breakfast 50F, served 0800-1030; half board 350-500F (per pers., 3 days min.) **Credit cards** Amex, Diners, Visa. **Pets** dogs allowed (+30F). **Facilities** swimming pool, parking. **Nearby** Le Bugue, cave of Bara-Bahau and Proumeyssac chasm, Limeuil, National Museum of Pre-history at Les Eyzies, 18-hole la-Croix-de-Mortemart golf course at Le Bugue. **Restaurant** service 1200-1400, 1930-2100; closed Wednesday lunchtime except public holidays; menus 130-350F, also à la carte; specialities: consommé de canard glacé, truffe en croustade.

This old coaching inn has been in the family for many generations. The two reception rooms, whose colours harmonise well with the open stonework and the wood of the ancient furniture, are full of charm. In one of them a small museum has been laid out. You can choose between a pretty dining room in local style, or another modern one which has been very well integrated. Good hearty cooking is complemented by a well chosen wine list. The bedrooms are comfortable and have character; for peace and quiet one would prefer those in the annexe, which all look out onto a very large garden with a swimming pool. A very warm welcome.

How to get there (Map 23): 45km south east of Périgueux via N89 and D710, then D47.

Hôtel Les Glycines★★★

24620 Les Eyzies–de–Tayac (Dordogne)
Tel. 53.06.97.07 – Fax 53.06.92.19
M. and Mme Mercat

Open 29 April – 3 Nov. **Rooms** 25 with telephone, bath and WC. **Price** single 300-380F, double 340-390F. **Meals** breakfast 48F, served 0800-1000; half board 377-420F, full board 470-510F (per pers., 3 days min.) **Credit cards** accepted. **Pets** dogs allowed. **Facilities** swimming pool, park, parking. **Nearby** Le Bugue, cave de Bara-Bahau and Proumeyssac chasm, Limeuil, National Museum of Pre-history at Les Eyzies, 18-hole la-Croix-de-Mortemart golf course at Le Bugue. **Restaurant** service 1200-1400, 1930-2130 (closed Saturday lunchtime except public holidays); menus 140-370F, also à la carte; specialities: côte de veau soufflée au foie gras, soufflé aux noix.

Dating back to 1862, this old coaching inn is a large house where stone, wood and prolific vegetation blend happily together. As the name indicates, there is a pergola covered with an abundance of wisteria; trimmed lime trees shade the terrace. The sitting room and bar have a restful atmosphere and have been furnished and decorated with great care. The lovely dining room opens onto the garden but meals may also be taken on a new verandah which gives on to the lawn. All the bedrooms are very comfortable and the furnishings have obviously been well selected; fabrics, papers and colours are in a contemporary style. The cooking makes good use of fresh produce from the kitchen garden.

How to get there *(Map 23): 45km south east of Périgueux via N89 and D710, then D47.*

Moulin de la Beune★★

24620 Les Eyzies-de-Tayac (Dordogne)
Tel. 53.06.94.33 - Fax 53.06.98.06
M. and Mme Soulié

Open end March – beg. Nov. **Rooms** 20 with telephone, bath or shower and WC. **Price** single 260F, double 280-400F. **Meals** breakfast 40F, served 0800-1030; half board 320F, full board 420F (per pers., 2 days min.) **Credit cards** Amex, MasterCard, Visa. **Pets** dogs allowed. **Facilities** parking, **Nearby** Le Bugue, cave of Bara-Bahau and Proumeyssac chasm, Limeuil, National Museum of Pre-history at Les Eyzies, 18-hole la-Croix-de-Mortemart golf course at Le Bugue. **Restaurant** service 1200-1430, 1900-2130 (closed Tuesday lunchtime); menus 85-315F, also à la carte: specialities: Saint-Jacques aux truffes, jarret de veau à l'ancienne, écrevisses.

When arriving at this old mill it is hard to believe that you are in one of the most visited areas of France. The river Beune runs quietly at your feet; the small garden dotted with tables is a peaceful haven. In the sitting room, beside the large fireplace, armchairs and little tables allow you to install yourself comfortably to read or write. To one side there is a room where drinks and breakfast are served, depending on the time of day. The decor of the recently refurbished bedrooms has been tastefully chosen. The restaurant, Le Vieux Moulin, occupies another adjacent mill, and is decorated with as much care. In the large dining room with its exposed stonework and beams, or in the garden at the foot of time worn cliffs, truffle-based Périgourdine specialities are served.

How to get there (Map 23): 45km south east of Périgueux via N89 and D710, then D47; in the middle of the village.

Au Bon Accueil
24510 Limeuil (Dordogne)
Tel. 53.63.30.97
M. and Mme Palazy

Open 15 March – end Oct. **Rooms** 10 (5 with shower). **Price** double 125-150F. **Meals** breakfast 25F, served 0800-0930; half board 160-190F, full board 200-225F (per pers., 3 days min.) **Credit cards** Eurocard. **Pets** dogs allowed. **Nearby** Le Bugue, cave of Bara-Bahau and Proumeyssac chasm, Limeuil, National Museum of Pre-history at Les Eyzies, 18-hole la-Croix-de-Mortemart golf course at le Bugue. **Restaurant** service 1200-1430, 1930-2130; menus 58-135F, also à la carte; specialities: filet de perche au Monbazillac, civet de lièvre ou sanglier, assiette gabare.

At the top of the magnificent medieval village of Limeuil M. and Mme Palazy have opened Le Bon Acceuil. The charm of this very simple inn is due to its owners' fervent wish to create a 'real' place. The welcome is warm and professional, the food simple and good, the atmosphere relaxed and calm. At these very reasonable prices the bedrooms are a bit basic, but for all that there is absolute peace. We recommend this inn especially in good weather, when you may enjoy a meal or a cup of tea sitting in its charming pergola. A pleasing terraced garden is being laid out at the base of an ancient battlement. Finally, for those in search of the real thing, weather permitting you can set out at dawn with M. Palazy to fish in the river, and later enjoy eating your catch at the hotel.

How to get there *(Map 23): 37km south of Périgueux via D710 towards Villeneuve-sur-Lot to Le Bugue, then D31 towards Trémolat.*

La Grande Marque★★

24220 Marnac-Saint-Cyprien
Tel. 53.31.61.63 - Fax 53.28.39.55
M. and Mme Devaux d'Hangest

Open April – All Saints. **Rooms** 16 (of which 4 duplex) with telephone, bath or shower, WC and TV. **Price** double 260-350F. **Meals** breakfast 35F, served 0830-0930; half board 250-352F, full board 325-370F (per pers., 3 days min.) **Credit cards** Visa. **Pets** dogs allowed. **Facilities** salt-water swimming pool, parking. **Nearby** châteaux of Veyrignac, Les Milandes and Montfort, Beynac and Cazenac, Domme, 9-hole Rochebois golf course at Vitrac. **Restaurant** service 1230-1330, 1930-2100; menus 95-200F, also à la carte; specialities: papitons de lotte et saumon, local cooking.

Buried in the middle of the country on the side of a hill, La Grande Marque offers an extraordinary panoramic view of the Dordogne. The bedrooms are in an old tobacco drying building which has been completely renovated. First, you enter a modern reception room almost bare of furniture and lit by immense picture windows. Exhibitions of paintings are held here. Upstairs the bedrooms, though comfortable, are also completely simple so as not to draw the eye away from the magnificent views of the landscape which can be seen from every window. The garden, dotted with sculptures by one of the sons, is a mass of flowers, and has many nooks and crannies to explore. On a shady terrace tables are laid for summer breakfasts, but if the weather is bad a pleasantly rustic dining room is used. The cooking is creative and excellent.

How to get there *(Map 23): 57km south east of Périgueux via N89 to Niversac, D710 to Le Bugue, D31 to Buisson and D25 to Siorac and D50.*

La Métairie★★★

24150 Mauzac (Dordogne)
Tel. 53.22.50.47 – Fax 53.22.52.93
Mme Vigneron and M. Culis

Open 1 April – 15 Oct. **Rooms** 10 with telephone, bath, WC, TV (6 with minibar).
Price double 390-750F (low season), 420-860F (high season), suite 990-1140F.
Meals breakfast 60F, served 0800-1000, half board 410-600F (per pers., 2 days
min.) **Credit cards** Visa, Eurocard. **Pets** dogs allowed (+30F). **Facilities** swimming
pool, parking. **Nearby** Les Eyzies, Limeuil, Le Bugue, Bergerac, 18-hole la-Croix-de-
Mortemart golf course at Le Bugue. **Restaurant** service 1230-1430, 1930-2100
(closed Tuesday 1 April – 15 June, and Tuesday lunchtime from 15 June); menus 95-
200F, also à la carte; specialities of Périgord.

A few kilometres from the famous horse–shoe shaped Cingle de
Tremolat, in a beautiful valley where great loops of the
Dordogne river wind through a mosaic of cultivated fields, lies La
Métairie. It is a charming and beautiful house converted with
comfort, delicacy and good taste. The garden is also very well done.
At the same level as the lawn a pleasant terrace runs along the side
of the house, and in summer a grill is lit near the swimming pool.
The restaurant cooking is very appetising and aromatic. Finally, it
is worth noting that the hotel is close to a superb boating lake
where every possible type of water sport is available.

How to get there *(Map 23): 68km south of Périgueux via N89 and D710
to Le Bugue, then D703 and branch off for Mauzac.*

Le Mas de Montet★★★

24600 Petit Bersac près Ribérac (Dordogne)
Tel 53.90.08.71 - Fax 53.90.55.87
Mme Duvert

Open all year. **Rooms** 14 with telephone, bath, shower, WC and TV. **Price** 380-550F.
Meals breakfast 38F, served 0700-1030; half board 400-500F, full board 500-650F
(per pers., 10 days min.) **Credit cards** Amex, Diners, Visa. **Pets** dogs allowed.
Facilities parking. **Nearby** Tourtoirac abbey, château de Hautefort, foie gras market
at Ribérac, 18-hole golf course at Périgueux. **Restaurant** service 1230-2000; menus
120-290F, also à la carte; specialities: Périgord cuisine, foie gras.

Lying in a great park planted with hundred-year-old sequoia
trees, this small château does not seem like a hotel. It is a family
home, with antique furniture, pottery, copperware, and so on...
The entrance is almost entirely glazed and contains a garden room
with white lacquered cane furniture and abundant green houseplants.
The good smell of polish accompanies the visitor into the sitting
room and the dining room, which are kept as they have been for
years by the owner, an elderly lady but still hale and hearty. The
bedrooms are as charming as one could wish, with pretty fabrics,
walnut wardrobes, draped dressing tables, old armchairs; each one
is arranged differently. The bathrooms can be huge. We preferred
No. 2 with its extension into the tower, and No. 9. A terrace on the
first floor means that you can have breakfast in the sunshine enjoying
a view of the park. Excellent gastronomic cooking, where foie gras
is unavoidable. A valuable address with an excellent restaurant.

How to get there *(Map 23): 50km west of Périgueux via D710 to Ribérac,*
D20 towards Aubeterre; Petit Bersac road, on the right.

148

L'Auberge du Noyer★★

Le Reclaud-de-Bouny-Bas
24260 Le Bugue (Dordogne)
Tel. 53.07.11.73 - Fax 53.54.57.44 - M. and Mme Dyer

Open Palm Sunday – All Saints. **Rooms** 10 with telephone, bath and WC. **Price** single 300F, double 500F. **Meals** breakfast 45F, served 0815-1000; half board 400F (per pers.) **Credit cards** MasterCard, Visa. **Pets** dogs not allowed. **Facilities** swimming pool, parking. **Nearby** Le Bugue, Proumeyssac chasm, Limeuil, Les Eyzies, Vézère valley from Limeuil to Montignac, Lascaux, 18-hole la-Croix-de-Mortemart golf course at Le Bugue. **Restaurant** service 1930-2100; menu 160F; specialities: coussin de truite farcie aux pleurotes, magret à l'orange, tarte aux noix.

Five kilometres from Le Bugue, this 18th-century Périgourdine farm has been completely renovated by an English couple, Paul and Jenny Dyer, who fell in love with the region. Auberge du Noyer is a charming and tranquil place in which to stay, even in the month of August. The bedrooms are spacious and have impeccable bathrooms: five have their own private terraces on which to have breakfast (ask for No. 8). The cooking is simple but refined and meals are served in a pretty, rustic dining room. Breakfast is a high point, with home made jams, freshly squeezed orange juice and toasted farmhouse bread.

How to get there *(Map 23): 37km south of Périgueux via D710 towards Villeneuve-sur-Lot, then D703 towards Lalinde.*

Hôtel de L'Abbaye★★★

Rue de l'Abbaye
24220 Saint-Cyprien-en-Périgord (Dorgogne)
Tel. 53.29.20.48 - Fax 53.29.15.85 - M. and Mme Schaller

Open 15 April – 15 Oct. **Rooms** 24 with telephone, bath or shower, WC (11 with TV and minibar). **Price** single 340-480F, double 360-660F, suite 650-800F. **Meals** breakfast 50F, served 0800-1000; half board 330-550F (per pers.) **Credit cards** Visa, Amex, Diners. **Pets** dogs allowed. **Facilities** swimming pool, parking. **Nearby** cave of Proumeyssac, Le Bugue, château de Campagne, Les Eyzies, 18-hole la-Croix-de-Mortemart golf course at Le Bugue. **Restaurant** service 1200-1400, 1930-2100; menus 140-320F, also à la carte; specialities: foie gras frais, poulet sauté aux langoustines, escalope de saumon grillé.

Situated in the pretty village of Saint-Cyprien, the exterior of this large house has been left untouched so that the local stone acts as is decoration. The same theme is echoed in the sitting room, with stone walls and fireplace and the original stone floor. The bedrooms are all of a good standard, some more luxurious than others. In one of the annexes bedrooms can be combined to form a family apartment. The bedrooms in the new building are excellent. Terrace and pleasant gardens with swimming pool.

How to get there *(Map 23): 54km south east of Périgueux via N89 and D710 to Le Bugue, then D703 and D35 to St-Cyprien.*

Hostellerie Saint-Jacques***

24470 Saint-Saud-Lacoussière (Dordogne)
Tel. 53.56.97.21 - Fax 53.56.91.33
M. and Mme Babayou

Open 1 April – 15 Oct (closed Sunday evening and Monday in low season). **Rooms** 22, and 3 apartments, with telephone, bath or shower, WC (10 with TV and minibar). **Price** single 300F, double 330-515F, suite 860F. **Meals** breakfast 45F, brunch by the swimming pool; half board 270-400F, full board 320-450F (per pers., 3 days min.) **Credit cards** MasterCard, Visa. **Pets** dogs allowed. **Facilities** heated swimming pool, tennis, parking. **Nearby** Brantôme abbey, Villars caves, St-Jean-de-Côle, 18-hole Saltgourde golf course at Marsac. **Restaurant** service 1230-1330, 1930-2100 (closed Sunday evening and Monday except for residents, and 15 Oct – Easter except Sunday and public holidays); menus 115-220F, also à la carte; specialities: foie gras maison aux figues, pied de porc farci aux ris de veau, parmentier au confit de canard.

The Hostellerie Saint-Jacques has the generous proportions of an 18th-century Périgourdine house. The bedrooms all have different fabrics and furniture. Those on the first floor are of uneven quality (some charming, some disappointing, and the corridor is a bit depressing). On the second floor all the bedrooms are perfect: gay, light and well decorated, most have beautiful views of the countryside. The dining room is also very attractive, and the cooking is excellent. It is a vast room which extends through glass doors into a well shaded garden generously provided with prettily laid tables. Full of flowers, the garden extends to the swimming pool and tennis court. Informal welcome.

How to get there *(Map 23): 58km north of Périgueux via N21 to La Coquille, then D79.*

Hôtel de La Hoirie***

La Giragne - 24200 Sarlat (Dordogne)
Tel. 53.59.05.62 - Fax 53.31.13.90
M. Sainneville

Open 15 March – 14 Nov. **Rooms** 15 with telephone, bath or shower, WC, TV and minibar. **Price** single and double 340-550F, suite 520-550F. **Meals** breakfast 53F, served 0800-1000; half board 360-465F (per pers., 3 days min.) **Credit cards** accepted. **Pets** dogs allowed. **Facilities** swimming pool, parking. **Nearby** old town and house of La Boétie at Sarlat, châteaux of Puymartin and Commarques, Carsac, Lascaux caves, 9-hole Rochebois golf course at Vitrac. **Restaurant** service 1200-1330, 1915-2100; menus 130-300F, also à la carte; specialities: assortiment de foie gras spécial mi-cuit, ris de veau aux truffes, filet mignon au foie gras et morilles, gâteau aux noix.

Near Sarlat, far from the crowds and the noise, this old hunting lodge of the Vienne family is a beautiful building in local stone. The most expensive bedrooms, those in the main body of the building, are spacious and have fine old furniture; some have the original stonework and fireplaces. The subtle colours of the walls and fabrics go well together. On the ground floor there is a small dining room which is welcoming and intimate. In the other part of the building there are smaller bedrooms, also pretty, among which we recommend the attic bedroom on the top floor. A small sitting room with a fireplace and a reading area is to be found on the ground floor. The garden is well shaded and has a swimming pool.

How to get there *(Map 23): 66km south east of Périgueux via N89 and D710 to beyond La Douze, then D47 to Sarlat-la-Canède via les Eyzies-de-Tayac.*

Le Relais de Touron★★

Le Touron
24200 Carsac-Aillac (Dordogne)
Tel. 53.28.16.70 – Mme Carlier

Open 31 March – 15 Nov. **Rooms** 12 with telephone, bath or shower and WC. **Price** double 265-375F, triple 385-475F. **Meals** breakfast 34F, served 0800-1000; half board 277-328F. **Credit cards** accepted except Amex and Diners. **Pets** dogs allowed. **Facilities** swimming pool, parking. **Nearby** walk along the valley of the Enéa from Carsac to Ste-Nathalène, old town and house of La Boétie at Sarlat, château de Puymartin, 9-hole Rochebois golf course at Vitrac. **Restaurant** closed lunchtime in low season except Sunday and national holidays; menus 90-245F, also à la carte; specialities feuilleté d'escargots au cèpes, œufs brouillés à la truite fumée, filet d'agneau au beurre de foie gras, sandre à l'orange.

The Relais de Touron is a peaceful country inn which lies at the end of the village. The rustling leaves of the poplar trees and the murmuring of the Enea as it flows tranquilly along create a romantic pastoral atmosphere. The comfortable bedrooms are all in the same building except No. 12, which is the most attractive (high ceiling, beams) but is for three or four persons. A good swimming pool surrounded by shaded lawns, and a terrace where meals and breakfast are served, are just a couple of the features which make the Relais de Touron a pleasant spot in which to stay.

How to get there *(Map 23): 75km south east of Périguex to Sarlat, then D704 towards Gourdon (600m before the village of Carsac).*

Château de Vieux-Mareuil★★★

Vieux-Mareuil - 24340 Mareuil (Dordogne)
Tel. 53.60.77.15 - Fax 53.56.49.33
M. and Mme Lefranc

Open 1 March – 15 Jan (closed Sunday evening and Monday 1 Nov – Easter). **Rooms** 14 with telephone, bath, WC, TV and minibar. **Price** double 400-1000F. **Meals** breakfast 60F, served 0800-1030; half board 450-750F, full board 550-850F (per pers., 3 days min.) **Credit cards** accepted. **Pets** dogs not allowed. **Facilities** swimming pool, parking. **Nearby** Brantôme abbey, château de Bourdeilles, St-Jean-de-Côle, Jumilhac-le-Grand, 18-hole Saltgourde golf course at Marsac. **Restaurant** service 1200-1430, 1900-2145; menus 120-320F, also à la carte.

Perched on a little hill in 20-hectares of woods and fields, this old château has been tastefully converted into a very comfortable hotel. In the main body of the hotel there are two attractive dining rooms, a sitting room (perhaps a bit too small) with a lovely fireplace, and in the tower of the château three beautiful bedrooms furnished in antique style. The other bedrooms are more modern but also very pleasing and are in a wing overlooking the park. For sunny days there is a swimming pool. The delicious cooking varies according to the season, and the very good demi-pension menu changes every day. The pleasant atmosphere created by the owners, and the excellent service, make this an ideal place to stay in one of the loveliest regions of France.

How to get there *(Map 23): 42km north west of Périgueux via D939 to Vieux-Mareuil.*

Hauterive Hôtel Saint-James★★★★

3, place Camille-Hostein
33270 Bouliac (Gironde)
Tel. 56.20.52.19 - Telex 573 001 - Fax 56.20.92.58 - M. Amat

Open all year. **Rooms** 17 with telephone, bath, WC, TV and minibar. **Price** single 600-800F, double 650-850F, suite 1150-1350F. **Meals** breakfast 70F, served from 0700. **Credit cards** accepted. **Pets** dogs allowed (+100F). **Facilities** swimming pool, tennis, sauna, health centre, parking. **Nearby** Museum of Contemporary Art, Museum of Fine Art, Port-de-la-Lune Theatre at Bordeaux, Le Bordelais, 18-hole Cameyrac golf course, 18-hole Bordelais golf course. **Restaurant** service 1200-1400, 2000-2200 (closed Sunday); menus 250-400F, also à la carte; specialities: fondant d'aubergine au cumin, pigeon aux épices et sa pastilla, salade d'huîtres au caviar et sa crépinette.

To make an exception and include this ultra-modern place means that it must be out of the ordinary. That it is, is due to the immense talents of two people: the owner and chef Jean-Marie Amat, and the architect Jean Nouvel. The result of their combined efforts is amazing. Occupying three buildings, all the bedrooms have picture windows with extensive views over vineyards and the plain of Bordeaux. The decor is in tones of white and cream, broken by brightly-coloured carpets or the flash of steel grey. This high-tech approach combines with bunches of flowers, sculptures and books to create the intimacy of a home: it could have been cold but is warm. There is no need to describe the famous cooking of Jean-Marie Amat. His celebrated restaurant and an excellent bistro adjoin the hotel.

How to get there *(Map 22): 5km east of Bordeaux; in the centre of le Pont-St-Jean head towards la Tresne; it's 2km from the Leclerc commercial centre in the Bouliac direction.*

Château du Foulon

33480 Castelnau-de-Médoc (Gironde)
Tel. 56.58.20.18 - Fax 56.58.23.43
M. and Mme de Baritault du Carpia

Open all year. **Rooms** 5 with bath and WC. **Price** double 400F, suite 500-600F. **Meals** breakfast incl. No restaurant. **Credit cards** not accepted. **Pets** dogs not allowed. **Facilities** parking. **Nearby** Médoc peninsula on the left bank of the Garonne then the Gironde (day trip, 150km), Mouton-Rothschild museum at Pauillac, 18-hole Bordelais golf course, 18-hole Bordeaux-le-Lac golf course.

From a small square close to the village cemetery in Castelnau-de-Médoc runs a long avenue lined with trees. At the end of this stands a small 19th-century château which, cut off by a small waterway crossing the estate, seems lost in the midst of the countryside. M. and Mme Baritault du Carpia have decided to share the experience of living in their château, and five comfortable and individual guest bedrooms are set aside for this purpose. Breakfast is taken at a large communal table, and you may have the use of the garden, with its swans and pheasants, to stroll there as if you were the Lords of the Manor.

How to get there *(Map 22): 28km north west of Bordeaux via N215 to Saint-Médard-en-Jalles, then D1 to Castelnau-de-Médoc; in the village, take D212 south to Foulon.*

Hostellerie du Vieux Raquine

Lugon
33240 Saint-André-de-Cubzac (Gironde)
Tel. 57.84.42.77 - Fax 57.84.83.77 - Mme de Raquine

Open all year. **Rooms** 7 with telephone, bath or shower, WC (3 with TV). **Price** single 450F, double 450-600F, suite 650F. **Meals** breakfast 50F, served 0800-1000. No restaurant. **Credit cards** Visa, Eurocard, MasterCard. **Pets** dogs not allowed. **Facilities** parking. **Nearby** church of St-André-de-Cubzac, château de Bouilh, Bourg, St Emilion, 18-hole Bordelais golf course.

The ground floor of this hotel covers the whole top of a hill. Completely renovated, it is furnished in an old fashioned style (not without a few failures). The bedrooms are impeccably kept and, except one, are all at ground level. There are two reception rooms. The one used as the dining room has windows all along one side opening on to a large terrace with an outstanding view of the vineyards of Fronsac, bordered by the Dordogne in the distance. Mme Raquine likes to make the hotel feel like a family house. Peace and fresh air are guaranteed: le Vieux Raquine was a rest home in times past.

How to get there *(Map 22): 23km north east of Bordeaux; A10 St-André-de-Cubzac exit, D670.*

Château Lardier★★

33350 Ruch - Castillon-la-bataille (Gironde)
Tel. 57.40.54.11 - Fax 57.40.70.38
M. and Mme Bauzin

Open March – end Nov (closed Sunday evening and Monday except July, Aug and Sept)
Rooms 9 with telephone, bath or shower, WC (2 with TV). **Price** double 200-305F; half
board 225-310F, full board 315-410F (per pers., 3 days min.) **Credit cards** Visa, Eurocard,
MasterCard. **Pets** dogs allowed. **Facilities** parking. **Nearby** Libourne and the Libournais
(Pomerol, Château Pétrus, St Emilion), Blasimon, Duras. **Restaurant** service 1200-1330,
1930-2130; menus 80-250F, also à la carte; specialities: croquants de Saint-Jacques,
foie gras, lamproie, symphonie de la mer, chausson de canard.

This charming country hotel on a little hill overlooking
vineyards is very peaceful, and you will receive a warm
welcome from the young owners, who have furnished it very
comfortably and in discreet good taste. The bedrooms vary in size;
they are light and airy and have pleasant turn–of–the–century
furniture. Ask for the 'Green' room as your first choice. The
cooking is good traditional fare, with some well prepared
specialities, and is served in a dining room where a log fire burns
in winter. In summer the tables are placed outside on the terrace,
in the shade of a cedar, with a fine view. The whole hotel is well
cared for and for guests' amusement there is a billiard table on the
first floor. This is a good family place from which to visit the
vineyards or explore the many Romanesque abbeys round about.

How to get there *(Map 22): 9km south of Castillon-la-bataille via D15 and
D17 towards Sauveterre, then D232 (2km from the town).*

La Closerie des Vignes★★

Village des Arnauds
33710 Saint-Ciers-de-Canesse (Gironde)
Tel. 57.64.81.90 - Mme Robert-Broy

Open all year (except Feb). **Rooms** 9 with telephone, bath, WC and TV. **Price** double 340F. **Meals** breakfast 30F, served 0800-1000; half board 295F (per pers., 3 days min.) **Credit cards** Visa, MasterCard, Eurocard. **Pets** dogs allowed. **Facilities** swimming pool, parking. **Nearby** citadel at Blaye, Bourg, cave of Pair-non-Pair near Prignac, château de Bouilh, church of St-André-de-Cubzac. **Restaurant** service 1200-1330, 1930-2100 (closed Sunday evening and Tuesday in high season); menus 115-150F, also à la carte; specialities: gambas flambées au whisky, lamproie bordelaise, magret confit, foie gras.

The Closerie des Vignes cannot claim to be an ancient building but this small auberge is truly delightful and the ambience so welcoming and friendly that it cries out to be included in this guide. Lying amid vineyards, it is very comfortable, admirably well cared for, and its decor contributes to its serenity: modern furniture with clean and simple lines, soft pastel colours, pretty floral fabrics and comfortable sofas and chairs. The dining room looks out over the vineyards and there is a pleasant swimming pool for summer visitors.

How to get there (Map 22): 8km south east of Blaye via D669 to Villeneuve, then D290.

Château de Commarque

33210 Sauternes (Gironde)
Tel. 56.76.65.94 – Fax 56.76.64.30
M. Reay-Jones

Open March – Jan. **Rooms** 10 with bath and WC. **Price** double 180-275F, suite 275F.
Meals breakfast 30F, served 0800-0915; half board 250F, full board 350F (per pers.,
3 days min.) **Credit cards** accepted. **Pets** dogs allowed. **Facilities** swimming pool,
parking. **Nearby** Sauternes vineyards, château de Malle, château de Roquetaille, St
Macaire, Cadillac. **Restaurant** service 1200-1400, 1930-2130; menus 75-175F, also
à la carte; specialities: cooking with Sauternes.

Commarque, surrounded by the leading Sauternes vineyards,
has retained the elegant rusticity of years gone by. Nearly all
the bedrooms are duplexes; their sleeping area is simple but
charming and is on the mezzanine (up a rather steep stairway). The
walls are white, the furniture is wooden and there are engravings
as decoration. Each room has a small, shaded private terrace which
looks out on the inner courtyard. An old barn has been converted
into a dining room with beams, stone walls and often a cheerful
wood fire. Here you will enjoy delicious traditional food, served
with a smile at a very reasonable price. The owner, M. Reay-Jones,
is English and gives his guests a cordial welcome; he is also an
enthusiastic wine producer and will be happy to discuss his favourite
subject with you.

How to get there *(Map 22): 50km south of Bordeaux via A62 (Autoroute
des Deux Mers), Langon exit.*

La Maison Rose★★

40320 Eugénie-les-bains (Landes)
Tel. 58.05.05.05 - Fax 58.51.13.59
M. Leclercq – M. and Mme Guérard

Open 14 Feb – 1 Dec. **Rooms** 22, and 5 suites, with telephone, bath, WC and TV. **Price** single 420-450F, double 520-550F, suite 650-800F. **Meals** breakfast 70F, served 0830-0915; full board 600-800F (per pers., 3 days min.) **Credit cards** accepted. **Pets** dogs allowed (+50F). **Facilities** swimming pool, tennis, sauna, health centre, parking. **Nearby** Aire-sur-Adour cathedral and organs, Mont-de-Marsan museums and keep, Samadet pottery museum, Saint-Sever Dominican monastery. **Restaurant** service 1300 and 2000; menus 170-190F.

Michel and Christine Guérard make a marvellous combination: he is the well known master of gastronomy who has made his restaurant Prés d'Eugénie one of the best in France; she is an accomplished hotelier and her three houses in Eugénie are models of what hotels should be. Les Prés has a colonial air, the Couvent des Herbes is exceptionally pretty, and in La Maison Rose she has opted for a country atmosphere. We have chosen La Maison Rose for its low weight, low price formula – meaning that for a very reasonable full-pension price you can choose a week's *cuisine minceur* cooking course or a week's thermal baths programme. Throughout your stay you can enjoy M. Guérard's delectable *cuisine minceur*, but you could also have a *fête gourmand* in his celebrated restaurant. This could be an unforgettable holiday, in charming surroundings.

How to get there *(Map 29): 35km south of Mont-de-Marsan via D124 towards Pau.*

La Vieille Auberge★★

Port-de-Lanne – 40300 Peyrehorade (Landes)
Tel. 58.89.16.29 – Fax 58.89.12.89
M. and Mme Lataillade

Open 31 May – 1 Oct (closed Monday). **Rooms** 8 with telephone, bath or shower, WC (2 with TV). **Price** single 200F, double 270-320F, suite 500F. **Meals** breakfast 35F, served 0830-1030; half board 270-320F (per pers.) **Credit cards** not accepted. **Pets** dogs allowed. **Facilities** swimming pool, parking. **Nearby** Biarritz, Peyrehorade, abbey of Arthous, Sorde-l'abbaye, Romanesque church at Cagnotte, Bonnat and Basque museums at Bayonne, 18-hole Hossegor golf course. **Restaurant** service 1200-1330, 1930-2100; menus 110-235F, also à la carte; specialities: magret, mousseline de saumon, saumon frais, confits de canard et de porc à l'ail.

This old coaching inn, where he was born, is as close to M. Lataillade's heart as it was to his father's. Above all La Vieille Auberge has the charm of an old establishment whose timbers, walls and floors have seen the march of time. The cosy reception rooms, which seem to live to the rhythm of a slow pendulum, are sometimes filled with the notes of an old piano. The bedrooms are in what used to be stables or barns. There is bags of charm, honest comfort, and a colourful garden with a swimming pool. M. Lataillade's absorbing museum is laid out in an old hay barn. Built up over the years, it contains objects and evidence retracing the history of the port of Lanne and its seafarers, who were known as 'Gabariers'. A good and friendly Gascon inn.

How to get there *(Map 29): 30km east of Bayonne via N117; on the church square.*

Auberge des Pins★★

Route de la Piscine
40630 Sabres (Landes)
Tel. 58.07.50.47 - Fax 58.07.56.74 - M. and Mme Lesclauze

Open all year (closed Sunday evening and Monday in low season). **Rooms** 26 with telephone, bath or shower, WC (21 with TV). **Price** single 160F, double 300F, suite 650F. **Meals** breakfast 40F, served 0730-1000; half board 300F (per pers., 3 days min.) **Credit cards** Visa. **Pets** dogs not allowed. **Facilities** parking. **Nearby** church at Sabres, local history museum at Marquèze, regional park of Les Landes de Gascogne. **Restaurant** service 1200-1400, 1930-2100; menus 90-380F, also à la carte; specialities: foie gras frais, filets de rouget, langoustines aux cèpes, pigeon en croûte.

You will be enchanted by this hotel amid the pines on the way out of the village of Sabres. Generations of good hotel keeping ensure high quality service and a faultless welcome. The bedrooms are in two buildings. The ones in the main building have every comfort and an old fashioned charm, but the bedrooms in the newer building, which blends very well with the old, are our favourites. They are large, light, airy and elegantly modern, with lovely fabrics, superb bathrooms and a small terrace. The dining room, with its antique furniture, copperware, ceramics and fireplace laden with a collection of rare old Armagnacs, is a place to linger in over the fine cooking of Michel Lesclauze. He uses the best local produce to make truly memorable meals. An absolute success which we strongly recommend.

How to get there *(Map 29): 40km east of Mimizan via D44.*

La Bergerie★★

Avenue du Lac
40140 Soustons (Landes)
Tel. 58.41.11.43 – Mme Clavier

Open 15 Mar – 15 Nov. **Rooms** 12 with telephone, bath, WC and TV. **Price** single 300F, double 350-400F, suite 500F. **Meals** breakfast 40F, served 0800-1000; half board 350-400F (per pers., 3 days min.) **Credit cards** Visa. **Pets** dogs not allowed. **Facilities** parking. **Nearby** the Marensin from Lit-et-Mixe to Dax (100km), Bonnat and Basque museums at Bayonne, 9- and 18-hole Côte d'Argent golf course. **Restaurant** for residents on half board only; specialities: foie gras et confit des Landes, vins de sable.

D rive past the village church, take the road lined with gigantic plane trees, and you will arrive at the Bergerie. A typically Landaise private house built at the beginning of the century, it is surrounded by large gardens. The oak floor in the entrance hall shines nearly as brightly as the polished copperware. There are two small and prettily furnished sitting rooms. The bedrooms are simple; their furnishings remind you that Spain isn't very far away. This homely charm is also found in the sitting room and dining room, where every morning the menu of the day is announced (fixed menu), prepared with fresh regional produce. On summer mornings a very pretty verandah opening on to the patio is laid for breakfast. The hospitality is such that you soon feel part of the household.

How to get there (Map 28): 38km north of Bayonne via A63 to St-Vincent-de-Tyrosse, then D112 to Tosse, D632 to Soustons.

A la Belle Gasconne★★

47170 Poudenas (Lot-et-Garonne)
Tel. 53.65.71.58 – Fax 53.65.87.39
M. and Mme Gracia

Open 1 Feb – 1 Jan (closed Sunday evening and Monday in low season). **Rooms** 7 with telephone, bath or shower, WC (3 with TV). **Price** single 420F, double 490-540F, suite 620F. **Meals** breakfast 45F; half board 540-715F (per pers.) **Credit cards** Amex, Diners, Visa, MasterCard. **Pets** dogs allowed. **Facilities** swimming pool. **Nearby** Auvillar (pottery museum), Nérac, 18-hole golf courses at Albret and Barbaste. **Restaurant** service 1200-1400, 1930-2130; menus 165-260F, also à la carte; specialities: foie gras frais, civet de canard au vin vieux.

Who hasn't dreamed of spending a few romantic days in an old mill with the sound of running water as a background? This one stands at the foot of a medieval village. Its vast living room, all wood and stone, retains some of the old mill machinery and you can actually see the water running under the floor through a glass paving stone. From this room there is access on to a little island where you can relax in the shade of the trees. The bedrooms, which have purpose-built elm furniture, rival each other in comfort and decoration. All the colours have been delicately selected, and in the bathrooms, tiled with Salernes tiles, even the dressing gowns are changed daily. At meal times you will enjoy food from one of the famous tables of France: each dish is an enchantment, and M. and Mme Gracia's hospitality is discreet and attentive.

How to get there *(Map 30): 47km south west of Agen via D656 through Nérac.*

Hôtel Ohantzea★★

Rue Principale
64250 Aïnhoa (Pyrénées-Atlantiques)
Tel. 59.29.90.50 - M. and Mme Ithurria

Open 15 Jan – 15 Nov (closed Sunday evening and Monday). **Rooms** 10 with telephone, of which 9 with bath, 1 with shower. **Price** single 210F, double 285F. **Meals** breakfast 30F, served 0800-0930; half board 280F, full board 340F (per pers., 3 days min.) **Credit cards** Eurocard, MasterCard, Visa. **Nearby** Espelette, Sare, Ascain, Villa Arnaga at Cambo-les-Bains, Bonnat and Basque museums at Bayonne, 18-hole Chantaco golf course at St-Jean-de-Luz. **Restaurant** service 1200-1400, 2000-2045; menus 120-205F, also à la carte; specialities: magret de canard aux cèpes, turbot braisé au Jurançon.

In the middle of the village, opposite the church, an attractive whitewashed facade hides this old 17th-century farm, renovated at the beginning of this century, and a lovely garden which is invisible from the road. The paintings hanging in the small sitting room were offered as payment by passing artists. To one side is the dining room, one of the most beautiful and authentic in the Pays Basque. Also notable are the old wooden stairs, the furniture, objects, coppers, prints, etc. The bedrooms and bathrooms are delightfully out of date and all are comfortable. Many retain their original wallpaper and those on the garden side have balconies covered with wisteria.

How to get there (*Map 28*): *26km south of Bayonne via D932 and D918 towards Espelette, then D20; in the main street.*

Le Château du Clair de Lune***

48, avenue Alan-Seeger
64200 Biarritz (Pyrénées-Atlantiques)
Tel. 59.23.45.96 - Fax 59.23.39.13 - Mme Beyrière

Open all year. **Rooms** 16 with telephone, bath, WC, TV (8 with minibar). **Price** double 400-650F. **Meals** breakfast 50F, served 0800-1100. No restaurant. **Credit cards** Visa, Amex, Diners. **Pets** dogs allowed (+35F). **Facilities** parking. **Nearby** rock of the Virgin, museum of the sea at Biarritz, Anglet and the forest of Chiberta, Arcangues, Bidard, 18-hole Biarritz golf course, 18-hole Chiberta golf course at Anglet.

This turn-of-the-century house above Biarritz is very peaceful and stands in a serene garden of rose beds, flower beds, trees and lawns. It is the sort of house which conjures up nostalgic memories of childhood. The bathrooms and baths have the huge proportions of another era, and the tiling and basins are ancient. The large sitting room on the ground floor opens on to and merges with the garden: gay, airy and bright, it is furnished with yellow sofas and a grand piano. The dining room, where guests breakfast together around a large table, makes you wish that you could dine here as well. A lovely family house on the Basque coast which, though a hotel, begins to feel as if it were your own.

How to get there *(Map 28): 4km south of the town centre via the pont de la Négresse and D255.*

Hôtel du Pont d'Enfer★★

64780 Bidarray (Pyrénées-Atlantiques)
Tel. 59.37.70.88 - Fax 59.37.76.60
M. Dufau

Open 1 March – 31 Jan (closed Monday evening and Wednesday in low season). **Rooms** 17 with telephone, bath or shower (13 with WC, 10 with TV). **Price** single 220F, double 270F. **Meals** breakfast 30F, served 0800-0930; half board 245F, full board 305F (per pers., 3 days min.) **Credit cards** accepted. **Pets** dogs allowed. **Facilities** parking. **Nearby** St-Jean-Pied-de-Port, caves of Isturits and Oxocelhaya, Bonnat and Basque museums at Bayonne, 18-hole Arcangues golf course at Argelous. **Restaurant** service 1200 and 1930; menus 92-158F, also à la carte; specialities: foie gras, confit de canard, salmis de palombe, sole au champagne.

To reach this hotel you cross the bridge, called Pont d'Enfer (Bridge of Hell), after which the hotel is named, spanning the Nive. Situated at the foot of a hill at the entrance to the village, the hotel is old but comfortable. We liked the huge dining room, furnished faithfully in Basque country style, as well as the atmosphere of the bedrooms. Some of the bedrooms are in a separate building and of these Nos. 14, 16 and 18 look out directly on to the river. In summer you can take your meals on the terrace beside the river Nive. Mme Gagnant's welcome is one of real kindness.

How to get there (Map 28): 35km south east of Bayonne via D932 and D918.

Hôtel Errobia★★★

Avenue Chantecler
64250 Cambo-les-Bains (Pyrénées-Atlantiques)
Tel. 59.29.71.26 - Fax 59.29.96.36 - Mme Garra

Open Easter and 1 May – 30 Oct. **Rooms** 15 with telephone, bath or shower, TV (9 with WC). **Price** single 300F, double 400F, suite 500F. **Meals** breakfast 30F, served 0730-1100. No restaurant. **Credit cards** Visa. **Pets** dogs allowed. **Facilities** swimming pool, parking. **Nearby** Villa Arnaga at Cambo, Artzamendi, church of Itxassou, Bonnat and Basque museums at Bayonne, 18-hole Arcangues golf course at Argelous.

In the residential area of Cambo-des-Bains, built on the edge of a plateau overhanging the river Nive facing the Pyrenees, this large Basque villa stands in magnificent gardens. The interior is of a very high standard and completely furnished in Basque style, from the antique furniture to the kitchens and the wall tiles (our only reservation: some of the bedding is uncomfortable). All around, the green and flowering gardens bear witness to the gentleness of the climate here. To enjoy the peace and beauty of this place, take a stroll through the gardens among the trees and the abundant hydrangeas, mimosas, and camellias.

How to get there *(Map 28): 20km south of Bayonne via D932; near the church.*

Artzaïn Etchea★★
Route d'Iraty
64220 Esterençuby (Pyrénées-Atlantiques)
Tel. 59.37.11.55 - Fax 59.37.20.16 - M. Arriaga

Open 20 Dec – 11 Nov (closed Wednesday in low season). **Rooms** 22 with telephone, bath or shower, WC (8 with TV). **Price** single 172F, double 208F, suite 276F. **Meals** breakfast 34F; half board 190-226F, full board 213-256F (per pers., 2 days min.) **Credit cards** not accepted. **Pets** dogs allowed (+20F). **Facilities** parking. **Nearby** St-Jean-Pied-de-Port (pilgrim's way), St-Etienne-de-Baïgorry, St-Jean-le-Vieux. **Restaurant** service 1230-1400, 1930-2100; menus 94-190F (child 60F), also à la carte; specialities: foie de canard chaud aux raisins, saumon frais au champagne, salmis de palombe.

Although Saint-Jean-de-Pied-de-Port is an undeniably charming town, you may wish to avoid the commotion and the crowds of holiday makers. If so, leave the town by a small road lined with low walls, trees and streams: it will bring you to the crossroads of Vallées where Artzaïn Etchea stands. As its Basque name indicates, it was once a shepherd's dwelling and has been converted into a simple but good country hotel. The bedrooms are comfortable but you will do well to choose one of the more recent ones, some of which have a wonderful view of the valley. The dining room is very pleasant and its windows allow you to enjoy the views at your leisure. In summer tables are placed outside, and you can hear the sound of the stream which runs below.

How to get there (*Map 28*): *52km south east of Bayonne via D918 to Saint-Jean-Pied-de Port then D301.*

Hôtel Arcé★★★

64430 Saint-Etienne-de-Baïgorry (Pyrénées-Atlantiques)
Tel. 59.37.40.14 - Fax 59.37.40.27
M. Arcé

Open 15 March – 15 Nov. **Rooms** 22 with telephone, bath or shower, WC and TV. **Price** single 370-430F, double 500-695F, suite 695-990F. **Meals** breakfast 50F, served 0745-1030; half board 335-540F, full board 385-630F (per pers., 3 days min.) **Credit cards** Eurocard, MasterCard, Visa. **Pets** dogs allowed. **Facilities** swimming pool, tennis, parking. **Nearby** St-Jean-le-Vieux, village of Béhérobie, 18-hole Arcangues golf course at Argelous. **Restaurant** service 1230-1345, 1930-2030; menus 110-230F, also à la carte; specialities: marinade de saumon et truite à la crème citronnée, sole farcie au fondant de cèpes, pigeon braisé sauce Madiran.

This old inn, typical of the region and luxuriously restored, has been managed by the same family for the last five generations. The large picture windows are in keeping with the beautiful proportions of the dining room, and outside long terraces are laid out at the water's edge. The bedrooms are extremely comfortable, newly decorated and overlooking the river and the Pyrenees; a variety of reading matter is supplied. Bouquets of flowers are placed all over the hotel. The little annexe is a pleasing addition, its balconies overhanging the river, so you can fish without even leaving your bedroom! Good classic regional cooking and the best of welcomes.

How to get there *(Map 28): 50km south of Bayonne via D932 and D918 to St-Martin d'Arossa, then D948 to St-Etienne-de-Baïgorry.*

La Devinière★★★

5, rue Loquin
64500 Saint-Jean-de-Luz (Pyrénées-Atlantiques)
Tel. 59.26.05.51. - M. Carrère

Open all year. **Rooms** 8 with telephone, bath and WC. **Price** 500-600F. **Meals** breakfast 50F, served all morning. No restaurant. **Credit cards** MasterCard, Eurocard, Visa. **Pets** dogs allowed by arrangement (+50F). **Nearby** St-Jean-Baptiste church at St-Jean-de-Luz, Basque coast road, Ciboure, Bayonne, Biarritz, 18-hole Nivelle and Chantaco golf courses.

There is no obvious reason why M. and Mme Carrère should have taken on and renovated this residential family hotel – he being a lawyer and she an antique dealer – other than the pleasure of opening a charming place in the heart of Saint-Jean-de-Luz. Good taste and discernment are apparent everywhere. The eight bedrooms are ravishingly pretty, furnished with beautiful antiques, and all, like the music room and library, are open for the use of their guests. The pedestrianised street and the garden ensure quiet nights even in the heart of the town. The welcome is warm. A good find.

How to get there *(Map 28): 15km south west of Biarritz via A63.*

Hôtel Arraya***

Place du village
64310 Sare (Pyrénées-Atlantiques)
Tel. 59.54.20.46 - Fax 59.54.27.04 - M. Fagoaga

Open 1 May – 6 Nov. **Rooms** 20 with telephone, bath or shower, WC and TV. **Price** single 395-450F, double 500-560F, suite 700-900F. **Meals** breakfast 50F, served 0800-1000. **Credit cards** Amex, Visa. **Pets** dogs not allowed. **Facilities** parking. **Nearby** Villa Arnaga at Cambo, Espelette, Ascain, St-Jean-de-Luz, Bonnat and Basque museums at Bayonne, 18-hole La Nivelle and Chantaco golf courses. **Restaurant** service 1200-1400, 1930-2200; menus 140-230F, also à la carte; specialities: ravioles de xanguro (crab) en son jumet, gâteau de morue.

D o not be put off by the sombre facade, which is typical of the region. This superb Basque hotel, set on the corner of two streets in the centre of the village, is made up of three old houses, and has a garden, invisible from the street and screened from its noise. On the ground floor the lovely sitting rooms and the comfortable dining room owe part of their charm to the patina of the rustic furniture and the bright colours of the bowls of flowers. The bedrooms are all different but equally attractively presented: the nicest is a room with a little wisteria-covered balcony on the garden side. There is a boutique selling regional delicacies which you can eat on the spot or take away. In the restaurant the menu is long and varied, but classic dishes and the delicious apple tart remain the best specialities of the house.

How to get there (*Map 28*): *36km south of Bayonne via A63, St-Jean-de-Luz exit, D918 to Ascain and D4 to Sare.*

Hôtel La Patoula★★★

64480 Ustaritz (Pyrénées–Atlantiques)
Tel 59.93.00.56 – Fax 59.93.16.54
M. Guilhem

Open 15 Feb – 5 Jan (closed Sunday evening and Monday in low season). **Rooms** 9 with telephone, bath or shower and WC. **Price** double 300-430F. **Meals** breakfast 55F, served 0800-1000; half board 325-390F, full board 445-510F (per pers., 3 days min.) **Credit cards** Visa, Eurocard, MasterCard. **Pets** dogs allowed (+35F). **Facilities** parking. **Nearby** Villa Arnaga at Cambo, Biarritz, Bonnat and Basque museums at Bayonne, 18-hole Biarritz golf course, 18-hole Chantaco golf course at St-Jean-de-Luz. **Restaurant** service 1200-1400, 2000-2200; menus 180-240F, also à la carte; specialities: alose grillée, saumon savage, palombes rôties, agneau de lait.

This hotel is set back from the road in a park bordered by the tranquil waters of the river Nive. This romantic view can be seen either from the dining room, from the pergola where breakfast tables are laid in summer, or from the sun loungers in the garden. In the winter, when there are fewer tourists about, the dining room with its open fire provides an intimate setting. The cooking is good and draws people from all over the district. The bedrooms are spacious, comfortable and very prettily decorated. We preferred the two which overlook the river and the four which overlook the garden. The modest number of rooms and Madame Guilhem's friendliness give La Patoula a very pleasant atmosphere.

How to get there *(Map 28): 11km south of Bayonne via A10, Bayonne-sud exit no.5, towards Cambo-les-Bains, then D982; in the centre of Ustaritz, opposite the church.*

Le Chalet***

03000 Coulandon (Allier)
Tel. 70.44.50.08 – Fax 70.44.07.09
M. Hulot

Open 1 Feb – 15 Dec. **Rooms** 28 with telephone, bath or shower, WC and TV. **Price** single 260-300F, double 320-400F. **Meals** breakfast 36F, served 0700-1100; half board 285-320F, full board 360-395F (per pers., 2 days min.) **Credit cards** accepted. **Pets** dogs allowed. **Facilities** lake, fishing, swimming pool, parking. **Nearby** Souvigny priory, châteaux of the valley of the Besbre and of Lapalisse at Dompierre (half day's journey), triptych of the Maître de Moulins at Notre Dame cathedral at Moulins, 9-hole Avenelles golf course at Moulins. **Restaurant** service 1230-1330, 1930-2100; menus 95-200F, also à la carte; specialities: filet de bœuf grillé aux échalotes confites, poêlée de langoustines aux pâtes fraîches.

Situated in the heart of the lush, green Bourbon countryside this very pretty hotel is surrounded by a large and peaceful garden and has the charm of an old fashioned country house. The food served in the dining room, which looks out on to the garden is simple and traditional of the region. The bedrooms have a rustic feel, with beams and wallpaper, and are all restful and comfortable. There is a lovely terrace in front of the hotel for enjoying summer days.

How to get there *(Map 18): 6km west of Moulins via D945.*

Château du Lonzat

Route du Donjon
03220 Jaligny-sur-Besbre (Allier)
Tel. 70.34.73.39 - Telex 989 000 - Fax 70.34.81.31 - M. Advenier

Open 1 March – 23 Dec. **Rooms** 5 with telephone, bath or shower, WC and TV. **Price** double 280-630F. **Meals** breakfast 46F, served 0730-1030; half board price on application. **Credit cards** Visa, MasterCard, Eurocard, Amex. **Pets** dogs allowed. **Nearby** Souvigny priory, châteaux of the valley of the Besbre and of Lapalisse at Dompierre (half day's journey), triptych of the Maître of Moulins at Notre Dame cathedral at Moulins, 9-hole Avenelles golf course at Moulins. **Restaurant** service 1930-2100; menu 136F; specialities: pâté aux pommes de terre, viande du charolais, légumes du jardin.

In this château there is a bathroom designed for those who can't stop talking: two baths are installed side by side so that conversation need never cease. In renovating the château, inherited from a great-aunt, Jacques and Valérie Advenier have done everything possible to beguile their guests. The bedrooms, hung with reproduction 18th-century fabrics, are as comfortable as they are well furnished. The oak panelling in the dining room has been restored and excellent meals are served there, but if the weather is good you may prefer to eat at tables under the umbrellas in the garden. The atmosphere is pleasant and relaxed.

How to get there *(Map 18): 30km south east of Moulins via N7 and D989 towards Le Donjon.*

Château de Boussac

Target
03140 Chantelle (Allier)
Tel. 70.40.63.20 – Fax 70.40.60.03 – M. and Mme de Longueil

Open 1 April – 15 Nov. **Rooms** 5 with bath and WC (1 with TV). **Price** single and double 600F, suite 950F. **Meals** breakfast 50F, served 0800-1000; half board 1100F (per pers., 5 days min.) **Credit cards** Visa, MasterCard, Amex. **Pets** dogs allowed (with suppl.) **Facilities** parking. **Nearby** church of Ste-Croix and Museum of the Vine at Saint-Pourçain-sur-Sioule, priory at Souvigny, triptych of the Maître de Moulins at Notre Dame cathedral at Moulins, 18-hole Val de Cher golf course at Montluçon. **Restaurant** set meal in the evening only; menu 260F incl. wine.

The many faces of this beautiful structure blend medieval austerity with the grace of the 18th century. The owners receive you like friends and do everything possible to include you in their country life. Each very comfortable bedroom is superbly furnished with antiques (often Louis XV or Louis XVI), family mementos, and beautiful fabrics. The sitting rooms have been restored to retain their character. Finally, the large dining room table sets the scene for sociable dinner parties which are very popular with sportsmen in the hunting and shooting seasons. The silver, the conversation, and the settings all contribute towards making each evening meal an echo of times past.

How to get there *(Map 25): 40km south of Moulins via A71, Montmarault exit, then D42 to Boussac (between Chantelle and Montmarault).*

Le Tronçais★★

Avenue Nicolas-Rambourg
Tronçais - 03360 Saint-Bonnet-Tronçais (Allier)
Tel. 70.06.11.95 - Fax 70.06.16.15 - M. and Mme Bajard

Open 15 March – 15 Dec (closed Sunday evening and Monday in low season). **Rooms** 12 with telephone, bath or shower, WC and TV. **Price** single 184F, double 235-312F. **Meals** breakfast 27F, served 0800-1030; half board 220-258F, full board 260-307F (per pers., 3 days min.) **Credit cards** Visa, MasterCard, Eurocard. **Pets** dogs allowed only in bedrooms. **Facilities** tennis, parking. **Nearby** oak forest of Tronçais, château de Culan, 18-hole Val de Cher golf course at Montluçon. **Restaurant** service 1200-1330, 1930-2100; menus 98-175F, also à la carte; specialities: terrine d'anguille aux mûres, sandre au gratin, côte de veau aux cèpes, game.

This hotel, once the private house of the owner of a forge in Tronçais, is located at the edge of the forest in a garden bordered by a lake. From the flight of steps leading to the entrance hall to the bedrooms everything is calm, comfortable and civilised. A small annexe close by is as attractive and comfortable as the house itself. The garden in front of the two buildings is gravelled and serves as the terrace and bar in the summer. The hotel grounds stretch all the way to the banks of the lake, in which you can do some fishing.

How to get there *(Map 17): 45km north of Montluçon via N144 towards Saint-Amand-Montrond, then D978a to Tronçais.*

La Thomasse★★★
28, rue du Docteur-Mallet
15000 Aurillac (Cantal)
Tel. 71.48.26.47 - Fax 71.48.83.66 - Mme Kusnierek

Open all year. **Rooms** 22 with telephone, bath, WC, TV (4 with minibar). **Price** single and double 320-370F, suite 450F. **Meals** breakfast 37F, served 0700-1200; half board 270-300F. **Credit cards** accepted. **Pets** dogs allowed. **Facilities** parking. **Nearby** church of Saint-Cernin, château d'Anjony, 9-hole Vezac golf club at Aurillac. **Restaurant** service 1930-2230; menus 120F and 160F, also à la carte; specialities: foie gras frais maison, charlotte aux griottes, fresh fish.

This hotel on the edge of Aurillac is situated in a quarter that lacks the charm of the old town, but you will be pleasantly surprised to find that behind the façade with its virginia creeper there is a delightful garden. The reception rooms are spacious and the old, dark brown furniture contrasts well with the whitewashed walls. The dining room has the same kind of rustic decor. Adjoining it is the bar, where the indirect lighting and cosy atmosphere invite you to linger over a drink. The bedrooms are very pleasant and comfortable, with small but well equipped bathrooms. The best are those facing the garden and there is one large suite with a fireplace and sitting area. Prices are reasonable, and this place is ideally suited for exploring the village or walking among the volcanic mountains of the Auvergne – unless you want to make yours a golfing holiday.

How to get there *(Map 24): 10 minutes from the centre of town.*

Auberge de Concasty***

15600 Boisset (Cantal)
Tel. 71.62.21.16 – Fax 71.62.22.22
Mme Causse

Open all year (on reservation). **Rooms** 16 with telephone, bath, WC and TV. **Price** single 240-270F, double 295-375F. **Meals** breakfast 39F, brunch 72F, served 0900-1130; half board 335-405F (per pers., 3 days min.) **Credit cards** accepted. **Pets** dogs allowed (+35F). **Facilities** swimming pool, jacuzzi, parking. **Nearby** château de Conros, valleys of the Lot and the Truyère, Champollion Museum at Figeac. **Restaurant** service 1230-1330, 2000-2130 on reservation (closed Wednesday except for residents); menus 135-195F; specialities: fresh local produce.

The Auberge de Concasty is an old country house with its own farm and fields around. Entirely restored, equipped with jacuzzi and swimming pool, the auberge has retained the atmosphere of a large family holiday house without losing its authenticity. It is comfortable throughout, from the bedrooms to the pleasantly decorated reception rooms. At Concasty you will be served with good seasonal cooking which favours local produce (cèpes, foie gras). A place to recommend in the Cantal.

How to get there (Map 24): *33km south west of Aurillac via N122 as far as Manhes, then D64.*

Château de Lavendès***

15350 Champagnac (Cantal)
Tel. 71.69.62.79 - Fax 71.69.65.33
Mme Gimmig

Open 1 March – 10 Dec (closed Monday in low season). **Rooms** 8 with telephone, bath or shower, WC and TV. **Price** double 420-520F. **Meals** breakfast 50F, served until 1000; half board 380-480F, full board 500-600F (per pers, 3 days min.) **Credit cards** Visa, Eurocard. **Pets** dogs not allowed. **Facilities** swimming pool, sauna (90F), parking. **Nearby** Bort-les-Orgues, Bort dam and château de Val, gorges of the Dordogne from Bort to the Aigle dam (3 hours), 9-hole Mont-Dore golf course. **Restaurant** service 1230-1345, 1930-2100; menus 145-260F, also à la carte; specialities: omble chevalier, saumon fontaine, fromages au lait cru, desserts aux fruits rouges et glacés.

Built on the site of an ancient manor house, this 18th-century building is set in the middle of 3-hectare grounds and was converted into an hotel-restaurant in 1986. In the lobby, which has an imposing fireplace, you can take afternoon tea. In the two dining rooms, one furnished in Louis XV style, the other in Louis XIII, you will enjoy gastronomic 'specialités de la maison' and modernised regional cooking. A splendid staircase (on which you will find many curiosities including old wooden mechanisms and children's toys) leads to the well-equipped bedrooms. There is absolute peace, apart from the sounds of the bells on the collars of the cows grazing the surrounding meadows.

How to get there (Map 24): 78km north of Aurillac via D922 to Vendes via Mauriac, then left on D12 or D112 to Champagnac (the château is on D15).

Auberge du Vieux Chêne★★

34, route des Lacs
15270 Champs–sur–Tarentaine (Cantal)
Tel. 71.78.71.64 – Fax 71.78.70.88 – Mme Moins

Open 15 March – 20 Dec (closed Sunday evening and Monday except July and Aug.)
Rooms 20 with telephone, bath or shower (16 with WC). **Price** double 210-300F.
Meals breakfast 40F, served 0800-1000; half board 250-280F, full board 270-300F
(per pers., 3 days min.) **Credit cards** Eurocard, Visa. **Pets** dogs allowed. **Facilities**
parking. **Nearby** Bort-les-Orgues, Bort dam and château de Val, gorges of the
Dordogne from Bort to the Aigle dam, 9-hole Mont-Dore golf course. **Restaurant**
service 1200-1330, 1900-2030; menus 120-220F, also à la carte; specialities: foie
gras d'oie maison, ris de veau aux morilles, escalope de saumon à l'oseille.

This old farmhouse, in which stone and timber predominate, is set well away from the road and has been enlarged and restored without losing any of its character. The bedrooms have been kept simple but are charming and comfortable. All have bathroom and telephone. At one end of the ground floor is a pleasant bar-sitting room, and all the rest of the space is taken up by a huge dining room whose end wall is one immense fireplace. Outside, a garden terrace is laid for breakfast. Very good welcome.

How to get there (*Map 24): 93km north of Aurillac via D922 to Bort-les-Orgues, then D979.*

Auberge du Pont de Lanau★★

Lanau 15260 Chaudes–Aigues (Cantal)
Tel. 71.23.57.76 – Fax 71.23.53.84 – M. Cornut

Open Feb – beg. Jan (closed Tuesday evening and Wednesday in low season). **Rooms** 8 with telephone, bath, WC and TV. **Price** single and double 270-350F. **Meals** breakfast 35F; half board 260-300F, full board 350-400F (per pers., 3 days min.) **Credit cards** Visa. **Pets** dogs allowed (+35F). **Facilities** parking. **Nearby** Saint-Flour, gorges of the Truyère. **Restaurant** service 1230-1400, 1930-2130; menus 90-300F, also à la carte.

Courtesy is the tradition in this old farmhouse-auberge built in 1855. Here, once upon a time, clients were served meals on the left (today the restaurant) and horses were stabled on the right (today the sitting room, breakfast room and bar). The well decorated restaurant has open stonework walls and is dominated by a large fireplace. Years ago guests slept in bed recesses close to the fireplace to keep warm, and you can still see traces of the original wooden partitions. Today the inn is primarily a restaurant serving very good, subtle and light regional cooking. M. Cornut likes to prepare specialities which are found nowhere else: these are often new and successful versions of traditional regional dishes. The eight bedrooms are pleasant, some flowery, while others, more elegant, are salmon pink. They have fabric-covered walls and are well insulated thanks to double-glazed windows. The auberge is located beside a minor road.

How to get there *(Map 25): 20km south of Saint-Flour via D921.*

Hostellerie de la Maronne★★★

Le Theil
15140 Saint-Martin-Valmeroux (Cantal)
Tel. 71.69.20.33 - Fax 71.69.28.22 - Mme Decock

Open 3 April – 5 Nov. **Rooms** 21 with telephone, bath, WC and minibar (6 with TV).
Price single 350-500F, double 350-550F, suite 700F. **Meals** breakfast 40-50F,
served 0830-1000; half board 355-455F. **Credit cards** MasterCard, Visa. **Pets** dogs
allowed. **Facilities** swimming pool, tennis, parking. **Nearby** medieval city of Salers,
basilica of Notre-Dame-des-Miracles at Mauriac, Puy Mary. **Restaurant** service
1930-2100; menus 200-280F, also à la carte; specialities: escalope de sandre aux
mousserons, foie gras chaud au caramel de porto.

This 19th-century Auvergnat house has been very well
converted into an hotel by M. and Mme Decock. Everything
is provided for guests' rest and recreation. Sitting room, reading
room and dining room have been tastefully and sensitively
decorated: there are lovely wall-coverings, the furniture is antique,
and the bedrooms are large and comfortable. The largest have a
terrace, some have a sitting room, and there is an apartment ideal
for families with a 20sq.m. terrace. The cooking has gone from
strength to strength. The surrounding countryside is ideal for
walking, but the swimming pool overlooking the valley is an
equally pleasant place to relax. Delightful welcome and service.

How to get there *(Map 24): 33km north of Aurillac via D922, then D37.*

Auberge de la Tomette★★

15220 Vitrac (Cantal)
Tel. 71.64.70.94 – Fax 71.64.77.11
M. and Mme Chauzi

Open 15 March – 31 Dec. **Rooms** 21 with telephone, shower or bath, WC and TV. **Price** single 240-260F, double 280-300F, suite 400-420F. **Meals** breakfast 28F; half board 220-270F, full board 280-330F (per pers., 3 days min.) **Credit cards** Visa, MasterCard. **Pets** dogs allowed in bedrooms only. **Facilities** swimming pool, sauna (40F). **Nearby** church of Saint-Cernin, château d'Anjony, Vic-sur-Cère. **Restaurant** service 1200-1400, 1900-2100; menus 62-160F, also à la carte; specialities: truite paysanne aux noix, caille forestière, ris de veau crémaillère.

Vitrac, in the midst of chestnut plantations, is a beauty spot in the south of the Cantal, and the Auberge de la Tomette is right in the heart of the village. The bedrooms are attractive. Some open onto a delightful little garden behind the auberge, but the greater part of the hotel is a few metres away in a large flowery park. The dining room, with panelling and exposed stonework, has a convivial atmosphere and the cooking is good. Children will enjoy the swimming pool and the garden, where many games are provided, while adults may appreciate the sauna. A picturesque stopping place in which to enjoy village life. Mme Chauzi is a kind hostess and is full of information about what to do and where to go.

How to get there *(Map 24): 25km south of Aurillac via N122 towards Figeac; at Saint-Mamet-La Salvetat take D66.*

Le Pré Bossu★★★

43150 Moudeyres (Haute-Loire)
Tel. 71.05.10.70 - Fax 71.05.10.21 - M. Grootaert

Open Palm Sunday – 11 Nov. **Rooms** 10 with telephone, bath or shower and WC.
Price double 320-400F. **Meals** breakfast 50F, served 0800-1000; half board 430-
590F (per pers., 3 days min.) **Credit cards** accepted. **Pets** dogs allowed in bedrooms
(+35F). **Facilities** parking. **Nearby** basilica of Notre-Dame-du-Puy at Puy-en-Velay,
Gerbier-des-Joncs, forest of the Mézenc, 9-hole Chambon-sur-Lignon golf course at
Romières. **Restaurant** service 1200-1330, 1930-2100; menus 165-360F (child 65F),
also à la carte; specialities: écrevisses aux petits légumes, andouillette d'escargot
au coulis de céleri.

Located in the lovely village of Moudeyres, this old thatched
cottage built in local stone gets its name from the meadow
which surrounds it. The atmosphere is cosy and welcoming. To
one side there is a reception room with a large fireplace, TV and
library. In the stone dining room delicious food is served, including
fresh produce from the kitchen garden. The wine list is good. Very
comfortable bedrooms, furnished in an attractive style. Garden and
terrace overlook the countryside and drinks can be served there.
If you want to go out for the day picnic baskets can be prepared.
Very friendly welcome.

How to get there *(Map 25): 25km east of Puy via D15 to les Pandreaux,*
then D36 to Moudeyres via Laussonne.

Relais de Saint-Jacques-de-Compostelle**

19500 Collonges-la-Rouge (Corrèze)
Tel. 55.25.41.02 - Fax 55.84.08.51 - M. Guillaume

Open March – Dec (closed Tuesday evening and Wednesday in low season). **Rooms** 24 (14 in the annexe) with telephone, of which 10 with bath or shower and WC (2 with TV). **Price** double 150-300F. **Meals** breakfast 35F. **Credit cards** accepted. **Pets** dogs allowed. **Facilities** parking. **Nearby** village and church of Collonges, church at Beaulieu-sur-Dordogne, Argentat, 18-hole Coiroux golf course at Aubazines. **Restaurant** service 1230-1330, 1930-2130; menus 100-250F, also à la carte; specialities: feuilleté de Saint-Jacques, filet de bœuf fourré au foie gras.

Its medieval houses in red sandstone make Collonges-la-Rouge an incredibly beautiful village. Located in the heart of the village, the hotel has just been very tastefully restored; the general effect is light and flowery. On the ground floor are two dining rooms, a small reception room furnished with amusing 'toad' armchairs, and an intimate bar. The small bedrooms are all very attractive. Excellent cooking is served with a smile (in summer, tables are laid on three lovely shaded terraces). A charming establishment which shows that even in a popular tourist resort hoteliers who love their work can be found: M. and Mme Guillaume's welcome is reason enough for a visit.

How to get there *(Map 24): 45km south of Tulle via D940 as far as 'Le Colombier', then right on D38 to Collonges-la-Rouge (the hotel is in the village).*

Au Rendez-Vous des Pêcheurs★★

Pont du Chambon
19320 Saint-Merd-de-Lapleau (Corrèze)
Tel. 55.27.88.39 – Fax 55.27.83.19 – Mme Fabry

Open 20 Dec – 11 Nov (closed Friday evening and Saturday lunchtime in low season).
Rooms 8 with telephone, bath or shower, WC and TV. **Price** single and double 230F.
Meals breakfast 30F, served 0800-0930; half board 225F, full board 260F (per pers.,
3 days min.) **Credit cards** Eurocard, Visa. **Pets** dogs allowed. **Facilities** parking.
Nearby cathedral at Tulle, Argentat, abbey church of Beaulieu-sur-Dordogne,
Collonges, 18-hole Coiroux golf course at Aubazines. **Restaurant** service 1215-1330,
1945-2100; menus 72-185F, also à la carte; specialities: sandre au beurre blanc,
ris de veau aux cèpes, mousse de noix glacée.

Built on the banks of the Dordogne, this large house, backing
onto wooded hills, owes much of its appeal to its exceptional
position. On the ground floor a light, large and well decorated
dining room (flowered curtains, pretty tables) has wide views across
the river. At one side a small lounge and bar gives access to a lovely
terrace overlooking the river. The bedrooms have been well
refurbished but again it is the view from them which makes them
special. They are comfortable but would be the better for
soundproofing. Fisherman cannot fail to be attracted by these
surroundings and to treat themselves, if they are out of luck, to
perch, pike and trout cooked by Elise. A good hotel, very
moderately priced.

How to get there *(Map 24): 45km east of Tulle via D978 to Saint-Merd-*
de-Lapleau via Marcillac-la-Croisille, then D13 to 'Pont-du-Chambon'.

La Maison Anglaise

Saint-Robert
19310 Ayen (Corrèze)
Tel. 55.25.19.58 - Fax 55.25.23.00 - M. and Mme Baldwin

Open all year. **Rooms** 6 with shower and WC. **Price** double 160-270F. **Meals** breakfast 35-55F, served 0800-1000; half board 220-275F (per pers., 2 days min.) **Credit cards** Visa, Amex. **Pets** dogs allowed (+15F). **Facilities** swimming pool, parking. **Nearby** château de Hautefort, abbey of Tourtoirac, Périgueux. **Restaurant** service 1200-1400, 1930-2130; menus 70-160F, also à la carte; specialities: magret de canard grillé aux cerises, foie de veau aux raisins.

The Maison Anglaise was established four years ago in Saint-Robert, a lovely little village perched on a green hill. The hotel, whose charm and quality have enriched the village, occupies a small and ancient house. It has a real country style bar with wooden furniture, a handsome dining room and, adjoining it, a comfortable lounge full of good furniture, paintings and objets d'art. The fireplaces are huge and fires are always lit in winter. There are six bedrooms on the first floor, some of them large. We liked their white walls, their curtains and their thick quilts, a good foil to the wooden furniture, wide floorboards and the pink tablecloths. The bathrooms are simple and well kept. Some of them are partitioned off the rooms but this has been done skilfully. The cooking is particularly good: in summer there is a grill by the swimming pool and tables are set on the panoramic terrace, where one can gaze over the landscape below.

How to get there *(Map 23): 30km north west of Brive-la-Gaillarde towards Objat, then Ayen, to Saint-Robert.*

Auberge des Prés de la Vézère**

19240 Saint-Viance (Corrèze)
Tel. 55.85.00.50 – Fax 55.84.25.36
M. Parveaux

Open May – mid-Nov. **Rooms** 11 with telephone, bath, WC and TV. **Price** single and double 230-290F. **Meals** breakfast 30F, served 0730-1000; half board 250-300F. **Credit cards** Visa. **Pets** dogs allowed. **Facilities** parking. **Nearby** abbey of Aubazines, Uzerches, Argentat, Collonges-la-Rouge, Pompadour stud farm, Beaulieu-sur-Dordogne, 18-hole Coiroux golf course at Aubazines. **Restaurant** service 1200-1400, 1930-2100; menus 105-205F, also à la carte; specialities: saumon fumé maison, dorade à l'ail et au thym, civet de canard tradition.

Saint-Viance is a very well preserved small town, with its old houses and the lovely bridge which spans the Vézère, a popular river with fishermen. The hotel is at the entrance to the village beside a quiet road. Its attractions are soon evident; there is a large dining room which extends into a shaded terrace, and on the first floor, although the corridor is a little gloomy, you will be agreeably surprised by the bedrooms, which have pale coloured wallpapers and pretty curtains matching the bedcovers. The rooms are cheerful and well cared for and all of them have well equipped bathrooms. This is a good place for a family holiday.

How to get there (Map 23): 11km north west of Brive-la-Gaillarde, towards Objat then Allassac.

La Borderie★★★

Le Pouret - 19270 Ussac (Corrèze)
Tel. 55.87.74.45 - Fax 55.86.97.91
M. and Mme Bordes

Open all year. **Rooms** 7 with telephone, bath , WC, TV and minibar. **Price** single and double 300-475F, suite 575-675F. **Meals** breakfast 50F, served 0730-1030; half board 375-480F. **Credit cards** Visa. **Pets** dogs allowed (+30F). **Facilities** swimming pool, parking. **Nearby** abbey church at Aubazines, Uzerches, Argentat, Collonges-la-Rouge, Pompadour stud farm, Beaulieu-sur-Dordogne, 18-hole Coiroux golf course at Aubazines. **Restaurant** service 1200-1330, 1930-2130; menus 125-350F, also à la carte; specialities: foie gras, pigeon, magret de canard.

This hotel is in a lovely part of the countryside near Brive, and in the 16th and 17th centuries, when the highway passed through here, it was a staging post. It still has old walls in rose coloured stone and some rooms of great character, like the dining room, which has two huge fireplaces and looks out on a flower-filled terrace – a lovely setting for discovering La Borderie's excellent cooking. The bedrooms are in a separate building which has been completely renovated. On the ground floor there is a small entrance lounge which opens onto the swimming pool. There are three bedrooms which do the same, and the others are on the first floor. They are all pleasingly decorated in pastel colours, with old engravings, comfortable soft furnishings and the occasional piece of antique furniture. Elegant bathrooms and perfect soundproofing add to the comfort of this hotel, where M. and Mme. Bordes make every effort to fill your stay with pleasant memories.

How to get there *(Map 23): 11km north of Brive-la-Gaillarde (direction Zone de Cana).*

Domaine des Mouillères★★

Les Mouillères
Saint-Georges-la-Pouge 23250 Pontarion (Creuse)
Tel. 55.66.60.64 - Fax 55.66.60.80 - M. and Mme Thill

Open 20 March – 1 Oct. **Rooms** 7 with telephone (3 with bath, 4 with basin, 4 with WC). **Price** single 110F, double 180-350F. **Meals** breakfast 38F, served 0800-0930. **Credit cards** Visa. **Pets** dogs not allowed. **Facilities** parking. **Nearby** hôtel de Moneyroux and Guéret museum, abbey church of Moutier-d'Ahun, 18-hole la Jonchère golf course at Montgrenier-Gouzon. **Restaurant** service 2000-2030 (residents only); menus 90-250F, also à la carte; specialities: truite montagnarde, feuilleté aux cèpes, rognons de veau au chinon.

This old Marchois dwelling stands alone in a 6-hectare park and is an ancient farm which has been restored by its inheritors, the owners of the hotel. The charming little sitting room has a mixture of furniture and old fashioned objects. We prefer the bedrooms with bathrooms, but the others have been totally refurbished and equipped with basins. They are all pretty and pleasant. In the warm and countrified dining room, the simple cooking uses fresh produce from the estate but the quality is sometimes uneven. If you want to explore the magnificent countryside, the owner will lend bicycles. Drinks and meals can be served on the lovely garden terrace. The best kind of welcome, and a very likeable place.

How to get there *(Map 24): 34km south of Guéret via D942 towards Aubusson; at Ahun take D13 towards La Chapelle-Saint-Martial, then D45.*

Hôtel Beau Site★★

Brignac - 87400 Royères (Haute-Vienne)
Tel. 55.56.00.56 - Fax 55.56.31.17
M. Vigneron

Open April – Dec (closed Friday evening in low season). **Rooms** 11 with telephone, bath or shower, WC (10 with TV). **Price** single 250F, double 290F. **Meals** breakfast 35F, served 0830-0930; half board 265F, full board 310F (per pers., 3 days min.) **Credit cards** Visa. **Pets** dogs allowed. **Facilities** heated swimming pool, parking. **Nearby** Saint-Etienne cathedral and Adrien-Dubouché ceramics museum in Limoges, church of Saint-Léonard-de-Noblat, lake Vassivière, abbey of Solignac, 18-hole Porcelaine golf course at Limoges. **Restaurant** service 1230-1345, 1945-2115 (closed Monday lunchtime, Friday evening and Saturday lunchtime in low season); menus 80-230F, also à la carte; specialities: fricassée d'escargot aux cèpes, truite au bleu d'Auvergne, charlotte à la châtaigne.

This big house, though now a hotel, has managed to hang on to its provincial family home character. The lace and embroidery in the smaller dining room, and its period furniture, irresistably evoke visions of the sort of house our grandparents might have lived in. The other, much larger, dining room overlooks the hotel's lovely grounds. The bedrooms are very attractive, their fabrics and wallpapers all well chosen, and the bathrooms are beyond reproach.

How to get there (Map 23): 17km east of Limoges via D941 towards Saint-Léonard-de-Noblat; at the lights at Royères take D124.

Au Moulin de la Gorce***

La Roche l'Abeille
87800 Nexon (Haute-Vienne)
Tel. 55.00.70.66 – Fax 55.00.76.57 – M. Bertranet

Open all year (closed Sunday evening and Monday 20 Sept – 30 April). **Rooms** 9, and 1 apartment, with telephone, bath, WC and TV. **Price** single 350F, double 650-700F, suite 1300F. **Meals** breakfast 65F, served from 0800; half board 1450F, full board 1780-1980F (2 pers., 3 days min.) **Credit cards** accepted. **Pets** dogs allowed. **Facilities** parking. **Nearby** Saint Etienne cathedral and Adrien-Dubouché ceramics museum at Limoges, abbey of Solignac, church of Saint-Léonard-de-Noblat, 18-hole Porcelaine golf course at Limoges. **Restaurant** service 1200-1330, 1930-2100; menus 160-450F, also à la carte; specialities: œufs brouillés aux truffes dans leur coque, foie poêlé aux pommes, lièvre à la royale.

Taken on and converted by a family of caterers and patissiers from Limoges, this flour mill dates back to 1569. It became a restaurant ten years ago and an hotel seven years ago. The sitting room derives its intimate atmosphere from a pretty collection of furniture. There are two dining rooms: one rather sophisticated, the other more countrified with exposed stonework and a fireplace. The bedrooms are tasteful and comfortable. Drinks are served on the terrace overlooking the lake and the garden. You will be won over by the delicious cooking and the welcome awaiting you in this historic corner of France.

How to get there *(Map 23): 30km south of Limoges via D704 then D17.*

Castel–Hôtel 1904★★

Rue du Castel
63390 Saint-Gervais-d'Auvergne (Puy-de-Dôme)
Tel. 73.85.70.42 - M. Mouty

Open Easter – 11 Nov. **Rooms** 17 with telephone, bath or shower, WC and TV (3 with minibar). **Price** single and double 240-260F. **Meals** breakfast 38F, served 0730-1000; half board 215-225F, full board 280-290F (per pers., 3 days min.) **Credit cards** Eurocard, MasterCard, Visa. **Pets** dogs not allowed. **Facilities** parking. **Nearby** gorges of the Sioule, church at Ménat, Fades viaduct, Mandet museum and museum of the Auvergne at Riom, 9- and 18-hole Volcans golf course at Orcines. **Restaurant** service from 1230 and 1930; menus 120-400F, also à la carte; specialities: tournedos roulé aux pieds de porc, sandre paysanne.

This ancient château, built in 1616, was converted into an hotel in 1904 and has been run by the same family ever since. It is now up to Jean-Louis Mouty to carry on the good work. All the charm of an old French hotel is to be found in its warm and welcoming rooms, the bar and above all the large dining room, whose wooden floors gleam. The fireplaces, the antique furniture and the ochre tones of the walls and curtains all contribute to the old-fashioned character of this place. The bedrooms, as comfortable as you could wish, are all different and in keeping with the rest of the hotel. Clients have the choice of two restaurants: the 'Castel' which has fine gastronomic fare, and the 'Comptoir à Mustache' which is an authentic country bistro. The sort of place you become attached to.

How to get there *(Map 24): 55km north west of Clermont-Ferrand via N9 to Châtelguyon, then D227 to Saint-Gervais-d'Auvergne via Manzat.*

Hôtel Clarion★★★

21420 Aloxe-Corton (Côte-d'Or)
Tel. 80.26.46.70 - Fax 80.26.47.16
M. and Mme Voarick

Open all year. **Rooms** 10 with telephone, bath, WC, TV and minibar. **Price** single 450F, double 450-770F. **Meals** breakfast 75F, served 0800-1300. No restaurant. **Credit cards** Visa, MasterCard. **Pets** dogs allowed. **Facilities** parking. **Nearby** Hôtel-Dieu, basilica of Notre Dame at Beaune, the Côte de Beaune between Serrigny and Chagny, château du Clos-Vougeot, Nolay, Rochepot, 18-hole Beaune-Levernois golf course.

At the Clarion, M. and Mme Voarick have achieved a successful blend of sophisticated comfort with natural beauty, creating a very appealing place to stay only 3km from Beaune. The hotel is behind the village of Aloxe-Corton, in a former gentleman's residence bordered by a large lawn, with vines beyond. Hidden beneath its traditional appearance lies the archetype of 1990s comfort. Completely decorated by the interior designer Pierre-Yves Prieu, who has chosen a pastel theme to accompany the ancient beams, this building offers the luxury of exceptionally comfortable bedrooms and excellent service. The best moment, although a bit expensive, is breakfast in the garden.

How to get there *(Map 19): 5km north of Beaune via N74.*

Chez Camille★★★

1, place Edouard-Herriot
21230 Arnay-le-Duc (Côte-d'Or)
Tel. 80.90.01.38 – Fax 80.90.04.64 – M. and Mme Poinsot

Open all year. **Rooms** 14 with telephone, bath and TV. **Price** double 395F, suite 600-800F. **Meals** breakfast 50F, served 0700-1200; half board 490F. **Credit cards** Visa, Amex, Diners. **Pets** dogs allowed (+30F). **Facilities** parking (+20F). **Nearby** basilica of Saint-Andoche at Saulieu, château de Commarin, Châteauneuf, 18-hole Château de Chailly golf course. **Restaurant** service 1200-1430, 1930-2200; menus 135-450F, also à la carte; specialities: rissoles d'escargots aux pâtes fraîches et champagne, le charolais.

Its location in the small town of Arnay-le-Duc does not affect the peace of this hotel with its many charms. The big lobby, with comfortable corners for sitting or talking, often echoes to the sound of piano music. Everything is warm and inviting – no long anonymous corridors but a lovely 17th-century staircase, and alcoves from which the bedrooms lead off. Restful, comfortable and well-decorated, the bedrooms occasionally contain antique furniture. If you can book well in advance, ask for No. 17, which is the bedroom we preferred. Apart from its excellent qualities as an hotel, Chez Camille has a great reputation for its cooking. The dining room, built under a glass roof like a winter garden, invites you to taste the best of Burgundy. Monique and Armand Poinsot have their own farm where they grow the produce with which you will be served. This gives the light, inventive cooking a typically local taste and makes this hotel a place not to be missed.

How to get there *(Map 19): 28km north east of Autun via N81.*

Hôtel Le Home**

138, route de Dijon
21200 Beaune (Côte-d'Or)
Tel. 80.22.16.43 - Fax 80.24.90.74 - Mme Jacquet

Open all year. **Rooms** 23 with telephone, bath or shower, WC (8 with TV). **Price** single 295F, double 295-430F. **Meals** breakfast 32F. No restaurant. **Credit cards** Visa. **Pets** dogs allowed. **Facilities** parking. **Nearby** Hôtel Dieu, basilica of Notre-Dame at Beaune, Côte de Beaune between Serrigny and Chagny, château du Clos-Vougeot, Nolay, Rochepot, 18-hole Beaune-Levernois golf course.

The inspiration for this small hotel, located at the entrance to Beaune, is definitely English. The Virginia-creeper covered house is surrounded by a green and flowering garden where breakfast is served. Well-chosen antiques, lamps and carpets give the personal touch to every room. The bedrooms are pretty, comfortable and quiet; the sitting room inviting. The proximity of the road is only noticeable from outside and the interior is well-insulated from noise. Mme Jacquet is very welcoming and loves her house, which is obvious in the well-cared-for appearance of all the rooms and the feeling of being received here as a friend.

How to get there *(Map 19): In Beaune, on the Dijon road; beyond the church of Saint-Nicolas.*

Hostellerie du Château★★

21320 Châteauneuf-en-Auxois (Côte-d'Or)
Tel. 80.49.22.00 – Fax 80.49.21.27 – M. and Mme Poirier

Open 15 Feb – 15 Nov (closed Monday evening and Tuesday in low season). **Rooms** 16 with telephone, bath or shower and WC. **Price** single 190-220F, double 380-450F, suite 450-500F. **Meals** breakfast 40F; half board 300-400F. **Credit cards** accepted. **Pets** dogs allowed. **Nearby** château de Commarin, basilica of Saint-Andoche at Saulieu, Hôtel-Dieu and basilica of Notre-Dame in Beaune, 18-hole Château de Chailly golf club at Chailly-sur-Armançon. **Restaurant** service 1200-1330, 1900-2130; menus 130-240F, also à la carte; specialities: émincé de veau aux morilles, langoustines poêlées aux deux poireaux.

This old parsonage is located at the top of an old market town which stands sentinel above the Bourgogne canal and overlooks the château. The ancient canal is visible from the terraced gardens, set out with tables and swings. Inside, an old fireplace and exposed stone walls recall the age of the place. The rest has been very well renovated. The restaurant has large windows overlooking the garden. The bedrooms are simply fitted out and comfortable, but it is best to avoid the ones in the annexe. The cooking varies according to the season and offers tempting Burgundian specialities. Don't leave without wandering through the village, whose old houses border a maze of narrow, quiet streets with an occasional vertiginous view over the plain below.

How to get there (Map 19): 30km north west of Beaune via A6, Pouilly-en-Auxois exit, then D977bis towards Vandenesse then Crugey; after the cemetry turn left, it's on the other side of the canal.

Le Manassès

21220 Curtil-Vergy (Côte-d'Or)
Tel. 80.61.43.81 – Fax 80.61.42.79
M. Chaley

Open 15 Feb – 15 Dec. **Rooms** 7 with telephone, bath, WC, TV and minibar. **Price** single and double 350F. **Meals** breakfast 50F, served 0745-1000. No restaurant. **Credit cards** Visa, Eurocard, MasterCard. **Pets** small dogs allowed. **Facilities** parking. **Nearby** abbey of Saint-Vivant at Curtil-Vergy, abbey of Cîteaux, château de Cussigny, château du Clos-Vougeot, Côte de Nuits, 18-hole Dijon-Bourgogne golf course.

To reach this small and tranquil hotel you must first go under a little porch and then across an inner courtyard. M. Chaley is a wine grower and a jovial host, as befits his profession. His house has been totally renovated and transformed into an hotel. References to wine abound: in the barn which houses an interesting wine museum, and in the big room where breakfast is served. In the corridors and in the bedrooms every single picture refers to wine. From the cellars close by comes the faint aroma of wine casks in which the grape harvest is maturing. The public rooms contain some fine old furniture; the comfortable bedrooms are more modern, with pretty colour combinations and marble-lined bathrooms. The view over the wild green valley is superb.

How to get there *(Map 19): 24km north of Beaune. A31, Nuits-Saint-Georges exit, D25 and D35.*

Les Grands Crus★★★
Route des Grands-Crus
21220 Gevrey-Chambertin (Côte-d'Or)
Tel. 80.34.34.15 - Fax 80.51.89.07 - Mme Farnier

Open 1 March – 1 Dec. **Rooms** 24 with telephone, bath and WC. **Price** single and double 330-410F. **Meals** breakfast 40F, served 0700-1030. No restaurant. **Credit cards** Visa, Eurocard. **Pets** dogs allowed (+10F). **Facilities** parking. **Nearby** church of Notre-Dame and art museum at Dijon, Côte de Nuits, châteaux du Clos-Vougeot and de Cussigny, abbey of Cîteaux, 18-hole Dijon-Bourgogne golf course.

Encircled as it is by the famous vineyards of Gevrey-Chambertin, the Les Grands Crus is aptly named. The bedrooms overlook the rows of vines (and some have a view of the old château). Opening off a wide corridor, the bedrooms are light and comfortable and are furnished with restrained, good-quality copies of Louis XV furniture. The almost traffic-free road and excellent sound-proofing ensure a quiet stay. On the ground floor a large living room acts as both breakfast room and sitting room. Mme Farnier herself will receive you there in her charming manner.

How to get there *(Map 19): 12km south of Dijon via N74 towards Beaune.*

Hôtel Le Parc★★

Levernois
21200 Beaune (Côte-d'Or)
Tel. 80.22.22.51/80.24.63.00 – Mme Oudot

Open all year (closed 20 Nov – 6 Dec). **Rooms** 25 with telephone, TV (19 with shower, 6 with bath, 18 with WC). **Price** double 195-420F. **Meals** breakfast 32F, served 0730-0930. No restaurant. **Credit cards** Visa, Eurocard, MasterCard. **Pets** dogs allowed. **Facilities** parking. **Nearby** museum at Châtillon, source of the Douix, Mont Lassois, forest of Châtillon, valley of the Ource, abbey at Molesmes, 9-hole golf course at Arc-en-Barrois, 18-hole Beaune-Levernois golf course.

Having tried the charms of Beaune and its wines, travel for 4km to the edge of the small village of Levernois, where the gates of the Hotel Le Parc give access to an old, ivy covered Burgundian house. It has a flowery courtyard where breakfast is served, and a garden with huge and ancient trees. Hotel Le Parc has the feel of a small hotel despite the number of bedrooms. The atmosphere of every bedroom is different, created in one by the wallpaper, in another by a chest of drawers and in yet another by the curtains and bedspread. Although not far from the town, you will feel as if you are in the country, and, most important, you will be very well looked after.

How to get there (Map 19): 4km south east of Beaune via D970.

Hostellerie du Val–Suzon★★★

R.N. 71 - 21121 Val-Suzon (Côte-d'Or)
Tel. 80.35.60.15 - Fax 80.35.61.36 - M. and Mme Perreau

Open 15 Jan – 15 Dec (closed Wednesday). **Rooms** 17 with telephone, of which 16 with bath and WC, 1 with shower, 10 with TV and minibar. **Price** single 300-350F, double 400-500F, suite 700F. **Meals** breakfast 48F, served 0730-0930; half board 428-478F, full board 608-658 (per pers., 3 days min.) **Credit cards** accepted. **Pets** dogs allowed (+50F). **Facilities** parking. **Nearby** château de Vantoux-lès-Dijon, Dijon, Carthusian monastery at Champmol, Côte de Nuits, 18-hole Dijon-Bourgogne golf course. **Restaurant** service 1200-1400, 1930-2145 (closed Thursday lunchtime in low season); menus 140-380F, also à la carte; specialities: œufs coque homard et foie gras, millefeuille d'escargots au beurre de persil.

Located at the edge of the village, the Hostellerie du Val-Suzon is composed of two separate buildings set in a flowery and undulating 1-hectare garden. In the main house there are several comfortable bedrooms and a simple but attractive dining room. The second building, a chalet, is situated at the end of the garden and contains a small sitting room and a very comfortable bedroom. It has TV and a minibar. Ideal for those in search of peace, The Hostellerie du Val-Suzon will welcome you most pleasantly. Finally, we suggest you take a drink on the shaded terrace, a delightful spot. Yves Perreau's cooking is always delicious.

How to get there *(Map 19): 15km north west of Dijon via N71 towards Troyes.*

Le Grand Monarque★★

10, rue de l'Etape
58220 Donzy (Nièvre)
Tel. 86.39.35.44 - M. Lesort

Open all year (Jan and Feb on reservation). **Rooms** 14 with telephone, of which 4 with bath, 6 with shower, 8 with WC, 7 with TV. **Price** double 160-250F. **Meals** breakfast 35F, served 0730-0930. **Credit cards** Visa. **Pets** dogs allowed (+25F). **Facilities** parking, garage. **Nearby** museum of La Meunière at Donzy-le-Pré, châteaux of Menou, la Motte-Josserand and Saint Fargeau (son et lumière in July and Aug), 9-hole Saint Satur golf course. **Restaurant** service 1200-1300, 1930-2100 (closed Sunday evening and Monday in low season); menus 95-195F, also à la carte; specialities: saupiquet donziais, magret de canard, coq au vin.

In the very lovely Burgundian village of Donzy, three beautiful old stone buildings form the hotel Grand Monarque. The bar-lounge is furnished with bistro tables and is next to the kitchen and its gleaming copper pans. Beside it is the dining room, where good regional cooking is served. A 15th-century spiral staircase leads to the small and charmingly simple bedrooms. Situated in the heart of the village, the hotel gives the impression of being a world away from the frenzied tourist migrations. Good value and good quality make this a useful place to stay.

How to get there *(Map 18): 65km south west of Auxerre via N151 to Courson-les-Carrières, then D104 to Entrain-sur-Nohain and D1 to Donzy (the hotel is near the church).*

Domaine de l'Etang

58450 Neuvy-sur-Loire (Nièvre)
Tel. 86.39.20.06 – M. and Mme Pasquet

Open all year. **Rooms** 10 with bath or shower (5 with WC). **Price** single 230F, double 280F, suite 600F. **Meals** breakfast incl. **Credit cards** not accepted. **Pets** dogs not allowed. **Facilities** parking. **Nearby** hunting and falconry museum at Gien, canal port at Briare, golf. **Restaurant** table d'hôtes on reservation for residents.

The Domaine de l'Etang is a pretty guest house lying in the Nevers countryside and owned by M. Pasquet, who also works in local tourism, and his wife who owns an art gallery in Paris. Lying among poppy fields, this is a good place to stay, with bedrooms under the roof and a very attractive garden. One idea distinguishes this hotel from others: breakfast is a help-yourself affair and is laid out in a splendid kitchen-dining room. Staying here is almost like renting a dream house in the country without having the problem of running it. Should you decide against the set menu for dinner, the owners will be happy to tell you where the good local restaurants are.

How to get there *(Map 17): 69km south west of Auxerre via D965 to Bonny-sur-Loire, then D7 to Neuvy-sur-Loire.*

Manoir de Sornat★★★

Allée de Sornat
71140 Bourbon-Lancy (Saône-et-Loire)
Tel. & Fax 85.89.17.39 - M. Raymond

Open all year (closed Sunday evening in low season). **Rooms** 13 with telephone, bath or shower, WC, TV and minibar. **Price** single 300F, double 600F, suite 700F. **Meals** breakfast 50F, served 0730-1100; half board 450-700F, full board 550-850F (per pers., 3 days min.) **Credit cards** Visa, Diners, Amex. **Pets** dogs allowed (+30F). **Facilities** parking. **Nearby** château de Saint-Aubin-sur-Loire, church at Ternant, abbey at Paray-le-Monial. **Restaurant** service 1200-1400, 1930-2130 (closed Monday lunchtime in low season); menus 140-360F, also à la carte; specialities: galette d'escargots de Bourgogne, filet de bœuf.

This house was built in the 19th century at the whim of an affluent Lyonnais who was fond of horse racing at Deauville. He chose a pure Anglo-Norman style of architecture, which though common in the channel resort is unusual here. Adjoining the Manoir are the remains of a racecourse where up to World War II the 'Bourbon Lancy' Prize was run. The bedrooms are spacious, light and airy and tastefully decorated. If you reserve a room with a terrace looking out over the park, you will be able to enjoy your abundant breakfast while watching the squirrels darting among the age-old trees. In the evenings you can descend the carved wooden staircase to enjoy the menus of Gérard Raymond, who combines traditional with new-style cuisine in a dining room with large bay windows that look out over the park. The owners are efficient and kind, and you may find it hard to leave.

How to get there *(Map 18): 25km north east of Moulins via N79 towards Chevagnes.*

Hostellerie du Château de Bellecroix***

6, route Nationale
71150 Chagny (Saône-et-Loire)
Tel. 85.87.13.86 - Fax 85.91.28.62 - Mme Gautier

Open 15 Feb – 20 Dec (closed Wednesday except July and Aug). **Rooms** 21 with telephone, bath or shower, WC, TV and minibar. **Price** single and double 500-950F. **Meals** breakfast 55F, served 0730-1030; half board 580F, full board 680-950F (per pers., 3 days min.) **Credit cards** Visa, Diners, Amex, MasterCard. **Pets** dogs allowed (+40F). **Facilities** swimming pool, parking. **Nearby** Hôtel-Dieu at Beaune, Côte de Beaune between Serrigny and Chagny, château du Clos-Vougeot, Nolay, Rochepot, 18-hole Beaune-Levernois golf course. **Restaurant** service 1200-1400, 1930-2100; menus 220-320F, also à la carte; specialities: poularde de Bresse pochée et morilles, escargots en cocotte luttée.

Built in the 12th and 18th centuries, and from 1199 Commanderie of the Knights of Malta, the Hostellerie is situated a little away from the town in a very lovely 2-hectare garden with shaded lawns and terraces. At the entrance, a large panelled room acts as both sitting room and dining room; two other more intimate rooms are to be found in the turrets. It is simply furnished: ancient and modern are sensitively combined and there is a measure of sophistication everywhere. The elegant bedrooms are well planned and all have a beautiful view over the grounds. At the back, in another building, a magnificent drawing room and some very comfortable bedrooms are to be found, but these are more expensive. Some of them are on the same level as the garden. Restaurant prices are on the high side.

How to get there (Map 19): 15km south of Beaune via N74, then N6.

Hôtel de Bourgogne★★★

Place de l'Abbaye
71250 Cluny (Saône-et-Loire)
Tel. 85.59.00.58 – Fax 85.59.03.73 – Mme Gosse

Open 1 March – 12 Nov (closed Monday evening). **Rooms** 15 with telephone, bath or shower, WC (11 with TV). **Price** single 400F, double 498F, suite 882-998F. **Meals** breakfast 55F, served 0730-0930; half board 478F, full board 608F (per pers., 3 days min.) **Credit cards** Amex, Visa, Diners. **Pets** dogs allowed (+40F). **Facilities** parking (+40F). **Nearby** abbey and Ochier museum at Cluny, caves at Azé, arboretum at Pézanin, château de Chaumont, 18-hole Château de la Salle golf course at Lugny. **Restaurant** service 1200-1400, 1930-2100; menus 130-440F also à la carte; specialities: foie gras frais de canard, chartreuse d'escargots, canard aux griottines.

This hotel was built on part of the site of the ancient Abbey of Cluny. Thus you will be staying in the very heart of the place which is the pride of the little town and attracts many visitors every summer. Here, however, the reasonable number of bedrooms and the arrangement of the rooms around a small inner garden safeguard the peaceful character of the place. There is a pleasantly proportioned sitting room, where several styles are nicely combined, a large dining room, and gastronomic cuisine which lives up to its excellent reputation. The bedrooms are comfortable and well decorated, and there is a bar where breakfast is served when the weather makes it impossible to use the garden. Everything, including the welcome, contributes to the pleasure of your stay. Lamartine enjoyed his stay here, and a number of well-known people have signed their names in the visitors' book in the past 30 years.

How to get there *(Map 19): 24km north west of Mâcon via N79 and D980.*

Auberge Aux Trois Saisons

Dracy-le-Fort – 71640 Givry (Saône-et-Loire)
Tel. 85.44.41.58 – Fax 85.44.46.53
MM. Völckers and Sobel

Open 1 April – 31 Oct. **Rooms** 5 with telephone, bath, WC (TV on request). **Price** single 400F, double 450F. **Meals** breakfast 42F. **Credit cards** Eurocard, MasterCard, Visa. **Pets** dogs allowed (+25F). **Facilities** parking. **Nearby** château de Germolles, château de Rochepot, Buxy, valley of les Vaux, 18-hole Chalon-sur-Saône golf course, Saint-Nicolas leisure park. **Restaurant** service 2000; menu 135F; Burgundian and American specialities.

D r Sobel left Harvard University to come and live in this old gentleman's residence. Five bedrooms have been furnished and decorated with perfect taste. They are spacious, with beams and white walls, while the zebra bedside rugs, patchwork quilts, fresh flowers, and chocolates on the bedside tables give a touch of sophistication. The bathrooms, with soft dressing gowns and perfumed soaps, are very luxurious. Around the house, apple, cherry and peach trees invite the visitor to stroll to the river which borders the grounds. At 7.30pm drinks are served, and then the host slips away to the kitchen to finish the preparation of dinner, served at 8pm. The candlelit tables, the quality of the food and the discreet background music make dinner a very pleasurable experience. However, it is sad to note that the auberge does not welcome children.

How to get there *(Map 19): 28km south of Beaune via N74 and N6 to Chagny, then D981 until 2km before Givry, turn left towards Dracy-le-Fort.*

Moulin de Bourgchâteau★★

Route de Chalon
71500 Louhans (Saône-et-Loire)
Tel. 85.75.37.12 - Fax 85.75.45.11 - M. Gonzales

Open 15 Jan – 20 Dec. **Rooms** 21 with telephone, bath or shower, WC and TV. **Price** single 200-240F, double 220-280F, suite 400-650F. **Meals** breakfast 35F, served 0700-1000. **Credit cards** accepted. **Pets** dogs allowed. **Facilities** parking. **Nearby** Côte Chalonnaise around Mercurey, Rully, château de Germolles, church at Givry, Buxy, Hôtel-Dieu at Louhans, 18-hole Lons-le Saunier golf course. **Restaurant** service 1200-1330, 1930-2100; menus 95-230F, also à la carte; specialities: foie gras chaud, poulet de Bresse.

Louhans is a large town in the part of the Bresse region that lies between Burgundy and the Jura. Once a month on big market days, when the streets and arcades are full of live poultry and farm produce, it is not unusual to hear the local patois spoken. The hotel occupies an old grain mill which was still working less than fifteen years ago; you can still see the impressive cog wheels in the bar. The huge building gives the impression of a rock standing on the water. The bedrooms are all similar in comfort and appearance. Their windows look out over the water and sometimes the mist gives you the feeling of being on a ship. You will have the same view from the restaurant, where you can enjoy the wines and food of Bresse and Burgundy. This is a good place to stay in a relatively unknown region of France.

How to get there *(Map 19): 33km south east of Chalon-sur-Saône via A6, Chalon sud exit (then D978), or Tournus exit (then D971).*

Moulin d'Hauterive★★★

Saint-Gervais-en-Vallière - 71350 Chaublanc (Saône-et-Loire)
Tel. 85.91.55.56 - Fax 85.91.89.65
M. Moille

Open 1 March – 30 Nov (closed Sunday evening and Monday in low season). **Rooms** 21 with telephone, bath or shower, WC, TV and minibar. **Price** double 500-650F, suite 600-800F. **Meals** breakfast 70F, served 0800-1100F. **Credit cards** Visa, Amex. **Pets** dogs allowed. **Facilities** swimming pool, tennis, sauna, parking. **Nearby** château de Germolles, château de Rochepot, Buxy, valley of Les Vaux, 18-hole Chalon-sur-Saône golf course, Saint-Nicolas leisure park. **Restaurant** service 1200-1400, 1900-2100; menus 150-280F, also à la carte; specialities: cassolette d'escargots à la purée de persil, foie gras poêlé à la purée de pomme de terre.

Located in the heart of the countryside, this old mill lies in three hectares of grounds through which the Dheune runs, and is an attractive house with two lovely dining rooms. In one of them armchairs are arranged around the fireplace. The bedrooms are exquisite and have all been decorated and furnished with care and good taste. Outside there are plenty of places to relax: beside the swimming pool, around the house, and on a more private terrace reached by crossing a little wooden bridge over the river. In summer, drinks and food are served outdoors. Christian Moille has a passion for cooking which adds to the pleasure of staying here.

How to get there (Map 19): 15km south east of Beaune via D970, then D94.

La Montagne de Brancion★★★

Brancion
71700 Tournus (Saône-et-Loire)
Tel. 85.51.12.40 - Fax 85.51.18.64 - M. and Mme Million

Open 15 March – 1 Nov. **Rooms** 20 with telephone, bath or shower, WC and minibar.
Price single 400-500F, double 400-580F. **Meals** breakfast 60F, served 0800-0930.
Credit cards accepted. **Pets** dogs allowed (+35F). **Facilities** swimming pool,
parking. **Nearby** church of Saint-Philibert at Tournus, church at Chapaize, Blanot,
Cluny, Taizé, château de Cormatin, 9- and 18-hole Château-la-Salle golf course.
Restaurant service 1915-2100; menus 150-250F, also à la carte; regional
specialities.

All the bedrooms in this hotel, which is perched on its own on
a hill, have views over the Maconnais vineyards and face the
rising sun. The landscape is magnificent, the silence impressive.
The building and its decor are modern. The cane furniture, a
different tint in each room, harmonises with the fabrics of the
cushions, bedcovers and curtains. Breakfasts are served in your
room, in the lounge or in the garden by the swimming pool and
are very good, with several kinds of buns, hot toast and fresh fruit
juice. Jacques and Nathalie Million are enthusiastic hoteliers,
paying great attention to their guests' needs and providing
information to ensure that you enjoy a visit to their part of the
country.

How to get there *(Map 19): 13km south of Chalon via A6, Tournus exit,*
then D14 towards Taizé (it's 1km from Brancion).

La Fontaine aux Muses**

Route de la Fontaine - 89116 La Celle-Saint-Cyr (Yonne)
Tel. 86.73.40.22 - Fax 86.73.48.66
Famille Pointeau-Langevin

Open all year (closed 1100 Monday – 1700 Tuesday). **Rooms** 17 with telephone, bath or shower and WC (4 with TV). **Price** single 320F, double 380F, suite 550-650F. **Meals** breakfast 35F, served 0800-1000; half board 350-510F (per pers., 3 days min.) **Credit cards** Eurocard, MasterCard, Visa. **Pets** dogs not allowed. **Facilities** swimming pool, golf (50F), tennis (35F), parking. **Nearby** Côte Saint-Jacques, Joigny, Othe forest, Saint-Cydroine, church of Saint-Florentin, cathedral of Saint-Etienne in Auxerre. **Restaurant** service 1230-1345, 2000-2115; menu 175F, also à la carte; specialities: ragoût de homard au foie gras, brasillade de pigeonneaux.

This old inn dates from the 17th century. Abandoned after the Second World War, it was renovated in 1960 by its present owners, M. Langevin who is a composer, and his wife who is a poet – hence the name of the establishment. In summer in the garden, or in winter by the fireside, they give musical recitals which occasionally lead to impromptu concerts. But in the dining room, around the fireplace, gastronomy rules. Comfortable armchairs await you beside the fire in the bar-lounge, and whether your beautiful bedroom is on the first floor or at ground level opening onto the garden, it will have a lovely view over the lush green countryside. More bedrooms have just been opened in a small house at the beginning of the golf course.

How to get there *(Map 18): 36km north west of Auxerre via N6 to Joigny, D943 for 7km, then D194.*

Le Castel★★

Place de la Mairie
89660 Mailly-le-Château (Yonne)
Tel. 86.81.43.06 - Fax 86.81.49.26 - M. and Mme Breerette

Open 15 March – 15 Nov (closed Wednesday). **Rooms** 12 with telephone, of which
8 with bath, 3 with shower, 8 with WC. **Price** single 160F, double 230-310F. **Meals**
breakfast 36F, served 0800-0930; 1 meal a day obligatory in high season. **Credit
cards** Visa, MasterCard, Eurocard. **Pets** dogs allowed (+25F). **Nearby** basilica of
Sainte-Madeleine at Vézelay, Saussois rocks, cathedral of Saint-Etienne in Auxerre,
Arcy caves, 18-hole Roncemay golf course at Chassy. **Restaurant** service 1215-1330,
1915-2030; menus 74-170F, also à la carte; specialities: escargots aux noisettes,
pavé de charolais, pétoncles à la bretonne, gratin de framboises.

A pretty garden with a lime-shaded terrace awaits you in front
of this late 19th-century house. The arrangement of the
ground floor means that the lounge lies between the two dining
rooms, the whole forming a single area. Around the fireplace are
Empire tables and armchairs, and although the furniture in the
dining rooms is in a different style, the ensemble works well. There
are no nasty surprises in the bedrooms, which are pretty and
individually decorated, and the food is good. It is quiet here, too,
facing the church in this tiny village. Drinks can be served on the
terrace, and the welcome is warm and relaxed.

How to get there *(Map 18): 30km south of Auxerre via N6 to Vincelles,
then D100 and D950; it's at the top of the village.*

Le Moulin des Templiers★★

Vallée du Cousin
Pontaubert - 89200 Avallon (Yonne)
Tel. 86.34.10.80 - Mme Hilmoine

Open 15 March – 30 Oct. **Rooms** 14 with telephone, bath or shower (11 with WC).
Price single 230F, double 330F. **Meals** breakfast 33F, served 0800-1000. No
restaurant. **Credit cards** not accepted. **Pets** dogs allowed (+40F). **Facilities** parking.
Nearby Avallon, Cousin valley, basilica of Sainte-Madeleine at Vézelay.

You take a quiet little tree-lined road winding along the valley
beside the river Cousin, and then you arrive at this mill, where
a kind welcome and all the comfort you could ask for are yours.
Breakfast is delicious and a copious affair, served in the garden on
the river bank when weather permits. There is toast, hot croissants,
good jams, and as much tea or coffee as you want. The bedrooms
are small but comfortable, and good taste is everywhere evident.
The car park is surrounded by a meadow in which a donkey, a
pony, chickens and pigs go about their routines, adding a further
flavour to this charming place. There is no restaurant, but
Pontaubert is only half a kilometre away.

How to get there *(Map 18): 46km south east of Auxerre, 4km west of
Avallon via D957 in the Vézelay direction.*

Château Hôtel de Brélidy★★★

Brélidy - 22140 Bégard (Côtes-d'Armor)
Tel. 96.95.69.38 - Fax 96.95.18.03
Mme Pémezec

Open Easter – All Saints. **Rooms** 14 with telephone, bath (1 with shower), WC (4 with TV). **Price** single 335-390F, double 360-650F, suite 880-950F. **Meals** breakfast 48F, served 0800-1000; half board 360-490F. **Credit cards** accepted. **Pets** dogs allowed (+30F). **Facilities** parking. **Nearby** Saint-Tugdual cathedral at Tréguier, basilica of Notre-Dame-de-Bon-Secours at Guingamp, château de Tonquedec, Kergrist, Rosambo, 18-hole Ajoncs d'or golf course at Saint-Quai-Portrieux. **Restaurant** service 1930-2100; menu 170F; specialities: pigeon aux pommes, moules au cidre.

From this old Breton château buried in the countryside you can see woods, wild hedgerows and deep lanes criss-crossing the hills. The granite walls rise out of banks of hydrangeas. At first this was a guest house offering a few bedrooms – now there are more, and of the level of comfort to be expected of a good hotel. The cooking is good too, but only a fixed menu is served in the two pleasant dining rooms. After dinner you can retire to the lounge or take advantage of the billiard room. Both are vast and, though a little bare, welcoming nonetheless. The bedrooms are named after flowers and the suite has a canopied bed and fine views; but for less money you might prefer the Jasmine or Iris rooms. A place to treasure in the most unspoilt Breton countryside.

How to get there *(see Map 5): 14km north west of Guingamp via D8, then D15 towards Bégard.*

Hôtel d'Avaugour★★★

1, place du Champ-Clos
22100 Dinan (Côtes-d'Armor)
Tel. 96.39.07.49 - Fax 96.85.43.04 - Mme Quinton

Open all year. **Rooms** 27 with telephone, bath, WC and TV. **Price** single 300-420F, double 420-480F. **Meals** breakfast 45F, served 0700-1000; half board 370-480F. **Credit cards** Visa, Amex, Diners. **Pets** dogs allowed. **Nearby** Léhon, Pleslin, Pléven, château de la Hunaudaie, 18-hole Dinard golf course at Saint-Briac-sur-Mer. **Restaurant** service 1230-1400, 1930-2115 (closed Sunday evening and Monday in low season); menus 95-300F, also à la carte; specialities: papillote de morue fraîche aux choux et lard, petit homard breton en salade, légumes croquants.

The fine grey stone facade of the Avaugour overlooks the ramparts in the middle of the town. Inside, the comfortable, intimate atmosphere of a family home reigns. All the rooms are charming, some facing the garden and the ramparts. You can choose between two restaurants: the hotel's own, opening onto the garden and offering good seafood specialities; or 'La Poudrière, recently opened in a very beautiful 15th-century room, where excellent grills are cooked before your eyes in the huge fireplace. Mme Quinton will look after you well.

How to get there *(Map 6): 29km south of Saint-Malo (in the centre of the town).*

Manoir du Cleuziou★★

22540 Louargat (Côtes-d'Armor)
Tel. 96.43.14.90 - Fax 96.43.52.59
M. and Mme Souvay

Open 1 March – 31 Jan. **Rooms** 28 with telephone, bath (1 with shower) and WC.
Price single 320-380F, double 420F. **Meals** breakfast 40F, served 0730-0930. **Credit
cards** Visa, Eurocard, Amex. **Pets** dogs allowed. **Facilities** tennis (25F), parking.
Nearby basilica of Notre-Dame-de-Bon-Secours at Guingamp, Menez-Bré, 18-hole
Saint-Samson golf course at Pleumeur-Bodou. **Restaurant** service 1200-1330,
1900-2130; menus 95-210F, also à la carte.

The oldest part of the manor dates back to the 15th century. It
is a beautiful building, the interior a match for its elegant
facade. There are magnificent carved stone fireplaces, lovely doors
and tapestries. All the small bedrooms are different and, like the
bathrooms, are of a good comfortable standard. If you have children
the prices are excellent because, for a small supplement, some
bedrooms can be arranged with two extra bunk beds. The dining
room is splendid but sadly the quality of the cooking is uneven.
The bar in the old cellars is open until 1am. We should point out
the presence of a small de luxe camping site a little way away which
belongs to the manor and has the use of its leisure facilities.

How to get there *(Map 5): 15km west of Guingamp via N12; in the village
follow signs.*

Le Repaire de Kerroc'h★★★

29, quai Morand
22500 Paimpol (Côtes-d'Armor)
Tel. 96.20.50.13 - Fax 96.22.07.46 - M. Broc

Open 16 Nov – 31 Jan, 16 Feb – 31 May, 8 June – 31 Oct. **Rooms** 12 with telephone, bath, WC, TV and minibar. **Price** single 250F, double 390F, suite 580F. **Meals** breakfast 45F, served 0800-1030; half board 395F, full board 495F (per pers., 3 days min.) **Credit cards** accepted except Amex. **Pets** dogs allowed (+50F). **Facilities** sea fishing (150F per pers.) **Nearby** abbey of Beauport, Guilben Point, l'Arcouest Point, Lanieff, Kermaria-an-Iskuit chapel, Lanloup, Plouézec, Bilfot Point. **Restaurant** service 1215-1400, 1915-2130; menus 95-350F, also à la carte; specialities: fraîcheur de raie bouclée aux légumes confits, caneton rôti au miel et aux épices.

Bréhat and Plougescant are only a few kilometres from the small town of Paimpol. On the quayside stands this very charming hotel, built in 1793 in typical St Malo architecture. The pretty bedrooms are named after islands off the Brittany coast and are well furnished in old-fashioned style. The hotel has been enlarged by the acquisition of the other part of this former corsair's house. There the bedrooms are larger and decorated with wallpapers and chintzes in bright, cheerful colours. The windows are double glazed, which together with the thick walls of the old house guarantees a peaceful night's sleep. Kerroc'h is famous for its excellent fish, unequalled in Paimpol. A very pleasant hotel in town, evoking the sea and Brittany.

How to get there (Map 5): 33km east of Lannion via D786 to Paimpol.

Hôtel Le Sphinx***

67, chemin de la Messe
22700 Perros-Guirec (Côtes-d'Armor)
Tel. 96.23.25.42 - Fax 96.91.26.13 - M. and Mme Le Verge

Open 15 Feb – 5 Jan. **Rooms** 20 with telephone, bath, WC and TV. **Price** single and double 430-500F. **Meals** breakfast 38.50F, served 0730-1000; half board 450-490F (per pers.) **Credit cards** Visa, Amex. **Pets** dogs not allowed. **Facilities** direct access to the sea, parking. **Nearby** footpath to Ploumanac'h, pink granite coast (chapel of Notre-Dame-de-la-Clarté), Sainte-Anne-de-Trégastel, boat excursions to the Sept Iles (Ile aux Moines), 18-hole Saint-Samson golf course at Pleumeur-Bodou. **Restaurant** service 1230-1400, 1930-2130 (closed Monday lunchtime except public holidays); menus 120-260F, also à la carte.

Located on a small coastal road, dominating the pink granite coastline of the Bay of Trestrignel, this hotel has practically everything: an exceptional position with a garden which goes down towards the sea, a cosily decorated bar-lounge, an adjoining dining room overlooking the ocean, and very welcoming proprietors. The bedrooms are all comfortable and well kept, although a bit impersonal. All of them enjoy the splendid view of the bay, the rocks and the sailing boats entering the port of Perros. Some bedrooms, newly built and furnished in English style, are really very pleasant, with bow windows right above the sea. These bedrooms are modern, but you will find them elegant and cheerful. Monsieur Le Verge's cooking is tasty and served with care. In summer, breakfast and drinks can be taken in the garden. A very good place.

How to get there *(Map 5): 11km north of Lannion, beside the sea.*

Domaine du Val★★★

22400 Planguenoual (Côtes-d'Armor)
Tel. 96.32.75.40 – Fax 96.32.71.50
M. Hervé

Open all year. **Rooms** 35 with telephone, bath, WC and TV. **Price** single and double 400-700F, suite 660-950F. **Meals** breakfast 40-50F; half board 380-550F, full board 500-700F (per pers.) **Credit cards** Visa, Amex. **Pets** dogs allowed. **Facilities** sauna (30F), health centre, parking. **Nearby** château de Bienassis, stud farm and church of Saint-Martin at Lamballe, 9-hole La Crinière golf course. **Restaurant** service 1230-1400, 1930-2130; menus 135-320F, also à la carte; specialities: saumon fumé maison, homard à l'armoricaine.

Set in large grounds stretching down to the sea, the Château du Val is well camouflaged. Covered tennis courts, squash courts, gymnasium, covered swimming pool, etc., are virtually hidden from sight. Amidst the greenery only a pretty Renaissance style building is visible. There is also a row of little granite houses, surrounded by shrubs. In these, every bedroom is at ground level and has its own terrace: they are peaceful and comfortable. The bedrooms in the Château are a bit more expensive and classic, and their bathrooms, tiled with Plancoët tiles, deserve a special mention. On the ground floor the dining room is comfortable and decorated in Neo-Gothic style. Beside it is an attractive verandah where in summer you can dine under bunches of grapes hanging from the vine. In all, the pleasant welcome and the many leisure activities available make the Domaine du Val a good place in which to spend a few days.

How to get there *(Map 6): 27km north east of St-Brieuc, exit autoroute at le Val-André; 1km from Planguenoual.*

Manoir du Vaumadeuc★★★★

Pléven
22130 Pléven (Côtes-d'Armor)
Tel. 96.84.46.17 - Fax 96.84.40.16 - M. O'Neill

Open Easter – 5 Jan. **Rooms** 14 with telephone, bath or shower and WC. **Price** single 490F, double 490-950F, suite 950F. **Meals** breakfast 45F, served 0800-1000; half board 430-660F, full board 615-845F (per pers., 3 days min.) **Credit cards** Visa, Amex, Diners. **Pets** dogs allowed (+50F). **Facilities** fishing in the lake, parking. **Nearby** château de la Hunaudaie, Dinan, Saint-Malo, Léhon, Preslin, 9-hole Pen Guen golf course at Briac-sur-Mer. **Restaurant** service 1900-2100 and on reservation Saturday and Sunday lunchtime (closed Wednesday in low season); menus 185-295F, also à la carte; specialities: filet de barbue au miel et aux oranges, live lobster from the fish tank.

Dating from the end of the 15th century, this manor has survived unscathed. In the main building are the dining room, a huge sitting room and delightful bedrooms, immaculately decorated and furnished. To one side there are two small houses in the same style, also comfortably arranged. In front of the manor in the 16th-century dovecote is the bar. Set in woods, but only 18km from the sea, this is an excellent place to stay. The regional cooking is good.

How to get there *(Map 6): 37km east of Saint-Brieuc via N12 to Lamballe; in the village, D28 to Pléven via La Poterie and the Hunaudaie forest.*

Le Fanal★★

Route du Cap Fréhel
Plévenon - 22240 Fréhel (Côtes-d'Armor)
Tel. 96.41.43.19 - M. and Mme Legros

Open 1 April – 30 Sept. **Rooms** 9 with telephone, shower and WC. **Price** single 230F, double 310F. **Meals** breakfast 32F. **Credit cards** Visa, Eurocard, MasterCard. **Pets** dogs not allowed. **Facilities** parking. **Nearby** cap Fréhel, fort of la Latte, rock of la Grande Fauconnière, market at Matignon (Wednesdays), 9-hole Sables-d'Or-les-Pins golf course at Cap Fréhel. **Restaurant** crêperie, service 1800-2100 weekends and school holidays.

In the middle of the Fréhel country, between Plévenon and the cape, the wooden architecture of Le Fanal blends perfectly with its surroundings. To experience its secret charm you must go inside: antique furniture, classical music, books about Brittany – everything contributes to peace and relaxation. The tastefully decorated bedrooms are modern and comfortable, and all have views over the moor and the sea. Nature lovers will appreciate the bird reserve and the walks, or they can just relax in the garden. The welcome is spontaneous and friendly.

How to get there *(Map 6): 40km west of St-Malo via D786, then D16.*

Hôtellerie de l'Abbaye

Bon-Repos - 22570 Saint-Gelven (Côtes-d'Armor)
Tel. 96.24.98.38 - M. Gadin

Open all year (closed Tuesday evening and Wednesday). **Rooms** 5 with bath and WC. **Price** single 230F, double 230-260F. **Meals** breakfast 30F, served 0830-0930; half board 225-240F (per pers., 5 days min.) **Credit cards** Visa, Eurocard, MasterCard. **Pets** dogs allowed (+20F). **Facilities** parking. **Nearby** Guerlédan lake, abbey of Bon-Repos, gorges of the Daoulas. **Restaurant** service 1215-1330, 1930-2030; menus 60-190F, also à la carte; specialities: filet de canard au cidre, brochet au beurre blanc, truite fumée de Quénécan.

This hotel occupies the old outbuildings of the Cistercian Abbey of Bon Repos, founded in 1184. There are plans for the restoration of the Abbey. The site is very peaceful and the main road is far enough away not to be heard, without access being difficult. The landscape is very green. The sight of the canal which joins Nante to Brest flowing tranquilly below, and the forest of Quénécan in front the Hôtellerie, makes a wonderful picture. It is an ideal spot for sportsmen in search of woodcock, and for fishermen (the nearby river Blanet is rated first class). All five bedrooms have bathrooms and are of a good, comfortable standard. However, you should note that three of them only have small round windows. Meals are served in a lovely dining room with big beams and solid stone walls. M. Gaudin does the cooking himself and prepares excellent dishes. Interesting prices and a friendly welcome.

How to get there *(Map 5): 46km south of Guingamp via D767 to Conlaix, then D44 to the abbey of Bon Repos via Laniscat and the gorges of the Daoulas.*

Ti Al-Lannec***

Allée de Mezo-Guen
22560 Trébeurden (Côtes-d'Armor)
Tel. 96.23.57.26 - Fax 96.23.62.14 - Telex 740656 - M. Jouanny

Open 15 March – 15 Nov. **Rooms** 29 with telephone, bath, WC and satellite TV. **Price** single 365-410F, double 600-950F. **Meals** breakfast 55-80F, served 0715-1030; half board 535-720F, full board 695-880F. **Credit cards** Amex, Visa, Diners, Eurocard. **Pets** dogs allowed (+40F). **Facilities** fitness centre, parking. **Nearby** le Castel, Bihit point, the Breton corniche from Trébeurden to Perros-Guirec, 9-hole Saint-Samson golf course at Pleumeur-Bodou. **Restaurant** service 1230-1400, 1930-2130; menus 125-370F, also à la carte; specialities: noix de coquilles Saint-Jacques dorées sauce curry, caneton rôti aux baies de cassis, la tentation de l'écureuil.

The interior of Ti Al-Lannec is exceptionally well decorated and the hotel has a wonderful view of the sea, easily accessible by a small path. The very comfortable bedrooms are beautifully furnished and decorated, some with English fabrics and wall-papers, and most have a sitting area, and a charming verandah or terrace. The same standard of decoration is apparent in the sitting rooms and the dining room, which extends on to a large verandah overlooking the Bay. The service here is perfect and the cooking totally successful. Outside are terraced gardens. Also worthy of note is the fitness centre.

How to get there (Map 5): 9km north west of Lannion via D65.

Manoir de Crec'h-Goulifen

Servel–Beg Leguer
22300 Lannion (Côtes-d'Armor)
Tel. 96.47.26.17 - Mme Droniou

Open all year. **Rooms** 7 with telephone, bath or shower and WC. **Price** single 250-280F, double 320-370F. **Meals** breakfast incl., served 0800-1030. No restaurant. **Credit cards** not accepted. **Pets** dogs allowed (+30F). **Facilities** tennis, parking. **Nearby** chapel of Kerfons, châteaux de Tonquédec, de Kergrist and de Rosambo, chapel of the Sept-Nains, 9-hole Saint-Samson golf course at Pleumeur-Bodou.

The manor of Crec'h-Goulifen was originally an 18th-century farm and has been lovingly renovated. The main room on the ground floor is arranged with regional country furniture, and here, or on the terrace, breakfast is served. The bedrooms are also in country style, small but comfortable although a little gloomy. We recommend two of the ones which have a bathroom (the third called 'Studio' is less pleasant); those with showers are a bit expensive. Apart from that, it is a pleasing and peaceful place, in a good position.

How to get there *(Map 5): 6km west of Lannion via D21, then towards Servel.*

Kastell Dinec'h★★★

22200 Tréguier (Côtes-d'Armor)
Tel. 96.92.49.39 – Fax 96.92.34.03
M. and Mme Pauwels

Open 15 March – 11 Oct and 27 Oct – 31 Dec (closed Tuesday evening and Wednesday in low season). **Rooms** 15 with telephone, bath and WC (6 with TV). **Price** single 300-320F, double 390-450F. **Meals** breakfast incl, served 0800-1000; half board 320-450F. **Credit cards** MasterCard, Eurocard, Visa. **Pets** dogs allowed (+25F). **Facilities** heated swimming pool 15 May – 15 Sept, parking. **Nearby** cathedral of Saint-Tugdual and the house of Ernest Renan at Tréguier, Pleubian, chapel of Saint-Gonéry at Plougescrant, château de la Roche-Jagu, 9-hole Saint-Samson golf course at Pleumeur-Bodou. **Restaurant** service 1930-2130; menus 130-300F, also à la carte; specialities: bar en croûte de sel, cassolette de moules aux mousserons, crêpes de seigle au homard.

In the countryside 2km from Tréguier stands this 18th-century manor farm. The main building – housing a good dining room, a small comfortable sitting room and some of the bedrooms – has two annexes containing the other bedrooms. Together they look on to a lovely garden where drinks and breakfast are served in summer. The bedrooms are small but tastefully decorated, some with antique furniture. The overall effect is simple but civilised. Mme de Pauwels' welcome is very warm and her husband's cooking is delicious. A very good address to have.

How to get there *(Map 5): 16km east of Lannion via D786, 2km before Tréguier; follow the signs.*

Domaine de Kéréven★★

Kéréven
29950 Bénodet (Finistère)
Tel. 98.57.02.46 – Mme Berrou

Open Easter – 15 Oct (on reservation Easter – 20 May and 20 Sept – 15 Oct). **Rooms** 16 with telephone, bath or shower and WC. **Price** single 300F, double 345-375F. **Meals** breakfast 35F, served 0830-1000; half board 295-325F (per pers., 3 days min.) **Credit cards** not accepted. **Pets** dogs not allowed. **Facilities** parking. **Nearby** boat trip on the Odet from Quimper to Bénodet, chapels of Gouesnac'h and le Drennec, châteaux of Bodinio and Cheffontaines, Quimper, îles de Glénan, 18-hole l'Odet golf course at Bénodet. **Restaurant** service 1930-2030; menu 115F; specialities: seasonal cooking, garden vegetables, fish.

This large Breton house has been restored and tastefully decorated by its owners. Set among fields, and with the farm buildings close by, it has kept its rural charm. In the spacious house the family has created a relaxed atmosphere. The bedrooms are all different and very comfortable. At lunchtime there is no restaurant, but in the evening dinner is served in a large dining room extended by a terrace. Self-catering appartments with a kitchen are available in another building and are very useful for family holidays. Comfort, tranquillity and great kindness are the order of the day.

How to get there *(Map 5): 14km south of Quimper via D34; 1km north of Bénodet.*

Castel Régis★★

Plage du Garo - 29890 Brignogan-Plage (Finistère)
Tel. 98.83.40.22 - Telex 940 941 - Fax 98.83.44.71
M. and Mme Plos

Open 4 April – 26 Sept. **Rooms** 21 with telephone, bath and WC. **Price** double 240-650F. **Meals** breakfast 33F, served 0730-1000; half board 380-460F, full board +98F (per pers., 3 days min.) **Credit cards** Visa. **Pets** dogs allowed (+35F). **Facilities** heated swimming pool, tennis, minigolf, sauna, parking. **Nearby** Pontusual point, church at Goulven, côte des Abers. **Restaurant** service 1230-1400, 1930-2100; menus 98-195F, also à la carte; specialities: blanquette Saint-Jacques, fricassée coquelet, cassolette de pommes chouchen.

Castel Régis has a marvellous position, on a tiny peninsula, with the restaurant at its very end by the water's edge. The bedrooms are scattered about in various buildings with a flowering garden and a mini-golf course in between. All the bedrooms are different, but try to get the ones directly overlooking the sea. There are bedrooms on the ground floor opening on to grass, and others suitable for families. Some are decorated with antiques, and some are more ordinary. When you make your reservation the management will be happy to give you descriptions of the bedrooms available. Certain external details are unattractive but you feel so good here and the welcome and cooking are so successful that you will easily forgive the defects, which will no doubt be dealt with in the future.

How to get there *(Map 5): 37km north east of Brest via D788 to Lesneven and D770.*

Auberge de Kervéoc'h★★

Route de Kervéoc'h
29100 Douarnenez (Finistère)
Tel. 98.92.07.58 - M. Guitton

Open Easter – Oct. **Rooms** 14 with telephone, bath or shower and WC. **Price** double 235-295F. **Meals** breakfast 38F; half board 285-295F. **Credit cards** Visa, Eurocard. **Pets** dogs not allowed. **Facilities** parking. **Nearby** boat museum, port of Rosmeur, church of Ploaré at Douarnenez, Leydé point, church of Confort and chapel of Notre-Dame of Kérinec, Quimper, 18-hole l'Odet golf course at Bénodet. **Restaurant** service 1230-1400, 1900-2100; menus 100-250F, also à la carte; specialities: homard crémé de son corail, émincé de Saint-Jacques aux algues.

The Auberge de Kervéoc'h is an old, nicely renovated farm located on a little road leading to the point of le Raz, five minutes from Locronan and the beaches bordering the bay of Douarnenez. There are two buildings. In one are the reception rooms and a number of bedrooms. In the other are larger and more comfortable bedrooms, though apart from the ones on the top floor some can be a bit depressing. The restaurant is excellent and serves fresh fish, sea food specialities and local produce. A fine garden with a pond surrounds the auberge, and in summer breakfast is served there. Only one problem: some bedrooms suffer from traffic noise.

How to get there *(Map 5): 18km north west of Quimper via D765.*

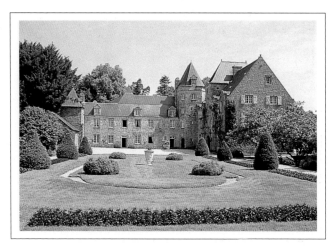

Manoir du Stang★★★★
29940 La Forêt-Fouesnant (Finistère)
Tel. 98.56.97.37 - M. Mme Hubert

Open May – Sept. **Rooms** 26 with telephone, bath or shower and WC. **Price** single 525F, double 590-860F, suite 1100F. **Meals** breakfast incl., served 0800-1000; half board price on request. **Credit cards** not accepted. **Pets** dogs not allowed. **Facilities** tennis, parking. **Nearby** Concarneau, Cabellou point, Saint-Corentin cathedral and art museum at Quimper, boat trips up the Odet and on the sea (îles des Glénans), 18-hole Cornouaille golf course adjoining the Manoir du Stang. **Restaurant** (residents only, on reservation) service 1930-2030; menu 150F, also à la carte.

L e Stang is an agricultural family estate of 40 hectares, with large formal gardens, a rose garden, lakes, woods, farm and fields, all very close to the sea. The manor is a civilised and comfortable 16th-century gentleman's residence. The 18th-century dining room opens on to a terrace overlooking the lakes. All the bedrooms are delightful, well furnished and with lovely views, and the cooking is enhanced by the quality of the home-grown produce.

How to get there *(Map 5): 12km south east of Quimper via D783 to the private drive of the Manoir, follow signs.*

Manoir de Kerhuel

Kerhuel
29720 Plonéour-Lanvern (Finistère)
Tel. 98.82.60.57 - Fax 98.82.61.79 - M. Vigliano

Open all year. **Rooms** 26 studio rooms and duplexes with telephone, bath, WC (12 with TV). **Price** double 550-600F. **Meals** breakfast 42F, served 0830-1030; half board 480F, full board 550F (per pers., 3 days min.) **Credit cards** Visa. **Pets** dogs allowed (+50F). **Facilities** heated swimming pool, tennis, sauna (50F), parking. **Nearby** Saint-Corentin cathedral and art museum at Quimper, 18-hole l'Odet golf course at Bénodet. **Restaurant** service 1200-1330, 1930-2230; menus 120-180F, also à la carte; specialities: saumon en croustille, feuilleté de fruits de mer.

Situated in the middle of a large, wooded, 6-hectare property, the Manoir de Kerhuel is a beautiful 18th-century building arranged in split-level apartments and guestrooms, the latter with period furniture in keeping with the style of the manor. The 16th-century outbuildings house a large reception room, a dining room and a bar, all enhanced by period panelling. The formal gardens add more than a touch of class to the fine buildings, and it is pleasant to walk or take afternoon tea here after swimming in the heated pool, which has a children's pool alongside.

How to get there *(Map 5): 10km south west of Quimper via D785 for 5km, then right on D156 towards Plonéour-Lanvern for 4km and left to Kerhuel.*

Hôtel Ker-Ansquer★★★

Lababan
29710 Pouldreuzic (Finistère)
Tel. 98.54.41.83 – Mme Ansquer

Open Easter – end Sept and school holidays. **Rooms** 11 with telephone, bath, WC and TV. **Price** double 290-310F. **Meals** breakfast 35F, served 0800-1000; half board 310F. **Credit cards** accepted. **Pets** dogs allowed (+30F). **Facilities** parking. **Nearby** Saint-Corentin cathedral and art museum at Quimper, 18-hole l'Odet golf course at Bénodet. **Restaurant** service 1230-1930; menus 90-295F; specialities: plateau de fruits de mer, coquilles Saint-Jacques en poêlon, langouste sauce armoricaine, canard à l'orange.

A good example of a modern building in traditional style, this hotel was built a few years ago and has just been enlarged by the addition of a new wing. The somewhat plain and austere architecture of slate roofs and grey stone walls has been enlivened by the newly built round tower. The furniture was made by a local cabinet maker and the crockery came from Quimper. The one-hectare garden ensures peace, and the view stretches out over fields and the countryside to the sea. A good place.

How to get there *(Map 5): 25km south west of Quimper via D784 to Landudec, then D143 towards Pouldreuzic and D40.*

Hôtel Porz–Morvan★★

29550 Plomodiern (Finistère)
Tel. 98.81.53.23 – M. and Mme Sihamdi–Nicolas

Open Easter – Oct. **Rooms** 12 with telephone, bath or shower and WC. **Price** double 280-300F, suite 500F (4 pers.) **Meals** breakfast 35F, served 0815-0930. **Credit cards** Visa. **Pets** dogs allowed. **Facilities** tennis (40F), parking. **Nearby** boat museum, port of Rosmeur, church of Ploaré and Leydé point at Douarnenez, chapel of Saint-Côme, church of Confort, 18-hole l'Odet golf course at Bénodet. **Restaurant** crêperie at the hotel.

Built in 1833, this farmhouse is in countryside in a popular tourist area and only 6 km from a magnificent beach. In the sitting room as well as the excellent creperie beside it there is an interesting assortment of country furniture. The bedrooms are comfortable and open on to the terrace, but with a single (rather than double) door only. If your are travelling with the family ask for bedroom 8, called 'Penty'. A charming place to stay, with a spontaneous welcome.

How to get there *(Map 5): 29km north west of Quimper via D63 to Plomodiern (the hotel is 3km east of the village).*

Manoir de Moëllien★★

29550 Plonévez-Porzay (Finistère)
Tel. 98.92.50.40 - Fax 98.92.55.21 - M. and Mme Garet

Open 20 March – 2 Jan. **Rooms** 10 with telephone, bath and WC (3 with TV). **Price** double 310-340F. **Meals** breakfast 35F, served 0800-0930; half board 335-365F, full board 390-420F (per pers.) **Credit cards** accepted. **Pets** dogs allowed (+30F). **Facilities** parking. **Nearby** Saint-Corentin cathedral and art museum at Quimper, Locronan, Sainte-Anne-la-Palud, church at Ploéven, 18-hole l'Odet golf course at Bénodet. **Restaurant** service 1230-1400, 1930-2100 (closed Wednesday in low season); menus 120-230F, also à la carte; specialities: fish and shellfish.

Invisible from the little road leading to it, this château is hidden by a pine forest. The dining room is on the ground floor of the main building, stone-built in the 17th century. Its rustic Breton furnishings are brightened with bunches of fresh flowers and house plants. Next door is a small, intimate bar. In the relaxing first-floor sitting room a stone fireplace takes pride of place. Opposite the noble facade of the manor is a building housing bedrooms at ground-floor level. They are comfortable, pretty and quiet. The views of the surrounding countryside and the excellent welcome will soon win your heart.

How to get there *(Map 5): 20km north west of Quimper via D63 to Locronan (the Manoir is 3km north west of Locronan via C10).*

Hôtel de l'Ermitage★★★

Manoir de Kerroch
29300 Quimperlé (Finistère)
Tel. 98.96.04.66 - Fax 98.39.23.41 - M. Ancelin

Open all year. **Rooms** 28 with telephone, bath or shower, WC (25 with TV, 16 with minibar). **Price** single 260-360F, double 340-380F, suite 680-750F. **Meals** breakfast 30F, served 0730-1000; half board 260-370F, full board 360-470F (per pers., 3 days min.) **Credit cards** Visa, Amex, Eurocard. **Pets** dogs allowed (+30F). **Facilities** heated swimming pool, parking. **Nearby** Sainte-Croix church and rue Dom-Maurice at Quimperlé, Carnoët forest, abbey of Saint-Maurice, 18-hole Quéven golf course at Lorient. **Restaurant** service 1200-1500, 1930-2200; menus 95-350F, also à la carte; specialities: gigot de lotte au beurre rouge, homard au sauternes.

In the heart of Carnoët forest, peaceful yet only 8km from the sea, L'Ermitage is a collection of houses set on a hillside. The bedrooms are in various buildings, and some are more luxurious than others. Some have an old-fashioned charm but could do with bright colours to cheer them up. For families the two large suites on the ground floor are ideal. Other bedrooms, in a more recent building, are very comfortable and have lovely terraces; these are decorated in a more modern style. The restaurant offers reasonably priced menus with cooking to match. The young owners love their hotel and know how to make the best of it. Their welcome and keenness to please are worth mentioning and have won them the Grand Prix de L'Acceuil.

How to get there *(Map 5): 42km south east of Quimper via N165, then D49 towards le Pouldu.*

236

Les Grandes Roches***

Route des Grandes-Roches
29910 Trégunc (Finistère)
Tel. 98.97.62.97 - M. and Mme Henrich

Open 15 Jan – 15 Dec. **Rooms** 22 with telephone, bath or shower and WC. **Price** single 230F, double 280-360F, suite 500F. **Meals** breakfast 40F, served 0800-0930; half board 300-400F, full board +150F (per pers., 3 days min.) **Credit cards** Visa. **Pets** dogs not allowed. **Facilities** parking. **Nearby** Pont-Aven, Nizon, Kérangosquer, Concarneau, Nevez, 18-hole l'Odet golf course at Bénodet. **Restaurant** service 1230-1430, 1915-2115 (closed Monday and Wednesday lunchtime); menus 98-250F, also à la carte; specialities: seafood, saumon à la peau, poissons fumés à l'auberge, filets de canard, nougat glacé maison.

In a large and well-shaded garden stands this old farmhouse, which has been renovated and is very comfortable. There is a bar with a terrace, two dining rooms and a sitting room with television. The thatched cottages, an unusual and interesting feature, have been very well restored and turned into apartments furnished in traditional style. A menhir can be found in the grounds – evidence of pre-historic times – and in the countryside around there are more dolmens, menhirs and monoliths. A number of beaches are close by. The owner's husband is German, which makes this a popular spot for visitors from beyond the Rhine.

How to get there (Map 5): *28km south east of Quimper via D783 to Trégunc via Concarneau (the auberge is just outside the village).*

Hôtel Ménez★★

Saint–Antoine
29252 Plouézoc'h (Finistère)
Tel. 98.67.28.85 – Mme Ménez

Open 1 June – 11 Sept. **Rooms** 8 with telephone, bath or shower and WC. **Price** single 150F, double 225-255F. **Meals** breakfast 25F, served 0800-1000. No restaurant. **Credit cards** not accepted. **Pets** dogs not allowed. **Facilities** parking. **Nearby** Plougonyen, parish enclosures of Saint-Thegonnec, Guimiliau and Lampaul-Guimiliau, 18-hole Saint-Samson golf course at Pleumeur-Bodou.

Here is another recently built hotel, but this one adheres scrupulously to the Breton style. Standing in a park with countryside around, it has ten very well furnished bedrooms with every imaginable facility. On the ground floor the light and cosy sitting room is peaceful and relaxing. The proprietors are most kind and welcoming.

How to get there *(Map 5): 9km north of Morlaix via D46.*

Château de Léauville

35360 Landujan (Ille-et-Vilaine)
Tel. 99.07.21.14 - Fax 99.07.21.80
M. and Mme Gicquiaux

Open 15 March – 15 Nov. **Rooms** 7 with telephone, bath and WC. **Price** single and double 470-720F. **Meals** breakfast 56F, served 0800-1000; half board from 476F (per pers.) **Credit cards** accepted. **Pets** dogs allowed (+60F). **Facilities** heated swimming pool, parking. **Nearby** museums of Brittany and of Art in Rennes, 18-hole la Freslonnière golf course at Le Rheu, 9-hole Rennes golf course. **Restaurant** service 1930-2030; menus from 185F; specialities: traditional seasonal cooking, fish, seafood on request.

Château de Léauville dates from the 16th and 17th centuries and incorporates a turret of the 11th-century manor of Pontelain, on whose ruins it was built. The 16th-century chapel now serves as an exhibition hall and there are traces of the old building everywhere. There is a friendly ambience in the dining room and the cosy, tastefully furnished bedrooms. In the garden is a large swimming pool, and there are terraces for relaxing and gazing at the countryside. The owners are very welcoming.

How to get there *(Map 6): 30km north west of Rennes via N12 to Bédée, then D72 to Irodouër and D21.*

Manoir du Tertre***

Paimpont
35380 Plélan-le-Grand (Ille-et-Vilaine)
Tel. 99.07.81.02 - Fax 99.07.85.45 - M. Gouguenheim

Open all year except Feb. **Rooms** 8 with telephone, bath and WC. **Price** double 300-500F. **Meals** breakfast 35F, served 0800-1100; half board 300-400F, full board 380-500F (per pers., 3 days min.) **Credit cards** Visa, Amex. **Pets** dogs not allowed. **Facilities** parking. **Nearby** Paimpont forest, les Forges-de-Paimpont, church at Paimpont, lake of le Pas-du-Houx, château de Comper, church at Tréhonrenteuc, Campénéac and château de Trécesson, 18-hole la Freslonnière golf course at Rheu, 9-hole Rennes golf course. **Restaurant** service 1230-1400, 1930-2100 (closed Monday); menus 120-175F, also à la carte; specialities: game, métamorphose de canard, écussons de Lancelot à la nage de volaille.

The interior of this house has much charm, as do the bedrooms, which have just been completely refurbished. Most have a big window overlooking the countryside and the 2-hectare grounds. This is an ideal place for a weekend, with walks along the tracks and paths of the forest of Paimpont in the footsteps of Merlin and the fairy Viviane.

How to get there *(Map 6): 40km south west of Rennes to Plélan-le-Grand, then D38 via N24.*

Château de la Motte Beaumanoir★★★

35720 Pleugeuneuc (Ille-et-Vilaine)
Tel. 99.69.46.01 - Fax 99.69.42.49
M. Bernard

Open all year except 5 weeks in winter (enquire). **Rooms** 6 and 2 suites with telephone, bath and WC (TV on request). **Price** double 700F, suite 800-900F. **Meals** breakfast 60F, served 0800-1000; half board 610F (per pers.) **Credit cards** Visa, Amex, MasterCard. **Pets** dogs allowed (+60F). **Facilities** heated swimming pool, boating, fishing, parking. **Nearby** Dinan, Léhon, Pleslin, château de la Hunaudaie, 18-hole Dinard golf course at Saint-Briac-sur-Mer. **Restaurant** service 1200-1300, 2000-2200 (closed Monday and Tuesday in low season, Tuesday in high season); menus 140-250F, also à la carte; specialities: traditional cooking.

A landscape of forests, lakes and fields surrounds this 15th-century château and gives it complete tranquillity. Behind the graceful austerity of its granite walls lies a cheerful and elegant interior. The bedrooms are huge, with high ceilings, beautiful furniture, and fabrics chosen to give a different personality to each room. Some have a view of the lake and the bathrooms are modern and comfortable. The young master of the house will welcome you more as a guest than a client. Do not hesitate to ask his advice about local tourist attractions. Quality cooking.

How to get there *(Map 6): 12km south east of Dinan via N137, then north of Pleugeuneuc turn left at first crossroads via D78.*

Manoir de la Rance★★★

Château de Jouvente
35730 Pleurtuit (Ille-et-Vilaine)
Tel. 99.88.53.76 - Fax 99.88.63.03 - Mme Jasselin

Open March – Dec. **Rooms** 10 with telephone, bath, WC (5 with TV). **Price** single 330-380F, double 380-700F, suite 750-950F. **Meals** breakfast 45F, served 0700-1100. No restaurant. **Credit cards** Visa. **Pets** dogs allowed (+40F). **Facilities** landing stage, parking. **Nearby** banks of the river Rance, Paimpont forest, les Forges-de-Paimpont, church at Paimpont, lake of le Pas-du-Houx, château de Comper, church of Tréhonrenteuc, 18-hole Dinard golf course at Saint-Briac.

Facing the Rance and surrounded by trees and flowers, this 19th-century manor stands in large and lovely grounds. The big sitting room is pleasantly furnished in a mixture of styles, and in the bar and the small sitting room, where tea is served, the atmosphere is really homely. Refreshments are served outside in the garden and on the terraces, which have reclining chairs. Whether on the first floor or on the second, attic floor, all the bedrooms are very comfortable and quiet. From all the rooms there is a stunning view of the sea, the cliffs and the countryside. Madame Jasselin the owner is very kind.

How to get there *(Map 6): 15km south west of Saint-Malo via D168, then left after the Rance dam on D114 to 'La Jouvente' (via Richardais). The manor is to the left on the way out of the village.*

La Malouinière des Longchamps★★★

35430 Saint-Jouan-des-Guérêts (Ille-et-Vilaine)
Tel. 99.82.74.00 - Fax 99.82.74.14
Mme Goger

Open all year, on reservation. **Rooms** 14 with telephone, shower, WC and TV. **Price** single and double 350-450F. **Meals** breakfast 40F, served any time. **Credit cards** Visa, Eurocard. **Pets** dogs not allowed. **Facilities** heated swimming pool, tennis, minigolf, parking. **Nearby** château and walled town of Saint-Malo, île de Cézembre, îles de Chaussey, 27-hole Saint-Malo golf course. **Restaurant** service at 1930; menu 140F. Traditional family cooking using fresh produce.

This long house in the typical architecture of the region has beautifully tended grounds with mini-golf, tennis and a swimming pool. The kindly welcome and the dinner prepared every evening for the residents (on reservation) give it a charming family character. The bedrooms on the first floor in the main body of the hotel are small but pleasing and comfortable, with a pretty view of the countryside. We prefer them to the bedrooms in the annexe building. The size of the dining room, and its fine granite walls, will amaze you, and the decor cleverly avoids making it seem cold. A small hotel a few minutes from St Malo which lends itself to an overnight stop as well as to a longer stay.

How to get there *(Map 6): 5km south of Saint-Malo in the Rennes direction; at Saint-Jouan follow the signs.*

La Korrigane★★★
39, rue Le Pomellec
35400 Saint-Malo (Ille-et-Vilaine)
Tel. 99.81.65.85 – Fax 99.82.23.89 – M. Marchon

Open all year. **Rooms** 12 with telephone, bath or shower, WC and TV. **Price** single 300-400F, double 400-650F. **Meals** breakfast 55F, served 0730-1000; brunch 100F. No restaurant. **Credit cards** accepted. **Pets** dogs allowed (+50F). **Facilities** parking. **Nearby** ramparts, castle and walled town of Saint-Malo, îles de Chaussey, île de Cézembre, Saint-Samson cathedral at Dol-de-Bretagne, 18-hole Dinard golf course at Saint-Briac.

This is without doubt one of the most charming little hotels in France. It lies within a turn-or-the-century house which from the outside looks like an old holiday house turned into a family *pension*. The atmosphere is so comfortable that you feel quite at home, and the welcome is warm, discreet and courteous. Everything is restful, exquisitely tasteful and unpretentiously aesthetic. Each bedroom has its own colour scheme, with perfectly harmonised colours and fabrics, and lovely furniture and paintings. Behind the house is a small garden where you can have breakfast or enjoy the sunshine. The large, book-lined sitting room is an invitation to relax. La Korrigane is better than a hotel: it is your own special pied-à-terre in Saint-Malo.

How to get there (Map 6): in the centre of town, take the Saint-Sevran road.

Hôtel Village La Désirade★★★

56360 Belle-Ile-en-Mer (Morbihan)
Tel. 97.31.70.70 – Fax 97.31.89.63
Mme Mulon

Open 1 March – 6 Jan. **Rooms** 24 with telephone, bath, WC and TV. **Price** double 390-470F. **Meals** breakfast 50-70F, served 0800-1100. No restaurant. **Credit cards** Amex, Visa, Diners. **Pets** dogs allowed. **Facilities** heated swimming pool, children's games, parking. **Nearby** Vauban fortifications, cave of l'Apothicairerie, port Donnan, les Aiguilles de Port-Coton, 18-hole Sauzon golf course.

Facing the Côte Sauvage, 500 metres from the sea, in one of those hamlets typical of Belle-Ile-en-Mer where Monet painted 'Les Aiguilles de Port-Coton', La Désirade has until now been the well-kept secret of regulars who came to enjoy its delicious seafood. Last year five small houses were built around a heated swimming pool close to the restaurant. Each of these has two bedrooms, giving a family or group of friends a place entirely to themselves. The decor is simple but in good taste, with brightly coloured chintzes creating a cheerful effect all year round. In the morning a breakfast buffet is set out by the swimming pool, allowing everybody to do his own thing. This is a relaxed place where privacy is respected. There is a restaurant adjoining the hotel.

How to get there *(Map 5): by car, take the Quiberon-Le Palais ferry; by air from Lorient by Finist-Air (20min. flight); 7km south of Le Palais via D190 through Bangor (the hotel is 2km from Bangor).*

Petit Hôtel Les Pougnots

Rue du Chemin-Neuf
Le Sauzon - 56340 Belle-Ile-en-Mer (Morbihan)
Tel. 97.31.61.03 - Fax 97.31.89.63 - Mme Guillouët

Open all year. **Rooms** 5 with telephone, shower and WC. **Price** single 450F, double 500F. **Meals** breakfast incl., served 0830-1200. No restaurant. **Credit cards** not accepted. **Pets** not allowed. **Nearby** Vauban fortifications, cave of l'Apothicairerie, Port Donnan, les Aiguilles de Port-Coton, 18-hole Sauzon golf course.

South of Quiberon lies a wild, romantic place of ocean-swept cliffs, gorse and heathland – Belle-Ile, an island which well deserves its name. You arrive on the island at le Palais, but the Hôtel des Pougnots is in Sauzon, a little port surrounded by whitewashed cottages with coloured shutters. Set high up in the village, this friendly little hotel looks rather like a chalet and has only five bedrooms to offer. Inside, the decoration is simple, even somewhat monastic in style, but tasteful and comfortable. Breakfast can be served on a small balcony overlooking the harbour. This is a precious address, until recently known by word of mouth only.

How to get there *(Map 5): by car, take the Quiberon-Le Palais ferry; by air from Lorient by Finist-Air (20min. flight); 5km from Le Palais, at the port of Le Sauzon.*

Auberge de Coët-Diquel**

Rue Coët-Diquel
56310 Bubry (Morbihan)
Tel. 97.51.70.70 - Fax 97.51.73.08 - M. Romieux

Open 15 March – 14 Dec. **Rooms** 20 with telephone, bath or shower and WC. **Price** single and double 254-304F. **Meals** breakfast 32F, served from 0800; half board 280-305F, full board 325-350F (per pers., 3 days min.) **Credit cards** MasterCard, Eurocard, Visa. **Pets** dogs allowed (+38F). **Facilities** swimming pool, tennis, fishing, parking. **Nearby** Hennebont, Île de Groix, Port-Louis, 18-hole Queven golf course, 18-hole Ploemeur-Océan golf course at Saint-Jude. **Restaurant** service 1230-1330, 1930-2030; menus 78-188F, also à la carte; specialities: viandes en sauce, fish, shellfish.

The Auberge de Coët-Diquel is built on the site of an old mill, on the banks of a river and in the middle of the forest. It would be not only a restful halt on your travels but also a pleasant place to stay for a while and make the most of the tennis court and covered swimming-pool. The dining room is very large but when there is a function part of it is divided off to maintain the residents' privacy. The owners are very friendly.

How to get there *(Map 5): 31km north east of Lorient via D769 to Plouay, then D2 (in the village take the road opposite the church porch).*

Hôtel de la Marine★★

7, rue du Général-de-Gaulle
56590 Ile-de-Groix (Morbihan)
Tel. 97.86.80.05 - Fax 97.86.56.37 - Mme Hubert

Open 1 Feb – 31 Dec. **Rooms** 22 with telephone, bath or shower and WC. **Price** single 172-193F, double 191-384F. **Meals** breakfast 30F, served 0800-1000; half board 190-297F, full board 373-397F (per pers., 2 days min.) **Credit cards** Visa, Eurocard. **Pets** dogs allowed (+30F). **Facilities** parking. **Nearby** museum at Groix, l'Enfer point, Saint-Nicolas point, Pen-Mer. **Restaurant** service 1200-1330, 1930-2130; menus 68-140F, also à la carte; specialities: barbecued fish, feuilleté de Saint-Jacques, marquise au chocolat.

This is a real find, because many of the hotels on the islands are neglected and seem to count on their isolation (and the sheer impossibility of leaving after the last boat) to keep their clientele. There is none of that attitude here. Mme Hubert, the owner, has lovingly designed and arranged this hotel, and we are certain that you will appreciate her taste. The reception room has pretty, old-fashioned furniture; the dining room, where you can eat very well at reasonable prices, has attractive coloured table linen; on the fireplace and the shelves is a collection of pottery; in a corner, a shell-encrusted clock is the only reminder of the passage of time. The bedrooms are simple, painted white and brightened with coloured curtains and bedspreads. Go for those facing the sea (especially No. 1), but all are very pleasant and comfortable. Outside, a paved garden offers drinks in the shade of the oldest tree on the island. An unreservedly kind welcome.

How to get there *(Map 5): boat from Lorient (45 min.), tel. 97.21.03.97.*

Manoir La Châtaigneraie★★★

Route de Moëlan-sur-Mer
56520 Guidel (Morbihan)
Tel. 97.65.99.93 – Mme Collet

Open all year. **Rooms** 10 with telephone, bath, WC, TV and minibar. **Price** single and double 450-650F. **Meals** breakfast 47F, served 0830-1030. No restaurant. **Credit cards** Visa, **Pets** dogs allowed (+30F). **Facilities** parking. **Nearby** Saint-Maurice, Hennebont, île de Groix, Port-Louis, 18-hole Queven golf course, 18-hole Ploemeur-Océan golf course at Saint-Jude.

Built as a family home, La Châtaigneraie has been a hotel for several years. Everything here is very comfortable. The atmosphere is restful in the reception rooms, intimate in the bedrooms (which all have minibar and TV) and generally peaceful, thanks to grounds of over one hectare. There is no restaurant, but you can get something light to eat between 8pm and 9pm if you order in advance. Breakfasts are ample and delicious, the welcome charming.

How to get there (Map 5): 10km north west of Lorient via D865 to Coatermalo, then D306; in the village take D162 in direction of Moëlan-sur-Mer.

Hôtel de Kerlon★★
56680 Plouhinec (Morbihan)
Tel. 97.36.77.03
M. and Mme Coëffic

Open 25 March – 31 Oct. **Rooms** 16 with telephone, WC, of which 15 with bath or shower, 10 with TV. **Price** single 220-250F, double 250-280F. **Meals** breakfast 30F, served 0800-1000; half board 250-270F (per pers.) **Credit cards** Visa, Eurocard. **Pets** small dogs allowed. **Facilities** parking. **Nearby** Hennebont, île de Groix, Port-Louis, 18-hole Queven golf course, 18-hole Ploemeur-Océan golf course at Saint-Jude. **Restaurant** service 1930-2100; menus 75-150F, also à la carte; specialities: fish, seafood.

This hotel is set in the middle of the countryside, 5km from the sea and mid-way between Lorient and Carnac. It is a farmhouse which has been completely renovated. The beams, exposed stonework and two fireplaces give a rustic air to the dining room, which has a small terrace where drinks are served or where you can relax beside the sloping garden. The bedrooms are plainly decorated and quiet. Being close to the beaches and resorts does not spoil this hotel's tranquil rural atmosphere.

How to get there *(Map 5): 30km south east of Lorient. Leave N165 at Hennebont, take D781 in direction of Port-Louis, at next roundabout take Carnac-Quiberon road.*

Hostellerie Les Ajoncs d'Or★★

Kerbachique
56720 Plouharnel (Morbihan)
Tel. 97.52.32.02 – Fax 97.52.40.36 – Mme Le Maguer

Open 15 Feb – 2 Nov. **Rooms** 20 with telephone, bath or shower and WC. **Price** double 240-350F, suite 600F. **Meals** breakfast 33F, served 0800-0930; half board 270-340F (per pers.) **Credit cards** Visa. **Pets** small dogs allowed (+suppl.) **Facilities** parking. **Nearby** menhirs of Carnac and Erdeven, church at Plouhinec, Belle-Ile, 18-hole Saint-Laurent-Ploëmel golf course. **Restaurant** service 1900-2130; menus 92-145F, also à la carte; specialities: rognons de veau au calvados, fish, seafood.

Les Ajoncs d'Or is a pink granite Breton farmhouse made up of three adjoining buildings and situated outside the village. On the ground floor a large restaurant with a lovely fireplace happily combines beams, exposed stonework, flowered curtains and pictures. Next door is another very pleasant room for breakfasts. The bedrooms are simple and comfortable. We recommend those above the restaurant which are well renovated, light and cheerful. Thanks to the hostess's personality the hotel has a family atmosphere. And the warmth of the welcome makes Les Ajoncs d'Or more than just a place to stop for a night – it's worth staying longer.

How to get there *(Map 5): 52km south east of Lorient via N165 to Auray, then D768.*

Moulin de Lesnehué★★

56890 Saint-Avé (Morbihan)
Tel. 97.60.77.77
Mme Cheval

Open 15 Jan – 15 Dec. **Rooms** 12 with telephone, bath or shower and WC. **Price** single 160F, double 210-230F. **Meals** breakfast 28F, served 0800-1000. No restaurant. **Credit cards** accepted. **Pets** dogs allowed. **Facilities** parking. **Nearby** chapel of Notre-Dame-du-Loc at Saint-Avé, ramparts and Saint-Pierre cathedral in Vannes, Conleau peninsula, fortress of Largoët, château du Plessis-Jossot, 18-hole Kerver golf course at Saint-Gildas de Rhuys.

This old 15th-century mill has a lovely position in the middle of the countryside on the banks of a stream. The bedrooms are arranged in the two buildings which form the hotel. All of them are simple and modern, with contemporary furnishings, but charming and comfortable. The hotel has no restaurant, but there is a *crêperie* in one of the buildings. Ferns, flowers, the sound of running water and birdsong provide nature's backdrop to this lovely place. A truly pleasant welcome.

How to get there *(Map 14): 5km north of Vannes via D126; turn right on the way out of the village of Lesnehué.*

Auberge du Moulin de Chaméron★★★

18210 Bannegon (Cher)
Tel. 48.61.83.80 – Fax 48.61.84.92
M. Candore

Open 1 March – 15 Nov. (closed Tuesday in low season). **Rooms** 13 with telephone, bath or shower, WC and TV. **Price** single 300F, double 440F, suite 550F. **Meals** breakfast 44F, served 0730-1000. **Credit cards** Amex, Visa, Eurocard. **Pets** dogs allowed (+30F). **Facilities** swimming pool, parking. **Nearby** basilica and château of Châteauneuf-sur-Cher, church of Saint-Amand-Montrond, abbey of Noirlac, châteaux of Meillant and Ainay-le-Vieil, Bourges, 18-hole Val-de-Cher golf course at Montluçon. **Restaurant** service 1215-1400, 1930-2100; menus 135-200F, also à la carte; seasonal cooking.

Renovated about ten years ago, this 18th-century mill lies deep in the countryside. The old milling machinery has been kept intact in the middle of the building and a museum displays a collection of tools and objects used by millers in the past. The bedrooms are very pleasant and comfortable, with antique or reproduction furniture. We particularly liked those on the ground floor with a private terrace where you can have breakfast. In the summer, lunch and dinner are served in the garden by the mill-pond, but if the weather is discouraging meals are taken in a delightful, intimate little dining room in the old mill. Excellent cooking and a charming welcome.

How to get there (*Map 17*): *42km south east of Bourges via N76 towards Moulins, then D953 and D41.*

La Solognote★★

18410 Brinon-sur-Sauldre (Cher)
Tel. 48.58.50.29 - Fax 48.58.56.00
M. and Mme Girard

Open all year (closed Wednesday and Tuesday evening Oct – June). **Rooms** 13 with telephone, bath or shower, WC and TV. **Price** double 280-360F, suite 450F. **Meals** breakfast 50F; half board 360-410F. **Credit cards** MasterCard, Visa. **Pets** dogs not allowed. **Facilities** parking. **Nearby** Orléans cathedral, la Source flower gardens at Olivet, châteaux of the route Jacques-Coeur, Aubigny-sur-Nère, le haut Berry from la Chapelle d'Angillon to Saint-Martin-d'Auxigny, Sancerre, 18-hole Sully golf course at Viglains, 18-hole Marcilly golf course. **Restaurant** service 1230-1400, 1930-2030; menus 150-310F, also à la carte; specialities: gratin de langoustines et grenouilles aux bettes, tarte fine aux pommes et au foie gras, game in season.

This tranquil village inn is barely 15 minutes from the RN20. It is a lovely brick house located in the village centre. The comfortable interior, combining antique and modern furniture, is simple and cheerful. The dining room is particularly attractive, with beams and a soft colour scheme. The bedrooms have every comfort and are all decorated differently. There are also small apartments for four people. The inn is also a restaurant with a reputation for good food.

How to get there *(Map 17): 60km south east of Orléans via N20 to Lamotte-Beuvron, then D923 towards Aubigny-sur-Nère.*

Château de la Beuvrière★★

18100 Saint-Hilaire-de-Court (Cher)
Tel. 48.75.14.63 - Fax 48.75.47.62
M. and Mme de Brach

Open 1 March – 10 Jan (closed Sunday evening). **Rooms** 15 with telephone, bath or shower, WC (4 with minibar). **Price** single 270F, double 330-460F, duplex 450F, suite 570F. **Meals** breakfast 38F, served 0730-1000. **Credit cards** Visa, Amex, Diners. **Pets** dogs allowed. **Facilities** swimming pool, tennis, parking. **Nearby** Saint-Etienne cathedral, hôtel Jacques-Coeur in Bourges, Aubigny-sur-Nère, 18-hole la Picardière golf course, 18-hole Vierzon golf course. **Restaurant** 1200-1400, 1930-2100 (closed Sunday evening and Monday); menu 140F, also à la carte; specialities: saumon fumé maison, foie gras frais maison, sandre braisé au beurre de truffes, ris de veau braisé à l'orange.

The château has kept its 1037-hectare estate intact since the Middle Ages. Inherited by the present owners, it is a very charming hotel today. The family furniture is authentic and dates from the 15th to the 19th century. The overall effect is one of excellent quality arranged with perfect taste. Lovely and very well kept, the bedrooms overlook the grounds. Those on the first floor are almost sumptuous, and if their bathrooms are a bit on the small side this is so as to preserve the wood panelled bed alcoves. The second floor bedrooms have original beams and some have a mezzanine. You will dine sitting on Empire armchairs at a beautifully laid table. The food is as excellent as the decor, and the welcome is spontaneous and cordial.

How to get there *(Map 17): 29km north west of Bourges via A71, Vierzon-Sud exit, then N20 towards Châteauroux.*

Hostellerie Saint-Jacques★★★

Place du Marché-aux-œufs
28220 Cloyes-sur-le-Loir (Eure-et-Loir)
Tel. 37.98.40.08 - Fax 37.98.32.63 - M. Thureau

Open 1 Feb – 15 Dec (closed Sunday evening and Monday in low season). **Rooms** 22 with telephone, bath or shower, WC, TV (1 with minibar). **Price** single and double 290-480F, suite 680F. **Meals** breakfast 50F, served 0800-1030; half board 540F, full board 740F (per pers., 2 days min.) **Credit cards** Visa, Eurocard, MasterCard. **Pets** dogs allowed. **Facilities** boats, table tennis, parking. **Nearby** chapel of Yrou at Châteaudun, Vendôme, valley of the Loir (Montoire-sur-le-Loir, Lavardin, Troo, manoir de la Possonnière), 9-hole la Bosse golf course at Oucques. **Restaurant** service 1200-1330, 1930-2100; menus 230-390F, also à la carte; specialities: gratinée de lotte au corail de homard, poitrail de canard à la gentiane.

Situated on the village square, l'Hostellerie Saint-Jacques is an old 16th-century coaching inn. Here you may go boating on the Loir, which crosses the shady half-hectare gardens. The 20 bedrooms have been completely modernised (perhaps a bit too much so) and redecorated. The tasteful and intimate dining room overlooks the garden. The Hostellerie has a reputation for good food and in summer you can enjoy the double pleasures of an excellent lunch eaten outside under the trees in beautiful surroundings.

How to get there *(Map 16): 53km north of Blois via D957 to Vendôme, then N10 (going north) to Cloyes-sur-le-Loir.*

Manoir de Boisvillers★★

11, rue du Moulin-de-bord
36200 Argenton-sur-Creuse (Indre)
Tel. 54.24.13.88 – M. and Mme Gonich

Open all year (closed 20 Dec – 15 Jan) **Rooms** 14 with telephone, bath or shower, WC and TV. **Price** single 170-260F, double 220-330F. **Meals** breakfast 35F, served 0730-0930. No restaurant. **Credit cards** Visa. **Pets** dogs allowed (+25F). **Facilities** swimming pool, parking. **Nearby** Pont-Vieux and Saint-Benoît chapel at Argenton, château de Nohant-Vic, Georges Sand museum at La Châtre, abbey church of Fontgombault, 18-hole Dryades and Pouligny-Notre-Dame golf courses.

The Manoir de Boisvillers stands in the centre of Argenton-sur-Creuse, in the old part of the town, by the river, and is reached through a maze of narrow streets. The 18th-century building is surrounded by extensive grounds which ensure peace and quiet. The entrance hall, where pink is the dominant colour, is particularly bright and pleasant, while the bedrooms are comfortable and prettily furnished, with well-chosen fabrics for the bedspreads and curtains. Some of the rooms command lovely views of the river and the houses on its banks. The dining-room, where breakfast is served, is not so attractive, but it has not yet been refurbished. Otherwise, both the setting and the decor of the hotel are fine, and hosts Monique and Jean-Pierre extend a warm welcome. It is well worth booking for a night... or more.

How to get there *(Map 16): 30km south of Châteauroux, in Limoges direction.*

Domaine de l'Etape★★★
Route de Bélâbre
36300 Le Blanc (Indre)
Tel. 54.37.18.02 – Mme Seiller

Open all year. **Rooms** 35 with telephone, bath or shower, WC (20 with TV). **Price** single 200-350F, double 210-410F. **Meals** breakfast 40F, served 0700-1100. **Credit cards** Visa. **Pets** dogs allowed. **Facilities** riding, fishing, shooting, boating, parking. **Nearby** museum of local history at Le Blanc, châteaux of Azay-le-Ferron, le Guillaume and le Bouchet, Benedictine abbey of Fontgombault. **Restaurant** residents only, service 1930-2130; menus 115-125F, also à la carte; specialities: coq en barbouille, pâté berrichon.

You will be delighted by the kind welcome in this 19th-century house standing in a 130-hectare estate. Everything is charming and a bit outdated. The sitting room, with Louis Philippe furniture, is ideal for reading or watching television. The pale wooden panelled dining room is often brightened by an open fire. There is a small garden terrace with a service bar. The bedrooms are simple and comfortable and differ from each other. Country-lovers will appreciate the bedrooms in the farmhouse, which are rustic but also comfortable. The farm provides fresh produce for the kitchen. Fishermen can try their luck in the lake and horse lovers can go riding or inspect the foals in the fields.

How to get there *(Map 16): 59km west of Châteauroux via N20 and N151 to Le Blanc, then D10 towards Bélâbre.*

Château de Bouesse
36200 Bouesse (Indre)
Tel. 54.25.12.20 - Fax 54. 25.12.30
M. and Mme Courtot-Atterton

Open Feb – Dec (closed Monday in low season). **Rooms** 11 with telephone, bath or shower and WC. **Price** single 280-350F, double 350-450F, suite 650F. **Meals** breakfast 45F, served 0800-1000; half board 345-425F (per pers., 3 days min.) **Credit cards** Visa, Amex. **Pets** dogs not allowed. **Facilities** parking. **Nearby** Pont-Vieux and Saint-Benoît chapel at Argenton, château de Nohant-Vic, Georges Sand museum at La Châtre, abbey church of Fontgombault, 18-hole Dryades and Pouligny-Notre-Dame golf courses. **Restaurant** service 1200-1400, 1930-2130; menu 125F, also à la carte; specialities: fish, foie gras, rognons de veau à l'ancienne, scallops.

M onsieur and Mme Courtot-Atterton are passionate about history, and have focussed their enthusiasm on the restoration of this superb 13th- and 15th-century château. The bedrooms' names refer to the château's history: 'Jeanne d'Arc', 'Raoul VI de Gaucourt', etc. The bedrooms are all very large, and often have stone fireplaces bearing coats of arms. Some rooms have been redecorated recently in the style of the Middle Ages, using furniture specially made for the château. Others are in the romantic style of the English 19th century. The hotel is totally comfortable and miraculously peaceful. The view cannot have changed for centuries. We particularly admired the dining room, which has pale blue and grey panelling picked out in white, and a 17th-century allegorical painting on the ceiling. In summer an excellent breakfast is served outside on the terrace.

How to get there *(Map 17): 33km south of Châteauroux, on D927 between Argenton-sur-Creuse and La Châtre.*

Château de la Vallée Bleue★★★

Saint-Chartier - 36400 La Châtre (Indre)
Tel. 54.31.01.91 - Fax 54.31.04.48
M. and Mme Gasquet

Open March – Jan (closed Sunday evening and Monday Oct – March) **Rooms** 13 with telephone, bath or shower, WC, TV and minibar. **Price** single 195-375F, double 315-550F. **Meals** breakfast 47F; half board 400-450F, full board 500-550F (per pers., 3 days min.) **Credit cards** Visa, MasterCard. **Pets** dogs allowed (+50F). **Facilities** swimming pool, parking. **Nearby** Georges Sand museum at La Châtre, château des Maître-Sonneurs at Saint-Chartier, château de Nohant-Vic, 18-hole Dryades golf course. **Restaurant** service 1200-1330, 1930-2100; menus 125-325F, also à la carte; specialities: home-smoked produce, carpe au beurre rouge, millefeuille aux poires.

The ghosts of George Sand and Chopin float over this small château, which was built by that couple's doctor in grounds of four hectares. The entrance hall is lovely, and M. and Mme Gasquet very welcoming. Everywhere there are pictures and memorabilia to do with the writer and the musician. The bedrooms are identified by small glass plaques with reproduction signatures of George Sand's artist friends. The bedrooms are comfortable, stylishly furnished and pleasantly decorated with Laura Ashley papers and fabrics. Lovely views over the park and the countryside. The English-style sitting room is warm and a glass of old cognac or liqueur beside the fire is a pleasure. The list of liqueurs is amazing. Off the sitting room there are two very attractive dining rooms opening onto the park with its two hundred year old oak tree. Good food.

How to get there *(Map 17): 27km south east of Châteauroux via D943 to St-Chartier. The hotel is outside the village on the Verneuil road.*

Château du Vivier

Le Vivier
36200 Argenton-sur-Creuse (Indre)
Tel. 54.24.22.99 - M. and Mme Longin

Open all year. **Rooms** 7 with telephone, bath, WC and TV. **Price** single and double 300-550F. **Meals** breakfast 65F, served until 1200; half board 500-650F, full board 650-900F (per pers., 3 days min.) **Credit cards** accepted. **Pets** dogs allowed (+60F). **Facilities** parking. **Nearby** Pont-Vieux and Saint-Benoît chapel at Argenton, château de Nohant-Vic, Georges Sand museum at La Châtre, abbey church of Fontgombault, 18-hole Dryades and Pouligny-Notre-Dame golf courses. **Restaurant** service 1200-1400, 1900-2300; menus 135-380F, also à la carte; specialities: fish, foie gras, unusual mushrooms.

There's a romantic air about this small château, built in the 17th century and renovated in the early 19th. Anxious to keep the family character of the place and to welcome their guests as friends, M. and Mme Longin have decorated it delightfully. In the dining room there is antique furniture, paintings, old photographs, curios and dried flower arrangements. The first floor bedrooms are large, with lovely materials used as wall or bed-hangings, as well as antique furniture. On the second floor the bedrooms are smaller but very sweet, with long windows reaching to the floor. In good weather tables are set outside under the big trees. There you can have tea, read Proust or lose yourself in the box maze in the garden.

How to get there *(Map 16): 30km south west of Châteauroux, on the way out of Argenton-sur-Creuse, at 'Le Vivier'.*

Hôtel du Bon Laboureur et du Château★★★

6, rue du Dr Bretonneau
37150 Chenonceaux (Indre-et-Loire)
Tel. 47.23.90.02 - Fax 47.23.82.01 - M. Jeudi

Open 15 March – 15 Nov. **Rooms** 36 with telephone, bath or shower, WC (18 with TV). **Price** single 200-500F, double 280-600F, suite 1000F. **Meals** breakfast 45F, served 0730-1030; half board 355-655F. **Credit cards** accepted. **Pets** dogs allowed. **Facilities** swimming pool, parking. **Nearby** château de Chenonceaux, châteaux of the Loire, Montlouis-sur-Loire via the valley of the Cher, 18-hole Touraine golf course at Ballon-Mire. **Restaurant** service 1200-1400, 1930-2130; menus 175-300F, also à la carte; specialities: tartare de saumon, sole farcie au vouvray, magret de canard au bourgueil, croustillant d'agneau, millefeuilles sablé aux fraises.

The hotel is located in the middle of the village 200 metres away from the château. Made up of various buildings on both sides of the road, and with gardens and a swimming pool, this property has been a hotel for many generations. The pleasant bedrooms are in traditional style; the ones in the small building overlooking the inner courtyard are really very charming and merit their higher prices. There are three very comfortable sitting rooms: the first is English-style, the other two are more contemporary with deep armchairs and soft colour schemes. The dining room is light and pleasant, and the food has been repeatedly praised in the visitors' book. The welcome is warm.

How to get there *(Map 16): 35km east of Tours via D410, or N76 to Bléré, then D40 to Chenonceaux (the hotel is in the centre of the town).*

Hôtel Diderot★★

4, rue Buffon
37500 Chinon (Indre-et-Loire)
Tel. 47.93.18.87 - Fax 47.93.37.10 - M. Kazamias

Open 15 Jan – 15 Dec. **Rooms** 24 (4 in annexe) with telephone, bath or shower, WC (TV on request). **Price** single 200-280F, double 250-380F. **Meals** breakfast 36F, served 0730-1000. No restaurant. **Credit cards** accepted. **Pets** dogs not allowed. **Facilities** parking. **Nearby** château de Chinon, château d'Ussé, Richelieu, Rabelais country (La Devinière), château du Coudray-Montpensier, Lerné, château de la Roche-Clermanet, 18-hole Touraine golf course at Ballon-Mire.

Its position close to the Place Jeanne D'Arc in the centre of Chinon does not spoil the appeal or the tranquillity of this hotel. On the contrary, the modest size of this 18th-century building (only 20 bedrooms, all different) gives visitors the impression of being in a particularly pleasing private house. There is no restaurant, but a delicious breakfast with a selection of home–made jams is served in front of a 15th-century fireplace.

How to get there *(Map 16): 48km south west of Tours via D751. Go along the Vienne to the Place Jeanne-d'Arc; it's on the corner of the rue Diderot.*

Hôtel George Sand★★

39, rue Quintefol
37600 Loches (Indre-et-Loire)
Tel. 47.59.39.74 - Fax 47.91.55.75 - M. and Mme Fortin

Open 28 Dec – 26 Nov. **Rooms** 20 with telephone, bath or shower, WC and TV. **Price** single 200-300F, double 250-400F. **Meals** breakfast 32F, served 0730-0930; half board 260-320F, full board 360-415F (per pers., 3 days min.) **Credit cards** Visa, MasterCard, EuroCard. **Pets** dogs allowed. **Nearby** château and keep of Loches, Carthusian monastery of le Liget in the forest of Loches, abbey church of Beaulieu-les-Loches, Montrésor, valley of the Indre, Cormery, Montbazon, Monts, Saché, 18-hole Touraine golf course at Ballon-Mire. **Restaurant** service 1200-1330, 1930-2130; menus 85-190F, also à la carte; specialities: tourte de chèvre au confit de poireau, sandre au beurre de Chinon.

Standing at the foot of the impressive Château de Loches, this ancient 15th-century house once marked the boundary of the medieval town. M. and Mme Fortin will welcome you with great kindness. Entering from the street you will be pleasantly surprised to find that the dining room and its large terrace are on the edge of the river Indre, which at this point passes over a weir. The hotel is decorated in a simple countrified style, and is especially recommended for families as each of the large first floor bedrooms contains several comfortable beds. Quite a few have stone fireplaces and beamed ceilings. Those on the second floor are smaller; the best overlook the river and the public gardens on the opposite bank. Some stone arches and a beautiful spiral staircase are reminders of the hotel's antiquity.

How to get there (Map 16): 42km south east of Tours via N143.

Domaine de la Tortinière★★★

Les Gués de Veigné
37250 Montbazon-en-Touraine (Indre-et-Loire)
Tel. 47.26.00.19 - Fax 47.65.95.70
Mme Olivereau-Capron - M. Olivereau

Open 1 March – 20 Dec. **Rooms** 21 with telephone, bath, WC and TV. **Price** double 435-880F, suite 1100-1460F. **Meals** breakfast 60F, served 0800-1100; half board 525-860F (per pers., 3 days min.) **Credit cards** Visa, Eurocard, MasterCard. **Pets** dogs not allowed. **Facilities** swimming pool, tennis, parking. **Nearby** keep of Fouques Nerra at Montbazon, valley of the Indre, Cormery, Monts, Saché, Tours cathedral, château d'Azay-le-Rideau, 18-hole Touraine golf course at Ballon-Mire. **Restaurant** service 1215-1345, 1930-2100; menus 195-345F, also à la carte; specialities: pigeon et foie gras en duo, gratinée de sandre aux poireaux, croustille de queue de bœuf au vin de Chinon.

La Tortinière, a Renaissance-style château built in 1861, is set in 15-hectare grounds dominating the Indre valley 10km from Tours. The two restaurants, the sitting room and most of the bedrooms are in the château. Many of the bedrooms (all are different) have been decorated successfully in contemporary style. Without doubt the most beautiful bedrooms are those in the towers – proper suites with their own sitting rooms attached. One can also stay in the Renaissance pavilion or the stables and enjoy looking across to the château. In autumn the undergrowth is carpeted with cyclamen. There is a heated swimming pool.

How to get there *(Map 16): 15km south of Tours via A10, Tours-sud exit, then N10 towards Montbazon; it's at 'Les Gués de Veigné'.*

Château de la Bourdaisière

25, rue de la Bourdaisière
37270 Montlouis-sur-Loire (Indre-et-Loire)
Tel. 47.45.16.31 - Fax 47.45.09.11 - M. de Broglie

Open 15 Feb – 15 Jan. **Rooms** 7 with bath or shower and WC. **Price** double 450-950F, suite 750-950F. **Meals** breakfast 45F. No restaurant. **Credit cards** Visa. **Pets** dogs allowed in kennel. **Facilities** swimming pool, tennis, riding, parking. **Nearby** Tours, grange de Meslay, wine cellars of Vouvray, châteaux of the Loire, 18-hole Touraine golf course at Ballon-Mire.

Built on the foundations of a 14th-century citadel by order of François I, the Château de la Bourdaisière was a gift from the king to his mistress, Marie Gaudin. Less than a century later, it was the birthplace of the beautiful Gabrielle d'Estrée, with whom Henri IV fell in love. It is no wonder, therefore, that the hotel's five bedrooms and two suites are named after women who had an influence on French history. The bedrooms are superb: large and all different, their decoration is bright and colourful while respecting the age of the building. Throughout the house there is a wealth of period furniture, with some truly sumptuous pieces in the lounge. This room is dedicated to the Princesse de Broglie, whose young descendants will welcome you. The hotel has splendid and extensive grounds, with formal gardens, a kitchen garden, an arboretum, and a rose garden. Those guests who do venture outside the estate will find that a stay in the château proves a fine introduction to the other châteaux of the Loire.

How to get there *(Map 16): 11km east of Tours via N152.*

Château de Rochecotte★★★

37130 Saint-Patrice – Langeais (Indre-et-Loire)
Tel. 47.96.91.28 - Fax 47.96.90.59
M. Pasquier

Open all year (closed 1 – 15 Feb.) **Rooms** 28 with telephone, bath or shower, WC and TV. **Price** single and double 350-830F, suite 1100F. **Meals** breakfast 50F, served 0800-1000; half board 970-1230F. **Credit cards** Visa, Diners, Amex. **Pets** dogs allowed. **Facilities** parking. **Nearby** château de Langeais, abbey of Fontevraud, châteaux of the Loire, 18-hole Touraine golf course at Ballon-Mire. **Restaurant** service 1200-1330, 1930-2130; menu 190F, also à la carte.

The Prince de Talleyrand certainly knew what he was doing when he used to come here in search of peace and quiet before facing the turmoil of the capital again. He enjoyed walking among the age-old trees in the vast park, he liked strolling through the formal gardens, and might have cherished above all the Italianate terrace commanding sweeping views of the Loire valley. Once left in a state of utter neglect, the estate has now been completely restored. The interior of the building has been refurbished to a very high standard of comfort but has lost its former style. You will be surprised by the size of the rooms and the amount of light in them. First, in the dining-room, where privacy is ensured by many small tables, separated by a plant or a column, and where traditional French cuisine is served. Then, in the bedrooms (even the smallest is a fair size) which have modern furnishings and luxuriously equipped bathrooms. The Château de Rochecotte is a fine hotel, in the very heart of Saint-Nicolas and Bourgueil country.

How to get there *(Map 16): 8km south west of Langeais via N152.*

Le Moulin Fleuri★★
Route du Ripault
Veigné - 37250 Montbazon (Indre-et-Loire)
Tel. 47.26.01.12 - M. and Mme Chaplin

Open 9 March — 31 Jan (closed Monday except public holidays). **Rooms** 12 with telephone, WC, of which 8 with shower, 10 with TV and minibar. **Price** single 165F, double 255-305F. **Meals** breakfast 43F, served 0800-1000; half board 235-325F, full board 288-375F (per pers., 2 days min.) **Credit cards** Amex, Eurocard, Visa. **Pets** dogs allowed. **Facilities** river fishing, parking. **Nearby** keep of Fouques Nerra at Montbazon, valley of the Indre, Cormery, Monts, Saché, Tours cathedral, château d'Azay-le-Rideau, 18-hole Touraine golf course at Ballon-Mire. **Restaurant** service 1230-1400, 1930-2100; menu 145F, also à la carte; cooking using local produce in season.

In the heart of the Touraine countryside and close to the Loire châteaux, this ancient 18th-century mill retains its original appearance. The entrance is enlivened by a courtyard garden. The Indre forms a large mill-pond encircling the terrace where breakfast is served. The interior decoration is simple, and the bedrooms, brightened with pleasing fabrics (especially on the second floor), have modern bathrooms or showers. From some bedrooms there is an exceptional view of the Indre. A very pleasant welcome.

How to get there *(Map 16): 18km south of Tours via A10, Tours-sud exit, then N10 towards Montbazan, then D98 for 5km to Le Moulin Fleuri.*

La Promenade★★★

1, place du 11 novembre
37290 Yzeures-sur-Creuse (Indre-et-Loire)
Tel. 47.94.55.21 - Mme Bussereau

Open March – Jan (closed Sunday evening and Monday in winter). **Rooms** 17 with telephone, bath, WC (10 with TV). **Price** single 210-250F, double 230-280F. **Meals** breakfast 35F and 42F, served 0730-1100; half board 252F, full board 297F (Per pers., 3 days min.) **Credit cards** accepted. **Pets** dogs allowed. **Facilities** parking. **Nearby** motor museum at Châtellerault, la Roche-Posay, château and museum at Le Grand-Pressigny, villages of Ingrandes, Saint-Gervais-Les-Trois-Clochers and Oyré, 18-hole La Roche-Posay golf course. **Restaurant** service 1200-1400, 1930-2100; menus 97-295F, also à la carte; specialities: foie gras frais de canard, ravioles de homard.

L a Promenade stands beside the square in the small village of Yzeures. The stout wooden framework of the ancient coaching inn has been retained and used to best advantage. All the ceilings are supported by long beams which, in the ground-floor dining room, rest on broad wooden pillars. The hotel has been completely and sensitively renovated. The bedrooms overlooking the street have been fitted with double glazing and are quiet. Although the hotel is not in the country, its atmosphere is so successfully rural that it feels as if it is.

How to get there (*Map 16*): *90km south of Tours via A10 to Châtellerault, then D725 (east) to beyond La Roche-Posay and D750 to Yzeures-sur-Creuse.*

Château de Chissay★★★★

Route de Pierrefitte-sur-Sauldre
41400 Chissy-en-Touraine (Loir-et-Cher) – Montrichard
Tel. 54.32.32.01 – Fax 54.32.43.80 – M. Savry

Open beg. March – beg. Jan. **Rooms** 31 with telephone, bath and WC. **Price** single 480F, double 550-910F, suite or apartment 950-1500F. **Meals** breakfast 50F, served 0730-1030; half board 480-680F, full board 670-860F (per pers.) **Credit cards** Amex, Diners, Eurocard, Visa. **Pets** dogs allowed (+45F). **Facilities** swimming pool, parking. **Nearby** Tours, grange de Meslay, Vouvray wine cellars, châteaux of the Loire, 18-hole Touraine golf course at Ballon-Mire. **Restaurant** service 1200-1330, 1930-2130; menus 160-280F, also à la carte; specialities: marbré de sandre et langoustines, feuilleté de noix de Saint-Jacques, pigeonneau rôti au jus de truffes, aumônière de fraises au rosé de Touraine.

This ancient fortified château is full of historical memories: Charles VII, Louis XI and the Duke of Choiseul all stayed here. More recently, General de Gaulle spent several days here in June 1940 before going to England. Entirely renovated in 1986, it has 31 luxurious bedrooms; those in the turrets are especially charming (Nos. 12, 22, 10, 30). The restaurant is good, and there are pleasant walks in the surrounding garden and woods, and in the Touraine countryside.

How to get there *(Map 16): 35km east of Tours via D40 to Chenonceaux, then D76; it's 4km before Montrichard.*

Hôtel Les Charmilles★★

Route de Pierrefitte-sur-Sauldre
41600 Nouan-le-Fuzelier (Loir-et-Cher)
Tel. 54.88.73.55 - Mme Sené

Open 15 March – 15 Dec. **Rooms** 14 with telephone, bath or shower, WC and TV. **Price** single 310F, double 330-390F, suite 480F. **Meals** breakfast incl., served 0730-0900. No restaurant. **Credit cards** Visa, MasterCard. **Pets** dogs allowed in the ground-floor bedrooms. **Facilities** parking. **Nearby** church of Saint-Viâtre, château du Moulin, lakes route to la Ferté-Saint-Aubin, La Source flower garden at Olivet, 9-hole Rivaulde golf and country club at Sallris.

This solid bourgeois house, built at the beginning of the century, has been a hotel for several years. The decor is warm but restrained, with recently laid thick fitted carpets. The bedrooms are big and comfortable, with good bathrooms. Breakfast is served in the bedrooms – just hang your breakfast order on the doorknob the evening before. The grounds are delightful. The large garden has a lake, cool shady areas under very old trees, comfy seats, and a lawn to relax on. The owners will greet you in a kind and friendly way. No restaurant... but you can picnic in the grounds.

How to get there *(Map 17): 44km south of Orléans via N20 towards Vierzon; it's on the way out of the village on D122.*

Hôtel Château des Tertres***
Route de Monteaux
41150 Onzain (Loir-et-Cher)
Tel. 54.20.83.88 - Fax 54.20.89.21 - M. Valois

Open 27 March – 14 Nov. **Rooms** 19 with telephone, bath or shower and WC. **Price** single and double 320-460F. **Meals** breakfast 37F, served 0800-1000. No restaurant. **Credit cards** Visa, Amex, MasterCard. **Pets** dogs not allowed. **Facilities** parking. **Nearby** châteaux of Chaumont, Blois, Amboise, Chambord, Beauregard and Chenonceaux, 9-hole la Carte golf course at Onzain, 18-hole château de Cheverny golf course.

This 19th-century château is a beautiful building and charmingly decorated. On the ground floor, overlooking the garden and the countryside, the reception area adjoins a sitting room with 19th-century furniture. To one side is a very attractive room where a delicious breakfast is served. The overall effect is that of a family house. The bedrooms are pretty and comfortable, and although in a popular tourist area, the château is quiet and reasonably priced. Excellent welcome. The hotel does not serve meals but there are some good restaurants in the village.

How to get there *(Map 16): 44km north east of Tours via N152 to the bridge of Chaumont-sur-Loire, then D1 to Onzain.*

Relais des Landes★★★

Ouchamps
41120 Les Montils (Loir-et-Cher)
Tel. 54.44.03.33 - Fax 54.44.03.89 - M. Badenier

Open all year except Dec. **Rooms** 28 with telephone, bath, WC, TV and minibar. **Price** single and double 495-685F. **Meals** breakfast 50F, served 0730-1000; half board 523-623F. **Credit cards** accepted. **Pets** dogs allowed (+35F). **Facilities** bicycle hire, parking. **Nearby** châteaux of Chaumont, Blois, Amboise, Chambord, Beauregard and Chenonceaux, 9-hole la Carte golf course at Onzain, 18-hole château de Cheverny golf course. **Restaurant** service 1230-1330, 1900-2130; menus 200-285F, also à la carte; specialities: foie gras fumé, petite salade aux langoustines, sandre Yvan Nataf, agneau de Pauillac rôti.

Lying in the middle of the countryside in grounds of 10 hectares, the Relais de Landes is a 17th-century house which has been well restored and is well kept. The lounge/reception also houses the bar and offers corners for conversation or reading. The TV room is set apart and will not bother you. The furniture is comfortable in these rooms and in the dining room, where a fire is lit in winter. In summer, meals are served on the shaded terrace overlooking the garden. The bedrooms are resolutely contemporary, mixing modern colour schemes with antique furniture. They are all extremely comfortable and have excellent bathrooms.

How to get there (Map 16): 56km north east of Tours via N151 to Condé-sur-Beuvron, then right on D7 to 1km before Ouchamps via Les Montils.

Auberge de la Chichone***

Place de l'Eglise
41210 Saint-Viâtre (Loir-et-Cher)
Tel. 54.88.91.33 - Fax 54.96.18.06 - M. and Mme Clément

Open 1 April – 28 Feb (closed Tuesday and Wednesday in low season). **Rooms** 7 with telephone, bath, shower and WC. **Price** single and double 290-320F. **Meals** breakfast 35F, served 0700-1100; half board 350F (per pers., 3 days min.) **Credit cards** Visa, Amex. **Pets** dogs allowed. **Nearby** church of Saint-Viâtre, château du Moulin, lakes route to la Ferté-Saint-Aubin, La Source flower garden at Olivet, 9-hole Rivaulde golf and country club at Sallris. **Restaurant** service 1230-1430, 1930-2200; menus 135-195F, also à la carte; specialities: game in season, girolles and cèpes mushrooms in season, fish from the lakes.

This hunting inn, very evocative of the Sologne, is situated in a small church square. The bar and dining room are done in a countrified style, with shelves of wine, hunting trophies, gleaming copperware, and small lamps on the tables. No detail has been overlooked in the creation of the overall effect. The bedrooms are warm, decorated in brown tones with cane furniture. The walls are covered with a velvety fabric resembling suede. A small television room opens on to a charming garden courtyard where breakfast can be served.

How to get there *(Map 17): 51km south of Orléans via A71, Lamotte-Beuvron exit, then D923, then D49.*

Château de la Voûte

Troo
41800 Montoire-sur-le-Loir (Loir-et-Cher)
Tel. 54.72.52.52 – MM. Clays and Venon

Open all year. **Rooms** 5 with bath or shower and WC. **Price** double 370-470F, suite 550F. **Meals** breakfast incl., served 0800-1000. No restaurant. **Credit cards** not accepted. **Pets** dogs not allowed. **Facilities** parking. **Nearby** Benedictine abbey of la Trinité and church of Rhodon at Vendôme, valley of the Loir, chapel of Saint-Gilles at Montoire, Gué-du-Loir, Lavardin, Saint-Jacques-des-Guérets, manoir de la Possonnière, 9-hole la Bosse golf course at Oucques.

Here is a place for the discerning. The rooms in this old manor are full of beautiful things, reflecting the owners' passion for antiques. The bedrooms are furnished and decorated with some of their finds. Every room is different and has its own style and charm; even the smallest is a success. Some are proper suites (named Pompadour, Louis XIII and Empire) and even apartments (Les Tours). The view is worthy of a 17th-century painting. This is an ideal place for exploring Touraine and the valley of the Loir and the Loire. A well managed hotel of great quality, and an address which one would rather keep to oneself.

How to get there *(Map 16): 48km north of Tours via D29 to La Chartre-sur-le-Loir, then right on D305 and D917 to Troo.*

Manoir de la Forêt★★

Fort-Girard
41160 La Ville-aux-Clercs (Loir-et-Cher)
Tel. 54.80.62.83 – Fax 54.80.66.03 – Mme Autebon

Open all year (closed Sunday evening and Monday Oct – March). **Rooms** 19 with telephone, bath or shower, WC and TV. **Price** single 240-310F, double 280-330F, suite 380-440F. **Meals** breakfast 40F, served 0730-0900; half board 450F, full board 500F. **Credit cards** Visa. **Pets** dogs allowed. **Facilities** fishing, parking. **Nearby** Benedictine abbey of la Trinité and church of Rhodon at Vendôme, valley of the Loir, chapel of Saint-Gilles at Montoire, Gué-du-Loir, Lavardin, Saint-Jacques-des-Guérets, manoir de la Possonnière, 9-hole la Bosse golf course at Oucques. **Restaurant** service 1215-1400, 1930-2100; menus 140-260F, also à la carte; specialities: foie gras frais au Muscat, grenadin de lotte et langoustines au coulis de poivrons.

A former hunting lodge of the Château de la Gaudinière, which dates from the 18th century, the Manoir de la Forêt stands in wooded 2-hectare grounds with a lake. The lounge/reception sets the scene: a restful atmosphere, fresh flowers and pleasant furniture. Two sitting rooms with deep armchairs and sofas are the ideal place for a drink, morning coffee or afternoon tea. The dining room, whose eleven windows open on to the garden, offers an excellent menu. Throughout, the choice of colours and fabrics is good. The bedrooms overlook the grounds or the forest and No.6 has a pretty terrace. In good weather drinks and meals are served outside.

How to get there (Map 16): *72km north east of Tours via N10 to 6km beyond Vendôme, then left on D141 to La Ville-aux-Clercs.*

Hôtel de l'Abbaye★★★

2, quai de l'Abbaye
45190 Beaugency (Loiret)
Tel. 38.44.67.35 – Fax 38.44.87.92 – M. Aupetit

Open all year. **Rooms** 18 with telephone, bath, WC and TV. **Price** single 420-480F, double 510-560F, suite 560-700F. **Meals** breakfast 42F, served 0700-1000. **Credit cards** Visa, Amex, Diners. **Pet** dogs allowed (+50F). **Facilities** parking. **Nearby** medieval and Renaissance quarters of Beaugency, château de Meung-sur-Loire, basilica and chapel of Saint-Jacques at Cléry-Saint-André, 18-hole Saint-Laurent-Nouan golf course. **Restaurant** service 1200-1400, 1900-2130; menu 195F, also à la carte; traditional cooking.

A discreet nameplate announces that this 17th–century former Augustine convent built on the banks of the Loire opposite the old bridge in Beaugency is... an hotel. You will be welcomed in an immense hall. Beside this is the bar and then comes the dining room, both very well furnished. In summer there are tables on the terrace overlooking the river. An extraordinary stone staircase leads to the bedrooms. The first floor bedrooms make use of their ceiling height to include a mezzanine, well designed to seem like part of the original building, and they contain some pieces of Louis XIII furniture. They are very comfortable and have pleasant bathrooms. The second floor bedrooms seem more classic, and some have interesting bathrooms. An unusual place.

How to get there *(Map 17): 29km south west of Orléans via A10, Meung-sur-Loire exit, then N152.*

Hôtel de la Sologne★★

Place Saint-Firmin
45190 Beaugency (Loiret)
Tel. 38.44.50.27 – Fax 38.44.50.27 – Mme Rogue

Open all year except Christmas and New Year. **Rooms** 16 with telephone, bath or shower, WC and TV. **Price** single and double 170-400F. **Meals** breakfast 40F, served 0700-0930. No restaurant. **Credit cards** Visa, MasterCard, Eurocard. **Pet** dogs not allowed. **Nearby** medieval and Renaissance quarters of Beaugency, château de Meung-sur-Loire, basilica and chapel of Saint-Jacques at Cléry-Saint-André, 18-hole les Bordes golf course at Saint-Laurent-Nouan.

This charming hotel in the heart of old Beaugency is very caringly managed by Mme Rogue. The bedrooms are plain but comfortable, and she has equipped them with television sets with headphones so as not to disturb the neighbours, wall lamps with pretty shades, hairdryers, and, in as many as possible, electric trouser presses. The sitting room is rustic in style and welcoming, with a fireplace, old beams and a huge selection of magazines. There is a pleasant verandah for sitting out.

How to get there *(Map 17): 29km south west of Orléans via A10, Meung-sur-Loire exit, then N152.*

L'Auberge de Combreux★★

45530 Combreux (Loiret)
Tel. 38.59.47.63 – Fax 38.59.36.19
Mme Gangloff

Open 20 Jan – 20 Dec. **Rooms** 20 with telephone, bath or shower, WC, TV (2 with jacuzzi). **Price** single 290F, double 350-490F, suite 640F. **Meals** breakfast 33F, served 0800-1000; half board 320-430F (per pers., 2 days min.) **Credit cards** Eurocard, MasterCard, Visa. **Pets** dogs allowed (+30F). **Facilities** heated swimming pool, tennis (30F), bicycles, parking. **Nearby** Orléans, arboretum and museum at Châteauneuf-sur-Loire, La Source flower gardens at Olivet, 18-hole Orléans golf course. **Restaurant** service 1200-1400, 1915-2115; menus 90-200F, also à la carte; specialities: mousseline de chèvre chaud au cresson, filet de brochet aux échalotes confites.

This is a lovely old inn. Inside there are white walls, white beds, bunches of reeds, and wood everywhere: beams, rustic furniture, mantlepieces. Throughout there is a gentle harmony between the colours of the curtains, the lampshades and, to add brighter tones, bouquets of flowers. The bedrooms too are very attractive, though some of them are in the annexe, on the other side of the street. In summer the arbour is perfect for a lazy breakfast or uplifting aperitifs. The food is good and of the real home-made variety. The warmth of the welcome is worth mentioning and so is the pleasure of excursions on the bicycles provided by the hotel.

How to get there *(Map 17): 35km east of Orléans via N60 and D709 to Fay-aux-Loges, then D9.*

VFB.

Domaine de Chicamour★★

45530 Sury-aux-Bois (Loiret)
Tel. 38.55.85.42 - Fax 38.55.80.43
M. Merckx

Open 1 March – 30 Nov. **Rooms** 12 with telephone, bath or shower, and WC. **Price** single 315F, double 350F. **Meals** breakfast 45F, served 0800-1000; half board 360F, full board 450F. **Credit cards** Visa. **Pets** dogs allowed (+25F). **Facilities** tennis, riding, bicycles, boules, parking. **Nearby** Orléans, arboretum and museum at Châteauneuf-sur-Loire, La Source flower gardens at Olivet, 18-hole Orléans golf course. **Restaurant** service 1200-1400, 1930-2100; menus 95-350F, also à la carte; specialities: foie gras, boudin de truite au vin de Montlouis, noisettes d'agneau.

Set in 8-hectare grounds in the heart of the Orléans forest, the small château of Chicamour has been turned into an hotel with the accent on simplicity and elegance. The result is remarkable. The lovely sitting room has deep sofas surrounding the fireplace and beautifully chosen curtains and fabrics. The collection of paintings and decorative objects help to make this a special place you will not want to leave. The bedrooms have everything you could want, with pale wood furniture and Laura Ashley fabrics matching the wallpapers and lampshades. They are all comfortable, overlook the grounds and have good bathrooms. In the elegant dining room good food based on regional produce is served. The cellar includes a great variety of Loire wines, and you can buy a few bottles. We have one reservation: the service is not always attentive.

How to get there *(Map 17): 39km west of Montargis on N60, between Bellegarde and Châteauneuf-sur-Loire.*

Hôtel de l'Abbaye★★

8, rue des Tourelles
02600 Longpont (Aisne)
Tel. 23.96.02.44 – M. Verdun

Open all year. **Rooms** 12 with telephone, of which 5 with bath or shower, 6 with WC. **Price** double 175-320F. **Meals** breakfast 35F, served any time; half board 290-390F, full board 360-460F (per pers., 3 days min.) **Credit cards** accepted. **Pets** dogs allowed. **Facilities** bicycle hire. **Nearby** abbey and château of Longpont, château, Hôtel de Ville and Alexandre Dumas museum at Villers-Cotterêts, château de Vierzy, forest of Retz, 9-hole Valois golf course at Barbery. **Restaurant** service 1200-1400, 1930-2100; menus 95-220F, also à la carte; specialities: wood grills, canard aux cerises, game and mushrooms in season.

This fine old house is situated in a village in the heart of the forest of Retz. Its large, heavy dining tables and its fireplace are the scene of warm and friendly gatherings for walkers and sportsmen. The food is not sophisticated, just plain delicious home cooking, and it owes a great deal to the proprietor, who does his best to make you feel at home. The few bedrooms vary in quality; five have full bathroom facilities, and all of them have a peaceful atmosphere and look out on the forest or the abbey. Other amenities of the hotel are a reading room, a TV room, a delightful garden and the availability of a wealth of tourist information about the region.

How to get there *(Map 10): 20km south of Soissons via N2 towards Villers-Cotterêts, then D2.*

Hostellerie Le Château★★★

Neuville-Saint-Amand
02100 Saint-Quentin (Aisne)
Tel. 23.68.41.82 – Fax 23.68.46.02 – M. Meiresonne

Open all year (closed Saturday and Sunday evening, 3 weeks in Aug, 1 week in Feb).
Rooms 15 with telephone, bath, WC, TV (6 with minibar). **Price** single and double
330-390F. **Meals** breakfast 45F, served from 0730. **Credit cards** Visa, Amex, Diners.
Pets dogs not allowed. **Facilities** parking. **Nearby** Antoine Lécuyer museum (pastels
by Quentin de la Tour), college and Hôtel de Ville of St-Quentin, 9-hole le Mesnil golf
course, 9-hole Homblières golf course. **Restaurant** service 1200-1330, 1900-2100;
menus 170-330F, also à la carte; specialities: cassolette d'escargots crème d'ail et
poivrons, mélange de ris et rognon au genièvre de Houlles, assiette gourmande.

In the north of France the title of château is given to the most
important house in a village. This château lies in the heart of a
beautiful wooded park. The ground floor rooms are occupied by
a restaurant well known for the quality of its cuisine. The nicely
furnished rooms extend into a modern wing, well provided with
bay windows which overlook the park; viewed from the outside,
however, the architectural effect is disappointing. The bedrooms
are very attractive, with pastel wallpapers, and furnished with flair
as well as being comfortable. The bathrooms are equally agreeable.
At the Hostellerie you can enjoy a restful and quiet stay in a
welcoming and attentive household.

How to get there *(Map 2): 120km south of Lille via A26, exit Saint-
Quentin-Gauchy or Saint-Quentin-Centre; Rue du General-Leclerc and
D12; in the centre 200m from the church.*

Château de Barive★★★★

Sainte-Preuve
02350 Liesse (Aisne)
Tel. 23.22.15.15 – Fax 23.22.08.39 – M. Ries

Open all year. **Rooms** 17 with telephone, bath or shower, WC and TV. **Price** single 380F, double 580-680F. **Meals** breakfast 55F, served from 0730; half board 460F (per pers., 5 days min.) **Credit cards** Visa, Amex, Diners. **Pets** dogs allowed. **Nearby** Laon cathedral, abbey of Prémontrés, forest of Saint-Gobain, ruins of abbeys of le Tortoir and St-Nicolas-aux-Bois. **Restaurant** service 1200-1400, 1900-2100; menus 175-210F, also à la carte; specialities: foie gras de canard au beaume de Venise, brochettes de queues de langoustines au saumon fumé.

Lost in the countryside, this 17th-century château was first a hunting lodge, then a boarding house, and has now been fully restored and opened as an impeccable hotel. The bedrooms are large and extremely comfortable, with thick continental quilts and luxuriously fitted bathrooms. There is no period furniture, but some fine copies recreate something of the historic atmosphere of the place. The big breakfast room opens wide onto the surrounding greenery and is arranged rather like a winter garden. The lounge and dining-room are still a little formal, but both rooms are comfortable, and the gourmet cuisine served in the latter certainly contributes towards warming up the atmosphere. Hotel facilities include a magnificent heated indoor swimming-pool, a sauna and a tennis court, so a stay here may provide the perfect opportunity to get back into shape. You will find a friendly and attentive welcome.

How to get there *(Map 3): 7km north east of Laon via D977.*

Auberge de la Scierie★★★

La Vove
10160 Aix-en-Othe (Aube)
Tel. 25.46.71.26 - Fax 25.46.65.69 - M. and Mme Duguet

Open all year. **Rooms** 15 with telephone, bath or shower, WC and TV. **Price** single and double 350-480F. **Meals** breakfast 40F, served 0800-1100; half board 480F (per pers., 3 days min.) **Credit cards** accepted. **Pets** dogs allowed. **Facilities** heated swimming pool, parking. **Nearby** Saint-Urbain basilica, cathedral of St Pierre et St Paul, modern art museum at Troyes, 18-hole la Cordelière golf course at Chaource. **Restaurant** service 1200-1400, 1930-2115 (closed Feb, Monday evening and Tuesday 15 Oct – 15 April); menus 120-210F, also à la carte; specialities: fish.

This inn is in unspoilt countryside in an old sawmill. The main structure has been restored and refurbished in such a way that it seems as if its present role is the one it was originally intended for. The surroundings, which are well cared for, provide places for al fresco meals and for walks in the wooded 2-hectare park, through which a stream flows. The bedrooms, which surround the swimming pool, are quiet and comfortable; some have old style furniture. So has the lounge, which contains a fine fireplace and a library. The food is excellent and guests are sure of a warm welcome.

How to get there *(Map 10): 33km west of Troyes via N60 towards Sens, then D374; it's on the way out of the village in the Villemoiron-en-Othe direction.*

Château d'Etoges

4, rue Richebourg – 51270 Etoges (Marne)
Tel. 26.59.30.08 - Fax 26.59.35.57
Mme Filliette-Neuville

Open all year. **Rooms** 19 with telephone, bath or shower, WC (TV on request). **Price** single 350F, double 480-620F, suite 950F. **Meals** breakfast 45F, served 0800-1100; half board 450-550F, full board 650-750F (per pers., 2 days min.) **Credit cards** accepted. **Pets** dogs allowed (+40F). **Facilities** parking. **Nearby** Champagne museum at Epernay, abbey of Hautvillers (where Dom Perignon invented champagne), 9-hole Val-Secret golf course at Château-Thierry. **Restaurant** service 1200-1400, 2000-2130; menu 160F; specialities: truite au champagne, pintade vigneronne.

The splendid Château d'Etoges is mostly an 18th-century building. It is set against a low hill under whose slopes flow water courses which emerge as fountains springing continuously from the ground. The interior of the château is equally enchanting; it has been refurbished with good taste to retain the building's character and provide a high standard of comfort (the bathrooms are irresistible). There is a grand staircase, spacious lounges with decorative panels, delightful percale table cloths in the dining room and superb bedrooms. Some are big and sumptuous, others more intimate, but in each of them there is a delightful blend of old furniture and pretty materials. There are romantic views over the moat. There is a warm personal welcome for all the guests at the Château d'Etoges, and a feeling of life in a rather more graceful age. An ideal base for exploring the vineyards of the Champagne country.

How to get there *(Map 10): 40km west of Châlons-sur-Marne via D33.*

Le Prieuré★★★

Chevet de l'Eglise
60440 Ermenonville (Oise)
Tel. 44.54.00.44 - Fax 44.54.02.21 - M. Treillou

Open all year (closed Feb). **Rooms** 11 with telephone, bath or shower and WC. **Price** double 450-500F. **Meals** breakfast 50F. No restaurant. **Credit cards** accepted. **Pets** small dogs allowed. **Nearby** abbey of Châalis, forest of Ermenonville, Astérix park.

Standing just next to the church, the Prieuré is a real little gem, hidden away in a marvellous landscaped garden. Its owners, Monsieur and Mme Treillou, have a weakness for beautiful antique furniture, paintings, curios and rugs. They have also selected fabrics to enhance the atmosphere of each room. The bedrooms are all, of course, extremely comfortable; in some of the ones on the top floor the fine ancient wooden framework of the building can be seen. The rooms are all quiet (the road through Ermenonville is not far away, but is not busy on weekends). On the ground floor, all the reception rooms lead out into the garden, and each one has a fireplace; while, throughout the house, the well-polished ancient tiled floor entrancingly captures the sunlight. Breakfast is served in a delightfully refined country style dining-room. This is a truly irresistible address.

How to get there *(Map 9): 51km north east of Paris via A1, exit Survilliers, then D922.*

A la Bonne Idée***

3, rue des Meuniers
60350 Saint-Jean-aux-Bois (Oise)
Tel. 44.42.84.09 - Fax 44.42.80.45 - M. Drieux

Open all year. **Rooms** 23 with telephone, bath, WC and TV. **Price** single and double 375-420F, suite 420F. **Meals** breakfast 55F, served 0730-1030; half board 620F, full board 695F. **Credit cards** accepted (except Diners). **Pets** dogs allowed (+25F). **Facilities** parking. **Nearby** château and forest of Compiègne, archery museum at Crépy-en-Valois, 18-hole golf course at Compiègne. **Restaurant** service 1200-1400, 1915-2100; menus 180-410F, also à la carte; specialities: la rabotte st-jeannaise, galette champignons sauvages, homard breton grillé sauce corail.

This hotel, once an historic 18th-century capitainerie, is situated in a charming little village in the heart of the forest of Compiègne. In the entrance hall and the bar the old and the new blend harmoniously. The lovely dining room provides a handsome setting for the enjoyment of fine food cooked by the chef. There is a choice of bedrooms; those in the main building are charmingly traditional in style, and the ones in the annexe are elegantly furnished and look out on flower gardens and the shaded terrace. A hospitable welcome, and a calm ambience (ensured by the fact that the hotel is in a cul-de-sac which leads to the forest paths), are appreciated by visitors.

How to get there *(Map 9): 75km north east of Paris via A1, exit Verberie, then D200 to Lacroix-Saint-Ouen and D85 through the forest of Compiègne to Saint-Jean-aux-Bois.*

Hôtel Dolce Vita★★★

Route des Sanguinaires
20000 Ajaccio (Corse-du-Sud)
Tel. 95.52.00.93 - Fax 95.52.07.15 - M. Federici

Open Easter – All Saints. **Rooms** 32 with telephone, bath, WC, TV and minibar. **Price** single and double 550-810F. **Meals** breakfast 50F, served 0700-1000; half board and full board (obligatory in July and August) 665-945F. **Credit cards** accepted. **Pets** dogs allowed (+40F). **Facilities** swimming pool, water ski-ing, beach. **Restaurant** service 1230-1345, 1930-2130; menu 255F, also à la carte; specialities: raviolis au broccio, fricassée de langouste.

The Dolce Vita is a modern hotel whose superb situation compensates for the functional style of its architecture and its rather flashy interior decor. All the rooms face the sea and some of them have been recently refurbished. They are situated on two levels and the lower ones have direct access to a small beach, where the presence of concrete is rather an eyesore to some. The hotel is very comfortable and the bathrooms have all the usual facilities. The gardens of the hotel are well stocked with flowers and it is a pleasure to stroll among the bougainvillea, oleanders and palm trees. The dining room is in two sections; a large interior room where the pink tablecloths seem to be waiting for some special occasion, and a spacious shaded terrace which overlooks the sea. At night, with the swimming pool floodlit, the twinkling lights in the bushes and the glimmer of lights across the bay, the scene is reminiscent of many a romantic movie.

How to get there *(Map 36): 8km west of Ajaccio via the Route des Sanguinaires. Ajaccio airport 15km away, tel. 95.21.03.64.*

Hôtel Genovese★★★

Quartier de la Citadelle
20169 Bonifacio (Corse-du-Sud)
Tel. 95.73.12.34 - Fax 95.73.09.03

Open all year. **Rooms** 14 with telephone, bath, WC, TV and minibar. **Price** double 700-1500F, suite 950-1700F. **Meals** breakfast 70-80F, served 0730-1100. No restaurant. **Credit cards** Visa, Amex, Diners. **Pets** dogs allowed. **Facilities** parking. **Nearby** boat trip to marine grottoes, cave of Sdragonato and tour of the cliffs, gulf of Santa-Manza, 18-hole golf course at Sperone.

Set out along the walls of the Bonifacio ramparts, this hotel is in an old naval building and has a fine view of the sea, the town and the harbour. It was recently opened and is luxuriously and elegantly furnished. The rooms are set round a delightful courtyard and are decorated in pastel shades with flowered curtains. The bathrooms are faultless and there is a jacuzzi in every suite. Room 2 also has a balcony which overlooks the port. There is no restaurant but the ground floor has a breakfast area and a lounge where a handsome white settee blends delightfully with the stone walls. An additional asset is that the hotel is fully air conditioned.

How to get there *(Map 36): in Bonifacio. Figari airport 21km away, tel. 95.71.00.22.*

Résidence du Centre Nautique★★★

Quai Nord
20169 Bonifacio (Corse-du-Sud)
Tel. 95.73.02.11 - Fax 95.73.17.47 - M. Lantieri

Open all year. **Rooms** 10 with telephone, shower, WC, TV and minibar. **Price** double 450-950F. **Meals** breakfast 50-60F. No restaurant. **Credit cards** Visa, Amex, Diners. **Pets** dogs allowed. **Facilities** parking. **Nearby** boat trip to the marine grottoes, cave of Sdragonato and tour of the cliffs, gulf of Santa-Manza, 18-hole golf course at Sperone.

This hotel on Bonifacio harbour looks out over the moored boats and lies below the upper town. Despite its name it is a place that gives a cordial welcome to tourists as well as to sailing enthusiasts. The height of the storeys of the house has made it possible to convert the rooms into small duplexes. On the lower level there is a small living room and on the mezzanine the bedroom and bathroom – more like a studio apartment than the conventional hotel bedroom. It will make you want to invite your neighbours in for cocktails in the living room. Some units have a view over the garden and others over the port, which is quiet and peaceful at night. You can have breakfast on the terrace overlooking the sailing boats and yachts.

How to get there *(Map 36): on the port. Figari airport 21km away, tel. 95.71.00.22*

Grand Hôtel Cala Rossa★★★

Cala Rossa - 20137 Porto-Vecchio (Corse-du-Sud)
Tel. 95.71.61.51 - Fax 95.71.60.11
M. Canarelli and Mme Biancarelli

Open 1 April – 10 Nov. **Rooms** 50 with telephone, bath, WC and TV. **Price** single 600F, double 640F, suite 1200F. **Meals** breakfast 65F, served 0730-1130; half board and full board prices on request. **Credit cards** accepted. **Pets** dogs not allowed. **Facilities** private beach, water ski-ing, windsurfing, boat trips, parking. **Nearby** Palombaggia beach and Piccovaggia peninsula, forest of l'Ospedale, 18-hole golf course at Sperone. **Restaurant** service 1230-1430, 1930-2100; menus 240-390F, also à la carte; specialities: croustillant d'agneau, tartare de denti au saumon fumé, consommé de homard.

The success of the Grand Hôtel Cala Rossa is due mainly to the enthusiasm of proprietor Toussaint Canarelli and his loyal and hard working team. At first the hotel concentrated on its restaurant, which is now one of the best in Corsica. The bedrooms are all comfortable, but the new suites decorated in Mediterranean style are very luxurious. The surroundings are magnificent: the garden with its shady pines, oleanders and plumbagos extends as far as the private beach. It is essential to book very early for the summer season. In spring and autumn you can enjoy the pleasures of the maquis and the forest of Ospedale as well as the sea.

How to get there *(Map 36): 10km north east of Porto Vecchio via N198, D568 and D468. Figari airport 33km away, tel. 95.71.00.22.*

L'Aïtone★★

20126 Evisa (Corse-du-Sud)
Tel. 95.26.20.04 – Fax 95.26.24.18
M. Ceccaldi

Open Jan – Nov. **Rooms** 32 with telephone, bath or shower and WC. **Price** single 150-200F, double 200-500F. **Meals** breakfast 35-38F, served 0800-0930; half board 250-450F, full board 380-550F. **Credit cards** Visa, Amex. **Pets** dogs allowed. **Facilities** swimming pool, parking. **Nearby** waterfall and pool in the forest of Aïtone, gorges of the Spelunca, forest of Aïtone, calanques of Piana, villages of Ota and Vico. **Restaurant** service 1200-1400, 1930-2200; menus 85-160F, also à la carte; specialities: terrine de sanglier aux châtaignes, omelette broccio et menthe.

The Aïtone is 850m above sea level on the edge of the spectacular forest of pines and larches covering Aïtone and the Valdo-Niello. Toussaint Cercaldi, the proprietor, has taken over from his parents and refurbished and enlarged the hotel. The building is not particularly attractive but it has a superb position and its great terrace overlooks the beautiful Spelunca valley. The bedrooms all have balconies and a magnificent view of the Gulf of Porto. There is good home cooking.

How to get there *(Map 36): 23km east of Porto via D84. Ajaccio airport 70km away, tel. 95.21.03.64.*

Les Roches Rouges★★

20115 Piana (Corse-du-Sud)
Tel. 95.27.81.81 - Fax 95.27.81.76
Mme Dalakupeyan

Open 1 April – 30 Oct. **Rooms** 30 with telephone, shower and WC. **Price** double 220-265F. **Meals** breakfast 40F, served 0730-1100; half board 300F (per pers.) **Credit cards** Amex, Diners, Visa. **Pets** dogs allowed. **Facilities** parking. **Nearby** calanques of Piana, boat to Girolata (dep. Porto), villages of Ota, Evisa and Vico, col de Lava, route de Ficajola. **Restaurant** service 1200-1400; menus 90-350F, also à la carte; specialities: fish, langouste.

This old Corsican house, on the edge of the village of Piana and three kilometres from the famous calanques, has been refurbished. There is a spacious, well-lit and handsome restaurant which extends onto a terrace, and from here as well as from the bedrooms there are superb views. The rooms themselves are rather plain and could do with a little improvement, but this is made up for by the cordial welcome given by Mady and the very reasonable prices.

How to get there *(Map 36): 71km north of Ajaccio via D81. Ajaccio airport, tel. 95.21.03.64.*

Hôtel Castel d'Orcino★★★

Tour d'Ancone
20111 Calcatoggio (Corse-du-Sud)
Tel. 95.52.20.63 – Fax 95.52.24.65 – Mme Jullien

Open all year. **Rooms** 38 with telephone, bath or shower and WC (12 with TV). **Price** single 265-525F, double 370-710F. **Meals** breakfast 37F, served 0800-1000; half board 325-495F, full board 435-605F (per pers., 3 days min.) **Credit cards** Visa. **Pets** dogs allowed (+20F). **Facilities** parking. **Nearby** gulf of Ajaccio via the Route des Iles sanguinaires, les Milelli, château de la Punta, Bastelica. **Restaurant** service 1200-1400, 1900-2100; menu 140F, also à la carte; specialities: fish, pot-au-feu de mer.

The hotel, which is by the sea on the south shore of the pretty little gulf of Liscia on the Palmentoio point, is made up of three houses. Here, in a setting full of luxuriant greenery, there is perfect peace. We recommend the bedrooms in the new building; each one has its own balcony, an attractively tiled bathroom and a fine view of the sea. The ones in the annexe and the main building are a little sombre and less appealing. Meals are served, according to the season, either on the extensive terrace overlooking the bay or in the dining room.

How to get there *(Map 36): 24km north of Ajaccio via D81 to the other side of Calcatoggio, then follow coast road to the point of Palmentoio. Ajaccio airport, tel.95.21.03.64.*

Le Maquis★★★★
20166 Porticcio (Corse-du-Sud)
Tel. 95.25.05.55 - Fax 95.25.11.70
Mme Salini

Open all year. **Rooms** 19 with air-conditioning, telephone, bath, WC, TV and minibar. **Price** half board only, double 1480-2300F. **Meals** breakfast incl., served 0800-1030. **Credit cards** accepted. **Pets** dogs allowed (+60F). **Facilities** heated swimming pool, tennis, gym, private beach, parking. **Nearby** gulf of Ajaccio via the Route des Iles Sanguinaires, les Milelli, château de la Punta, Bastelica. **Restaurant** service 1230-1400, 1930-2200; à la carte 300-450F.

The Maquis is one of the outstanding hotels in this guide. It is splendidly situated on a small inlet off the gulf of Ajaccio, two kilometres from Porticcio. Its pretty private beach, the elegance of its decor, the comfort of its public rooms and its bedrooms (ask for a room with a terrace facing the sea) make it just the place for a relaxing and satisfying holiday. The terrace, the covered swimming pool and a tennis court complete the picture. At midday there is a delicious buffet lunch on the terrace and in the evenings an excellent menu, changed every day, is served. What more could one want? Thanks to the proprietor, Mme Salini, Le Maquis is an oasis on a coast which unfortunately has been rather spoiled, but if you do want to explore outside the haven of the hotel you can take a trip into the interior of Corsica.

How to get there *(Map 36): 18km south east of Ajaccio via N196, D55 along the coast. Ajaccio airport, tel. 95.21.03.64.*

Hôtel L'Aiglon**

20147 Serriera (Corse-du-Sud)
Tel. 95.26.10.65 – Fax 95.26.14.77
M. Colonna-Ceccaldi

Open 1 May – end Sept. **Rooms** 18 with telephone, bath or shower (4 with WC). **Price** 200-350F. **Meals** breakfast 30F, served 0800-0930; half board 200-300F, full board 250-360F (per pers., 3 days min.) **Credit cards** accepted. **Pets** dogs allowed. **Facilities** parking. **Nearby** waterfall and pool in the forest of Aïtone, gorges of the Spelunca, forest of Aïtone, calanques of Piana, boat to Girolata, villages of Ota and Vico. **Restaurant** service 1230-1400, 2000-2130; menus 85-130F, also à la carte; specialities: omelette au broccio, daube de sanglier, cannellonis à la corse.

The Hôtel L'Aiglon was built about thirty years ago out of the lovely Porto stone. It is a place for lovers of peace and tranquillity and is set in the heart of the Maquis. To reach it you take a winding road across hilly countryside; but it is not as isolated as this might suggest for the sea is only five kilometres away. Because it is patronised by a regular clientele the bedrooms have not been updated. They are fairly plain and the furniture is very 1950s. The bathrooms are behind rather thin partitions. To one side of the building there are six rooms in bungalows, each one with its own terrace. The moderate rates encourage visits from those who want to explore the interior of Corsica or those who want inexpensive proximity to the sea.

How to get there (Map 36): 5km north of Porto via D81; follow signs. Calvi airport 80km, tel. 95.65.08.09.

Hôtel Balanéa★★★

6, rue Clémenceau
20260 Calvi (Haute-Corse)
Tel. 95.65.00.45 - Fax 95.65.29.71 - M. Ceccaldi

Open all year. **Rooms** 37 with air-conditioning, telephone, bath, WC, TV (9 with minibar). **Price** double 300-1200F, suite 700-1200F. **Meals** breakfast 60F, served 0730-1030. No restaurant. **Credit cards** accepted. **Pets** dogs allowed (+100F). **Facilities** parking. **Nearby** citadel of Calvi, tour of the villages of Balagne (Calenzana, Zilia, Montemaggiore, Sant'Antonino, church of the Trinity at Aregno, convent of Corbara), Scandola national park, 9-hole Lumio golf course.

The Balanéa is beside the harbour in Calvi. Recently renovated, it is the most pleasant hotel in the centre of town. The bedrooms, which are very comfortable, are spacious and well decorated, and have large bathrooms. Most of them have balconies, some of them even terraces from which there are marvellous views of the fort and citadel. All the rooms are air-conditioned, a boon for summer nights. The Balanéa is the only hotel open in Calvi during the winter.

How to get there *(Map 36): on the port in Calvi. Calvi airport 7km, tel. 95.65.08.09*

Auberge de la Signoria★★★
Route de forêt de Bonifato
20260 Calvi (Haute-Corse)
Tel. 95.65.23.73 – Fax 95.65.38.77 – MM. Ceccaldi

Open 4 April – 15 Oct. **Rooms** 10 with telephone, bath, WC, TV and minibar. **Price** single and double 450-1100F, suite 1000-1500F. **Meals** breakfast 70F, served 0800-1100; half board 575-900F (per pers., 2 days min.) **Credit cards** Amex, Eurocard, Visa. **Pets** dogs allowed. **Facilities** swimming pool, tennis, hammam, parking. **Nearby** citadel of Calvi, tour of the villages of Balagne (Calenzana, Zilia, Montemaggiore, Sant'Antonino, church of the Trinity at Aregno, convent of Corbara), Scandola national park, 9-hole Lumio golf course. **Restaurant** service 1200-1330, 1930-2230; menu 320F (child 130F), also à la carte; specialities: carpaccio de saumon aigre doux, mérou à la brousse, noisettes d'agneau à la croute d'herbes du maquis.

The Signoria is the kind of hotel one dreams about; it is in a fine old house in large grounds planted with eucalyptus and palm trees. The proprietors have recently refurbished the house but without detracting from its special character. The bedrooms in the main building are the more comfortable but you will not be disappointed by those in the annexe. A high point of your dream holiday will be the candlelit dinners under the palm trees on the terrace, and you will also enjoy the swimming pool in the garden. The Signoria is a quiet place even in August, and it is as well to have your own means of transport for getting about.

How to get there *(Map 36): 5km from Calvi on the airport road. Calvi airport 7km, tel. 95.65.08.09.*

Marina d'Argentella

L'Argentella
20260 Calvi (Haute-Corse)
Tel. 95.65.25.08 - M. Grisoli

Open 30 May – 3 Oct. **Rooms** 25 with bath and WC. **Price** double room with half board 350-500F (per pers.), reduced rate for children. **Meals** breakfast incl. **Credit cards** Visa. **Pets** dogs allowed. **Facilities** parking. **Nearby** citadel of Calvi, tour of the villages of Ballagne (Calenzana, Zilia, Montemaggiore, Sant 'Antonino, church of the Trinity at Aregno, convent of Corbara), Scandola regional park, 9-hole Lumio golf course. **Restaurant** service 1230-1430, 2000-2200; menu 120F, also à la carte; specialities: fish and Corsican dishes.

The Argentella is a very special place, not only because it is beautifully situated by the beach on the Crovani bay, but also due to the care that Pièrre and Dorine take to ensure that you have a good holiday. The bedrooms, which are in small bungalows in a eucalyptus grove, are simple but charming and all of them have private bathrooms. Dhair, the chef, plans new dishes every year: at midday the menu offers a light meal, freshly cooked and interesting. In the evening the menu is more extensive and deliciously tempting. Daytime entertainments include bathing, wind-surfing, picnics and boat excursions. At seven in the evening you can join in the traditional volleyball game, and refresh yourself afterwards with a glass of wine as you watch the wonderful sunsets. One of the high points of life at the Argentella are the nights out in Calvi.

How to get there *(Map 36): 22km south of Calvi towards Porto by coast road. Calvi airport 25km away, tel. 95.65.08.09.*

Hôtel Mare e Monti★★

20225 Feliceto (Haute-Corse)
Tel. 95.61.73.06 - Fax 95.61.78.79
M. Renucci

Open 1 May – 30 Sept. **Rooms** 18 with telephone, of which 14 with shower and WC, 2 with bath. **Price** single 252-265F, double 283-297F. **Meals** breakfast 30F, served 0800-1000; half board 276F, full board 385F (per pers., 3 days min.) **Credit cards** accepted. **Pets** dogs allowed. **Facilities** parking. **Nearby** citadel of Calvi, tour of the villages of Ballagne (Calenzana, Zilia, Montemaggiore, Sant 'Antonino, church of the Trinity at Aregno, convent of Corbara). **Restaurant** service 1200-1400, 1930-2200; menus 80-180F, also à la carte; specialities: truite à la Calamenti, agneau de lait à la mode corse.

This lovely house, which lies between the sea and the mountains, was built in 1870 and is still lived in by the same family. Behind the hotel there are steep rocky cliffs, and in the distance one can see the sea behind Ile Rousse. On one side of the hotel is a fine terrace where you will enjoy your meals. Nearby are two magnificent cedar trees, and in an orchard there are apple trees whose fruit is much enjoyed at breakfast time. The second floor bedrooms, with high ceilings, simple decor and old paintings, are preferable to those on the third floor, where the lino covered floor is not very attractive. M. Renucci gives a cordial welcome to all his guests and the traditional and tasty food provided by his chef is an attraction for people who want to know the true Corsica rather than that found in its seaside resorts.

How to get there *(Map 36): 26km north east of Calvi via N197 to beyond Alcajola, then right on D13 to Feliceto via Santa Reparata. Calvi airport, Tel. 95.65.08.09.*

La Bergerie★★

Route de Monticello
20220 L'Ile-Rousse (Haute-Corse)
Tel. 95.60.01.28 - M. Caumer

Open 15 March – 1 Dec (closed Sunday evening and Monday in low season). **Rooms** 19 chalets/rooms with bath or shower and WC. **Price** single and double 280-460F. **Meals** breakfast 30F, served 0800-1000; half board 400-460F (per pers., 5 days min.) **Credit cards** Visa. **Pets** dogs allowed. **Facilities** swimming pool, parking. **Nearby** citadel of Calvi, tour of the villages of Ballagne (Calenzana, Zilia, Montemaggiore, Sant 'Antonino, church of the Trinity at Aregno, convent of Corbara). **Restaurant** service 1200 and 1930; à la carte; specialities: brochettes de liche, araignées farcies, omelette aux oursins, sardines farcies, mérou à la juive.

La Bergerie is an old sheep farm converted into a small hotel 800 metres from Ile Rousse and the beach. The place is already well known as a restaurant and bungalow accommodation has been added in the peaceful depths of the garden. The proprietor, a keen fisherman, likes to offer his guests the fruits of his fishing expeditions. You will have the opportunity to taste such unusual dishes as sea urchin omelette and sea anemone fritter. Relaxed and friendly atmosphere.

How to get there *(Map 36): 24km north east of Calvi via N197 to L'Ile Rousse. Calvi airport, tel. 95.65.08.09.*

U Sant' Agnellu

20247 Rogliano (Haute-Corse)
Tel. 95.35.40.59
M. and Mme Albertini

Open Easter – Oct. **Rooms** 9 with bath and WC. **Price** double 220-300F. **Meals** breakfast 25F; half board 250-300F. **Credit cards** Visa. **Pets** dogs allowed. **Facilities** parking. **Nearby** Romanesque cathedral of la Canonica and San Parteo church, villages of Cap Corse from Bastia to Saint-Florent. **Restaurant** service 1200-1500, 1930-2300; menu 90F, also à la carte; specialities: brandade, boulettes au broccio, cannelonis, tourte Sant 'Agnellu.

Young M. Albertini set up a restaurant in this old town hall in 1984, then, three years later, converted it into an hotel. He should be congratulated for his enterprise. The food he serves is delicious and abundant and unbeatable value. The bedrooms, with roughcast cut white walls and solid wooden furniture, are simple but of a good standard and very comfortable. The tiled bathrooms are also excellent. Five of the rooms look out onto the sea and the others to the mountains. During fine weather meals are served on the panoramic terrace: the spacious indoor dining room with its semicircle of large windows also has fine views. Visitors who enjoy old buildings will find plenty to interest them in the picturesque 17th-century village, which has two churches, a convent and the ruins of a château as well as various Genoese towers.

How to get there *(Map 36): 42km north of Bastia via D80 towards Macinaggio (free boat from port of Macinaggio to the hotel). Bastia airport, tel. 95.54.54.54.*

Hôtel de la Corniche★★

San-Martino-di-Lota
20200 Bastia (Haute-Corse)
Tel. 95.31.40.98 – Fax 95.32.37.69 – Mme Anziani

Open 1 Feb – 20 Dec. **Rooms** 16 with telephone, bath or shower and WC. **Price** single 200-270F, double 250-350F. **Meals** breakfast 30-35F, served 0730-1000; half board 230-320F, full board 290-380F (per pers., 3 days min.) **Credit cards** accepted. **Pets** dogs not allowed. **Nearby** Romanesque cathedral of la Canonica and San Parteo church, villages of Cap Corse from Bastia to Saint-Florent. **Restaurant** service 1200-1400, 1930-2130 (closed Sunday evening and Monday, Oct – end March); menus, also à la carte; specialities: gratin de fruits de mer, raviolis au broccio et aux herbes, ragout de sanglier aux pâtes fraîches.

This hotel at San Martino-di-Lota lies along a winding road ten minutes' drive from Bastia. It has been owned by the same family since 1935 and has wonderful views of the sea. The first thing you will notice is the beautiful terrace and its splendid plane trees. Meals are served here in fine weather and on clear days you can see as far as the Italian coast. Home cooking and Corsican specialities are the keynotes of the menu. The bedrooms were refurbished four years ago and are excellent for their price range: here good taste and comfort come together with traditional wooden furniture and attractive bathrooms. They all look out to sea. You will find a cordial welcome here.

How to get there *(Map 36): 6km north of Bastia via D80, then D131 at Pietranera. Bastia airport, tel. 95.54.54.54.*

Auberge Le Moulin du Plain★★

25470 Goumois (Doubs)
Tel. 81.44.41.99
M. Choulet

Open 25 Feb. – 2 Nov. **Rooms** 22 with telephone, bath or shower (19 with WC). **Price** single 152-184F, double 180-246F. **Meals** breakfast 30F, served 0800-0930; half board 194-220F, full board 250-278F (per pers., 3 days min.) **Credit cards** Eurocard, Visa. **Pets** dogs allowed. **Facilities** parking. **Nearby** circuit from Maîche (D437) to Gière and Indevillers, corniche of Goumois via the gorges of the Doubs to the Echelles de la Mort, art and clock-making museums in Besançon, 18-hole Prunevelle golf course. **Restaurant** service 1200-1330; menus 94-165F, also à la carte; specialities: truite à l'échalote, feuilleté aux morilles, jambon du pays, coq au savagnin.

This hotel is a great favourite with anglers. It stands on the banks of the Doubs river with its sand and pebble beach, at the foot of the mountains and facing Switzerland. The emphasis here is on calm and simplicity: the steep roof of the building is a typical feature of farmhouses in the Haut-Jura, and the bedrooms are attractively unpretentious. The Auberge du Moulin du Plain is ideal for those seeking a peaceful retreat. It has a small lounge, several fireplaces and a bar area and its exceptional location has a lot to offer not only to anglers but also to all those in search of simple pleasures: bathing in crystal-clear waters and stunning walks and excursions (Switzerland is within easy reach). The hotel serves good food.

How to get there (Map 20): 53km south of Montbéliard via D437 towards Maîche, at Maison Rouge D437b to Goumois; 4km before Goumois beside the river Doubs.

Hôtel Taillard★★★
25470 Goumois (Doubs)
Tel. 81.44.20.75 – Fax 81.44.26.15
M. Taillard

Open March – Nov (closed Wednesdays in March and Oct). **Rooms** 17 with telephone, bath or shower, WC and TV (6 with minibar). **Price** double 270-310F, suite 400-420F. **Meals** breakfast 42F, served 0800-0930; half board 325-365F (per pers., 3 days min.) **Credit cards** Amex, Diners, Visa. **Pets** dogs allowed (+30F). **Facilities** swimming pool, parking. **Nearby** circuit from Maîche (D437) to Gière and Indevillers, corniche of Goumois via the gorges of the Doubs to the Echelles de la Mort, art and clock-making museums in Besançon, 18-hole Prunevelle golf course. **Restaurant** service 1200-1400, 1945-2045; menus 130-320F, also à la carte; specialities: escalope de foie gras aux griottes de Fougerolles.

Staying in this hotel you will benefit from the hotel-keeping and gastronomic experience of four generations of Taillards. The hotel stands on the side of a small valley in the middle of the Jura countryside, and commands views of the bluish skyline of Switzerland opposite. The bedrooms are comfortable, and most of them have a balcony overlooking the mountains. The green pastures of the Haut-Doubs still resound with the jingling bells of grazing cattle, while the river Doubs is noted for its trout fishing. Calm and simplicity prevail. We particularly enjoyed M. Taillard's cooking: regional, with an imaginative range of dishes which will appeal to even the most refined palate. The service is excellent too, and this large chalet is well worth a visit.

How to get there *(Map 20): 53km south of Montbéliard via D437 towards Maîche, at Maison Rouge D437b to Goumois; it's near the church.*

Château de Rigny★★

Rigny – 70100 Gray (Haute-Saône)
Tel. 84.65.25.01 – Fax 84.65.44.45
M. and Mme Maupin

Open all year. **Rooms** 24 with telephone, bath, WC and TV. **Price** single 300F, double 390-550F. **Meals** breakfast 50F, served 0730-1000. **Credit cards** accepted. **Pets** dogs allowed. **Facilities** heated swimming pool, tennis, bicycles, parking. **Nearby** town hall, church of Notre-Dame and Baron-Martin museum in Gray, art and clock-making museums in Besançon. **Restaurant** service 1200-1400, 1930-2130 (closed 5-30 Jan); menus 180-300F, also à la carte; specialities: petite marmite du pêcheur, mignon de veau jurassien, ris de veau au savagnin.

Steeped in history, Château de Rigny was rebuilt in the reign of Louis XIII, and after several eventful centuries as a private residence became a hotel in 1962. It is set in 5 hectares of landscaped gardens, complete with lake and river. The magnificent entranceway with a lounge area and a remarkable wooden fireplace sets the style for the entire building. Both dining-rooms are delightful: a subtle pink colour scheme has been chosen for one of them, while the other is decorated in bolder greens and blues. The bar area is rather more modern in conception and leads out on to the terrace facing the garden and its immaculate lawns. The bedrooms are perfect. Those in the main house have period furniture and decoration; those in the annexe are newer, but have received the same care as the rest of the château. They all have colour television and the usual amenities. Drinks can be served outside. The hotel is noted for its owners' warm welcome.

How to get there *(Map 19): 45km north east of Dijon via D70 towards Combeaufontaine; take D2 out of Gray.*

Hôtel de la Vouivre***

39 bis, rue Gédéon-David
39300 Champagnole (Jura)
Tel. 84.52.10.44 – Mme Pernot

Open 1 May – 30 Nov. **Rooms** 20 with telephone, bath or shower, WC and TV. **Price** single 283-350F, double 283-390F. **Meals** breakfast 35F, served 0700-0930; half board 270-300F, full board 390-420F (per pers., 3 days min.) **Credit cards** Visa. **Pets** dogs allowed (+35F). **Facilities** swimming pool, tennis, parking. **Nearby** lake of Chalain, cirque of Beaume-les-Messieurs, château de Syam, Billaude waterfall, Langouette and Malvaux gorges, 9-hole Val-de-Sorne golf course at Lons-le-Saunier. **Restaurant** service 1200-1400, 1930-2130 (closed Wednesday lunchtime); menus 98-140F, also à la carte; specialities: truite au vin jaune, filet de bœuf aux morilles.

Ever since the hotel opened ten years ago, Virginia creeper has been trying to cover its façade, and the bitterly cold Jura winters have been blighting its progress. The lake, set on the edge of four hectares of parkland, provides good fishing. The hotel has comfortable rooms, and facilities include a swimming-pool and a tennis court. Standing just outside Champagnole, it is a peaceful retreat for those wishing to relax or explore the beautiful Jura countryside.

How to get there *(Map 20): 43km south west of Pontarlier via D471.*

Le Moulin de la Mère Michelle★★

Les Planches – 39600 Arbois (Jura)
Tel. 84.66.08.17 – Fax 84.37.49.69 – M. Delavenne

Open all year. **Rooms** 22 with telephone, bath or shower, WC, TV and minibar. **Price** double 300-600F. **Meals** breakfast 55F, served 0800-1030; half board 400-515F (per pers., 3 days min.) **Credit cards** Amex, MasterCard, Visa. **Pets** dogs allowed (+60F). **Facilities** swimming pool, tennis, parking. **Nearby** wine and vineyard museum, Pasteur's house, Planches cave, 9-hole Val-de-Sorne golf course at Lons-le-Saunier. **Restaurant** service 1200-1330, 1930-2100 (closed Thursdays in low season); menus 75-350F, also à la carte; specialities: poularde aux morilles et vin jaune, pochouse de truite.

The Moulin de la Mère Michelle stands well off the beaten track, on the way to Switzerland, and not far from Arbois, a town that delights the visitor with the opulent provincial charm that prospering business and vineyards confer. Formerly a mill where walnuts used to be ground, the building has been carefully restored by its current owner, who has decorated the bedrooms with much taste and attention to detail. Some of these are extremely comfortable, and have beamed ceilings, stone walls, minibars and four–posters (in rooms 5 and 10). The rooms located beneath the terrace, however, are not as comfortable and have no view, but they are cheaper, and can be perfectly suitable for children, for instance. This is a good hotel, in a peaceful and superb setting near a spectacular waterfall. It should be noted that half-board is compulsory in summer, particularly for guests staying for one night only.

How to get there *(Map 19): 42km north east of Lons-le-Saunier via N83 to Arbois via Poligny, D107 to Mesnay then D247.*

Auberge de Courpain★★★

Courpain
91690 Fontaine-la-Rivière (Essonne)
Tel. (1) 64.95.67.04 - Fax (1) 60.80.99.02 - Mme Tewe

Open 1 March – 31 Jan (closed Sundays and Mondays unless reserved). **Rooms** 18 with telephone, bath or shower and WC (4 with TV). **Price** single and double 350F, suite 500-600F. **Meals** breakfast 45F. **Credit cards** accepted. **Pets** dogs allowed. **Facilities** helicopter landing pad, parking. **Nearby** church of Saint-Basile at Etampes, Dourdan, Arpajon and the valley of the Renarde, château de Farcheville, 18-hole Belesbat golf course at Boutigny-sur-Essonne. **Restaurant** service 1230-1400, 1930-2100; menus 130-180F, also à la carte; specialities: pigeonneau rôti au poivre vert, émincés de Saint-Jacques au beurre blanc.

This former coaching inn consists of a number of buildings lying within a large garden in the middle of the countryside. Unfortunately the road beside the hotel has been considerably widened and the garden can therefore be a bit noisy. A path leads from the inn to a delightful valley which provides the opportunity for many pleasant walks on the banks of its trout streams. You will appreciate reading or relaxing in the lounge or by the fireplace of the Auberge de Courpain, where a warm and cosy atmosphere prevails. There are three dining rooms to choose from, all spacious and pleasantly furnished (our favourite one is the summer dining-room, for its vast windows looking out on to the garden.) The bedrooms are all different and have been tastefully decorated, and the same amount of care and attention to detail has been devoted to the bathrooms. The cooking is good.

How to get there *(Map9): 58km south of Paris via N20 to Etampes, then D721 for 8km (towards Pithiviers).*

Hostellerie de Villemartin★★★

1, allée des Marronniers
91150 Morigny-Champigny (Essonne)
Tel. (1) 64.94.63.54 – Fax (1) 64.94.24.68 – M. Savignet

Open all year (closed Sunday evenings and Mondays except public holidays). **Rooms** 14 with telephone, bath or shower (13 with WC) and TV. **Price** single 260-410F, double 300-450F. **Meals** breakfast 41F, served 0730-1100. **Credit cards** accepted. **Pets** dogs allowed (+60F). **Facilities** tennis, parking. **Nearby** church of Saint-Basile at Etampes, Dourdan, Arpajon and the valley of the Renarde, château de Farcheville, 18-hole Belesbat golf course at Boutigny-sur-Essonne. **Restaurant** service 1200-1330, 2000-2130; menus 190-340F, also à la carte; specialities: foie gras frais de canard, blanc de turbot en écaille de pommes rôties, feuilleté de pintadeau aux pleurotes, glacé de nougat au coulis de framboise.

Backing on to a 16th-century fortified farmhouse, this elegant manor is set in 17 hectares of parkland and woods by the river Juine. The interior decoration is classic, although of uneven quality. Most of the bedrooms are spacious, and all of them command fine views of the grounds. They are comfortable and have vast en suite bathrooms. In some of them an extremely old terracotta tiled floor can be seen. The pleasant candlelit dining-room provides an appropriate setting for the top quality food served here. This is a quiet, welcoming hotel, only minutes away from the hustle and bustle of the capital.

How to get there *(Map 20): 45km south of Paris via N20 towards Etampes; at Etréchy D148 and D17 towards Morigny; it's in the hamlet of Villemartin.*

Auberge Les Alouettes★★

4, rue Antoine-Barye
77630 Barbizon (Seine-et-Marne)
Tel. (1) 60.66.41.98 - Fax (1) 60.66.20.69 - M. and Mme Cresson

Open all year. **Rooms** 22 with telephone, bath or shower, WC and TV (6 with minibar). **Price** double 200-520F. **Meals** breakfast 40F, served 0800-1030. **Credit cards** accepted. **Pets** dogs allowed. **Facilities** tennis, parking. **Nearby** house of Théodore Rousseau, forest and palace of Fontainebleau, 18-hole Fontainebleau golf course at Barbizon. **Restaurant** service 1200-1430, 1930-2130 (closed Sunday evenings in low season); menus 150-190F, also à la carte; specialities: fricassée de médaillons de langouste aux arômes d'anis, petites queues de homard façon normande aux saveurs d'estragon, gâteau de ris de veau aux crêtes de coq.

The hotel lies a little way from the main street lined with small art galleries where tourists like to stroll. Scattered through the house are souvenirs of the comfortably bohemian existence of a professor of philosophy at the Sorbonne who once lived there and received, among others, Mallarmé, Paul Painlevé and Gaultier-Boissière. He was also an amateur painter, and the paintings on the bedroom doors date back to the time when the rooms were used as studios. They are charming, and quite comfortable, but those located in the Villa Simone, the hotel annexe, are even more comfortable and cosy. The dining-room has been refurbished, and a large verandah leading out into the garden has been added. This is an interesting place to stay, conveniently close to Paris.

How to get there (Map 9): 57km south east of Paris via A6, Fontainebleau exit; then N37 and D64 to Barbizon.

Hostellerie de la Clé d'Or★★★

73, Grande-Rue
77630 Barbizon (Seine-et-Marne)
Tel. (1) 60.66.40.96 - Fax (1) 60.66.42.71 - M. Gayer

Open all year (closed Sunday evenings in low season). **Rooms** 16 with telephone, bath or shower, WC, TV and minibar. **Price** single 280F, double 420F, suite 850F. **Meals** breakfast 45F, served 0745-1100. **Credit cards** accepted. **Pets** dogs allowed. **Facilities** parking. **Nearby** house of Théodore Rousseau, forest and palace of Fontainebleau, 18-hole Fontainebleau golf course at Barbizon. **Restaurant** service 1200-1400, 1730-2100; menus 180-230F, also à la carte; specialities: frites de langoustines au gingembre, ris de veau aux jeunes légumes, croustade de turbot à graine de moutarde de Meaux.

Located in Barbizon, on the edge of the forest, the Hostellerie de la Clé d'Or is a traditional kind of hotel, evocative of opulence and comfort. Formerly a coaching-inn, it is the oldest establishment in a village whose peace and beauty have inspired so many artists. The food certainly constitutes the highlight of a visit. Skilfully prepared gourmet cuisine is served here, admirably complemented by an interesting wine list. Besides that, however, the hotel has much to offer: a beautiful dining-room with a fireplace, a terrace looking out across the garden where meals can be served in summer, and fully-equipped bedrooms with access to the lawn. The elegant atmosphere of the place is enhanced by such features as beautiful antique furniture, copperware, pottery and tastefully hung paintings.

How to get there *(Map 9): 57km south east of Paris via A6, Fontainebleau exit; then N37 and D64 to Barbizon.*

Château des Bondons★★★

47/49, rue des Bondons
77260 La Ferté-sous-Jouarre (Seine-et-Marne)
Tel. (1) 60.22.00.98 - Fax (1) 60.22.97.01 - M. Busconi

Open all year. **Rooms** 8 with telephone, bath, WC, TV and minibar. **Price** double 300-400F, suite 500-800F. **Meals** breakfast 40F, no restaurant. **Credit cards** Visa, Amex. **Pets** dogs allowed (+30F). **Facilities** parking. **Nearby** Jouarre, Eurodisney.

Set in extensive grounds, this small 19th-century château was about to sink into oblivion, but thanks to a thorough renovation programme under the supervision of owners M. and Mme Busconi it has been brought back to life. The reception rooms on the ground-floor look out onto the surrounding gardens. The entrance hall has an elaborate marble mosaic floor evocative of Vienna in the days of Klimt or Hoffmann, and the same geometrical patterns can be seen in ivory inlay in the panelling. In the dining-room some delightful panelling inlaid with small landscape pictures has also been preserved. There is a wealth of 18th-century style furniture – modern copies, but elegant. The lounge is vast and flooded with light, but the tiled floor could do with a few rugs to warm it up. A fine wooden staircase leads up to the bedrooms. The atmosphere there is extremely warm and cosy, with thick carpets and lovely flowery fabrics for the curtains. The bedrooms are all individually decorated and have luxuriously equipped bathrooms. Rooms 4 and 8 are particularly noteworthy (more expensive but exceptional). Extremely friendly welcome and large and excellent breakfasts.

How to get there *(Map 10): 65km east of Paris via A4, Ferté-sous-Jouarre exit, then N3; its in the villgae in Chalons-sur-Marne, Montménard direction.*

Hostellerie du Moulin de Flagy★★★

2, rue du Moulin
77940 Flagy (Seine-et-Marne)
Tel. (1) 60.96.67.89 - Fax (1) 60.96.69.51 - M. and Mme Scheidecker

Open 22 Jan – 12 Sept and 25 Sept – 19 Dec. (closed Sunday evenings and Mondays). **Rooms** 10 with telephone, bath and WC. **Price** single 200-245F, double 250-435F. **Meals** breakfast 40F, served 0745-1100; half board 305-385F, full board 465-545F (per pers., 4 days min.) **Credit cards** accepted. **Pets** dogs allowed. **Facilities** parking. **Nearby** palace and forest of Fontainebleau, Moret-sur-Loing, 18-hole La Forteresse golf course. **Restaurant** service 1215-1415, 1915-2115; menus 160-200F, also à la carte.

This 13th-century flour mill has been well restored. Beneath the rendering the ancient masonry was discovered in a remarkable state of conservation. Thus the original half-timbering, the cob walls, the ground-floor stonework and the fine vaulted gable have all been stripped bare and greatly contribute to the strong period atmosphere of the building. The hotel accommodates guests in ten fully-equipped and carefully decorated bedrooms. The dining-room looks out on to the river, and there are also a terrace and a garden. Dinner is served by candlelight in the evening and log-fires are lit in winter. You are assured of a comfortable stay in this hotel where quiet rural setting and beautiful architecture combine to create an ambience of warmth and well-being only an hour away from Paris.

How to get there *(Map 9): 88km south east of Paris via A6, Fontainebleau exit, then N6 to Moret-sur-Loing, D218 to Villecerf and D22 to Flagy.*

Hostellerie Aux Vieux Remparts***

3, rue Couverte
77160 Provins (Seine-et-Marne)
Tel. (1) 64.08.94.00/(1) 64.00.02.89 - Fax (1) 60.67.77.22 - M. Roy

Open all year. **Rooms** 25 with telephone, bath or shower, WC, TV and minibar. **Price** single 340-430F, double 390-560F. **Meals** breakfast 50F, served 0700-1100; half board 450-520F, full board 630-700F (per pers., 3 days min.) **Credit cards** accepted. **Pets** dogs allowed (+60F). **Facilities** parking. **Nearby** ramparts, tower of César, church of Saint-Quiriace in Provins, church of Saint-Loup-de-Naud, 18-hole Fontenaille golf course. **Restaurant** service 1200-1430, 1930-2130; menus 180-350F, also à la carte; specialities: duo de foie gras de canard et oie au marc de champagne, medley de rognon et ris de veau au brie de Provins, levée de truites marinées aux herbes odoriférantes, parfait glacé à la rose.

The Hostellerie Aux Vieux Remparts has long been known as a gourmet restaurant. It is now also a hotel, accommodating guests in pleasant rooms in an adjoining modern building which successfully blends in with the town's medieval architecture. The dining-room still has its big oak beams but the decoration in the bedrooms is more modern, and everything has been devised to make them comfortable and welcoming: warm colours, quilted bedspreads, thick carpets. The menu features a tempting range of dishes which, in summer, can be enjoyed in the shade on the terrace. Despite being centrally located the hotel is very quiet. A warm welcome.

How to get there *(Map 10): 86km south east of Paris via N19 (Pont-de-Charenton) to Provins.*

Auberge Casa del Sol★★

63, rue des Canches
77760 Recloses (Seine-et-Marne)
Tel. (1) 64.24.20.35 - Mme Hude-Courcoul

Open 15 Jan – 16 Aug and 1 Sept – 20 Dec (closed Tuesdays). **Rooms** 10 with telephone, bath or shower, 7 with WC, 9 with TV and 3 with minibar. **Price** single 250F, double 340-360F, suite 615F. Meals breakfast 40F, served 0800-1000; half board 365F, full board 510F (per pers., 3 days min.) **Credit cards** accepted. **Pets** dogs allowed. **Facilities** parking. **Nearby** palace and forest of Fontainebleau, Barbizon, Milly-la-Forêt (chapel of Saint-Blaise decorated by Cocteau, and covered market), Moret-sur-Loing, 9-hole Fontainebleau golf course. **Restaurant** service 1200-1430, 1900-2130; menus 140-160F, also à la carte; fresh and local products.

The Casa del Sol is 40 minutes away from Paris and just a few miles from Fontainebleau. This is an old building, modest in proportions, and well restored. The bedrooms are extremely pretty, comfortable and decorated in country style; some are in the attics. All the rooms are very quiet. The lounge and the dining-room have recently been refurbished and improved. In summer meals are served outside on the terrace. The cooking, using fresh homegrown produce, combines the traditional with the modern. Colette Courcoul, the owner, is an active and efficient host, and a warm, convivial atmosphere prevails.

How to get there *(Map 9): 75km south east of Paris via A6, Ury exit, then D63e to Recloses.*

Hostellerie Le Vieux Logis

5, rue Sadi-Carnot
77810-Thomery (Seine-et-Marne)
Tel. (1) 60.96.44.77 - Fax (1) 60.96.42.71 - M. Plouvier

Open all year. **Rooms** 14 with telephone, bath, WC and TV. **Price** single and double 380F. **Meals** breakfast 45F, served 0700-1000. **Credit cards** Visa, MasterCard, Amex. **Pets** dogs allowed (+35F). **Facilities** parking. **Nearby** palace and forest of Fontainebleau, Barbizon, Milly-la-Forêt (chapel of Saint-Blaise, decorated by Cocteau, and covered market), Moret-sur-Loing, 9-hole Fontainebleau golf course. **Restaurant** service 1215-1445, 1930-2130; menus 120-220F, also à la carte.

Having restored and opened the beautiful "Moulin de Flagy", M. and Mme Plouvier decided to apply all their energy and flair to this handsome late 18th century house, set in a village once famous for its vineyards and close to the forest of Fontainebleau. The fourteen fully-equipped bedrooms are decorated in a muted contemporary style combining painted wood and mellow fabrics. The chef's inspired efforts in the kitchen result in exquisite, imaginative food, served in a magnificent dining-room, an appropriate setting for such gourmet cuisine. In the conservatory, white tables, a white piano and potted plants create an elegantly modern atmosphere which is carried through to the pleasant bar area. Not even the slightest details are overlooked by Madame Plouvier, and she will ensure you have an enjoyable stay. The hotel sometimes hosts private concerts.

How to get there *(Map 9): 71km south east of Paris via A6, 9km west of Fontainebleau via N6 towards Sens, then D137 towards Champagne.*

Auberge du Gros Marronnier**

3, place de l'Eglise
78720 Senlisse (Yvelines)
Tel. (1) 30.52.51.69 – Fax (1) 30.52.55.91 – Mme Trochon

Open all year. **Rooms** 19 with telephone, bath or shower and WC. **Price** single 290F, double 325-385F. **Meals** breakfast 45F, served 0700-1130; half board 220F, full board 490F. **Credit cards** accepted. **Pets** dogs allowed (+50F). **Facilities** parking. **Nearby** châteaux of Dampierre and Breteuil, abbeys of Vaux-le-Cernay and Port-Royal-des-Champs, 27-hole Château de la Couharde golf course at Yvelines. **Restaurant** service 1200-1430, 1930-2200; menus 135-305F, also à la carte; specialities: foie gras et confit de canard maison, Saint-Jacques à la provençale.

This charming inn stands in a small street in Senlisse, one of the pretty villages set amidst the natural beauty of the Chevreuse valley. Across the courtyard from the hotel a porch leads into a lovely walled garden with fruit trees, a well and small benches where one can sit and admire the neighbouring church. The peace of the countryside pervades the house as well. The bedrooms are being refurbished and improved this year. As soon as the weather permits, tables are set up in the garden. The hotel is only 35 minutes away from the centre of Paris and there is a métro station just 6 km from Senlisse (R.E.R. line B), making it an ideal weekend destination for those anxious to avoid the hassle of driving to and from the capital.

How to get there *(Map 9): 46km south west of Paris via A13 and A12 to Versailles, N10 to Maurepas, D58 to Dampierre and D91 to Senlisse.*

Hôtel Dame Carcas★★★

15, rue Saint-Louis - La Cité
11000 Carcassonne (Aude)
Tel. 68.71.37.37 - Fax 68.71.50.15 - M. Luraschi

Open all year. **Rooms** 30 with telephone, bath or shower, WC and TV. **Price** single 300-420F, double 350-650F, suite 900-1200F. **Meals** breakfast 52F, served 0700-1100. **Credit cards** Visa, Amex, Diners. **Pets** dogs allowed. **Facilities** parking. **Nearby** La Cité, churches of Saint-Vincent and Saint-Nazaire in Carcassonne, château de Pennautier, 9-hole Auriac golf course at Carcassonne. **Restaurant** in Hôtel de la Cité, adjacent; service 1200-1400, 1900-2200 (closed Wednesdays); menus 100-150F, also à la carte; seasonal specialities.

Formerly an annexe of the Hôtel de la Cité, the 'Dame Carcas' is now a hotel in its own right, and a very pleasant one, too. It has been entirely refurbished with as much flair and attention to detail as its neighbour, but is rather more sober in style. The 30 bedrooms are all comfortably fitted, with cherrywood beds and good furniture, and their decoration is charming and fresh. Rooms 215 to 219 are resolutely rustic in character with tiling and a flowery decor, whereas rooms 201 to 210, lavishly equipped with marble *en suite* bathrooms, are elegance epitomised. The hotel doesn't have a restaurant of its own, but a footbridge allows easy access to the restaurant in the Hôtel de la Cité.

How to get there *(Map 31): at Carcassonne, inside the ramparts.*

Hostellerie du Grand Duc★★

2, route de Boucheville
11140 Gincla (Aude)
Tel. 68.20.55.02 - Fax 68.20.61.22 - M. and Mme Bruchet

Open 25 March – 15 Nov. **Rooms** 10 with telephone, bath or shower and WC. **Price** single 195-240F, double 230-320F. **Meals** breakfast 35F, served 0800-1100; half board 230-270F, full board 310-370F (per pers., 3 days min.) **Credit cards** Visa, Eurocard, MasterCard. **Pets** dogs allowed. **Facilities** parking. **Nearby** forest of Fanges, Saint-Paul-de-Fenouillet, gorges of Galamus. **Restaurant** service 1215-1400, 1930-2100 (closed Wednesdays in low season); à la carte; specialities: baignades de sépiole au Fitou, caille au muscat, faux-filet au foie gras et aux griottes, regional specialities.

This hotel of great charm – a carefully restored family mansion – is set in a small village. Their guests' well-being is the young and friendly owners chief concern and they pride themselves on their warm welcome. There are ten bedrooms, all individually designed and decorated in a wide range of styles. Whitewashed walls, exposed stonework and beamed ceilings highlight the rustic character of the pleasant dining-room. The lounge and the bar area are particularly cosy. In summer, breakfast and dinner can be served in the garden, with candles on the tables in the evening.

How to get there (Map 31): 63km north west of Perpignan via D117 to Lapradelle, then D22 to Gincla.

Relais du Val d'Orbieu★★★

11200 Ornaisons (Aude)
Tel. 68.27.10.27 – Fax 68.27.52.44
M. and Mme Gonzalvez

Open Feb – Dec (closed Sunday evenings Nov – Feb). **Rooms** 20 with telephone, bath, WC, TV and minibar. **Price** single 450F, double 590-750F, suite 750-1450F. **Meals** breakfast 68F, served 0730-1030; half board 750-850F (per pers.) **Credit cards** accepted. **Pets** dogs allowed (+80F). **Facilities** swimming pool, tennis, golf practice, parking. **Nearby** cathedral of Saint-Just in Narbonne, mountain of la Clape, African reserve of Sigean, abbey of Fontfroide, Lagrasse, 9-hole Auriac golf course at Carcassonne. **Restaurant** service 1215-1345 and 1930-2100; menus 210-410F, also à la carte; specialities: canon d'agneau au basilic, dos de palangre aux aromates.

Facing the stunningly picturesque Montagne Noire, the location of the Relais couldn't be better. The building itself, formerly a mill, has been carefully restored: the rooms are elegantly decorated and an atmosphere of calm and cosiness prevails. The bedrooms at garden level are all very comfortable and in the morning delicious and ample breakfasts are served there with, on the menu, fresh fruit juices, cheese, pâtisseries and home-made jams, with a large choice of teas and coffees. As for the restaurant, Chef JP Robert's much praised cuisine has earned it a reputation as one of Languedoc's top eating-places, and his talent is admirably set off by JP Gonzalvez's remarkable selection of regional wines. Guests find an attentive welcome.

How to get there *(Map 31): 47km east of Carcassonne via A61, Lézignan exit then D611 to Lézignan and D24 (eastward) to Ornaisons; signposted.*

Castel de Villemagne★★

Villemagne
11310 Saissac (Aude)
Tel. 68.94.22.95 - Mme de Vézian Maksud

Open 15 March – 15 Nov. **Rooms** 7 with telephone, bath or shower and WC. **Price** single 245-335F, double 300-415F, suite 580F. **Meals** breakfast 38F, served 0800-1000; half board 283-340F (per pers., 3 days min.) **Credit cards** Visa, Eurocard, MasterCard. **Pets** dogs allowed in bedrooms. **Facilities** parking. **Nearby** la Montagne Noire, abbey of Villelongue, belvedere of the châteaux of Lastours, gorges of la Clamoux, 9-hole Auriac golf course at Carcassonne. **Restaurant** service 1930-2030; menus 98-185F, children 55F, also à la carte; specialities: cassoulet, civet de marcassin.

In a pretty village in the Montagne Noire area, between Mazamet and Carcassonne, Mme de Vezian–Maksud accommodates guests in a manor built in the 14th and 18th centuries. The Castel de Villemagne has throughout the centuries been a private house, opening as a hotel only ten years ago, and it retains the distinctive character of a long-established and much-loved family home. In the bedrooms, tall wardrobes and Napoleon III wing-chairs create that old-fashioned charm associated with country living. In summer, the garden is the best place to have breakfast, for the lovely view of the Pyrenees and the pleasant grounds. Mme de Vézian Maksud is very much attached to her native region and will be delighted to tell you all you want to know about the Languedoc area and the fascinating Cathars.

How to get there *(Map 31): 31km north west of Carcassonne via N113, then D629 to Saissac and D103.*

Hôtel Les Arcades★★★

23, bd Gambetta
30220 Aigues-Mortes (Gard)
Tel. 66.53.81.13

Open all year (closed 3-28 Feb). **Rooms** 6 with telephone, bath and WC. **Price** double 460-550F. **Meals** breakfast incl. **Credit cards** Visa. **Pets** small dogs allowed. **Nearby** the Camargue, Arles, Saintes-Maries-de-la-Mer (gipsies' pilgrimage 24-25 May). **Restaurant** closed Mondays in low season; menus 120-200F, also à la carte; specialities: gardiane de taureau à l'ancienne, crêpes pralinées à l'orange.

We really like this 16th-century house set in a quiet street in the old town. Inside, everything is neat and charming. A lovely aged and patinated paint effect, in colours ranging from lime green to brown, enhances the corridors and the bedrooms, where curtains, bedspreads and antique furniture are in perfect harmony with it. The bedrooms are vast, with high, elaborate ceilings and tall mullioned windows, and fully equipped bathrooms provide all the modern comforts. Breakfast and dinner – which are excellent – are served in a pleasant dining-room with an ancient terracotta tiled floor. It opens on one side into a little garden, and on the other into an arcade where a few tables are set up. A warm, family atmosphere prevails.

How to get there (Map 32): *48km west of Arles towards Saintes-Maries-de-la-Mer, then D58.*

Hôtel Marie d'Agoult★★★

Château d'Arpaillargues
30700 Uzès (Gard)
Tel. 66.22.14.48 – Fax 66.22.56.10 – M. Savry

Open 15 March – 15 Nov. **Rooms** 28 with telephone, bath, WC, TV and minibar. **Price** single and double 380-1080F, suite 900-1080F. **Meals** breakfast 55F, served 0730-1030; half board 430-780F, full board 625-975F. **Credit cards** accepted. **Pets** dogs allowed (+60F). **Facilities** swimming pool, tennis, parking. **Nearby** le Duché, churches of Saint-Etienne and Saint-Théodorit in Uzès. **Restaurant** service 1230-1330, 1930-2100; menus 130-200F, also à la carte; specialities: minestrone de homard glacé parfumé aux ravioles.

The beautiful 18th-century Château d'Arpaillargues was once the home of Marie de Flavigny, composer Franz Liszt's companion. The bedrooms are comfortably fitted and tastefully decorated. If you want one with its own terrace, try room no 1 on the roof of the main building, or rooms 15 or 16 with access to the garden. In the annexe, room 28 is a small duplex complete with a covered terrace. The extremely high standards of everything here make up for the somewhat formal atmosphere that prevails. A pleasant bar area, lunch by the swimming-pool, and breakfast and dinner in the garden in summer make a stay here a delightful prospect. The food matches its surroundings: it is exquisite.

How to get there *(Map 33): 40km west of Avignon via N100 to Remoulins, then D981 to Uzès and D982 (westward) to Arpaillargues.*

Mas Quayrol★★

Aulas
30120 Le Vigan (Gard)
Tel. 67.81.12.38 - Fax 67.81.23.84 - M. Grenouillet

Open April – Nov. **Rooms** 16 with telephone, bath, WC and TV. **Price** single and double 350F. **Meals** breakfast 35F. **Credit cards** Visa. **Pets** dogs allowed. **Facilities** swimming pool, tennis, parking. **Nearby** château de Roquebois at Meyrueis, cave of the Demoiselles, cirque of Navacelles, la Couvertoirade, Cévenol museum at Le Vigan, Cévennes national park; 9-hole Bombequiols golf course at Ganges. **Restaurant** service 1200-1400, 1900-2100; menus 135-250F, also à la carte; specialities: champignons de la forêt, truites, foie gras de canard, coquelet au citron et morilles, pélardon de chèvres.

Set on a hillside above the village of Aulas, this hotel commands stunning views of the valley below. The layout of the building follows the slope, and the different levels have been skilfully put to use to accommodate terraces, small lounges and a panoramic restaurant. Beamed ceilings and wood-panelling create a pleasant atmosphere. The brown colour scheme chosen to decorate the bedrooms was fashionable in the Seventies but makes the rooms seem a bit dark when the sun is not shining. Everywhere else in the hotel, large picture windows afford unimpeded enjoyment of the natural surroundings (the most remarkable of these many windows is the one in the entrance hall which looks out on to the swimming pool).

How to get there *(Map 32): 60km north of Montpellier via D986, then D999 to le Vigan, then Aulas.*

Hôtel Le Mas du Termes***
Route de Bagnols–sur-Cèze
30430 Barjac (Gard)
Tel. 66.24.56.31 – Fax 66.24.58.54 – M. and Mme Marron

Open 1 March – 31 Dec. **Rooms** 14 (and 6 apartments) with telephone, bath or shower, WC (3 with TV). **Price** double 320-370F, suite 600-800F. **Meals** breakfast 40F, served 0730-1100; half board 360-385F, full board 510-535F (per pers., 3 days min.) **Credit cards** Visa, Eurocard, MasterCard. **Pets** dogs allowed. **Facilities** swimming pool (55F), parking. **Nearby** museum of modern art at Bagnols-sur-Cèze, Prafrance bamboo garden at Anduze, gorges of the Ardèche. **Restaurant** service 1200-1400, 1900-2200; menus 90-280F, also à la carte; specialities: panaché d'agneau de lait à la sauge et au romarin, suprême de saumon au confit de poireaux.

This hotel lies only minutes away from the gorges of the Ardèche and the Cèze valley, both very popular with visitors in search of beautiful scenery. Yet its location amidst its own extensive vineyards ensures you will find peace and quiet. The gourmet restaurant is one of the best eating-places in the area and serves home-produced wine. The building was once used for silkworm breeding, and its character is still evident in the vaulted lounge, the bar in the interior courtyard, and the stone walls. Besides comfortable, pleasant bedrooms there are three flats to let. The young owners are considerate and friendly hosts.

How to get there *(Map 32): 84km north west of Avignon via A7, Bollène exit, then D994 to Pont-Saint-Esprit, then N86 and turn left after 3km onto D901 to Barjac via Aiguéze.*

Hostellerie Le Castellas★★★

Grand' Rue
30210 Collias (Gard)
Tel. 66.22.88.88 - Fax 66.22.84.28 - M. and Mme Aparis

Open 10 March – 6 Jan. **Rooms** 14 with telephone, bath or shower, WC, TV and minibar. **Price** single 400-440F, double 500-590F. **Meals** breakfast 50F, served 0730-1100; half board 495-535F. **Credit cards** accepted. **Pets** dogs allowed (+50F). **Facilities** swimming pool, parking. **Nearby** Pont du Gard, Uzès, Nîmes, 9-hole golf course at Uzès. **Restaurant** service 1200-1400, 1900-2115; menus 160-300F, also à la carte; specialities: foie gras poêlé et plateau de pommes de terre à la truffe, suprême de pigeon rôti à la provençale, champignons et jus de ses abats.

In a little street in the centre of Collias two venerable 17th-century dwellings house the Hostellerie Le Castellas. The layout of the buildings forms an enclosed courtyard which proves the perfect location for a fine swimming-pool, the terrace of the restaurant, and a delightful little garden "à la Monet". A favourite haunt of artists and sculptors, the second house displays some remarkable interior decoration and has extraordinary bathrooms. The bedrooms in the main building are also very pleasant, but more classical in style. A friendly welcome and a restaurant serving a refined and imaginative cuisine add to the many attractions of the hotel. A good place to stay.

How to get there *(Map 33): 26km north east of Nîmes via A9, Remoulins exit; at Remoulins D981 then D112 to Collias.*

A l'Auberge Cévenole★★★

30110 La Favède (Gard)
Tel. 66.34.12.13 - Fax 66.34.50.50
Mme Burlon

Open 1 Apr – 1 Oct **Rooms** 20 with telephone, bath or shower, WC (6 with TV and minibar). **Price** single 300-350F, double 300-600F, suite 550-650F. **Meals** breakfast 45F, served 0730-1030; half board 335-500F (per pers., 3 days min.) **Credit cards** Visa, Eurocard, MasterCard. **Pets** dogs not allowed. **Facilities** swimming pool, tennis, parking. **Nearby** Mas-Soubeyran and Desert museum, Prafrance bamboo garden at Anduze, caves of Trabuc, 18-hole Haut de Nîmes golf course. **Restaurant** service 1200-1400, 1930-2100; menus 165-265F, also à la carte; specialities: fricassée de moules aux cèpes des Cévennes, gourmande de ris de veau aux morilles, salade de filet de canard aux grillotines.

There is nothing here to remind you of the austere "Cévennes noires": it is an island of greenery in which the garden gradually merges with the surrounding hills. In the bedrooms and the lounge, fitted carpets and wall–fabrics create a warm and cosy atmosphere. The decoration shows a meticulous attention to detail and your hosts' desire to ensure you have a comfortable and enjoyable stay. The garden full of flowers, the large swimming–pool and the secluded location make the hotel a peaceful and pleasant summer retreat. The restaurant serves excellent food.

How to get there *(Map 32): 14km north west of Alès via N106 to La Grande-Combe and D283.*

L'Hacienda★★★

Mas de Brignon - 30320 Marguerittes (Gard)
Tel. 66.75.02.25 - Fax 66.75.45.58
M. and Mme Chauvin

Open all year. **Rooms** 11 with telephone, bath or shower, WC, TV and minibar. **Price** single 350-450F, double 400-500F. **Meals** breakfast 60F, served 0745-1030; half board 400-500F (per pers., 3 days min.) **Credit cards** accepted. **Pets** dogs allowed (+50F). **Facilities** swimming pool, tennis (70F), archery, boules, bicycles, sauna (70F), parking. **Nearby** Maison Carrée, art museum in Nîmes, Pont du Gard, château de Villevieille at Sommières, chapel of Saint-Julien-de-Salinelles, 18-hole Hauts-de-Nîmes golf course. **Restaurant** service 1200-1300, 1930-2130; menus 140-290F, also à la carte; specialities: feuillantine de noix de Saint-Jacques au champagne, magret de canard à l'aigre doux et au miel.

Built around a patio with a swimming-pool, this large farmhouse within easy reach of Nîmes has just been entirely refurbished. It has eleven bedrooms, differing in quality: two of them are a bit dark. The room with a terrace, on the first floor, is one of the nicest, and rooms 5 and 6 communicate with one another, which can be very convenient for families. Around the hotel, among rose-bushes and oleanders, you will find many facilities for outdoor games. M. Chauvin does the cooking himself, using only fresh produce and changes his menu according to what is available. A friendly family atmosphere prevails in this hotel, well located just on the outskirts of Nîmes.

How to get there *(Map 33): 6km east of Nîmes via A9, Nîmes-Est exit; then N86 and D135; go through Marguerittes and follow signs.*

Hôtel Plazza★★

10, rue Roussy
30000 Nîmes (Gard)
Tel. 66.76.16.20 – Fax 66.67.65.99 – M. Viallet

Open 10 Jan – 31 Dec. **Rooms** 28 with air conditioning, telephone, bath or shower, WC and TV. **Price** single 250-300F, double 315-420F. **Meals** breakfast 45F. **Credit cards** accepted. **Pets** small dogs allowed (+30F). **Facilities** parking (+45F). **Nearby** Maison Carrée, art museum in Nîmes, Pont du Gard, château de Villevieille at Sommières, chapel of Saint-Julien-de-Salinelles, 18-hole Hauts-de-Nîmes golf course. **Restaurant** brunch and light meals on request.

There is nothing left of the earlier Hôtel Plazza except an elegant Art Deco wrought iron door. Otherwise, the hotel has been thoroughly and carefully refurbished by Bernard and Annie Viallet and many thoughtful details ensure that guests have a comfortable and enjoyable stay. The bedrooms are not large but have every modern amenity, including air-conditioning. The bathrooms are also well equipped. The decoration shows a 1930s influence and creates a pleasantly warm atmosphere. A garage and a peaceful location add further appeal, and the hotel offers good value for money.

How to get there *(Map 32): Rue Roussy runs parallel to the Boulevard Amiral Courbet in the town centre.*

Royal Hôtel★★
3, Boulevard Alphonse-Daudet
30000 Nîmes (Gard)
Tel. 66.67.28.36 – Mmes Riera and Morel

Open all year. **Rooms** 32 with telephone, bath or shower and WC (18 with TV). **Price** single and double 240-355F. **Meals** breakfast 35F, served 0700-1200; half board 245F, full board 345F. **Credit cards** Amex, Diners, Visa. **Pets** dogs allowed (+30F). **Nearby** Maison Carrée, art museum in Nîmes, Pont du Gard, château de Villevieille at Sommiéres, chapel of Saint-Julien-de-Salinelles, 18-hole Haut-de-Nîmes golf course. **Restaurant** service 1200-1500 (also evenings in summer); menu 100F; Mediterranean cooking.

This small hotel is located close to the Quai de la Fontaine and the Maison Carrée, and looks out on to the Place d'Assas renovated by Martial Raysse. The hotel has a clientele of artists and designers and the atmosphere is relaxed and informal. The decoration sets the style of the house: it is a humorous mixture of furniture bought in flea-markets and of kitsch. Some of the spacious bedrooms have 1930s bronzes, others have 1950s sycamore–wood furniture (our favourites are rooms 2, 18 and 21). An attractive restaurant serves salads and brunches and tables are set up outside in the square in summer. It is better to take a room at the back of the hotel if you don't want to listen to the clattering of forks deep into the night. During the "férias" everyone goes a bit mad and the bar and the restaurant stay open late. There are jazz sessions some evenings.

How to get there *(Map 32): in the town centre.*

Le Mas d'Oléandre

Saint-Médiers - 30700 Uzès (Gard)
Tel. 66.22.63.43 - M. Törschen

Open 16 March – 31 Oct. **Rooms** 3 rooms, 2 apartments and 1 studio, with bath or shower and WC. **Price** single 160F, double 230F, suite 320-380F. **Meals** breakfast 40F, served 0900-1000; no restaurant. **Credit cards** not accepted. **Pets** dogs not allowed. **Facilities** swimming pool, parking. **Nearby** le Duché, churches of Saint-Etienne and Saint-Théodorit in Uzès, Pont du Gard, Nîmes, Avignon, 9-hole golf course at Uzès.

A secluded location and a stunning view are the main features of this hotel tucked away at the end of a peaceful little village. All around it cypresses, vineyards and hills combine to create a beautifully harmonious landscape and that may be what kept the owners from returning to their native Germany once they had set eyes on it. This doesn't feel like a hotel at all. The farmhouse has been carefully restored to make your stay as pleasant as possible. There are comfortable and cosy bedrooms, fully-fitted flatlets, and well-equipped apartments which easily accommodate families with children. The hotel is an ideal base for exploring the beautiful Uzès area, and the swimming-pool proves an irresistible invitation to laze in the sun. In the evening your hosts will gladly point you towards the best local restaurants. The flatlets and apartments have small kitchens.

How to get there *(Map 33): 40km west of Avignon via N100 to Montaren, then D337 to Saint-Médiers (the Mas is on the edge of the hamlet).*

Auberge du Pont Romain★★★

2, rue Emile-Jamais – 30250 Sommières (Gard)
Tel. 66.80.00.58 – Fax 66.80.31.52 – Mme Michel

Open 15 March – 15 Jan (closed Wednesdays in low season). **Rooms** 18 with telephone, bath or shower (16 with WC). **Price** single 260-395F, double 260-420F. **Meals** breakfast 45F, served 0745-1000; half board 395F. **Credit cards** accepted. **Pets** dogs allowed. **Facilities** swimming pool, parking. **Nearby** château de Villevieille, chapel of Saint-Julien-de-Salinelles, church of Notre-Dame-des-Pommiers in Beaucaire, Pont du Gard, Nîmes; 18-hole Nîmes-campagne golf course. **Restaurant** service 1215-1315, 2015-2130; menus 155-220F, also à la carte; specialities: petit gris des garrigues au roquefort, foie gras maison.

The facade that looks out onto the street is austere and barracks-like, betraying something of the history of the building. It was a carpet factory in the 19th century, then a laundry, then, until 1968, a distillery. But as soon as you walk through the porch you enter a different world. A marvellous garden (all the more so for its unlikely location) full of trees and flowers provides an agreeable setting for a terrace and a swimming-pool, and leads down to the Vidourle river. The vastness of the bedrooms can prompt memories of hostels or boarding schools, but the best rooms are the ones with views of the garden, and our favourite is room no 8 with a terrace among the branches of the plane trees overlooking the river. In the restaurant the menu features traditional food in generous helpings, but the service can be a bit casual. This must be the only hotel in France to boast a factory chimney!

How to get there *(Map 32): 28km south east of Nîmes via D40.*

Hôtel d'Entraigues★★★

8, rue de la Calade – 30700 Uzès (Gard)
Tel. 66.22.32.68 – Fax 66.22.57.01 – Mme Georges

Open all year. **Rooms** 36 with telephone, bath, WC, TV and minibar. **Price** single 180-190F, double 280-650F. **Meals** breakfast 42F, served 0730-1000; half board +220F (per pers., 3 days min.) **Credit cards** accepted. **Pets** dogs allowed (+40F). **Facilities** swimming pool, parking (+50F). **Nearby** le Duché, churches of Saint-Etienne and Saint-Théodorit in Uzès, Pont du Gard, Nîmes, Avignon, 9-hole golf course at Uzès. **Restaurant** service 1215-1400, 1930-2130; menus 110-185F, also à la carte.

The Hôtel d'Entraigues is a fine 15th-century house in the centre of Uzès, just opposite the ancient seat of the barons of Castille and the bishop's palace. Some of the bedrooms have views of those impressive buildings (such as room no 9) or of the surrounding countryside, but those without a view make up for it in other ways. The rooms are all attractive and pleasant although different in style and size: some nestle under the eaves, others are a lot bigger (rooms 14, 15, 16, 18). A small lounge close to the reception area and a vaulted breakfast room provide all the comfort guests can wish for. The restaurant which has opened recently is just across the street. Its decor is quite surprising, combining frescoes and stone pillars crowned with somewhat 'post-modernist' illuminated capitals. The food, however, is very good, and upstairs there is a large flowery terrace with a superb view. A hotel and a town full of charm and character.

How to get there (Map 33): 16km north west of the Pont du Gard via D981; opposite the cathedral.

Hôtel de l'Atelier★★

5, rue de la Foire
30400 Villeneuve-lès–Avignon (Gard)
Tel. 90.25.84.01 - Fax 90.25.80.06 - M. and Mme Gounaud

Open March – Nov. **Rooms** 19 with telephone, bath or shower, WC (11 with TV). **Price** double 220-400F. **Meals** breakfast 30-34F, served 0700-1000; no restaurant. **Credit cards** accepted. **Pets** dogs allowed. **Nearby** "the Crowning of the Virgin" by Enguerand Quarton in the Musée Municipal in Villeneuve, Carthusain monastery of the Val-de-Bénédiction, fort Saint-André in Villeneuve, chapel of Notre-Dame-de-Belvezet, Avignon, 18-hole Châteaublanc-les-Plans golf course at Avignon.

The Hôtel de l'Atelier is in Villeneuve-lès-Avignon, a small town gathered at the foot of the impassive fort Saint-André which faces Avignon across the Rhône. Avignon was once the city of the popes, Villeneuve was home to the cardinals. Outwardly a quiet village house, the building has many hidden charms: a sequence of flowery patios where fig-trees provide welcome shade, a roof terrace – the perfect setting for a cup of tea, or an evening drink – and delightful bedrooms. The latter have all been carefully and individually designed, and their shape and size vary, as do the pieces of period furniture they contain. Our favourite is room 42 on the top floor: it has all the character of attic rooms (with air-conditioning!), and if you stand on the little platform you can see Avignon from it through the high window. The hotel doesn't have a restaurant of its own but Avignon is just on the doorstep and in Villeneuve itself there are some good and very affordable eating places. The drawback is a somewhat inattentive welcome.

How to get there *(Map 33): 3km west of Avignon via N100; if on A6, Avignon-Nord exit.*

Mas de Couran★★

Route de Fréjorgues
34970 Lattes (Hérault)
Tel. 67,65.57.57 – Fax 67.65.37.56 – M. Cohuau

Open all year. **Rooms** 18 with telephone, bath or shower, WC, TV and minibar. **Price** single 335-355F, double 380-400F, suite 400-520F. **Meals** breakfast 35F, served 0730-1000; half board 720F, full board 920F (2 pers.) **Credit cards** Visa, Amex, Diners. **Pets** dogs allowed (+40F). **Facilities** parking. **Nearby** Fabre museum in Montpellier, châteaux of Castries, Flaugergues and la Moyère, 9-hole Coulondres golf course at Montpellier. **Restaurant** service 1200-1400, 1930-2130 (closed Sunday evenings); menus 99-225F, also à la carte; specialities: feuilleté de Saint-Jacques au curry, magret de canard aux figues, foie gras de canard maison.

First of all, do not be put off by the unnattractive surroundings, for once you are at the hotel – blue with wisteria in season – you will be rewarded for your perseverance. The rooms are comfortable and most have pretty floral fabrics. We recommend No 4 with its vast private terrace. The attic bedrooms are beamed, but avoid these rooms in summer and go instead for the ground floor rooms which are cooler and open directly into the garden. The dining room and lounge have that cosy feel that a good family pension had in former times. Outside, the lawn, shaded by some old pines, ends in a lovely swimming pool; unfortunately the buffet served there at lunchtime in summer attracts a large number of visitors, who can intrude.

How to get there *(Map 32): 5km south of Montpellier via D986 towards Palavas-les-Flots.*

Château de Madières★★★

Madières
34190 Ganges (Hérault)
Tel. 67.73.84.03 – Fax 67.73.55.71 – M. and Mme Brucy

Open 3 Apr – 14 Nov. **Rooms** 10 with telephone, bath or shower, WC, TV and minibar. **Price** double 505-850F, suite 850-975F. **Meals** breakfast 68F, served 0830-1030; half board 530-695F (per pers., 3 days min.) **Credit cards** accepted. **Pets** dogs allowed (extra charge). **Facilities** swimming pool, fitness room, parking. **Nearby** Brissac, gorges of the river Vis, cirque de Navacelles, cave of the Demoiselles, chapel of Saint-Etienne-d'Essensac, church of Saint-Guilhem-le-Désert. **Restaurant** service 1230-1400, 1930-2100; menus 180-335F, also à la carte; specialities: truite au picpoul, magret de canard flambé.

Set on the southern slopes of the Cévennes among the gorges of the river Vis, this 14th-century fortified house juts out like a balcony on the side of the mountain, only 40 minutes away from the cirque de Navacelles. The Château has been carefully restored to become a hotel of great character. The bedrooms are luxuriously equipped and look out onto a patio. They are extremely comfortable and pleasant, and their individual decoration shows great attention to detail. The elegant lounge still has a Renaissance fireplace and leads out onto a terrace overlooking the river and the village. There are two dining-rooms (one with panoramic views) to choose from to enjoy Mme Brucy's excellent cooking. In summer, meals can be served by the swimming-pool which has just been completed on a terrace below the hotel.

How to get there *(Map 32): 60km north west of Montpellier via D986 towards Le Vigan to Ganges, then D25 towards the cirque de Navacelles.*

Relais Chantovent

34210 Minerve (Hérault)
Tel. 68.91.14.18
Mme Evenou

Open 15 March – 1 Jan (closed Sunday evenings and Mondays in low season). **Rooms** 7 with shower (1 with bath) and WC. **Price** single 180F, double 220F. **Meals** breakfast 28F, served 0800-1000; half board 280F, full board 320F (per pers., 3 days min.) **Credit cards** Visa, Eurocard, Access. **Pets** on dogs allowed. **Nearby** Lagrasse, château de Gaussan, abbey of Fontfroide, African reserve of Sigean, gorges of the Tarn. **Restaurant** service 1230-1400, 1930-2100; menus 90-210F; specialities: croustillant aux deux saumons sur coulis de poivrons doux.

Minerve is a village high up between the gorges of the rivers Cesse and Briand, and the hotel buildings are scattered in its narrow alleys. The annexe is a tastefully restored old village house next to the post-office cum library and the rooms in it are not remotely second-best to the ones in the main building. Two of them share a terrace, and the one in the attic has kept its original layout, with the bathroom more or less in the room; all have charm and character. Those facing the restaurant have just been fully refurbished: fabrics and contemporary lithographs create a cheerful atmosphere, and the bathrooms have been refitted. The restaurant serves good, simple, local specialities. The village and its surroundings are splendid and the welcome is very friendly.

How to get there *(Map 31): 45km north west of Carcassonne via N113 and D160 to Homps, then D910 to Olonzac and D10 to Minerve (northward).*

Domaine de Rieumege★★★

Route de Saint-Pons
34390 Olargues (Hérault)
Tel. 67.97.73.99 - Fax 67.97.78.52 - M. Sylva

Open 1 Apr. – 1 Nov. **Rooms** 14 with telephone, bath or shower (12 with WC). **Price** single 278-354F, double 358-465F, suite 731-849F. **Meals** breakfast (buffet) 55F, served 0830-1000; half board 354-471F, full board 449-566F (per pers., 2 days min.) **Credit cards** Visa, Eurocard, MasterCard. **Pets** dogs allowed (+35F). **Facilities** swimming pool, tennis, parking. **Nearby** abbey of Fontcaude, mountains of l'Espinouse, cave of la Devèze. **Restaurant** service 1200-1400, 1900-2130; menus 79-195F, also à la carte; specialities: soufflé de perche au coulis d'écrevisses, poêlée de coquillages, pavé de bœuf en croûte.

The mountains of the Haut–Languedoc provide an impressive backdrop for the Domaine de Rieumege, a pleasant place to stay in an area where good hotels are few and far between. This is an old 17th-century house which has been restored by the owners with great taste and a feeling for comfort. The terraces and lounges have been improved this year. The interior decoration skilfully combines country style antiques with more modern pieces of furniture, exposed stonework with well-chosen colours on the walls. Despite the nearby road the hotel is quiet. The Domaine now also features a farmhouse large enough to accommodate four to eight people, complete with private swimming-pool and tropical garden, which can be rented on a half-board basis.

How to get there (Map 31): 50km north west of Béziers via D14, then D908 towards Olargues; it's 3km before Olargues in the Saint-Pons-de-Thomières direction.

Le Sanglier★★★

Domaine de Cantourras
Saint-Jean-de-la-Blaquière - 34700 Lodève (Hérault)
Tel. 67.44.70.51 - Mme Plazanet et M. Lormier

Open 15 March – 1 Nov. **Rooms** 10 with telephone, bath and WC. **Price** double 330-370F. **Meals** breakfast 40F, served 0800-1000; half board 350-400F, full board 390-460F (per pers., 3 days min.) **Credit cards** Visa. **Pets** dogs allowed. **Facilities** swimming pool, tennis, parking. **Nearby** church of Saint-Guilhem-le-Désert, cirque de Navacelles, la Couvertoirade, chapel of Gignac, Villeneuvette. **Restaurant** service 1200-1330, 1930-2030 (closed Tuesdays and Wednesday lunchtime in low season); menus 135-205F, also à la carte; specialities: coquille Saint-Jacques sur chiffonade au Noilly Prat, côtes d'agneau grillées au feu de bois et crème d'ail, cassolette d'escargots aux noisettes.

In the very heart of the Hérault, the Sanglier lies well off the beaten track and close to an extraordinary mini-canyon, all sand and red rocks, which looks as if it got lost on the way to Arizona. Formerly a shepherd's house, the building has been completely renovated. The ten bedrooms are all on the first floor – try to get one with a terrace facing the mountain. Despite their outdated seventies decor they are all pleasant and comfortable. The large dining-room is in rustic style and the tables face a big fireplace where meat is grilled on vine branches. Meals can also be served outside. The house is surrounded by a pretty terraced garden which leads down to a swimming-pool. You will be warmly welcomed by attentive hosts.

How to get there *(Map 32): 45km west of Montpellier via N109 towards Lodève to Rabieux, then D144 on the right.*

Château de Pondérach***

Route de Narbonne
34220 Saint-Pons-de-Thomières (Hérault)
Tel. 67.97.02.57 - Fax 67.97.29.75 - Mme Counotte

Open 1 Apr – 15 Oct. **Rooms** 9 with telephone, bath and WC. **Price** double 400-470F.
Meals breakfast 73F, half board 550F, full board 680F (per pers., 3 days min.) **Credit
cards** Amex, Diners, Eurocard, Visa. **Pets** dogs allowed (extra charge). **Facilities**
parking. **Nearby** regional park of the Haut-Languedoc, cave of la Devèze, mountains
of l'Espinouse. **Restaurant** service 1230-1330 and 1930-2100; menus 180-390F,
also à la carte; specialities: regional cuisine, cassoulet.

The Château de Pondérach lies within a 160–hectare estate at
the foot of the Mediterranean slopes of the Cévennes, where
palm trees, firs, beeches and olive trees blend their many shades of
green. Nothing has changed since the days when it was a private
residence and that accounts for its intimate atmosphere. There are
delightful bedrooms in the main building and the annexe, the latter
having a flowery terrace. Attentive welcome and service.

How to get there *(Map 31): 51km north west of Béziers via N112.*

Manoir de Montesquiou★★★

48210 La Malène (Lozère)
Tel. 66.48.51.12 - Fax 66.48.50.47
M. and Mme Guillenet

Open 1 Apr – end Oct. **Rooms** 12 with telephone, bath or shower, WC (5 with TV).
Price double 390-520F, suite 720F. **Meals** breakfast 50F, served 0800-1000; half
board 415-580F (per pers.) **Credit cards** Visa, Diners. **Pets** dogs allowed (+35F).
Facilities parking. **Nearby** gorges of the Tarn, gorge of the Jonte-du-Rozier at Les
Vanels, cave of Dargilan, from La Malène excursions to the Point Sublime (viewpoint)
and to Les Hourtous rock. **Restaurant** service 1200-1400 and 1930-2100; menus
170-265F, also à la carte; specialities: poire à la poitrine fumée sur son croûton doré
au bleu des causses, fondant au chocolat.

This 15th- and 16th-century manor set in the marvellous gorges
of the Tarn is a splendid building with stonework of a lovely
colour. On the ground floor a vaulted hall has been turned into a
dining-room. Its walls are whitewashed and unadorned, yet it
conveys an impression of extreme refinement. At the far end, guests
can relax or watch television in the hotel's games-room. The
bedrooms are furnished with antiques and combine period charm
with modern comfort. The bedroom named 'du seigneur' is a truly
sumptuous affair with a four-poster bed. The 'Regency' bedroom
is more intimate and the nicest of the cheaper rooms. The food is
excellent and quite inexpensive considering its quality.

*How to get there (Map 32): 41km south east of Mende via N88 and D986
to Sainte-Enimie, then D907 bis to La Malène via the gorges of the Tarn.*

Château d'Ayres***

48150 Meyrueis (Lozère)
Tel. 66.45.60.10 – Fax 66.45.62.26
M. de Montjou

Open 1 Apr – 15 Nov. **Rooms** 26 with telephone, bath or shower, WC and TV (13 with minibar). **Price** double 350-800F, suite 800F. **Meals** breakfast 55F; half board 375-550F, full board 480-655F (per pers.) **Credit cards** Amex, Diners, Visa. **Pets** dogs allowed (+45F). **Facilities** swimming pool, tennis, parking. **Nearby** gorges of the Tarn, gorge of the Jonte de Rozier at les Vanels, cave of Dargilan, Cévennes national park. **Restaurant** service 1230-1345, 1930-2200; menus 140-300F, also à la carte; specialities: feuilleté aux deux saumons, émincé de pigeonneau rôti au choux et au foie gras.

The Château d'Ayres has not been spared the many vicissitudes of history. Rebuilt in the 18th century by the Nogaret family, it was later sold and turned into a hotel. But the heiress of the estate, a Miss Roussel, married one of the Nogarets' cousins, thus bringing the castle back into the family. One can easily understand why the family is so attached to it. Set amidst 5 hectares of beautiful parkland planted with age-old oaks and gigantic sequoias, it is lovely. The lounges, bedrooms and library are decorated with fine period furniture and attractive paintings. Exquisite taste is in evidence throughout the house, including the lovely dining room which is rather more rustic in style. This is a special place.

How to get there (*Map 32*): *55km south of Mende via N88, and D986 to Meyrueis via Sainte-Enimie.*

Hôtel Chantoiseau★★★

rue Chantoiseau
Vialas – 48220 Le Pont-de-Montvert (Lozère)
Tel. 66.41.00.02 – Fax 66.41.04.34 – M. Pagès

Open 10 Apr – 11 Nov (closed Tuesday evenings and Wednesdays). **Rooms** 15 with bath or shower, WC, TV and minibar. **Price** single and double 400-420F. **Meals** breakfast 50F, served 0800-0930; half board 360F, full board 400F (per pers., 3 days min.) **Credit cards** accepted. **Pets** dogs not allowed. **Facilities** swimming pool, parking. **Nearby** ridgeway to Alès via Portes; La Garde, Guérin, Florac. **Restaurant** service 1200-1330, 1900-2030; menus 70-670F, also à la carte; specialities: ravioles au pélardon, carré d'agneau, suprême au chocolat.

The Chantoiseau is one of the best hotels in the region. This former 17th- century coaching inn, set 600 metres up on the steep Mediterranean slopes of the Cévennes, provides a sunny stopping place on the doorstep of the Cévennes national park. The bedrooms are comfortable and look out onto peaceful valleys and mountains. The dining room retains the austere character of houses in the area: walls built in large slabs of granite, deep embrasures, the warm presence of wood. It commands beautiful views over the valley. The menu features specialities of the Cévennes only, prepared by the owner whose talent has earned wide recognition, and who has chosen the finest wines to accompany them. The wine list has a lot to offer, ranging from modest but charming 'vins de pays' to great vintages.

How to get there *(Map 32): 60km south east of Mende via N88 and N106, just before Florac turn left on D998 to Pont-de-Montvert.*

La Terrasse au Soleil****

Route de Fontfrède
66400 Céret (Pyrénées-Orientales)
Tel. 68.87.01.94 - Fax 68.87.39.24 - Mme Leveillé-Nizerolle

Open 6 March – 2 Jan. **Rooms** 27 with telephone, bath, WC, TV and minibar. **Price** single 495F, double 595-695F, suite 995-1095F. **Meals** breakfast 60F, served 0800-1100; half board 530-580F, full board 630-680F. **Credit cards** Eurocard, MasterCard, Visa. **Pets** dogs allowed. **Facilities** heated swimming pool, tennis, golf practice, parking. **Nearby** museum of modern art and church of Saint-Pierre in Céret, Cabestany, Prats-de-Mollo, château de Quéribus, Quilhac and the château de Peyrepertuse, Perpignan, 27-hole Saint-Cyprien golf course. **Restaurant** service 1200-1430, 1930-2130; menus 120-350F, also à la carte; specialities: foie gras au Banyuls, magret de canard aux cerises, saumon aux morilles.

La Terrasse au Soleil is an old farmhouse which has been completely restored. It occupies an enviable position crowning the village among cherry trees. The bedrooms have all the modern comforts. The largest and best are the upstairs ones with a terrace and views of the mountains. The restaurant's reputation is firmly established and the cuisine is as tempting as ever. In good weather meals can be served in the garden. A heated swimming-pool and tennis court add to the many assets of this hotel, where a friendly and informal atmosphere encourages guests to relax. An excellent place.

How to get there *(Map 31): 31km south west of Perpignan via A9, Le Boulou exit, then D115 towards Céret; it's 2km from the centre of the village via D13f in the Fontfrède direction.*

Le Mas Trilles***
66400 Céret-Reynès (Pyrénées-Orientales)
Tel. 68.87.38.37 - Fax 68.87.42.62
M. and Mme Bukk

Open Easter-end Oct. **Rooms** 12 with telephone, bath, WC and TV. **Price** double 370-850F. **Meals** breakfast 55F, served 0830-1030; half board 380-620F. **Credit cards** MasterCard, Visa. **Pets** dogs allowed (extra charge). **Facilities** swimming pool, parking. **Nearby** museum of modern art and church of Saint-Pierre in Céret, Cabestany, Prats-de-Mollo, château de Quéribus, Quilhac and the château de Peyrepertuse, Perpignan, 27-hole Saint-Cyprien golf course. **Restaurant** service 1930-2100; table d'hôte dinner 130-180F.

The Mas Trilles is a very ancient house surrounded by a garden with fruit trees. From the swimming-pool, when there is a lot of traffic and the wind is blowing in the wrong direction the rumble of cars on the road above the hotel can sometimes be heard. The bedrooms, however, are silent at all times. Inside, the house has been fully refurbished and decorated with exquisite taste: there are terracotta floors, the walls in some rooms have been sponge painted and in others whitewashed, and each fabric has been carefully chosen by Madame Bukk to blend in with, and round off, the decor. The bedrooms have very nice bathrooms and many of them also have a private terrace where breakfast (which always includes fresh fruit) can be served. Dinner (for residents only) is served in a charming dining-room. A friendly welcome adds to the pleasant homely atmosphere that prevails. This is a fine and comfortable hotel.

How to get there *(Map 31): 31km south west of Perpignan via A9, Le Boulou exit, then D115 towards Céret; it's 3km from the centre, in Amélie-les-Bains direction.*

Hôtel Casa Païral★★★

impasse des Palmiers
66190 Collioure (Pyrénées-Orientales)
Tel. 68.82.05.81 - Fax 68.82.52.10 - Mmes De Bon et Lormand

Open 3 Apr – 31 Oct. **Rooms** 27 with air-conditioning, telephone, bath or shower, WC, TV and minibar. **Price** single 300-600F, double 350-680F, suite 650-850F. **Meals** breakfast 40F. No restaurant. **Credit cards** Visa, Eurocard, MasterCard, Amex. **Pets** dos allowed (+30F). **Facilities** swimming pool, parking (+30F). **Nearby** the Vermeille coast between Argelès-sur-Mer and Cerbère, balcon de Madeloc, mountain road between Collioure and Banyuls, château de Salses, museum of modern art in Céret, 27-hole Saint-Cyprien golf course.

An absolute gem. Tucked away in a small blind alley in the centre of Collioure, Casa Païral provides peace and quiet just minutes from the beaches, restaurants and *cafés*. It is a lavish town house built in the 19th century in an elaborate Moorish style. Wrought ironwork, marble and ceramics are essential features of the decorative theme. The patio has a palm-tree, a hundred-year-old magnolia and lush vegetation. The bedrooms are all comfortable, but those in the main building have more character. The breakfast room and the lounges, which look out into the walled garden with its swimming-pool, are also extremely pleasant. The hotel is very much in demand and it is essential to book.

How to get there *(Map 31) 26km south east of Perpignan via N114.*

Auberge L'Atalaya★★★

Llo - 66800 Saillagouse (Pyrénées-Orientales)
Tel. 68.04.70.04 - Fax 68.04.01.29
M. and Mme Toussaint

Open 20 Dec – 5 Nov. **Rooms** 13 with telephone, bath or shower, WC, TV and minibar.
Price single 480F, double 560F, suite 640F. **Meals** breakfast 50F, served 0730-1030;
half board 435-515F, full board 820-900F (per pers., 3 days min.) **Credit cards** Eurocard,
MasterCard, Visa. **Pets** dogs allowed in the bedrooms. **Facilities** swimming pool,
solarium, parking. **Nearby** Odeillo solar furnace, lake of Les Buoillouses north of Mont-
Louis, gorges of the river Aude, château de Quérigut, 18-hole Real Club de Cerdana golf
course, 9-hole golf course at Font-Romeu. **Restaurant** service 1230-1430, 1930-2130
(closed Mondays and Tuesday lunchtimes in low season); menus 143-370F, also à la
carte; specialities: mesclun de homard et gésiers grillés, filet mignon de biche sauce
foie gras.

L lo is the most typical pastoral village of the Cerdagne region on
the border between Andorra and Spain, which can be glimpsed
from some of the bedrooms. Clustered around its watchtower – called
an 'atalaya' in old Castilian – and the ruins of its 11th-century castle,
the village stands above the gorges of the river Sègre. Needless to say,
its location is one of the memorable features of the Auberge. But the
building itself is well worth the stay. The house has been tastefully
decorated throughout and the bedrooms are comfortable and
attractive. In summer, meals are served outside on a terrace among
geraniums and hollyhocks, and there is now also a swimming-pool.
In winter, the closest ski stations are Eyne and Err-Puigmal, and there
are at least eight others within easy reach. The food is good.

How to get there *(Map 31): 90km west of Perpignan via N116 to Saillagouse,
then D33.*

Lou Raballou

66210 Mont-Louis (Pyrénées-Orientales)
Tel. 68.04.23.26
M. and Mme Duval

Open June – Oct (closed Wednesdays in Sept). **Rooms** 14 with bath or shower (8 with WC). **Price** double 150-300F. **Meals** breakfast 30F; half board 200-240F, full board 240-270F (per pers., 3 days min.) **Credit cards** Visa. **Pets** small dogs allowed. **Nearby** Romanesque church of Planès, lake of Les Bouillouses, gorges of the river Aude, château de Quérigut, pass of Saint-Georges. **Restaurant** service 1230-1300 and 1930-2000; menus 100-190F, also à la carte; Catalan cooking.

Louis XIV was the king of France when Madame Duval's ancestor left his native Bigorre region to work on one of Vauban's projects as a carpenter. The splendid fortifications in Mont-Louis are still standing, and the carpenter's craftsmanship is still in evidence... You will find this auberge amongst the village houses. Its façade doesn't stand out, but as soon as you walk through the door you will feel at ease. Inside, the decor is rustic in style, cosy and authentic. Some of the bedrooms are more comfortable than others, so we recommend rooms 3, 18, 19, 20, 21, which Christiane Duval has lovingly fitted out with antique furniture, extremely comfortable beds and pleasant bathrooms. But Lou Raballou is also renowned for its gourmet cuisine. Pierre Duval does the cooking. The menu features excellent traditional dishes, prepared with only the freshest of products according to ancient recipes. In the autumn, Pierre will take you mushrooming, and then serve the mushrooms in some delicious form at mealtimes. This is a charming, friendly and unpretentious inn.

How to get there (Map 31): 10km east of Font-Romeu via N116 (in the old part of the town).

Château de Camon
09500 Camon (Ariège)
Tel. 61.68.28.28 - Fax 61.68.81.56
M. du Pont

Open March – Nov. **Rooms** 7 with bath or shower and WC. **Price** single and double 500-1000F, suite 1500F. **Meals** breakfast incl. **Credit cards** accepted. **Pets** dogs allowed. **Facilities** swimming pool, parking. **Nearby** Mirepoix, châteaux of Lagarde, Caudeval, Montségur and Foix. **Restaurant** table d'hôtes dinner on reservation; menu 300F.

This château lies in the beautiful region of Ariège, on the wooded road into Spain which is worth a detour. At the château you are treated more like a guest than a customer. Château Camon has been in the family of M. du Pont for two centuries – "Only two hundred years," he says as if to apologise for so recent an acquisition. The château is closed to the public unless, of course, you are a guest, but there is an abbey next to it which can be visited; they both overlook the village below. A terraced garden with many species and colours of plants descends to the lawn where there is a swimming pool. The bedrooms have been admirably decorated by the owner, who is a man of taste and skill (he is an interior designer). They have antique and family furniture and beautiful proportions. You will be delighted with every aspect of this château, even with the corridors which lead to your room!

How to get there *(Map 31): 59km south west of Carcassonne via D119 to Mirepoix, then D7 towards Chalabre. If on A61, Castelnaudary exit.*

Château de Castelpers★★

Castelpers - 12170 Ledergues (Aveyron)
Tel. 65.69.22.61 - Fax 65.69.25.31 - Mme Tapié de Celeyran

Open 1 Apr – 1 Oct. **Rooms** 9 with telephone, bath or shower (8 with WC, 6 with TV).
Price single 240F, double 370-455F, suite 500F. **Meals** breakfast 40F, served 0800-
0930; half board 225-340F, full board 290-405F (per pers., 3 days min.) **Credit cards**
Amex, Eurocard, MasterCard, Visa. **Pets** dogs allowed (+20F). **Facilities** parking.
Nearby châteaux of Le Bosc and Taurines, Sauveterre, viaduct and valley of Le Viau,
lakes of Pareloup, 18-hole golf course at Albi. **Restaurant** service 1230-1400, 1930-
2100 (closed Tuesdays except for residents); menus 130-260F, also à la carte;
specialities: confit aux ceps, beignets au roquefort, faux-filet aux morilles, foie gras
poêlée au jus de truffes.

The Château de Castelpers is tucked away in a verdant corner
of Rouergue, in the peaceful Viaur valley, a region where inns
are scarce. The rusic dry-stone building is adjoining another with
Gothic arches where the main lounge has a ceiling resembling a
ship's hull. The terrace overlooks a large park with centuries-old
trees bordered by a trout stream. Handsome old furniture gives
character to the dining room, the lounge and the very comfortable
bedrooms. Room 5 has leaded windows and a canopied bed; the
others are more modern, like number 9 and its neighbour on the
ground floor, which open onto the garden.

How to get there *(Map 31): 40km from Rodez and Albi via N88, then
take D80 at 'Les Peyronnies', 3km from Nancelle-Gare.*

Château de Creissels★★

Creissels - 12100 Millau (Aveyron)
Tel. 65.60.16.59 - Fax 65.61.24.63
Mme Austruy

Open all year except Jan. **Rooms** 33 (2 for disabled persons) with telephone, of which 21 with bath, 7 with shower, 26 with WC, 14 with TV. **Price** single 160F, double 275-350F. **Meals** breakfast 35F, served 0800-1000; half board 240-310F, full board 340-410F (per pers., 3 days min.) **Credit cards** accepted. **Pets** dogs allowed. **Facilities** parking. **Nearby** Millau, Montpellier-le-Vieux, Causses du Larzac (from Millau to Caylar), gorges of the Tarn, Roquefort cellars. **Restaurant** service 1200-1330, 1930-2130 (closed Tuesdays in low season); menus 103-187F, also à la carte; specialities: truites aux gésiers et jambon, tourte au roquefort, agneau des Causses.

Within easy reach of Millau, in the old village of Creissels, the Château de Creissels provides an ideal stopping place for travellers. The origins of this ancient viscountcy can be traced back to the 11th century, and those of the château itself to the 12th. Although the château and its grounds now lie in a somewhat urban setting, once inside the building all is peace and quiet. Traces of the long history of the place can be seen everywhere, as in the vast "Bishop's bedchamber', remarkable for its perfectly preserved 19th-century character. But all the bedrooms are charming and comfortable, and for once we would almost advise taking the rooms with bathrooms and lavatories on the landing, for they are as just as beautifully decorated as those with en suite bathrooms. The annexe also has some very nice rooms (18, 19, 30 and 31). In the château our favourites are 4, 7 and 14 (the bishop's room). More care could be taken with the cooking.

How to get there *(Map 31): 70km south east of Rodez via D911; 3km south of Millau, road to Saint-Affrique.*

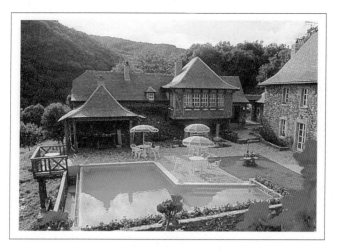

Hôtel Longcol★★★

La Fouillade
12270 Najac (Aveyron)
Tel. 65.29.63.36 - Fax 65.29.64.28 - Famille Luyckx

Open all year (closed Tuesday in low season). **Rooms** 15 with telephone, bath or shower, WC, TV and minibar. **Price** double 450-700F. **Meals** breakfast 50F, served 0730-1030; half board 490-565F, full board 655-730F (per pers., 3 days min.) **Credit cards** Amex, MasterCard, Visa. **Pets** dogs allowed. **Facilities** swimming pool, tennis, fishing, parking. **Nearby** château de Najac, gorges of the Aveyron; Carthusian monastry, chapel des Pénitents noirs and Place des Cornières in Villefranche-de-Rouergue. **Restaurant** service lunchtime residents only, 1945-2130; menus 120-210F, also à la carte; specialities: seasonal cuisine, home-made foie gras, salade Longcol.

This old Rouergue country house is like a miniature village sitting on a wild mountain pass with the Aveyron flowing below. Recently restored and decorated in fine taste, each room is furnished with beautiful oriental objects, antique rugs and furniture and old studded doors – all elegantly arranged, comfortable and not too overwhelming. The lounge and billiard room are particularly gracious, a corner fireplace and large leather armchairs creating a convivial atmosphere. The bedrooms are all different, bright and cheerful. All the rooms have views of either the swimming pool or the valley. In summer you can fish in the river that runs through the land and lunch can be taken by the pool, looking out over the beautiful countryside.

How to get there (Map 31): *19km south of Villefranche-de-Rouergue via D922, at 'La Fouillade'.*

L'Oustal del Barry**

Place du Bourg
12270 Najac (Aveyron)
Tel. 65.29.74.32 - Fax 65.29.75.32 - M. and Mme Miquel

Open Apr – Oct (closed Monday, except public holidays, from April – June and Oct).
Rooms 21 with telephone, bath or shower, WC and TV. **Price** single 226-252F, double
270-420F. **Meals** breakfast 44F, served 0800-1030; half board 285-316F, full board
345-362F (per pers., 2 days min.) **Credit cards** Amex, Visa. **Pets** dogs allowed.
Facilities parking. **Nearby** château de Najac, gorges of the Aveyron; Carthusian
monastery, chapel des Pénitents noirs and Place des Cornières in Villefranche-de-
Rouergue. **Restaurant** service 1230-1400, 1930-2100; menus 95-320F, also à la
carte.

Five generations of the same family have looked after the Oustal
del Barry, which has all the charms of a traditional French hotel.
On the whole the bedrooms are rustic but with a curious mixture
of other styles, principally Art Deco. The dining room has a
panoramic view of the flowers and greenery of the six-hectare
grounds. A vegetable garden has been cultivated by M. and Mme
Miguel where they grow several types of herbs used in the excellent
cuisine, which also incorporates other local produce. The kindness
of your hosts will make you sad to leave this simple and charming
hotel. It is noteworthy that the tarif of the hotel includes free
admission to the swimming pool at Najae, one hour of tennis a
day and the use of bicycles.

How to get there *(Map 31): 24km south of Villefranche-de-Rouergue via*
D922, then D39.

Hostellerie Les Magnolias

12550 Plaisance (Aveyron)
Tel. 65.99.77.34 – Fax 65.99.70.57
M. Roussel

Open 15 March – 15 Nov. **Rooms** 6 with telephone, bath, WC and TV. **Price** single and double 200-300F. **Meals** breakfast 35-55F; half board 200-260F, full board 260-330F (per pers.) **Credit cards** Amex, Eurocard, MasterCard, Visa. **Pets** dogs allowed (+25F). **Nearby** churches in Plaisance, abbey of Sylvanes, château du Bosc, Toulouse-Lautrec museum in Albi, 18-hole golf course at Albi. **Restaurant** service 1215-1400, 2000-2130; menus 68-300F, also à la carte; cuisine based on traditional local products.

This is one of the best places in this guide. A beautiful 14th-century dwelling, once owned by Paul Valéry's brother, it will enchant you at first glance. Carefully chosen, delicate decor has transformed this village house into a hotel with an intimate character. The cooking here is a labour of love. M. Roussel talks with enthusiastic fervour about the ingredients that go into the sauces and succulent dishes which he will serve to you. All the produce is local, fresh and home-made. It is with the same enthusiasm that he has collected the materials and furnishings with which he has decorated and restored his hotel. It is a place where people will go to great pains to ensure that you are pleased. At the top of the lovely staircase are the delightful bedrooms, all renovated to further enhance the charm and comfort of this hotel.

How to get there *(Map 31): 42km east of Albi via D999 to Saint-Sernin-sur-Rance, then D33.*

Hôtel du Midi-Papillon★★

12230 Saint-Jean-du-Bruel (Aveyron)
Tel. 65.62.26.04 - Fax 65.62.12.97
M. and Mme Papillon

Open Palm Sunday – 11 Nov. **Rooms** 19 with telephone, of which 11 with bath, 3 with shower, 17 with WC. **Price** single 73-93F, double 90-182F. **Meals** breakfast 21F, served 0800-1000; half board 152-206F, full board 182-236F (per pers., 3 days min.) **Credit cards** Eurocard, MasterCard, Visa. **Pets** dogs allowed. **Facilities** swimming pool. **Nearby** Millau belfry, Montpellier-le-Vieux, gorges of the Tarn. **Restaurant** service 1230-1400, 1930-2130; menus 67-183F, also à la carte; specialities: soufflé à l'artichaut et saumon fumé, pigeon en cocotte garni de cèpes, tarte chaude aux pommes, confiture de lait.

Saint-Jean-du-Bruel is a good stopping place in the gorges of the Dourbie on the road to Mont Aigoual, the highest point in the Cévennes. The hotel is an old coaching inn run by the same family for four generations. Well situated on an outcrop above the river it offers an outstanding picture-postcard view of the old houses of the village and an old stone bridge. This hotel has all the qualities of a good French inn: comfort and good taste in the house, good food and a friendly atmosphere. Our favourite rooms were numbers 3, 4 & 5 which have terraces overlooking the river; there are also larger rooms ideal for families.

How to get there *(Map 32): 99km north west of Montpellier via N109 and N9 in Le Caylar direction to La Cavalerie, then D999 (it's at the beginning of the village).*

Hôtel des Trois Lys★★★

38, rue Gambetta
32100 Condom (Gers)
Tel. 62.28.33.33 - Fax 62.28.41.85 - Mme Manet

Open all year. **Rooms** 10 with telephone, bath or shower, WC and TV. **Price** single 280F, double 380-550F. **Meals** breakfast 38F, served 0730-1030. No restaurant. **Credit cards** Amex, Visa, MasterCard, Eurocard. **Pets** dogs allowed. **Facilities** swimming pool, parking. **Nearby** Armagnac museum in Condom, châteaux, churches and bastides of Armagnac; Flaran, Larresingle, Fourcès, Tillac, Bassoues, Lavarders, collegiate church of La Romieu; 9-hole Guinlet golf course in Eauze.

When they converted this 18th-century manor house into a hotel M. and Mme Manet followed their own taste for the decoration and furnishings, so everything has been done to a very high standard. The hotel has ten rooms each one decorated in co-ordinated colours and furnished with antiques or excellent reproductions finished in splendid fabrics. The rooms are big, sometimes very big, and some of them retain their wood panelling, and Louis XV alcoves, whilst double doors, thick carpeting and double glazing ensure absolute silence. The bathrooms are also good: gleaming taps, coloured tiles and low-tension lighting. For breakfast you descend a monumental stone staircase to the ground floor. Pleasingly decorated in pastel tones, the dining room and the lounge take you through to the back of the house where a swimming pool tempts you to plunge into its refreshing depths, especially in the height of summer. Need we say more?

How to get there *(Map 30): 40km south west of Agen.*

Hôtel de Bastard★★

Rue Lagrange
32700 Lectoure (Gers)
Tel. 62.68.82.44 - Fax 62.68.76.81 - M. Arnaud

Open 1 March – 7 Jan. **Rooms** 29 with telephone, bath or shower, WC and TV. **Price** single 180-265F, double 210-310F. **Meals** breakfast 32-38F; half board 260-310F (per pers., 3 days min.) **Credit cards** Visa, Amex, Diners, Eurocard. **Pets** dogs allowed (+15F). **Facilities** swimming pool, parking. **Nearby** château de Gramont, châteaux, churches and bastides of Armagnac, Flaran, Larresingle, Fourcès, Tillac, Bassoues, Lavarders, collegiate church of La Romieu; 9-hole Fleurance golf course. **Restaurant** service 1215-1330, 1930-2130 (closed Friday, Saturday lunchtime and Sunday evening 1 Oct – 30 Apr); menus 80-270F, also à la carte; specialities: foie frais, carpaccio de magret.

Lectoure is a magnificent small fortified town overlooking the undulating countryside of the Gers. Setting out to explore the narrow streets lined with old houses you will come across a large carved stone gateway which is the entrance to this 18th-century house. On the other side a large paved terrace with a swimming pool overlooks the last rooftops of the village and then the open countryside. This is the view from the reception rooms. They are beautifully decorated, with pretty fabrics, high ceilings and handsome furniture in the 18th-century style. You may be surprised by the bedrooms; they are small but comfortable and given the personal touch by attractive coloured fabrics. Choose a room on the first floor and make sure that the hotel is not doing a wedding if it is a weekend. Bearing all this in mind the Hôtel de Bastard is a charming place to stay.

How to get there *(Map 30): 35km north of Auch via N21.*

Le Demeure d'en Jourdou★★

31480 Cadours (Haute–Garonne)
Tel. 61.85.77.77
M. Lachambre

Open all year. **Rooms** 7 with telephone, bath or shower, WC, TV and minibar. **Price** single 250-390F, double 280-420F. **Meals** breakfast 37F, served 0800-1000; half board 380-500F, full board 480-600F (per pers., 3 days min.) **Credit cards** Amex, Visa. **Pets** dogs allowed. **Facilities** parking. **Nearby** châteaux of Laréole, Larra and Launac, abbey of Sainte-Marie-du-Désert, bastide of Grenade, 9-hole Las Martines golf course. **Restaurant** service 1200-1400, 1930-2130; menus 77-377F, also à la carte; specialities: salade périgourdine, cratère d'escargots à la crème d'ail doux, noix de Saint-Jacques au safran, soufflé glacé à l'armagnac.

This elegant pink brick house is a little set back from the road surrounded by beautiful countryside and fields as far as the eye can see. A skilful restoration has preserved its old world charm. The large bedrooms on the first floor retain their original flooring and fine Louis XIV doors. They are comfortable, the furnishings tasteful and the bathrooms well appointed. The other bedrooms, smaller but well done, are in the attic. Soft blue carpet and cane furniture lend these rooms an intimate charm. In the dining room, with its pastel fabrics and dark blue walls, an elegant table setting awaits. The cooking is in keeping with the rest of the hotel, refined and creative but also classical. Relaxed and pleasant welcome.

How to get there (Map 30): 39km west of Toulouse via D1.

Auberge du Poids Public★★★

31540 Saint-Félix-Lauragais (Haute-Garonne)
Tel. 61.83.00.20 - Fax 61.83.86.21
M. Taffarello

Open all year. **Rooms** 13 with telephone, bath or shower, WC, TV and minibar. **Price** double 240-290F. **Meals** breakfast 38F, served 0800-1000; half board 250-300F (per pers.) **Credit cards** Amex, Visa, Eurocard. **Pets** dogs allowed. **Facilities** parking. **Nearby** cathedral of Saint-Papoul, Toulouse-Lautrec museum in Albi, Toulouse, route du Pastel, Midi Canal route, 9 and 18-hole golf courses at Toulouse. **Restaurant** service 1200-1315, 1930-2115 (closed Sunday evening Oct – April); menus 125-200F, also à la carte; specialities: terrine de foie gras aux poireaux, gigotin d'agneau de lait des Pyrénées, croustillant aux fruits rouges.

Situated on the outskirts of the village, this old inn makes a pleasant stopping place. The bedrooms are fairly large and simply furnished with some antique pieces. Six of them enjoy a very fine view. On the whole they are quiet and those that look onto the street are only used if the others are full. There is a private bar-lounge. Depending on the time of year lunches and dinners are served either in the large, bright and prettily decorated dining room or in the shade of wide umbrellas on the lovely terrace. In either case the marvellous view is matched by the fine cooking, some of the best food in the region.

How to get there *(Map 31): 40km south east of Toulouse via D2 towards Revel.*

Hostellerie des 7 Molles★★★

31510 Sauveterre-de-Comminges (Haute-Garonne)
Tel. 61.88.30.87 - Fax 61.88.36.42 - M. Ferran

Open mid-March – end Oct and mid-Dec – mid-Jan. **Rooms** 19 with telephone, bath, WC, TV and minibar. **Price** single 570F, double 600-760F, suite 900-1100F. **Meals** breakfast 70F, served 0800-1100; half board 560-675F, full board 750-900F (per pers., 3 days min.) **Credit cards** accepted. **Pets** dogs allowed. **Facilities** heated swimming pool, tennis, parking. **Nearby** Saint-Bertrand-de-Comminges, Montréjeau, Gallo-Roman villa of Montmaurin; 18-hole Lannemezan golf course, 9-hole golf course in Luchon. **Restaurant** service 1200-1400, 1930-2130; menus 170-300F, also à la carte; specialities: pastis gersois de foie gras à la pomme reinette, agneau de lait des Pyrénées et sa moulinade de haricots.

The seven watermills of Sauveterre beside the Roussec were once a feature of this pretty corner of Comminges. The mills have disappeared but the millstones remain and lend their name to the hotel. The location is interesting. Above all the immediate environment is superb: meadows, vines and groves of trees surround the house. The bedrooms are spacious. The 18th-century style furniture and pale blue decor create a homely and pleasant atmosphere. There is a similar ambience in the dining room and the reception rooms. The cooking is both traditional and nouvelle, of an excellent standard and largely home made including the charcuterie (cold meats), patisserie, jams and foie gras.

How to get there *(Map 30): 74km south east of Tarbes via N117 to Saint-Gaudens, then D8 to Valentine and D9 (follow signs).*

Hôtel des Beaux-Arts★★★

1, place du Pont-Neuf
31000 Toulouse (Haute-Garonne)
Tel. 61.23.40.50 - Fax 61.22.02.27 - Mme Cazorla

Open all year. **Rooms** 20 with telephone, bath or shower, WC and TV. **Price** single and double 340-575F. **Meals** breakfast 45F, served any time. **Credit cards** accepted. **Pets** dogs allowed (+50F). **Facilities** parking. **Nearby** Saint-Sernin basilica, church of the Jacobins, Saint-Raymond and Augustinian museums, the Capitole (town hall) in Toulouse, bastide of Grenade, cathedral of Lombez, 9- and 18-hole golf courses at Toulouse. **Restaurant** room service 2000-0100.

The Hôtel des Beaux Arts stands facing the Garonne, its back to old Toulouse with its narrow brick lanes. Apart from three bedrooms which we cannot recommend, all the others have views of the river, the most charming room having a small balcony. Small but comfortable and pleasant, they are air-conditioned and insulated from the noisy street, but we advise against opening the windows. Being so close to the Beaux Arts, the corridors and rooms always have exhibitions of paintings. The decor features contemporary steel-framed furniture reminiscent of the Empire style, a pleasing combination of grey and dusky pine, and the clever use of mirrors. The overall effect is muted, sophisticated, and very modern.

How to get there (Map 30): near the Pont Neuf and next to the Beaux-Arts.

Le Relais de Saux★★★

Saux
65100 Lourdes (Hautes-Pyrénées)
Tel. 62.94.29.61 – Fax 62.42.12.64 – Mme Heres

Open all year. **Rooms** 7 with telephone, bath, WC, TV and minibar. **Price** double 500-600F. **Meals** breakfast 45F, served from 0800; full board 425-475F (per pers., 3 days min.) **Credit cards** Amex, Visa. **Pets** dogs allowed (+50F). **Facilities** parking. **Nearby** mill of Boly (home of Bernadette Soubirou) in Lourdes, Cirque de Gavarnie, 18-hole golf course at Lourdes. **Restaurant** service 1200-1400, 1900-2130; menus 140-310F, also à la carte; specialities: foie frais de canard aux poires, homard rôti aux herbes, pigeon aux choux croquants, confit de canard aux cèpes, magret.

Away from the crowds of Lourdes, Le Relais de Saux is both calm and quiet. It is an old house full of rustic charm, very pleasantly furnished and decorated by its owners. A small bar-lounge welcomes you before you dine, the cooking is of a high standard and the service attentive. If the weather permits you can also dine or enjoy an aperitif on the terrace overlooking the countryside. The cooking is regional with some specialities of the South West. The bedrooms, although not all equally comfortable, are nevertheless welcoming and full of charm.

How to get there (Map 29): 18km south of Tarbes via N21 towards Lourdes; it's 3km before Lourdes. If on A64, take Tarbes-Ouest exit.

Hôtel du Château*

46500 Alvignac (Lot)
Tel. 65.33.60.14 – Fax 65.33.69.28 – M. Darnis

Open 1 Apr – mid Nov. **Rooms** 36 with telephone, bath or shower and WC. **Price** single 150F, double 200-260F. **Meals** breakfast 25F, served 0730-0930; half board 220-240F, full board 240-290F. **Credit cards** accepted. **Pets** dogs allowed. **Facilities** parking. **Nearby** Padirac chasm, Rocamadour, Gramat (truffle market). **Restaurant** service 1200-1330, 1900-2030; menus 60-180F, also à la carte; specialities: duck, saumon à l'aneth.

Situated in a corner of the Quercy famous for its waters since the 18th century, this hotel is built on the foundations of an ancient château. The flower-decked terrace of the restaurant extends from the large dining room, and there is a small bar hung with paintings by M. Darnis' brother. A courtyard shaded by large trees ensures quiet and coolness. The bedrooms have been redecorated in pale colours. Nostalgics may yearn for the charms of yester year but the bedrooms have gained in comfort, quiet and practicality. The annexe is similarly styled but we would only recommend it as a last resort since it lacks the friendliness of the main house. Guests also have the use of extensive grounds on the other side of the road. The welcome is a warm one.

How to get there *(Map 24): 58km south of Brive-la-Gaillarde via N20 to Cressensac, then N140 and D673.*

Hôtel Les Falaises★★

Gluges
46600 Martel (Lot)
Tel. 65.37.33.59 – M. Dassiou

Open 1 March – 30 Nov. **Rooms** 14 with telephone, bath or shower and WC. **Price** single 160-200F, double 220-290F. **Meals** breakfast 35F, served 0800-1000; half board 220-250F, full board 280-350F (per pers., 3 days min.) **Credit cards** Visa. **Pets** dogs not allowed. **Facilities** parking (+30F). **Nearby** Quercy region of the Dordogne from Souillac to Saint-Céré, Rocamadour, 9-hole Mas del Teil golf course at Souillac. **Restaurant** service 1230-1400, 1930-2100; menus 100-250F, also à la carte; specialities: magret de canard au verjus et raisins confits.

At the foot of the cliffs bordering the Dordogne, here is an old residence that has been converted into a hotel. At the entrance is a little house serving as a television/reading room. A large terrace with ornamental pool separates it from the main building, and in summer meals are served here in the shade of the trees. The dining room has just been renovated; predominantly blue, its large windows open out on to the terrace. The bedrooms are comfortable and sensibly furnished, and we particularly recommend 10 and 11, both having terraces on the front of the house. So that guests may enjoy a peaceful stroll before dinner the hotel has just purchased grounds of one hectare. The beautiful location, warm welcome, excellent cooking and particularly good breakfasts are the trump cards of this family hotel.

How to get there *(Map 24): 70km south of Brive-la-Gaillarde via N140 towards Martel (on the banks of the Dordogne).*

Le Pont de L'Ouysse★★★
46200 Lacave (Lot)
Tel. 65.37.87.04 – Fax 65.32.77.41
M. and Mme Chambon

Open 1 March – 11 Nov (closed Monday in low season). **Rooms** 13 with telephone, bath, WC, TV and minibar. **Price** single 350F, double 450F, suite 750F. **Meals** breakfast 50F, served 0800-1000; half board 550F (per pers.) **Credit cards** Amex, Diners, Visa. **Pets** dogs allowed. **Facilities** parking. **Nearby** Quercy region of the Dordogne from Souillac to Saint-Céré, Rocamadour, 9-hole Mas del Teil golf course at Souillac, 9-hole Rochebois golf course at Vitrac. **Restaurant** service 1230-1400, 1930-2100; à la carte; specialities: écrevisses, foie gras, pigeon aux cèpes, poulette rôtie aux truffes.

The same family has run this hotel for 35 years. The house clings to the rock smothered in greenery. The large, light bedrooms are very comfortable, with an attractive decor based on English wallpapers and fabrics. The bathrooms are equally pleasing. The road which goes over the river and up to the hotel is a dead end, so peace and quiet are assured. The charm of this place is enhanced by its lovely terrace, shaded by a horse chestnut and a lime, where you can dine out in summer. The menu is not extensive but often changes, and the excellent cooking owes everything to the imagination and skill of M. Chambon. As for Mme Chambon, she is sure to give you a friendly welcome.

How to get there *(Map 23): 37km south of Brive-le-Gaillarde via N20 to Souillac, then D43.*

Hôtel Les Vieilles Tours★★

Lafage – 46500 Rocamadour (Lot)
Tel. 65.33.68.01 – Fax 65.33.68.59
M. and Mme Zozzoli

Open 9 Apr – 7 Nov. **Rooms** 17 with telephone, bath or shower and WC. **Price** double 210-440F. **Meals** breakfast 36-56F, served 0800-1130; half board 235-360F. **Credit cards** Eurocard, MasterCard, Visa. **Pets** dogs allowed (+25F). **Facilities** swimming pool, parking. **Nearby** old town, Francis Poulenc museum in Rocamadour, truffle market in Gramat, Padirac chasm, Lascaux caves, 9-hole Mas del Teil golf course at Souillac. **Restaurant** service 1930-2100 (at lunchtime on reservation); menus 110-250F, children 55F, also à la carte; specialities: cailles au foie gras, agneau des Causses, foie gras poêlé, truite au vin, poule au pot truffée.

This hotel is only 2 km from Rocamadour. It has been well restored using fine local stone and enjoys exceptional views and absolute peace. The reception and dining room have retained their stone walls and the tables are tastefully laid. There are bedrooms in both the old building and its modern annexe, which has been built in the local style. Pleasantly furnished, with some 19th-century pieces, the bedrooms are all different but of the same high standard of comfort, which extends to the bathrooms. M. Zozzoli is a painter, engraver and lithographer; his work is to be seen around the hotel. The menu offers first class regional dishes, changing according to season and Mme Zozzoli's creative flair.

How to get there (Map 24): 53km south of Brive-la-Gaillarde via N20 to Cressensac, then N140 and D673; 2.5km from Rocamadour, in Payrac direction.

Hostellerie Le Vert**

Le Vert – 46700 Mauroux (Lot)
Tel. 65.36.51.36
M. and Mme Philippe

Open 14 Feb – 30 Nov. **Rooms** 7 with telephone, bath or shower, WC and TV. **Price** single 200F, double 240-340F. **Meals** breakfast 35F, served 0730-1030; half board 260-310F, full board 340-390F (per pers., 3 days min.) **Credit cards** Amex, Eurocard, MasterCard, Visa. **Pets** dogs allowed (+25F). **Facilities** parking. **Nearby** cathedral of Saint-Etienne in Cahors, Cahors wine route (château de Bonaguil), valley of the Lot. **Restaurant** service 1200-1315, 1930-2030 (closed Thursdays and Friday lunchtime); menus 95-190F, also à la carte; specialties: foie gras frais aux fruits frais, salade de gésiers et langoustines, poêlée de cèpes aux petits gris.

The Hostellerie Le Vert is in an old converted farmhouse. Its modest windows, overhanging roof and the beautiful mullion window in the dining room shed a soft and gentle light on the spacious, comfortable and refined interior. A lovely terrace looks out over the surrounding countryside and it is pleasant to have breakfast here in the summer. The cooking is very good and the atmosphere welcoming. In summer, choose the bedroom that has been made in the old vaulted cellar (no. 6), which is cool and unusual. Above it a new bedroom has just been created, large and light, with a beamed ceiling, stone floor, a fine fireplace and a piano. The bedrooms in the main hotel are not so original but are no less inviting and comfortable.

How to get there *(Map 30): 58km west of Cahors via D911 to Fumel, then D139; it's 1km from the village, on the road to Puy-l'Evêque, at 'Le Vert'.*

Relais de la Dolse★★★

Montcabrier - 46700 Puy-l'Evêque (Lot)
Tel. 65.36.53.42 - Fax 65.24.61.25

Open Easter – 31 Oct. **Rooms** 11 with telephone, bath, shower and WC. **Price** single and double 360-390F. **Meals** breakfast 30F, served 0830-1000; half board 510-690F (1-2 pers., 3 days min.) **Credit cards** Amex, Diners, Visa. **Pets** dogs allowed. **Facilities** swimming pool, parking. **Nearby** Cahors wine route from Mercues to Montcabrier. **Restaurant** service 1200-1400, 1900-2130; menus 120-190F, also à la carte.

This hotel stands in the middle of the countryside, amongst clumps of trees and small valleys. It is composed of two buildings about 100 metres apart. The older building accommodates the reception area and the restaurant. A sympathetic renovation programme has laid the emphasis on features such as the beamed ceilings and exposed stonework. In the dining room, period furniture and finely-worked Indian fabrics combine to create a warm atmosphere, while an impressive many-coloured wooden horse prances above the big fireplace. There is only one bedroom (our favourite) in the old building, otherwise the bedrooms occupy a more recent construction which blends in well with its natural setting. They are large and comfortable, and decorated in shades of pink and white. Each one has a small private garden, very pleasant in summer. Breakfast is served in an adjoining room. You will be warmly welcomed, and prices are reasonable.

How to get there *(Map 30): 8km north of Puy-l'Evêque via D68 (3km from the village).*

Hôtel de la Pelissaria★★★

46330 Saint-Cirq-Lapopie (Lot)
Tel. 65.31.25.14 – Fax 65.30.25.52 – Mme Matuchet

Open 10 Apr – 12 Nov. **Rooms** 7 with telephone, bath, WC and TV. **Price** double 380-450F, suite 640F. **Meals** breakfast 47F, served 0800-1000. **Credit cards** Eurocard, MasterCard, Visa. **Pets** dogs allowed (+15F). **Nearby** valleys of the Lot and the Célé. **Restaurant** service 1230-1330, 1930-2030 (closed Thursday and Friday); à la carte; specialities: home-made pasta and sorbets, confit de canard.

There is something quite magical about the village of Saint-Cirq-Lapopie, one of the most beautiful medieval villages in France and classed as a historic monument. So it is good to find one of the best hotels in this guide here. Built in the 13th century using the fine local stone, this house has been sympathetically restored and tastefully decorated by its young owners. Overall there is an atmosphere of refinement. In the dining room you can sit close to the fireplace on comfortable sofas by the piano as you wait to be seated at your table. All the rooms are perfect. Our favourite was no. 4 which has a small window looking out over the village and valley of the Lot. Two little cottages nestling in a wild garden each contain a charming bedroom. Very good cooking and excellent value for money. The number of tables is limited so it is essential to book if you want to eat in the restaurant.

How to get there *(Map 31): 33km east of Cahors via D653 towards Saint-Géry, then D662.*

Auberge du Sombral★★
46330 Saint-Cirq-Lapopie (Lot)
Tel. 65.31.26.08 - M. and Mme Hardeveld

Open 1 Apr – 11 Nov (closed Tuesday evening and Wednesday). **Rooms** 8 with telephone, bath or shower and WC. **Price** single 300F, double 400F. **Meals** breakfast 45F, served until 0930. **Credit cards** Eurocard, MasterCard, Visa. **Pets** dogs allowed. **Nearby** valleys of the Lot and the Célé. **Restaurant** service 1200-1400, 1930-2100; menus 95-230F, also à la carte; specialities: truite au vieux Cahors, feuilleté d'asperges aux morilles, escalope de foie chaud aux pommes, terrine de foie de canard confit.

This auberge is in an old house which has been perfectly restored. It faces the town square at the heart of this village, now classed as a historic monument. The village is on an escarpment overlooking the valley of the Lot. The atmosphere is calm, the surroundings exceptional, and the furniture and decor harmoniously chosen. There are no harsh contrasts in the colours of the dining room on the ground floor or the bedrooms, which are pleasant and comfortable. Whilst you can explore the village with its alleys and picturesque houses, the auberge has its own museum with a permanent display of paintings by local artists. The restaurant is noteworthy, with good cooking and regional specialities, so this is another outstanding place to stay in Saint-Cirq-Lapopie.

How to get there *(Map 31): 33km east of Cahors via D653 towards Saint-Géry, then D662.*

Domaine de la Rhue★★★

La Rhue
46500 Rocamadour (Lot)
Tel. 65.33.71.50 – Fax 65.33.72.48 – M. and Mme Jooris

Open 9 Apr – 17 Oct. **Rooms** 12 with telephone, bath or shower and WC (4 with TV).
Price single 370F, double 370-570F. **Meals** breakfast 42-60F, served 0800-1000.
No restaurant. **Credit cards** Eurocard, MasterCard, Visa. **Pets** dogs allowed (+30F).
Facilities swimming pool, parking. **Nearby** old town, Francis Poulenc museum in
Rocamadour, truffle market in Gramat, Lascaux caves, 9-hole Mas del Teil golf course
at Souillac.

This hotel is in the splendid stables of a château, in beautiful,
undulating countryside. Taste and comfort abound. The vast
entrance hall retains its original paving and traces of the stalls.
Pleasantly furnished in an antique, rustic style, this hotel makes
relaxing easy – unless of course you would rather sit out by the
pool. Each bedroom is named after a different colour of horse.
They are all spacious, quiet and attractive, with some antique
furniture, elegant fabrics and frequently the original beams. The
bathrooms are similar in style; truly a relaxing atmosphere. Some
of the rooms on the ground floor have a private terrace.
Throughout there is a modern standard of comfort but this hotel
has not lost the charm of an earlier age. Courteous welcome.

How to get there (*Map 24*): *55km south of Brive-la-Gaillarde via N20
towards Cressensac, then N140; 1km before junction with D673, road on
the right.*

La Source Bleue★★★

Touzac
46700 Puy-l'Evêque (Lot)
Tel. 65.36.52.01 – Fax 65.24.65.69 – M. and Mme Bouyou

Open 2 April – 15 Nov. **Rooms** 12 with telephone, bath and WC (5 with TV). **Price** single 250F, double 250-430F. **Meals** breakfast 35F, served 0730-0930; half board from 260F, full board from 360F (per per., 3 days min.) **Credit cards** Amex, Eurocard, Visa. **Pets** dogs allowed (+30F). **Facilities** swimming pool, sauna (100F), health centre (100F), parking. **Nearby** Marguerite Moréno museum, Cahors wine route (château de Bonaguil), 18-hole La Chapelle golf course at Auzac, 18-hole Castelnaud-de-Gratecambe golf course. **Restaurant** service 1200-1330, 1930-2115 (closed Tuesday lunchtime); menus 135-200F, also à la carte; specialities: saumon cuit sur sa peau, rôti de lotte et sa concassée de tomates fraîches, agneau de pays au parfum de gingembre.

La Source Bleue is in a converted 14th-century paper mill on the left bank of the Lot and has been tastefully restored by its owners. The bedrooms, some with modern furniture, are comfortable, and the bathrooms are beyond reproach. The cooking is sophisticated and served in a beautiful dining room. The service is attentive but discreet, and on occasion there is some well chosen music. The gardens and grounds of the hotel have their own allure; they are stocked with many varieties of plants and you will be impressed by a forest of giant bamboo.

How to get there (Map 30): 48km west of Cahors via D911 towards Fumel; at Touzac, cross the Lot.

Hostellerie Saint-Antoine****

17, rue Saint-Antoine
81000 Albi (Tarn)
Tel. 63.54.04.04 - Fax 63.47.10.47 - MM. Rieux and fils

Open all year. **Rooms** 48 with air-conditioning, telephone, bath, WC and TV. **Price** single 360-450F, double 450-750F, suite 850-950F. **Meals** breakfast 60F; half board 420-720F (per pers.) **Credit cards** accepted. **Pets** dogs allowed (+55F). **Facilities** parking. **Nearby** cathedral of Sainte-Cécile, Toulouse-Lautrec museum in Albi, Viaur viaduct, Ambialet, Gaillac, Cordes, 18-hole golf course at Albi. **Restaurant** service 1200-1400, 1900-2130 (closed Saturday and Sunday lunchtime); menus 160-280F, also à la carte; specialities: foie gras, salade de homard, daube de bœuf à l'albigeoise, tournedos Périgueux, tarte à l'ancienne, glace aux noix.

Founded in the 18th century and run as a business by the same family for five generations, this inn was restored in 1960. Elegantly modernised, each room is enhanced by antique furniture, often Directoire or Louis-Phillippe, and the fabrics are bright and fresh. The bedrooms are extremely comfortable, quiet, sophisticated in detail, and more often than not have a view of the flower garden. Some of the larger ones have a small sitting room area. On the ground floor the dining room is similarly decorated and opens into the garden. Good traditional cooking, attentive service and hospitality.

How to get there *(Map 31): in the town centre.*

Demeure de Flore★★

106, route Nationale
81240 Lacabarède (Tarn)
Tel. 63.98.32.32. – Fax 63.98.47.56 – Mme Tronc

Open 20 March – 21 Nov. **Rooms** 8 with telephone, bath, WC and TV. **Price** single 320F, double 380F. **Meals** breakfast 45F. **Credit cards** MasterCard, Eurocard, Visa. **Pets** dogs not allowed. **Facilities** swimming pool, parking. **Nearby** Goya museum in Castres, le Sidobre and the Monts Lacaune de Castres at Mazamet, 18-hole La Barouge golf course at Pont-de-l'Arn. **Restaurant** service 1930-2130; menus 100-200F, also à la carte.

This small hotel is hidden from the road by lush vegetation. Indoors, the elegant decor denotes taste and design flair. Antique furniture, paintings and curios combine to create a warm and cosy atmosphere. The comfortable bedrooms are all individually decorated with colourful designer fabrics and antiques bought locally. The bathrooms are modern, elegant and luxuriously equipped. Our favourite rooms are those with a small terrace and access to the garden and swimming-pool. Table d'hôte evening meals, based on fresh local produce, are served with a smile in the lovely dining-room. This is a wonderful address.

How to get there *(Map 31): 15km east of Mazamet via N112.*

Château de Montlédier***

Route d'Anglès - 81660 Pont-de-L'Arn (Tarn)
Tel. 63.61.20.54 - Fax 63.98.22.51
Mme Thiercelin

Open 1 Feb. – 31 Dec. **Rooms** 9 with telephone, bath, WC (8 with TV and minibar). **Price** single 330-360F, double 430-590F. **Meals** breakfast 48F; half board 340-490F, full board 430-580F (per pers., 3 days min.) **Credit cards** Amex, Diners, Visa. **Pets** dogs allowed. **Facilities** swimming pool, parking. **Nearby** Goya museum in Castres, le Sidobre and the Monts Lacaune de Castres at Mazamet; 18-hole La Barouge golf course at Pont-de-l'Arn. **Restaurant** service 1200-1330, 1930-2130 (closed Sunday evening and Monday except July – Aug); menus 100-195F, also à la carte; specialities: foie gras maison, carré d'agneau, feuilleté aux petits légumes, magret de canard.

From one side the château seems to be comfortably settled on a hillside but on the other side there is a vertiginous drop. One still enters through the grand courtyard. Inside there are a number of small sitting rooms, arranged so that there is something to please everyone. The bedrooms are spacious and beautifully decorated. Each has an individual style and great attention has been paid to comfort. The smallest and least expensive rooms (Victoria and Alexandra) are as charming as the others, and the Raymond IV bedroom has a particularly nice bathroom – it is huge and from its window one can see through the trees into the ravine. Meals are served in the small dining room or on a shady terrace which forms an extension to the lounge. There is a warm welcome here.

How to get there *(Map 31): 19km south east of Castres via N112 towards Mazamet, then D65 at Bout-du-Pont-de-l'Arn.*

Le Métairie Neuve***

81660 Pont-de-L'Arn (Tarn)
Tel. 63.61.23.31
Mme Tournier

Open 15 Jan – 15 Dec. **Rooms** 11 with telephone, bath, WC and TV (9 with minibar). **Price** single 290-430F, double 310-450F. **Meals** breakfast 50F, served 0700-0930; half board 330-350F, full board 425-520F (per pers., 3 days min.) **Credit cards** Diners, Eurocard, MasterCard, Visa. **Pets** dogs allowed. **Facilities** swimming pool, tennis court, parking. **Nearby** Goya museum in Castres, le Sidobre and the Monts Lacaune de Castres at Mazamet; 18-hole La Barouge golf course at Pont-de-l'Arn. **Restaurant** service 1200-1330, 1930-2100 (closed Saturday in low season, Saturday lunchtime in high season); menus 100-230F, also à la carte; specialities: terrine de foie gras frais, ris de veau à l'ancienne, fish, game.

This is a lovely old farmhouse on the outskirts of a village which today is expanding. Commercial developments are spreading but this hotel is in a leafy and quiet backwater. The bedrooms are all well equipped and there is a pleasing attention to detail in the furnishings. The colours are harmonious and the old furniture blends perfectly with the more modern pieces. The hotel has a fine courtyard, a large garden with a terrace, and a swimming pool close to the vegetable garden. One of the restaurant's two rooms is reserved for non-smokers. The food itself makes the journey worthwhile.

How to get there *(Map 31): 19km south east of Castres via N112 towards Mazamet.*

Château de l'Hoste**

Saint-Beauzeuil
82150 Montaigu-de-Quercy (Tarn-et-Garonne)
Tel. 63.95.25.61 - Fax 63.95.20.50 - M. Naulet

Open 16 March – 15 Oct. **Rooms** 32 with telephone, bath and WC. **Price** single 200F, double 250-400F. **Meals** breakfast 40F, served 0800-1000; half board 270F, full board 370F (per pers., 3 days min.) **Credit cards** Visa, MasterCard. **Pets** dogs allowed (+20F). **Facilities** swimming pool, parking. **Nearby** Agen museum, Port-Sainte-Marie, Villeneuve-sur-Lot, Beauville, 18-hole château de Terrides golf course. **Restaurant** service 1200, 1945 (closed Sunday evening and Monday in low season); menus 110-240F, also à la carte; specialities: lamproie bordelaise, alose sauce mousseline, cassoulet d'antan.

After a long search M. and Mme Naulet fell in love with this 18th-century house and the countryside around it. You too will also be charmed by its pale stone walls, lovely interior courtyard, and the proximity of the swimming pool. The conversion has been less successful in the bedrooms where the antique-style furniture disappoints. They are nevertheless large, well kept rooms with comfortable beds and impeccable bathrooms. We recommend rooms 204 and 210, which are smaller but charming. In summer avoid the rooms that overlook the terrace where dinner is served; the enthusiasm of the diners enjoying the chef's excellent cooking (especially the Lamproie à la Bordelaise) may disturb you if you want an early night.

How to get there *(Map 30): 40km north east of Agen via D656; between Agen and Cahors – 8km east of Montaigu.*

Château de la Motte Fénelon★★★

Square du Château
59403 Cambrai (Nord)
Tel. 27.83.61.38 - Fax 27.83.71.61 - Mme Delevallée

Open all year. **Rooms** 40 with telephone, bath, WC, TV and minibar. **Price** double 290F (annexe), 440-540F (château), suite 950F. **Meals** breakfast 50F, served 0700-1000; half board price on request. **Credit cards** accepted. **Pets** dogs allowed (+20F). **Facilities** tennis, parking. **Nearby** church of Saint-Géry in Cambrai ('Entombment' by Rubens), abbey of Vaucelles, Matisse museum at le Cateau-Cambrésis, art museum in Valenciennes, 9-hole golf course at Valenciennes. **Restaurant** service 1200-1330, 1930-2130 (closed Sunday evening); menus 150-225F, also à la carte; specialities: noisette d'agneau en croûte de sel, feuillantine de langoustines, croustillant praliné.

The Château de la Motte Fénlon stands at the gate of Cambrai. Large, well kept grounds separate this classic 18th-century building from its less elegant neighbours. On the ground floor there is a superb suite of lounges with period furniture and tall windows opening onto the grounds. Less ornate but just as comfortable and quiet, the bedrooms are well done and have impeccable bathrooms. Situated on the second floor, they benefit from a fine view but are not as light as the rooms currently being refurbished on the first floor. We do not recommend the little bungalows in the grounds. The huge dining room is in the basement. The welcome here is courteous and the château is well run, making it a pleasant place to stay.

How to get there *(Map 2): Via A2, Cambrai exit.*

Château de Ligny★★★

4, rue Pierre-Curie
59191 Ligny-Haucourt (Nord)
Tel. 27.85.25.84 - M. and Mme Boulard

Open all year (closed Monday in low season). **Rooms** 6 rooms and 3 suites with telephone, bath WC, TV (suites with minibar). **Price** single and double 460-590F, suite 680-1100F. **Meals** breakfast 50F, served 0745-0930. **Credit cards** Amex, Visa, Diners. **Pets** dogs allowed in bedrooms (+50F). **Nearby** church of Saint-Géry in Cambrai ('Entombment' by Rubens), abbey of Vaucelles, Matisse museum at le Cateau-Cambrésis, art museum in Valenciennes, 9-hole golf course at Valenciennes. **Restaurant** service 1230-1345, 1930-2130 (closed Monday lunchtime and Saturday lunchtime); menus 190-360F, also à la carte; specialities: foie gras de canard en terrine, noisette d'agneau à la menthe poivrée.

Beside the village church the gates of the château open onto a charming courtyard in the centre of which a magnolia overhangs a stone fountain. The size of the building makes this an easy place to stay, for the atmosphere is less grandiose than in some other château hotels. The bedrooms are all decorated differently. The 'Rustique' bedroom is entirely green, including the carpet; the 'Royal' suite is more modern in inspiration with its pale colours. The owner is an antiques enthusiast and the 'Regent' bedroom in particular has benefitted from his expeditions, a superb carved wood ram claiming attention. A small park around the château guarantees tranquility.

How to get there (Map 2): 15km south east of Cambrai via A2, Cambrai exit.

Le Jardin Fleuri★★

23, rue du Moulin
59990 Sebourg (Nord)
Tel. 27.26.53.31 - Fax 27.26.50.08 - Mme Delmotte

Open all year (closed 1-15 Sept). **Rooms** 13 with telephone, bath or shower (9 with WC, 6 with TV). **Price** double 190-250F. **Meals** breakfast 25F, served 0700-1000; half board 260-320F, full board 360-420F (per pers., 4 days min.) **Credit cards** Visa. **Pets** dogs allowed. **Facilities** parking. **Nearby** art museum in Valenciennes, Bavay, Le Quesnoy, glass museum in Sars-Poterie, 9-hole golf course at Valenciennes. **Restaurant** service 1200-1300, 1900-2200 (closed Wednesday evening); menus 110-180F, also à la carte; specialities: langue Lucullus, saumon à l'unilatérale, tarte aux pommes.

In the small rue du Moulin one first catches sight of the restaurant and then, behind it, a colourful and charming garden; the little stream with its wooden bridge and the beautiful fir trees are eye catching. Beyond is the hotel, a small brick house. It contains 13 bedrooms on two floors; cosy and comfortable they look out over the garden and two of them have a balcony. Good cooking and very reasonable prices.

How to get there *(Map 3): 9km east of Valenciennes via A2, Curgies exit, then D8.*

Auberge du Bon Fermier★★★

64–66, rue de Famars
59300 Valenciennes (Nord)
Tel. 27.46.68.25 – Fax 27.33.75.01 – M. and Mme Paul

Open all year. **Rooms** 16 with telephone, bath or shower WC, TV and minibar. **Price** single 380-480F, double 430-580F. **Meals** breakfast 45F, served 0700-1100. **Credit cards** accepted. **Pets** dogs allowed. **Facilities** parking (+50F). **Nearby** remains of the ancient abbey at Saint-Amand-les-Eaux, fortifications of Le Quesnoy, valley of l'Helpe, 9-hole golf course at Valenciennes. **Restaurant** service 1200-1430, 1900-2230; menus 160-200F, also à la carte; specialities: langue Lucullus, cochon de lait à la broche, tarte au maroilles.

Make a stop at the Auberge du Bon Fermier and you will spend a comfortable evening in this former royal coaching inn which in the 17th century was on the route from the Tuileries to Brussels. An inn since 1840 and now classed a historic monument, it has been scrupulously restored by its present owners. The red bricks of which the outer walls and often the interior walls are made, the oak beams and floors, all conjure up a past age. The bedrooms are spacious and have a sitting-room area; they are all delightful but the quietest are those that overlook the grounds. Comfort and style are blended well. The restaurant serves regional specialities and offers a good choice of spit roasted meats as well as the hotel's own fresh lobster speciality. The ambience is a little theatrical but this is nevertheless a stopping place not to be missed.

How to get there *(Map 3): in the town centre, near the town hall.*

Grand Hôtel Clément★★★

91, esplanade du Maréchal-Leclerc
62610 Ardres (Pas-de-Calais)
Tel. 21.82.25.25 - Fax 21.82.98.92 - M. Coolen

Open 15 Feb – 15 Jan (closed Monday). **Rooms** 17 with telephone bath or shower, WC, TV and minibar. **Price** single and double 225-325F. **Meals** breakfast 35F, served 0730-0930; half board 235-285F, full board 335-385F. **Credit cards** accepted. **Pets** dogs allowed. **Facilities** parking. **Nearby** the 'Bourgeois de Calais', art and lace museum in Calais, basilica of Notre-Dame and Sandelin museum in Saint-Omer, church of Saint-Eloi and museum in Hazebrouck, 18-hole golf course at Wimereux. **Restaurant** service 1200-1400, 1900-2100; menus 95-320F, also à la carte; specialities: volaille de Licques, ragoût et produits de la mer, foie gras.

This hotel is situated beside a small esplanade which although busy during the day is calm and silent at night. It has been run by the same family since 1917 and François Coolen, a member of the 'Young Restaurateurs of France', has assured its reputation with his culinary skill. The bedrooms are simple, but a piece of old furniture, a lovely mirror, or a beamed ceiling give each room a unique feel. Our favourites were numbers 19, 20 and 21, which look out over the grounds at the rear of the hotel, but all the rooms are attractive. There is a nostalgic feel to the bar, the lounge and the beautiful dining room. The welcome is full of kindness.

How to get there *(Map 2): 97km north west of Arras via A26, Nordausque exit; then N43. 17km south east of Calais.*

Chartreuse du Val Saint–Esprit***

1, rue de Fouquières
62199 Gosnay (Pas-de-Calais)
Tel. 21.62.80.00 - Fax 21.62.42.50 - M. and Mme Constant

Open all year. **Rooms** 23 with telephone, bath, WC, TV and minibar. **Price** single 330-500F, double 400-600F. **Meals** breakfast 50F, served 0630-1000. **Credit cards** Visa, Amex, MasterCard. **Pets** dogs allowed (+45F). **Facilities** parking. **Nearby** Aa golf course. **Restaurant** service 1200-1430, 1900-2200; menus 115-375F, also à la carte; specialities: turbot à la fondue de poireaux, feuilleté de foie gras et ris de veau, médaillon de lotte aux endives, pied de porc truffé, suprême de bar aux fenouils.

At first sight this splendid brick and stone edifice, with its great courtyard and large park, may seem rather austere. This first impression is however immediately dispelled by a warm and friendly welcome and the refinement of the interior decoration. Most of the rooms are vast, and the first-floor bedrooms are impressively high-ceilinged. They are extremely comfortable, with fine bathrooms. Lavish amounts of attention have been devoted to features such as bed spreads, curtains and wallpapers, which all blend to perfection. The second-floor rooms tend to be less bright, but this makes them more cosy and intimate. The breakfast room is delightful, with a row of arched windows looking out into the gardens. An extension is being added to the hotel (it should be ready for the summer season). There will be more rooms available, and their decor and ambience are intended to be perfectly in tune with the character and charm of the Chartreuse.

How to get there (Map 2): 5km south of Béthune via A26, exit 6.

Château de Cocove***

62890 Recques-sur-Hem (Pas-de-Calais)
Tel. 21.82.68.29 - Fax 21.82.72.59 - Mme Calonne

Open all year (closed 25 Dec). **Rooms** 24 with telephone, bath or shower, WC and TV. **Price** single and double 415-660F. **Meals** breakfast 45F, served 0730-1030; half board 358-580F, full board 463-785F. **Credit cards** Amex, Visa, Diners. **Pets** dogs allowed (+45F). **Facilities** sauna (25F), parking. **Nearby** basilica of Notre-Dame and Sandelin museum in Valenciennes, blockhouse at Eperlecques, church of Saint-Eloi and museum in Hazebrouck, the 'Bourgeois de Calais', art and lace museum in Calais; 27-hole Saint-Omer golf course at Lumbres. **Restaurant** service 1200-1400, 1930-2130; menus 105-205F, also à la carte; specialities: fricassée de soles et langoustines, croustillant de poissons.

Only a few minutes from Calais, this 18th-century château is deep in the countryside surrounded by extensive grounds. You will find yourself very welcome. The interior has been sympathetically restored in keeping with the age of the building. In the same spirit the dining room has been converted from the old stables, its wide doors replaced by bay windows and the pale subdued decor adding to the elegance of the room. The bedrooms are light and pleasantly furnished and some of them are very spacious. M. Calonne is gradually introducing antique furniture which he has found after scouring the antique shops. You will enjoy the quiet and the excellent bathrooms. Before you leave, amateur wine enthusiasts can visit the cellars where a large selection of fine wines can be purchased at a reasonable cost.

How to get there *(Map 1): 17km south east of Calais via N43 towards Saint-Omer.*

Hôtel Cléry★★★

62360 Hesdin-l'Abbé (Pas-de-Calais)
Tel. 21.83.19.83 - Fax 21.87.52.59
Mme Osseland

Open 15 Jan – 20 Dec. **Rooms** 19 with telephone, bath or shower, WC and TV. **Price** single 340F, double 420-560F. **Meals** breakfast 50F, served 0700-1000. No restaurant. **Credit cards** accepted. **Pets** no dogs allowed. **Facilities** parking. **Nearby** castle-museum and national marine centre in Boulogne-sur-Mer, pottery museum in Desvres, Opal coast, Cap Gris-Nez, Cap Blanc-Nez; 18-hole golf course at Hardelot.

It was at this small château that Napoleon would have decided to strike camp at Boulogne. There are three rooms on the ground floor: a large, light room where breakfast is served, a bar and a beautiful room where you can sit in deep leather armchairs by an open fire. An elegant staircase with a Louis XV style wrought iron banister leads to the first floor. The bedrooms are comfortable and the decor simple. The rooms on the second floor have the feel of attic rooms, but whether they look out on the chestnut trees in the park or on the drive, all the bedrooms are quiet. Behind a beautiful courtyard with old stone paving and banks with geraniums there are seven other bedrooms in the former stable block. Room eight is on the ground floor and among the others, on the first floor, are two pretty single bedrooms. A short distance from the main road, this hotel is ideal for travellers to or from Britain.

How to get there *(Map 1): 9km south east of Boulogne via N1.*

Hostellerie du Moulin du Pré★★

14860 Bavent (Calvados)
Tel. 31.78.83.68
Famille Hamchin–Holtz

Open all year (except 1-15 March and 1-15 Oct; closed Sunday evening and Monday except July, August and national holidays). **Rooms** 10 with telephone, bath or shower (5 with WC). **Price** double 200-315F. **Meals** breakfast 40F, served 0800-1000. **Credit cards** accepted. **Pets** dogs not allowed. **Facilities** parking. **Nearby** Deauville, Caen, Normandy landing beaches, Houlgate, 18-hole Le Home Varaville golf course at Cabourg. **Restaurant** service 1230-1330, 1930-2100; menus 250-280F, also à la carte; specialities: gaspacho aux huîtres pochées, turban de sole soufflé au homard, ris d'agneau aux morilles.

This renovated farmhouse in the countryside on the borders of the Auge region stands in large grounds with a small lake. The sea is only 4 km away and one can therefore easily enjoy a country and seaside holiday here. The interior of the hotel is comfortable. The small bedrooms are delightful, some in a rustic style, and all of them look out on the peaceful countryside. The bathroom facilities and soundproofing vary from room to room. The large dining room and lounge on the ground floor are very welcoming and mealtimes provide an opportunity to sample some excellent seasonal home cooking.

How to get there *(Map 7): 14km north east of Caen via D513 towards Cabourg, then D95 towards Gonneville-en-Auge.*

Hôtel d'Argouges★★

21, rue Saint-Patrice
14400 Bayeux (Calvados)
Tel. 31.92.88.86 – Fax 31.92.69.16 – M. and Mme Auregan

Open all year. **Rooms** 25 with telephone, bath or shower, WC and minibar (18 with TV). **Price** single 190-320F, double 190-380F. **Meals** breakfast 35F, served 0730-1030. No restaurant. **Credit cards** accepted. **Pets** dogs allowed (+35F). **Facilities** parking. **Nearby** Bayeux cathedral, Port-en-Bessin, 27-hole Omaha Beach golf course at Bayeux.

If you are stopping at Bayeux you will feel at home in this old private hotel run by the Argouges family. It is on the quiet outskirts of the old town and within walking distance of all points of interest. The hotel has 25 rooms, all very quiet and plainly but comfortably furnished. They are in two buildings and have high ceilings and exposed beams. Most are quite large. Rooms 23 and 24, built in old barns, are actually small, well designed apartments, each one with a large main bedroom and a small bedroom for children. At the rear of the hotel, behind an 18th-century facade, there is an extensive garden where you can have your breakfast, unless you prefer the delightful dining room. This is a fine hotel; and good value.

How to get there (Map 7): 27km west of Caen via N13.

Auberge de la Boule d'Or

14430 Beuvron-en-Auge (Calvados)
Tel. 31.79.78.78
M. and Mme Duval

Open all year (closed Sunday evening and Monday except July – Aug). **Rooms** 3 with bath or shower and WC. **Price** double 220F. **Meals** breakfast 30F, served 0700-1000; half board 220F, full board 300F (per pers., 7 days min.) **Credit cards** accepted. **Pets** small dogs allowed. **Nearby** Lisieux, pays d'Auge from Lisieux to Deauville and Lisieux to Cabourg. **Restaurant** service 1200-1330, 1900-2130 (closed Dec and Jan); menus 95-135F, also à la carte; Norman cooking.

In summer, every street and square in Beuvron-en-Auge seems to be in bloom, and the houses are decked out with geraniums to such an extent that their ancient half-timbering itself seems to be blossoming. The Boule d'Or is a small, modest inn well known for its traditional cuisine. There is no reception area as such, so you should go straight into the dining-room, which is rustic in style, with pink table cloths striking a note of simplicity and conviviality. A small staircase leads up to the hotel's three bedrooms, which have recently been refurbished. They are small but comfortable, bright and neat, and have pleasant bathrooms. This is a friendly, unpretentious address in one of the most beautiful villages in Normandy.

How to get there *(Map 8): 25km west of Lisieux via A13, exit Dozulé.*

Château du Baffy★★

Le Bourg-Creully
14480 Colombiers-sur-Seulles (Calvados)
Tel. 31.08.04.57 – Fax 31.08.08.29 – M. Baheux

Open all year. **Rooms** 35 with telephone, bath or shower and WC (TV +20F). **Price** single 315-380F, double 400-535F. **Meals** breakfast incl., served 0800-1015; half board 310-373F, full board 420-493F (per pers., 3 days min.) **Credit cards** accepted. **Pets** dogs allowed (+30F). **Facilities** tennis, swimming pool, sauna, parking. **Nearby** Caen, Normandy landing beaches, 18-hole golf course at Garcelles. **Restaurant** service 1200-1330, 1900-2100 (closed Sunday evening and Monday in low season); menus 90-190F; specialities: grenadin de veau 'Marie Harel', méli-mélo de poissons aux petits légumes.

Before even entering this hotel you will be charmed by its flowering gardens, through which run streams crossed by romantic little bridges. The interior of the château is no less appealing. A happy atmosphere pervades the lounges and dining rooms, decorated in pastel shades and with cane furniture and pretty fabrics. The naïve paintings on the walls add a cheerful note. The bedrooms are simply furnished and comfortable. They look out over the grounds, and the ones in the outbuildings overlook the swimming pool The latter have recently been delightfully refurbished. If you plan a holiday here, don't hesitate, there are plenty of things to do: sightseeing, relaxation and the delights of good food, as well as a highly professional and cordial welcome.

How to get there *(Map 7): 26km north west of Caen via D7 to Douvres-la-Délivrande, then D35.*

Hostellerie du Château de Goville★★★

14330 Le-Breuil-en-Bessin (Calvados)
Tel. 31.22.19.28 – Fax 31.22.68.74
M. Vallée

Open all year. **Rooms** 10 with telephone, bath or shower, WC and minibar. **Price** double 395-695F, suite 695F. **Meals** breakfast 50F, served 0830-1130; half board 425-550F (per pers., 2 days min.) **Credit cards** Visa, Amex, Diners. **Pets** dogs allowed (+75F). **Facilities** parking. **Nearby** Bayeux tapestry and cathedral, châteaux of Creullet and of Creully, church of St-Loup-Hors, abbey of Mondaye, 27-hole Omaha Beach golf course. **Restaurant** service 1130-1430, 1930-2130 (closed Tuesday in low season); menus 115-245F, also à la carte; specialities: traditional cuisine.

The château in which Monsieur Vallée's family have lived since 1813 has retained the charm of a private house. The interior decoration of the house is highly elegant: there is hardly a piece of furniture, objêt d'art or picture which is not genuine and old. The curtains and wall coverings all contribute, and no corner has been overlooked. There is something of the atmosphere of an English country house here. The spacious dining room is lit, as if by candlelight, by a huge crystal chandelier, and you will be enchanted by the lounge while you enjoy your aperitif or perhaps a glass of Calvados. A hospitable welcome completes the enjoyment of a stay at one of the most attractive hotels in Normandy.

How to get there *(Map 7): 38km north west of Caen via N13 to Bayeux, then D5 towards Molay-Littry.*

Ferme Hôtel La Rançonnière★★

Route d'Arromanches
14480 Crépon (Calvados)
Tel. 31.22.21.73 – Fax 31.22.98.39 – Mme Vereecke

Open all year. **Rooms** 35 (25 with telephone, 30 with bath or shower and WC, 5 with TV). **Price** single and double 180-340F. **Meals** breakfast 40F, served 0745-1000; half board 205-295F, full board 290-380F. **Credit cards** accepted. **Pets** dogs allowed. **Facilities** parking. **Nearby** Bayeux tapestry and cathedral, châteaux of Creullet and of Creully, church of St-Loup-Hors, abbey of Mondaye, 27-hole Omaha Beach golf course. **Restaurant** service 1200-1400, 1900-2130; menus 60-235F, also à la carte; specialities: homard breton flambé, poularde aux morilles.

The Bessin region is full of old manor houses and Crépon has more than its share in terms of both numbers and interest. You enter this old farm through a crenellated carriage gate into a vast courtyard around which are reception, restaurant and the bedrooms of the hotel. The interior is decidedly rustic with wooden furniture and exposed timbers everywhere. The comfortable bedrooms have small windows and old furniture whose dark tones are at times a little heavy... We particularly like rooms 29, 30, 31 and 32. The rooms above the restaurant are a little small but very pleasant. The food is good and abundant and served in a vast hall, often brightened by a cheerful wood fire. In summer you can dine in the courtyard. The cordial welcome will make you feel at home.

How to get there (Map 7): 21km north west of Caen via D22 towards Arromanches, then D112 towards Couseulles.

Hôtel du Pavillon de la Poste★★

25, rue Fossorier
14800 Deauville (Calvados)
Tel. 31.88.38.29 - Mme Bazire

Open all year. **Rooms** 15 with telephone, bath or shower, WC, TV and minibar. **Price** single and double 350-400F. **Meals** breakfast 35F, served 0830-1030. No restaurant. **Credit cards** Visa. **Pets** dogs allowed (+60F). **Nearby** Trouville museum, Honfleur, Houlgate, Cabourg, 27-hole New-Golf, 18-hole and 9-hole St-Gatien golf courses at Deauville.

Were it not for the two small palms and the flowers bordering the steps up the to front door, the lovely interior decor of the hotel might come as a complete surprise. It is a magical place whose lounge, breakfast room and each small bedroom leave one lost for words. Charm and comfort are the keynotes of this place, with its pictures, lovely fabrics and wallpapers, old furniture (often of English origin) and mass of other personal touches. The whole is close to perfection, and the cordial welcome, plus its location at Deauville, make it all the more appealing. Book well in advance.

How to get there (Map 8): 40km north east of Caen via A13, Deauville exit.

Hôtel l'Ecrin★★★

19, rue Eugène-Boudin
14600 Honfleur (Calvados)
Tel. 31.89.32.39 - Fax 31.89.24.41 - Mme Blais

Open all year. **Rooms** 20 with telephone, bath or shower, WC and TV (10 with minibar). **Price** double 300-650F, suite 800F. **Meals** breakfast 40-45F, served 0800-1100. No restaurant. **Credit cards** accepted. **Pets** dogs allowed (+50F). **Facilities** sauna (40F), parking. **Nearby** old dock, church of Sainte-Catherine, Eugène Boudin museum in Honfleur, Deauville, Trouville, 27-hole New-Golf, 18-hole and 9-hole St-Gatien golf courses at Deauville.

You can truly relax in the courtyard and lovely gardens of this elegant Napoleon III mansion. Although in the centre of the town, the hotel is out of the way of the hordes of tourists who head for Honfleur when summer begins. The ground floor rooms still retain their original layout and much of the style of their period. In the Proustian lounge the gilt of the plasterwork echoes the gilt on the armchairs, and the delicate tints of the numerous paintings are repeated in the silks, the curtains and the carpets. Indoor plants give a foretaste of the adjoining conservatory. The bedrooms are a little overdone (no. 2 is extraordinary) but very comfortable. Avoid the ones on the second floor but do not reject the ones in the lodges, where the cheaper rooms are not necessarily the least pleasant. Breakfast is served in a room full of paintings, many in the style of the school of Honfleur (Boudin, etc), or in the conservatory, which opens into the garden, itself as attractive as the rest of the house.

How to get there *(Map 8): 97km west of Rouen via A13, Beuzeville exit, then D22(it's in the town centre).*

Auberge Saint–Christophe★★
14690 Pont-d'Ouilly (Calvados)
Tel. 31.69.81.23
M. Lecoeur

Open all year, except All Saints and 15 Feb – 13 March (closed Sunday evening and Monday). **Rooms** 7 with telephone, bath or shower, WC and TV. **Price** double 250F. **Meals** breakfast 40F, served 0800-0930; half board 260F, full board 360F (per pers., 2 days min.) **Credit cards** Amex, Eurocard, Visa. **Pets** dogs allowed (+25F). **Facilities** parking. **Nearby** castle of Falaise, 'La Suisse Normande', Thury-Harcourt, Clécy (châteaux of La Pommeraye and Placy), Oëtre rock, gorges of St-Aubert, château de Pontécoulant; 18-hole Clécy-Cantelou golf course. **Restaurant** service 1200-1330, 1930-2100; menus 88-230F, also à la carte; specialities: nonnettes de saumon au beurre de cidre, salade tiède de queues de langoustines, crème brûlée.

This hotel is in an elegant house in the Suisse Normande. Its interior has been carefully designed to provide every comfort. Plants and flowers adorn every corner. There is a small lounge, a breakfast room which becomes a bar in the evening, and many places to sit and talk, read, contemplate or snooze. The bedrooms are small but charming and have recently been renovated in a more modern style. They look out over the peaceful gardens but the soundproofing in the hotel could be better. During the summer lunch can be taken on the terrace. The food is up to the high standards of the hotel and the young owners will give you a very cordial welcome.

How to get there *(Map 7): 26km south of Caen via D562 towards Flers, or N158 towards Falaise, then D1; it's 1.5km from Pont-d'Ouilly via D23 towards Thury-Harcourt.*

Hostellerie du Haras de la Hauquerie**

Quetteville
14130 Pont-l'Evêque (Calvados)
Tel. 31.64.14.46 – Fax 31.64.24.52 – Mme Lombard

Open all year. **Rooms** 20 with telephone, bath or shower, WC and minibar (10 with TV). **Price** single 230F, double 200-480F, suite 500-600F. **Meals** breakfast 38F, served 0800-1030; half board 280-600F, full board 380-700F (per pers., 15 days min.) **Credit cards** Visa, MasterCard, Eurocard. **Pets** dogs allowed (+50F). **Facilities** parking. **Nearby** villages of St-Hymer, Pont-l'Evêque, Beaumont-en-Auge, manors of Glatigny and Canapville, 27-hole St-Julien golf course at Pont-l'Evêque. **Restaurant** service 1200-1415, 1900-2130; menus 120-180F, also à la carte; specialities: langoustines flambées.

This is a genuine Normandy stud farm and in the surrounding fields some of the stars of French racecourses have shown their paces. M. Lombard is still a breeder of horses but is often there to greet his guests. Mainly, however, it is his charming wife who looks after the hotel and restaurant. The decor of the hotel is delightful, full of carefully thought out details, and all the rooms are comfortable. The hotel has recently been very discreetly extended, and you would only know it from the inside. In the new wing the bedrooms are more conventionally like hotel rooms, but no less pleasant than the others. Many of them have small terraces which look out on the fields. There are two huge ones under the roof, with plenty of room for a family or a party of friends. The restaurant is very pleasant and good value.

How to get there *(Map 8): 90km west of Rouen via A13, Beuzeville exit, then N175 towards Pont-l'Evêque.*

La Chaîne d'Or★★★

27, rue Grande
27700 Les Andelys (Eure)
Tel. 32.54.00.31 - Fax 32.54.05.68 - M. and Mme Foucault

Open 2 Feb – 31 Dec. **Rooms** 10 with telephone, bath or shower, WC and TV. **Price** single 290F, double 490-540F, suite 710-740F. **Meals** breakfast 48F, served 0800-0930. **Credit cards** Amex, Access, Eurocard, MasterCard, Visa. **Pets** dogs not allowed. **Facilities** parking. **Nearby** church of Notre-Dame and Château Gaillard at Les Andelys, Giverny, 18-hole Vaudreuil golf course. **Restaurant** service 1200-1400, 1930-2130 (closed Sunday evening and Monday and one week in Sept.); menus 135-280F, also à la carte; specialities: filet de sole en écaille de homard, noisette et son pied d'agneau au pistou, gratin de fruits.

This friendly hostelry was founded in 1751. Once you have walked inside through the porch and across the inner courtyard, a stunning view of the river Seine is revealed. Most of the bedrooms are large and light. The ones overlooking the river have just been entirely refurbished: very elegant and refined, they have gained in comfort what they have lost in authenticity. In the rooms looking out over the church or the courtyard, there are items of period furniture, rugs and engravings. Foreign guests prefer them for their old-world atmosphere and they are equally comfortable. The breakfast room has a high ceiling with polished beams, and is sometimes used in the evening as a convivial lounge. In the dining-room, half timbering, paintings and flowers combine to create a warm and cosy ambience, while the pink table-cloths compliment the silvery green of the Seine. The traditional dishes served there are light and delicious.

How to get there *(Map 8): 72km north west of Paris via A13, Gaillon exit, then D316.*

Relais Moulin de Baline★★

Baline - 27130 Verneuil-sur-Avre (Eure)
Tel. 32.32.03.48 - Fax 32.60.11.22
M. Gastaldi

Open all year. **Rooms** 10 with telephone, bath and WC (6 with TV, 8 with minibar). **Price** double 320-350F. **Meals** breakfast 45F, served 0800-1100; half board 320-350F, full board 450-470F (per pers., 2 days min.) **Credit cards** accepted. **Pets** dogs allowed. **Facilities** lake and river fishing, supervised parking. **Nearby** Senonches forest, châteaux de Beauménil and d'Anet, 9-hole golf course at Coulonges. **Restaurant** service 1200-1500, 1930-2200 (closed Monday); menus 140-250F, also à la carte; specialities: duo de sole et langouste, cassolette d'escargots et gambas aux petits lardons, 'œuf d'autruche farci'.

When you first see the hotel from the road you may worry about its proximity to the traffic, but as soon as you enter peace reigns and the only noise is of the meeting of the waters of the rivers Avre and Iton, which flow into each other here. The Moulin possesses ten hectares of land with a small lake and boats are available for fishing enthusiasts. The bar–dining room, littered with the spoils of trips to antique shops, has Persian tablecloths and a splendid fireplace. The bedrooms are just as appealing – some of them in the attic seeming to be perched in the trees. You will be warmly welcomed at the Relais and its proximity to Paris makes it a useful place to stay.

How to get there (Map 8): *45km south west of Evreux via N154 to Nonancourt, then N12 towards Verneuil-sur-Avre.*

Château de la Rapée★★★

27140 Bazincourt-sur-Epte (Eure)
Tel. 32.55.11.61
M. Bergeron

Open 16 Feb – 15 Jan. **Rooms** 14 with telephone, bath or shower and WC (8 with TV). **Price** single 350-380F, double 450-480F, suite 600-800F. **Meals** breakfast 45F, served 0800-1000; half board 500-630F, full board 640-735F (per pers., 3 days min.) **Credit cards** accepted. **Pets** dogs not allowed. **Facilities** parking. **Nearby** châteaux d'Harcourt and de Gisors, A.G. Poulain museum in Vernon and Nicolas Poussin museum at Les Andelys, Monet museum in Giverny, 18-hole Bertuchère golf course. **Restaurant** service 1230-1400, 1930-2100; menus 140-190F, also à la carte; specialities: tarte légère au livarot, douillons, anguille en matelote au cidre brut.

This 19th-century Norman mansion is less than an hour from Paris and a few kilometres from Gisors. Lost in the midst of woods and fields, at the end of a dirt track, with a stud farm its only neighbour, it is ideal for seekers of tranquillity in a beautiful setting. The bedrooms are comfortable (the largest are on the first floor and number 15 has a terrace) and there arc two dining rooms; one for summer and another with a large fireplace for the winter months. Monsieur Bergeron is a good cook and Madame will make you feel like one of the family. Tables in the garden allow you to have breakfast and snacks in the open air, weather permitting.

How to get there *(Map 9): 70km north west of Paris via A15, Pontoise exit, then D915 to Gisors; it's 4km north of Gisors via D915.*

Auberge de l'Abbaye★★★

27800 Le Bec-Hellouin (Eure)
Tel. 32.44.86.02
Mme Sergent

Open 20 Feb – 5 Jan (closed Monday evening and Tuesday in low season). **Rooms** 10 with telephone, bath and WC. **Price** double 350-380F, suite 450F. **Meals** breakfast 35F, served from 0800; half board 335F. **Credit cards** Eurocard, MasterCard, Visa. **Pets** dogs allowed. **Facilities** parking. **Nearby** abbey of Bec-Hellouin, insect collection in the Canel museum at Pont-Audemer, 18-hole Champ de Bataille golf course at Neubourg. **Restaurant** service 1215-1430, 1915-2130; menus 125-250F, also à la carte; specialities: cassolette de homard, lapin au cidre, ris de veau aux morilles, tarte aux pommes.

This hotel is in an 18th-century building close to the abbey and in the centre of a very pretty village. There are ten bedrooms furnished in a rustic style, all small but comfortable and quiet and with full bathroom facilities. The dining room is attractive, with whitewashed walls and a fireplace, and the food lives up to the promise of the setting. As well as all this there is an interior courtyard colourful with flowers, a small terrace on the front where you can enjoy the fresh air and watch the life of the village square, and hospitable proprietors who have built up a loyal clientele and are full of enthusiasm for their job. You will not be disappointed in this good, simple and genuine inn.

How to get there (Map 8): 38km north west of Evreux via N13 to Feuguerolles, then D130 to Le Bec-Hellouin.

Château de Brécourt★★★★

Douains
27120 Pacy-sur-Eure (Eure)
Tel. 32.52.40.50 - Fax 32.52.69.65 - MM. Savry and Charpentier

Open all year. **Rooms** 29 with telephone, bath, shower and WC. **Price** single 375-480F, double 610-810F, suite 960-1210F. **Meals** breakfast 60F, served 0630-1200; half board 1145-1500F, full board 1590-1785F. **Credit cards** Amex, Diners, Visa. **Pets** dogs allowed (+50F). **Facilities** swimming pool, jacuzzi, tennis, parking. **Nearby** A.G. Poulain museum and church of Notre-Dame in Vernon, château de Gaillon, Monet museum in Giverny, 9-hole golf course at Gaillon. **Restaurant** service 1200-1330, 1930-2130; menus 225-350F, also à la carte; specialties: escalope de cabillaud en brandade à l'huile d'olive, dos de bar cuit à la vapeur en couscous, fish.

The Château de Brécourt is an ideal place for a weekend; it is a Louis XIII building only 60 km from Paris on the borders of Normandy. The lovely 17th-century moated château has a 22-hectare park where it is a pleasure to stroll at any time of the year. More active guests will enjoy the swimming pool and tennis courts. There are two dining rooms, both with a fine view of the woods and the countryside and both with a menu featuring good Normandy specialities. The decor is in keeping with the elegant and comfortable atmosphere of the house.

How to get there *(Map 8): 21km east of Evreux via N13, Pacy-sur-Eure exit, then D181 and D533. 70km west of Paris via A13, Vernon exit.*

Auberge du Vieux Puits★★

6, rue Notre-Dame-du-Pré - 27500 Pont-Audemer (Eure)
Tel. 32.41.01.48
M. and Mme Foltz

Open 20 Jan – 28 June and 8 July – 20 Dec (closed Monday evening and Tuesday). **Rooms** 12 with telephone, bath or shower (10 with WC, 6 with TV). **Price** single 160-350F, double 230-390F. **Meals** breakfast 38F, served 0800-0930. **Credit cards** Eurocard, MasterCard, Visa. **Pets** dogs not allowed. **Facilities** parking. **Nearby** insect collection in the Canel museum at Pont-Audemer, abbey of Le Bec-Hollouin, 18-hole Champ-de-Bataille golf course at Neubourg. **Restaurant** service 1200-1400, 1930-2100; menus 175F (weekday lunch only) - 280F, also à la carte; specialities: canard aux griottes, truite 'Bovary'.

This auberge at Pont–Audemer is easily accessible from the autoroute and makes a perfect stop for anyone who wants to get to know Normandy. The buildings, in perfect Norman style with 17th-century timbering, encircle a flower garden with an old well and two impressive willows under which you can enjoy an aperitif, a coffee or a snack in summer. Inside the buildings there are several small lounges where you can take tea or read a book. The dining room is larger and is decorated with old pottery and shining copper. Here you will enjoy a very personal cuisine drawing upon regional recipes. Your choice of bedrooms will depend on whether you like the simple rustic charm of the old buildings or the modernity of the new wing recently built in a sympathetic style.

How to get there *(Map 8): 52km west of Rouen via A13, Pont-Audemer exit, then D139 and N182 (it's 300m from the town centre).*

Hostellerie du Moulin Fourest

27300 Saint-Aubin-le-Vertueux (Eure)
Tel. 32.43.19.95 - Fax 32.45.55.50
M. and Mme Deduit

Open all year (closed Sunday evening and Monday). **Rooms** 8 with shower and WC. **Price** single 180F, double 200F. **Meals** breakfast 30F, served 0730-0930. **Credit cards** Visa, Amex. **Pets** dogs allowed (+35F). **Facilities** parking. **Nearby** Lisieux, Bernay, 18-hole Champ-de-Bataille golf course. **Restaurant** service 1200-1400, 1930-2130; menus 95-250F, also à la carte: specialities: lapereau à la crème camembert, flan de foie gras au confit de poireaux, feuillantine de mousse au chocolat.

The small river flowing past the foot of the mill winds hither and thither, creating small spurs of land perfect for fishing or simply relaxing on. Inside the hotel the rustic decoration of the bar and the dining-room combines fine pieces of furniture, ancient beams and paintings to create a warm and cosy atmosphere. François Deduit, who is both the chef and the owner of the hotel, is a promising young cook, and his traditional cuisine has gained him a solid reputation throughout the region. The bedrooms command fine views of the surrounding countryside. Their modern furnishings, however, are a disappointment after the charm and authenticity of the period furniture in the reception rooms and on the landings, but the rooms certainly have gained in comfort. In the spring, parasols are set up on a neat and flower terrace which then becomes the ideal setting for breakfast and dinner, enhanced by the distant babble of water gushing through the weir hatches.

How to get there *(Map 8): 3km south of Bernay via D833.*

Les Saisons***

Route des Saisons
Vironvay - 27400 Louviers (Eure)
Tel. 32.40.02.56 - Fax 32.25.05.26 - M. Guillet

Open all year. **Rooms** 12 with telephone, bath, WC, TV and minibar. **Price** single 490-590F, double 590-690F, suite 850-950F. **Meals** breakfast 50F, served 0715-1100; half board 770F, full board 1005F. **Credit cards** Visa. **Pets** dogs allowed (+30F). **Facilities** tennis, children's games, parking. **Nearby** church of Notre-Dame in Louviers, Rouen cathedral, Monet museum in Giverny, 18-hole le Vaudreuil golf course. **Restaurant** service 1200 and 1900 (closed Sunday evening); menus 98-270F, also à la carte; specialities: homard grillé au porto, truite de rivière gratinée à la crème de livarot.

This hotel in the midst of the green Normandy countryside has bedrooms in a leafy park in which there are rosebeds and fruit trees. Here you can enjoy the delights of solitude in your own chalet among the trees, or spend hours at any time of day either reading or in conversation in one of the little sitting rooms. In the dining room you can eat typical regional dishes, varying according to season, and prepared from the fresh produce of the hotel's kitchen garden.

How to get there *(Map 8): 21km south of Rouen via A13, Louviers-Sud exit, then N154.*

Hôtel du Golf★★

Golf du Vaudreuil
27100 Le Vaudreuil (Eure)
Tel. 32.59.02.94 - Fax 32.59.67.39 - Mme Launay

Open all year. **Rooms** 20 with telephone, bath or shower (17 with WC and TV, 10 with minibar). **Price** single 160-220F, double 220-350F. **Meals** breakfast 25-40F, served 0700-1100. No restaurant. **Credit cards** Amex, Eurocard, MasterCard, Visa. **Pets** dogs allowed (+20F). **Facilities** 18-hole golf course, parking. **Nearby** Rouen, Château Gaillard, 18-hole golf course at Le Vaudreuil.

The Château de Vaudreuil was destroyed during the Revolution and all that remains of it are two lodges beside an avenue that leads nowhere. The château's large park is now a golf course and one of the lodges a hotel. It is quiet here, and you can enjoy views over the greens. The bedrooms, with big windows and almond green wallpaper, are simply furnished but pleasant. They are small on the first floor but considerably larger on the second. The decor is modern but elegant and the breakfast room and the adjoining sitting area look out on the grass. There is no restaurant at the hotel but golfers can eat at the golf club. Guests are cordially welcomed.

How to get there *(Map 8): 15km south east of Rouen via A13, exit 18 or 19; then D77 to the entrance of Le Vaudreuil.*

Hôtel du Château d'Agneaux★★★

Avenue Sainte-Marie
50180 Saint-Lô - Agneaux (Manche)
Tel. 33.57.65.88 - Fax 33.56.59.21 - M. and Mme Groult

Open all year. **Rooms** 12 with shower, WC and TV (10 with minibar). **Price** double 360-880F, suite 950F. **Meals** breakfast 55-65F. **Pets** dogs allowed (+50F). **Facilities** tennis (30F), sauna (80F), parking. **Nearby** church and museum in Saint-Lô, château de Torigni-sur-Vire; 9-hole golf course at Courtainville. **Restaurant** service 1930-2100; menus 180-260F, also à la carte; specialities: fish and desserts.

Leave behind the ghastly suburbs of Saint-Lô: Agneaux has escaped the bunglings of the town planners. You reach it along a narrow gravel lane which quickly carries you away from the main road to the old chapel, the château and the watchtower looking out over the unspoilt and peaceful valley, with nothing in view but copses of trees and the river Vire flowing gently through the green countryside. M. et Mme Groult owned a farmhouse inn for many years. Agneaux is their dream come true, and they have refurbished it with love. The bedrooms are very comfortable and prettily though not overwhelmingly decorated, with some four-poster beds, some fine floor tiling and lovely wood floors. Rooms 11 and 12 are very quiet and Room 4 has five windows through which the daylight shines from three of the four points of the compass. The château is a haven of peace.

How to get there *(Map 7): 1.5km west of Saint-Lô via D900.*

Manoir de Roche Torin***
50220 Courtils (Manche)
Tel. 33.70.96.55 - Fax 33.48.35.20
Mme Barraux

Open 15 March – 15 Nov. **Rooms** 12 with telephone, bath or shower, WC and TV (3 with minibar). **Price** single 380F, double 420-580F, suite 750F. **Meals** breakfast 48F, served 0800-1030. **Credit cards** Amex, Diners, Visa. **Pets** dogs allowed (+35F). **Facilities** parking. **Nearby** orientation viewpoint table in the Jardin des Plantes in Avranches, Mont Saint-Michel. **Restaurant** light meals only; local specialities.

This turn of the century gentleman's residence combines old and contemporary styles in a happy compromise. Flowered fabrics brighten the lounge and its accommodating sofas and in the dining room there is a splendid fireplace where the chef grills lobsters, beef and salt-meadow lamb. The bedrooms follow the style of the rest of the house mixing modern furniture with cane chairs and period pieces. They are all very comfortable. The terrace and garden are very pleasant and during the fine weather a bar and meal service is provided there. This is a lovely spot and between the hotel and Mont Saint-Michel, which can be seen in the distance, there is nothing but fields crossed by small inlets and dotted with sheep.

How to get there *(Map 7): 22km south west of Avranches via N15, then towards Mont Saint-Michel via D43.*

Auberge de la Sélune**

2, rue Saint-Germain
50220 Ducey (Manche)
Tel. 33.48.53.62 - Fax 33.48.90.30 - M. Girres

Open all year (closed Monday 1 Oct – 1 March). **Rooms** 19 with telephone, bath and WC. **Price** double 240-260F. **Meals** breakfast 32F, served 0700-0930; half board 260-270F, full board 370-380F (per pers., 3 days min.) **Credit cards** Eurocard, MasterCard, Visa. **Pets** dogs not allowed. **Facilities** parking. **Nearby** orientation table in the Jardin des Plantes in Avranches, Mont Saint-Michel. **Restaurant** service 1200-1400, 1900-2100; menus 72-180F, also à la carte; specialities: pie au crabe, paupiettes de saumon au poiré, rable de lapereau farci au vinaigre de cidre.

The Auberge de la Sélune is a well-proportioned former almshouse. It is in a country setting on the edge of the village in a large garden by the river Sélune, where you could possibly catch a salmon. The auberge has large high-ceilinged rooms and the pleasant bedrooms are furnished with coloured cane furniture and pretty fabrics. A good number of them look out on a delightful vista of the flowering garden and the tranquil river. The rooms situated in the small annexe are also very attractive and open onto the lawn. The auberge is well kept, elegant and comfortable; you will have a cordial and hospitable welcome there.

How to get there *(Map 7): 10km south east of Avranches via N175, then N176 towards Saint-Hilaire-du-Harcouët (follow signs as you enter Ducey).*

Hôtel de France et des Fuchsias★★

18, rue du Maréchal-Foch
50550 Saint-Vaast-la-Hougue (Manche)
Tel. 33.54.42.26 – Fax 33.43.46.79 – M. and Mme Brix

Open March – 6 Jan (closed Monday in low season). **Rooms** 33 with telephone (28 with bath or shower, WC and TV). **Price** single 270F, double 270-370F. **Meals** breakfast 38F, served 0800-1030; half board 265-315F, full board 335-400F (per pers., 3 days min.) **Credit cards** accepted. **Pets** dogs allowed (+40F). **Facilities** bicycle hire. **Nearby** Valognes, Barfleur, Thomas Henry museum in Cherbourg; 9-hole golf course at Fontenay-en-Cotentin. **Restaurant** service 1200-1400, 1900-2115 (closed Tuesday lunchtime in Nov, Dec, March, April); menus 75-230F, also à la carte; specialities: choucroute de la mer au beurre blanc, raviole de homard et son coulis.

At Saint Vaast-la-Hougue on the eastern side of the Cotentin peninsula the climate is so mild that mimosas flourish. The bedrooms in this old coaching inn are simple but elegant, with muted colours and good furniture (though Room 14 is a bit small). The food is excellent and happily combines the products of the sea with those of the nearby farm at Quettehou. There is a small fishing port quite close, a sandy beach, and pretty countryside with hedgerows and woods. This part of Normandy has a particularly kind climate and in the last two weeks of August there are open-air chamber concerts in the garden. These are free for hotel guests.

How to get there (Map 7): 37km south east of Cherbourg via N13 to Valognes, then D902 and D1 to Saint-Vaast-la-Hougue (it's in the town centre).

La Verte Campagne**

50660 Trelly (Manche)
Tel. 33.47.65.33
M. and Mme Bernou

Open 1 Feb – 30 Nov and 20 Dec – 6 Jan (closed Sunday evening and Monday in low season). **Rooms** 8 (4 with bath, 1 with shower, 3 with WC). **Price** single 100F, double 200-350F. **Meals** breakfast 30F, served 0830-1000; half board +170F, full board +270F (per pers., 3 days min.) **Credit cards** Visa. **Pets** dogs not allowed. **Facilities** parking. **Nearby** Mont Saint-Michel, valley of the Vire, 18-hole Granville golf course at Bréhal. **Restaurant** service 1230-1430, 1930-2130; menus 140-320F, also à la carte; specialities: filet de canette aux épices et aux figues, vinaigrette tiède de rougets aux artichauds, moelleux au chocolat et mousse chicorée.

This hotel in an authentic Normandy farmhouse of the 18th century and, situated as it is in the heart of wooded countryside, deserves its name. It is not a large place but its size gives it an intimate, family-home atmosphere. The stone walls, beams and furniture, antique ceramics and copperware create an ambience which is rustic yet civilised, comfortable and welcoming. All the bedrooms are different, but whether large or small they are furnished with an eye to harmony and comfort. There is an air of English elegance in the delightful fabrics used and the charming furniture. Meals are not served in the garden but it is a good place for quiet relaxation. The food is well thought of by guests and so is the outstanding friendliness of Madame Bernou, who makes this a rather special place.

How to get there *(Map 7): 42km south west of Saint-Lô via D972 to Coutances, then D971 towards Bréhal to Quettreville-sur-Sienne, then D35 and D49.*

Manoir du Lys★★★

La Croix Gauthier
61140 Bagnoles–de–l'Orne (Orne)
Tel. 33.37.80.69 – Fax 33.30.05.80 – M. and Mme Quinton

Open 28 Feb – 10 Jan (closed Sunday and Monday 1 Jan – Easter and 1 Nov – 10 Jan). **Rooms** 23 with telephone, bath or shower, WC, TV and minibar. **Price** single and double 300-650F, suite 650-1000F. **Meals** breakfast 50F; half board 350-550F, full board 500-680F (per pers., 3 days min.) **Credit cards** accepted. **Pets** dogs allowed (+35F). **Facilities** tennis, golf (3 greens), parking. **Nearby** Andaine forest, Bonvouloir lighthouse, château de Carrouges, Sées cathedral, 9-hole golf course at Bagnoles-de-l'Orne. **Restaurant** service 1230-1430, 1930-2130; menus 120-350F, also à la carte; specialities: raviolis de grenouilles, duo de boudin, carré d'agneau de pré-salé.

The Manoir du Lys is in the midst of the Andaine forest near Bagnoles de l'Orne, the only spa in western Normandy. In this peaceful place you will be captivated by the blend of tranquility and luxury. The bedrooms are light and airy and well furnished. Number 1 is ideal for families with children as it has a mezzanine with two extra beds, while Number 2 has a large terrace. The attic rooms look out onto the orchard where you can sometimes see deer attracted by the fruit. There are beautiful lawns around the hotel and sometimes meals are served outside. M. Quinton looks after the cooking and his excellent food features Normandy specialities.

How to get there *(Map 7): 53km west of Alençon via N12 to Pré-au-Pail, then N176 and D916.*

Auberge du Val au Cesne

Le Val au Cesne
76190 Croix-Mare (Seine-Maritime)
Tel. 35.56.63.06 – Fax 35.56.92.78 – M. Carel

Open all year. **Rooms** 5 with telephone, bath, WC and TV. **Price** double 350F. **Meals** breakfast 45F, served 0800-1100; half board 300F, full board 350F (per pers., 3 days min.) **Credit cards** Visa. **Pets** dogs allowed. **Facilities** parking. **Nearby** Rouen cathedral, church and museum in Yvetot, abbey of Saint-Wandrille; 18-hole golf course at Etretat. **Restaurant** service 1200-1400, 1900-2100; menu 150F, also à lar carte; specialities: terrine de raie, tête et fraise de veau, sole farcie à la mousse de langoustines, escalope de dinde 'Vieille Henriette', feuilleté aux pommes.

Primarily this is a splendidly furnished restaurant with a fine reputation. M. Carel set up five comfortable bedrooms in a nearby house at the request of his clientele. The house is in a pretty little valley and thanks to the good taste of the furnishings, which are in the style of the region, and the charm of the architecture, you will feel quite at home here. You will find some of the garden occupied by animals; there are a couple of peacocks, an aviary and a cattery. Though there is a road nearby it will not disturb you, for there is hardly any traffic when night falls.

How to get there *(Map 8): 11km north west of Rouen via A15 towards Barentin, then N15 towards Yvetot.*

Le Donjon

Chemin de Saint-Clair
76790 Etretat (Seine-Maritime)
Tel. 35.27.08.23 - Fax 35.29.92.24 - Mme Abo Dib

Open all year. **Rooms** 8 with telephone, bath or shower and WC. **Price** single and double 380-580F. **Meals** breakfast 50F, served 0800-1000; half board and full board 600-800F. **Credit cards** Amex, Diners. **Pets** dogs allowed (+50F). **Facilities** swimming pool, parking. **Nearby** Etretat cliffs, châteaux of Valmont and Bailleul, Trinity church and Bénédictine museum in Fécamp, 18-hole golf course at Etretat. **Restaurant** service 1200-1400, 1930-2200; menus 130-260F, also à la carte; specialities: seafood, fish.

Overlooking the charming town of Etretat, with its cliffs and pebble beach, this small ivy-covered château is a seductive place by any standards. The bedrooms have recently been refurbished, and are all equally pretty. They have original names: there is the Koala Room (a suite with a children's bedroom), Arsène's bedroom, the Serge room, which is the smallest and overlooks the swimming pool, and the Rétro Room, aptly named as it contains photos of the wedding of the grandparents of Mme Abo Dib, the owner. The ground floor has several small lounges decorated in a turn-or-the-century style. From one of them there are panoramic views of the Etretat cliffs. The chef is full of ideas and his cooking is first rate.

How to get there (Map 8): 17km west of Fécamp via D940.

Auberge du Clos Normand*

22, rue Henri IV
76370 Martin-Eglise (Seine-Maritime)
Tel. 35.82.71.01 - M. and Mme Hauchecorne

Open 1 Jan – 23 March, 31 March – 22 Nov, 22-31 Dec (closed Monday evening and Tuesday). **Rooms** 7 with telephone, bath or shower, WC and TV. **Price** double 260-360F, suite 450F. **Meals** breakfast 32F, served 0800-1000; half board 342-392F (per pers., 3 days min.) **Credit cards** Access, Amex, Diners, Visa. **Pets** dogs allowed (+50F). **Nearby** castle and museum in Dieppe, church and graveyard in Varengeville, château de Mesnières-en-Bray, St-Säens, valley of the Varenne and Eawy forest, 18-hole golf course at Etretat. **Restaurant** service 1215-1400, 1930-2100; à la carte; specialities: tarte aux moules, filets de sole dieppoise, turbotin sauce crème estragon, tarte aux pommes.

This is a beautiful little hotel, dating back to the 15th century, on the edge of the forest of Arques, a few kilometres from the sea. From the pretty rustic dining room you can watch the chef at his stove; just the scene for a relaxed and intimate atmosphere. The garden borders the river and you can lunch in the open. There are seven bedrooms in the annexe at the bottom of the garden, all of them havens of tranquility. All are different, enlivened with floral wallpaper, and they look out on the green landscape. As is often the case with overnight stops you will be asked to dine in the hotel.

How to get there *(Map 1): 5km south east of Dieppe via D1 towards Neufchâtel-en-Bray.*

Auberge de la Rouge★★★

Route du Havre-Goderville – Saint-Léonard
76400 Fécamp (Seine-Maritime)
Tel. 35.28.07.59 – Fax 35.28.70.55 – M. and Mme Guyot

Open all year except February school holiday. **Rooms** 8 with telephone, shower, WC, TV and minibar. **Price** single and double 280F. **Meals** breakfast 30F, served 0700-1000. **Credit cards** accepted. **Pets** dogs allowed. **Facilities** parking. **Nearby** Etretat cliffs, châteaux of Valmont and Bailleul, Trinity church and Bénédictine museum in Fécamp, 18-hole golf course at Etretat. **Restaurant** service 1200-1430, 1900-2130 (closed Sunday evening and Monday); menus 105-260F, also à la carte; specialities: sardines fraîches au gros sel, filet du pêcheur mousseline, morue fécampoise à la crème, ris de veau aux morilles, sabayon.

Although this hotel is situated on a main road 2 km from Fécamp you need not worry about being disturbed by noise. The bedrooms, recently converted from the old ballroom, look out on the garden and are soundproofed. They are all identical, modern, comfortable and have a mezzanine with an extra bed. The bathrooms have showers. The food is delicious and plentiful. The tasteful rustic decor and the cordial welcome from the owner make this a very agreeable place to stop.

How to get there (Map 8): 2km south of Fécamp via D925 towards Goderville.

Château de Sassetot–le-Mauconduit

Sassetot-le-Mauconduit
76540 Valmont (Seine-Maritime)
Tel. 35.28.00.11 - Fax 35.28.50.00 - Mlle Dormet

Open Feb – Dec (closed Sunday evening and Monday, Nov – Feb). **Rooms** 30 with telephone, bath or shower, WC and TV. **Price** double 415-730F. **Meals** breakfast 50F, served 0730-0930; half board 760F (2 pers.) **Credit cards** Visa, Amex. **Pets** dogs allowed (+60F). **Facilities** parking. **Nearby** church of the Trinité and Benedictine museum at Fécamp, St-Valéry-en-Caux, Châteaux of Valmont and Bailleul, church and château of Cany-Barville, 18-hole golf course at Etretat. **Restaurant** service 1930-2130 (closed Sunday evening and Monday); menus 115-300F; also à la carte; specialities: foie gras and home smoked salmon.

This elegant classical château once welcomed Empress Sissi of Austria. The interior does not overwhelm and there are some nice, well-proportioned rooms overlooking the vast English-style park. The bedrooms, reached via a double landing wooden staircase, are often hung with green or pink paper and have been thoroughly and comfortably refurbished. The bathrooms are equally good. The furniture, antique and reproduction, varies from room to room but fits in well with the decor. You will enjoy the creatively cooked food in the panelled dining room or, in summer, on the terrace. In the evenings you can play bar billiards. A cordial and attentive welcome awaits you.

How to get there *(Map 8): 74km north west of Rouen via N15 to Valliquerville, then D926 and D17.*

Hôtel Sud-Bretagne★★★★

42, Bd de la République
44380 Pornichet (Loire-Atlantique)
Tel. 40.11.65.00 – Fax 40.61.73.70 – M. Bardouil

Open all year. **Rooms** 30 with telephone, bath, WC and TV. **Price** single 450F, double 550-1000F, suite 1200-1500F. **Meals** breakfast 60F; half board 550-850F, full board 750-1050F. **Credit cards** accepted. **Pets** dogs allowed (+35F). **Facilities** swimming pool, tennis, parking. **Nearby** La Baule, La Brière and the Guérande marshes, 18-hole La Baule golf course at St-Denac. **Restaurant** menus 190-450F, also à la carte.

Ideally located not far from the beaches at La Baule, the Hôtel Sud-Bretagne has been run by the same family since 1912, and to this day every member of the family joins in running and improving the hotel. The family's contributions range from interior decoration to the organisation of excursions aboard 'Ia Orana' ('welcome' in Tahitian), a 17-metre teak and mahogany ketch. The atmosphere that prevails in the hotel owes a lot to the family's dedication. You will feel at home. And a magnificent home it is, where each room has its own style. There is a lounge with a cosy fireplace, a billiard room, and several dining-rooms looking out onto the turquoise waters of an indoor swimming-pool. Outside, elegant garden furniture invites you to relax in the sun. Each bedroom has a different theme (ducks, cherries, Empress Josephine, for example) reflected in the choice of fabrics, furniture and objects. There are some small apartments, with a lounge, a terrace, and typical Breton box beds for children. The Sud-Bretagne is one of a few luxury hotels which has retained all its charm and character.

How to get there *(Map 14): 5km east of La Baule.*

Auberge de Kerhinet★★

Le Kerhinet
44410 Saint-Lyphard (Loire–Atlantique)
Tel. 40.61.91.46 – Mme Pebay-Arnauné

Open all year (closed Tuesday evening and Wednesday). **Rooms** 7 with bath and WC. **Price** single 240F, double 260F. **Meals** breakfast 40F, served 0800-1100; half board 295F. **Credit cards** Visa, Diners, Amex. **Pets** dogs allowed. **Facilities** parking. **Nearby** medieval town of Guérande, marshes, La Brière regional park, Croisic aquarium, 18-hole La Bretesche golf course, 18-hole La Baule golf course at St-Denac. **Restaurant** service 1200-1500, 1900-2300; menus 80-200F, also à la carte; specialities: émincés de pimpenneaux, anguilles au roquefort, persillade de cuisses de grenouilles fraîches, petits foies de canard aux pleurottes, matelote d'anguille à la Brièronne.

This lovely little auberge lies in a listed village which has been immaculately rebuilt and restored. Thatched roofs and stone walls are commonplace and create an atmosphere of a place built with loving care. The auberge has a rustic style, with the spirit of the countryside in the bar, dining room and the bedrooms, which are in a separate and quiet chalet. The food is good, the welcome cordial, and this is a good place to know in this region.

How to get there *(Map 14): 23km north of St-Nazaire via D47 to Saint-Lyphard via Saint-André-des-Eaux.*

Abbaye de la Villeneuve★★★★

Route des Sables-d'Olonne
44840 Les Sorinières (Loire–Atlantique)
Tel. 40.04.40.25 – Fax 40.31.28.45 – M. Lesmarie

Open all year. **Rooms** 20 with telephone, bath, WC (12 with TV). **Price** single 470F, double 515-890F, suite 1090-1245F. **Meals** breakfast 65F, served 0645-1030; half board 410-925F, full board 615-1130F. **Credit cards** accepted. **Pets** dogs allowed. **Facilities** swimming pool, parking. **Nearby** art museum and Jules Verne museum at Nantes, valley of the Erdre, Clisson, 18-hole golf course at Nantes. **Restaurant** service 1200-1330, 1900-2130; menus 170-460F, also à la carte; specialities: saumon fumé à l'abbaye crème de raifort, corne d'abondance de sandre aux beurres du Val-de-Loire, noisettes de canard de challans aux pêches acidulées.

The abbey was founded in 1201 by Constance of Brittany, destroyed during the French Revolution then rebuilt in 1977. Today this old Cistercian abbey is a hotel. The great hall of the monastery is now the restaurant and the bedrooms retain the magnificent timbers of the building's frame. In the lounges plaster ceilings and stone fireplaces give the room a grand air but as places to relax in they are less forbidding then the austerity of the original abbey. An air of elegant comfort pervades this place, which is only ten minutes from the centre of Nantes. You will be looked after in grand hotel style.

How to get there *(Map 14): 10km south of Nantes via N137 towards La Roche-sur-Yon. It's 4km from Les Sorinières.*

Relais du Gué de Selle★★★

Route de Mayenne
Evron – 53600 Mézangers (Mayenne)
Tel. 43.90.64.05 – Fax 43.90.60.82 – MM. Paris and Peschard

Open 1 March – 20 Jan (closed Sunday evening and Monday in low season). **Rooms** 26 with telephone, bath, shower, WC and TV. **Price** single 260-342F, double 300-380F, suite 438F. **Meals** breakfast 39F, served 0700-0930; half board 236-380F, full board 300-480F (per pers., 3 days min.) **Credit cards** Visa, Eurocard, Amex, Diners. **Pets** dogs allowed (+38F). **Facilities** tennis (25F), sauna (42F), parking. **Nearby** basilica of Evron, fortified town of Sainte-Suzanne, château du Rocher, Clermont abbey, 9-hole golf course at Laval. **Restaurant** service 1200-1400, 1945-2100; menus 88-200F; also à la carte; specialities: chausson de homard au foie gras, pigeonneau farci et ses pâtes fraiches, rosace de pommes tièdes au caramel.

This hotel has been converted from an old U-shaped farm built in 1843, the date being carved in a beam in the entrance hall. Though close to the road the hotel has about 80 hectares, including a lake, around it. There are many things to do (bicycles are provided) and there is even a gym. The bedrooms, like the bathrooms, are very well equipped and the ones that look out over the lake are particularly recommended. The dining room, where good food and a fine Anjou wine are served, is a huge room with a pleasant atmosphere. It was formerly a cow-shed and grain store.

How to get there *(Map 7): 39km north east of Laval via A81, Vaiges exit then D24 and D20 to Evron via la Chapelle-Rainsoin, and D7 to beyond Mézangers.*

Hôtel L'Ermitage★★★
53340 Saulges (Mayenne)
Tel. 43.90.52.28 – Fax 43.90.56.61
M. and Mme Janvier

Open all year except Feb (closed Sunday evening and Monday in low season). **Rooms** 36 with telephone, bath or shower, WC, TV and minibar. **Price** single 250-300F, double 280-390F, suite 450F. **Meals** breakfast 42F, served 0730-1000; half board 300-420F, full board 390-520F (per pers., 3 days min.) **Credit cards** accepted. **Pets** dogs allowed (+40F). **Facilities** heated swimming pool, sauna (40F), health centre, parking. **Nearby** caves of Roquefort and Margot at Saulges, basilica of Evron, fortified town of Sainte-Suzanne, château du Rocher, abbey of Clermont, 9-hole golf course at Laval. **Restaurant** service 1200-1400, 1915-2100; menus 95-240F, also à la carte; specialities: foie gras poêlé au pomme, langoustines sauce orange, escalope de silure au vin de Loire, filet de daguet grand veneur.

L'Ermitage is situated in the region of the Evre and Vegre, two charming fishing rivers in the heart of the Mayenne. It is a modern building in the centre of the small and quiet market town of Saulges. Major refurbishment has done much to improve the comfort of this hotel. The bedrooms have been completely renovated and all look out onto the countryside. The garden has been enlarged by the addition of a meadow, and the restaurant with its views of the park has also been refurbished to celebrate the arrival of Thierry Janvier, the son of the family, who has been in Paris for two years studying with the best chefs.

How to get there (Map 15): *37km east of Laval via A81, Vaignes exit, then D24 and D20.*

Relais Cicéro★★★

18, boulevard d'Alger
72200 La Flèche (Sarthe)
Tel. 43.94.14.14 - Fax 43.45.98.96 - Mme Levasseur

Open 4 Jan – 19 Dec. **Rooms** 21 with telephone, bath or shower, WC and TV. **Price** single 380-425F, double 495-675F. **Meals** breakfast 45F, served from 0700. No restaurant. **Credit cards** Amex, Eurocard, Visa. **Pets** small dogs allowed. **Nearby** chapel of Notre Dame-des-Vertus, Tertre Rouge zoological park, château de Lude, Solesmes abbey.

This hotel isn't really a country hotel since it is in the small, pretty town of La Flèche, yet the Relais Cicero has various advantages that make it a first-class place to stay. It is situated on a peaceful tree-lined street away from the bustle and noise of the town. Its large garden is tranquil and the beautiful 16th- and 18th-century building is both comfortably and elegantly furnished. There is a bar, a reading room and a television room. In the dining room a very good breakfast is served – in winter to the accompaniment of a blazing fire in the fireplace. The bedrooms are comfortable and tastefully furnished. Our favourite rooms are those in the main building.

How to get there *(Map 15): 52km north west of Angers via A11, Durtal exit, then N23 to La Flèche.*

422

Auberge du Port-des-Roches★★

72800 Luché-Pringé (Sarthe)
Tel. 43.45.44.48 – Fax 43.45.39.61
M. Martin

Open all year (closed Sunday evening and Monday). **Rooms** 13 with telephone, bath or shower (11 with WC, 6 with TV). **Price** double 200-290F. **Meals** breakfast 30F, served 0800-0900; half board 230-270F, full board 300-340F (per pers., 5 days min.) **Credit cards** accepted. **Pets** dogs not allowed. **Facilities** parking. **Nearby** châteaux of Montmirail, Courtanvaux and Saint-Calais, 18-hole Le Mans golf course at Lulsanne. **Restaurant** service 1200-1330, 1900-2030; menus 135-160F, also à la carte; specialities: filet de sandre au vinaigre de cidre, terrine maison, charlotte aux fruits.

L ocated by the side of a pretty road in the valley of the Loir, this comfortable, unpretentious hotel has a charming terrace (on the other side from the road) which overlooks the Loir. There are 13 comfortable, light bedrooms. Mme Martin welcomes you with a smile and the cooking of M. Martin relies on the local market produce. The television room, the large dining room and most of the bedrooms look out over the entrance courtyard. Only three bedrooms have views of the Loir. A friendly place to stay for visiting the valley of the Loir or the châteaux of the Loire.

How to get there *(Map 16): 40km south west of Le Mans in La Flèche direction, then D13 to Luché-Pringé and D214 to "Le Port-des-Roches".*

Hôtel du Martinet★★

Place de la Croix–Blanche
85230 Bouin (Vendée)
Tel. 51.49.08.94 – Mme Huchet

Open all year. **Rooms** 16 with telephone, bath or shower and WC (10 with TV). **Price** single 180-200F, double 245-310F. **Meals** breakfast 30F. No restaurant. **Credit cards** accepted. **Pets** dogs allowed (+20F). **Facilities** bicycles, swimming pool, parking. **Nearby** church of St-Philbert-de-Grand-Lieu, Machecoul, oyster beds, 18-hole golf courses at St-Jean-de-Monts and at Pornic.

One can only be enchanted by this late 18th-century residence where the atmosphere of a well run household reigns and the smell of wax mingles with that of bowls of cut flowers. The furniture in the bedrooms on the ground and first floors is plain but very comfortable. There are two other bedrooms under the eaves which are ideal for families of four. A large garden to the rear of the house has good views of the countryside and the marshes of the Vendée. There isn't a restaurant in the hotel but the husband of the owner, an oyster breeder, is pleased to let you taste the oysters from his oyster beds.

How to get there *(Map 14): 51km south west of Nantes via D751 and D758 in the direction of Noirmoutier.*

Château de la Vérie★★★
Route de Saint-Gilles-Croix-de-Vie
85300 Challans (Vendée)
Tel. 51.35.33.44 - Fax 51.35.14.84 - M. Martin

Open all year. **Rooms** 11 with telephone, bath, shower, WC, TV and minibar. **Price** single and double 350-850F. **Meals** breakfast 48-70F, served 0730-1030. **Credit cards** Visa, Mastercard. **Pets** dogs allowed (+50F). **Facilities** swimming pool, tennis, parking. **Nearby** château and market at Clisson, church of St-Philbert-de-Grand-Lieu, Machecoul, St-Gilles-Croix-de-Vie, la Fromentine (boats for Ile d'Yeu). **Restaurant** service 1230-1400, 1930-2130 (closed Sunday evening and Monday in low season); menus 100-280F, also à la carte; specialities: pommes de terre de Noirmoutier farcies aux langoustines, canard de challans aux sang en deux services.

The sea used to come this far but has retreated, leaving behind some lush marshland. Recently converted into a hotel, the château boasts some exquisite bedrooms, both comfortable and well renovated. Japanese wickerwork, vivid colours, charming little engravings and antique furniture – nothing is lacking: even the mirrors in the bathrooms have china frames. The dining room and lounge have been decorated in the same spirit; they are welcoming rooms, very like a private house. These two rooms look out onto a large terrace where breakfast is served and you can contemplate the lush greenness of the grounds. There is a swimming pool not far away, useful because this is the second most sunny part of France.

How to get there *(Map 14): 60km south of Nantes via D937 to Rocheservière, then D753; it's 2.5km from the town hall in the direction of Saint-Gilles-Croix-de-Vie.*

Flux Hôtel★★

27, rue Pierre-Henry, Port Joinville
85350 Ile-d'Yeu (Vendée)
Tel. 51.58.36.25 - Mme Cadou

Open 1 Jan – 29 Nov (closed Sunday evening in low season). **Rooms** 16 with telephone, bath or shower and TV. **Price** double 260-280F. **Meals** breakfast 32F, served 0830-0900; half board 290F, full board 360F (per pers., recommended in July, Aug.) **Credit cards** Visa. **Pets** dogs allowed (+25F). **Facilities** parking. **Nearby** Ker-Chalon beach, lighthouse, Saint-Sauveur church, ruins of the old château. **Restaurant** service 1200-1400, 1930-2100 (closed Sunday evening in low season); menus 80-160F; specialities: fish, shellfish, tarte aux pruneaux.

A short distance from Port-Joinville, there is a small hotel whose name, jealously guarded by generations of guests, is the Flux Hôtel. The bedrooms are all quiet and comfortable, those in the annexe have a terrace, and the furnishing is simple and modern. The shellfish you and your children catch during the afternoon are cooked and served to you in the evening. However, if you want to be one of these lucky people, you must book far in advance and agree to half board and even full board during July and August.

How to get there *(Map 14): steamer connections with Port-Joinville (tel. 51.58.36.66) and Fromentine (tel. 51.68.52. 32).*

Hôtel du Général d'Elbée★★★

Place d'Armes
85330 Noirmoutier-en-l'Ile (Vendée)
Tel. 51.39.10.29 - Fax 51.39.08.23 - M. Savry

Open 1 April – 1 Oct. **Rooms** 28 with telephone, bath and WC. **Price** single 375-640F, double 425-670F, suite 880-1100F. **Meals** breakfast 55F, served 0730-1130. **Credit cards** accepted. **Pets** dogs allowed (+60F). **Facilities** swimming pool. **Nearby** art and folk museum at La Guérinière, L'Herbaudière, salt marshes. **Restaurant** service 1200-1400, 1930-2200; menus 90-240F, also à la carte; specialities: plateau de fruits de mer, maquereaux frais en marinade, huîtres gratinées.

The Hôtel du Général d'Elbée is in a large old building on the edge of a small canal. The antique furniture in the cosy and comfortable bedrooms adds to the charm of this place. A walled garden contains a large swimming pool The cooking is good, unpretentious, and benefits from produce fresh from the market. Attentive service.

How to get there *(Map 14): 82km south west of Nantes via D751 and D758. Access by the bridge from Fromentine. The hotel is in the centre of the town.*

Hôtel Les Prateaux★★

Bois de la Chaize
85330 Noirmoutier-en-l'Ile (Vendée)
Tel. 51.39.12.52 - Fax 51.39.46.28 - M. Blouard

Open 15 March – 30 Sept. **Rooms** 13 with telephone, bath or shower (9 with WC).
Price single 265F, double 275-380F. **Meals** breakfast 36F, served 0800-0900; half
board 270-362F, full board 300-440F (per pers., obligatory from 15 June – 15 Sept.)
Credit cards Diners, Visa. **Pets** dogs not allowed. **Facilities** parking. **Nearby** church
of St-Philbert-de-Grand-Lieu, Machecoul, oyster beds, 18-hole golf courses at St-
Jean-de-Monts and Pornic. **Restaurant** service 1230-1330, 1930-2030; à la carte;
specialities: fish and shellfish.

This hotel has the feel of a family boarding house, which it once
was. The pleasant, old-fashioned bedrooms and the fairly rigid
meal times are part of its appeal, but above all it is the location that
makes this hotel so attractive. Built in 1939 on the end of the Île
du Noirmoutier in the middle of the forest of la Chaize, it is totally
peaceful. The sea is only about 300 metres away and a walk through
the woods will bring you down to a pretty little beach. The main
house contains the restaurant, lounge and some of the bedrooms,
the others being a few steps away in the garden. The atmosphere
is very summery and there is a scent reminiscent of the côte d'Azur
from the pines, mimosa and superbly coloured arbutus.

How to get there *(Map 14): 82km south west of Nantes by D751 and
D758. Access by road bridge from Fromentine, 1.5km from Noirmoutier to
Bois de la Chaize then follow signs.*

Logis de la Couperie★★

85000 La Roche-sur-Yon (Vendée)
Tel. 51.37.21.19
Mme Oliveau

Open all year. **Rooms** 7 with telephone, bath or shower, WC and TV. **Price** single 260-420F, double 285-470F, suite 420-470F. **Meals** breakfast 38F, served 0730-1000. No restaurant. **Credit cards** Visa, Amex. **Pets** dogs not allowed. **Facilities** parking. **Nearby** history museum and château of Chabotterie, Saint-Sulpice-le-Verdon, Tiffauges.

The Logis de la Couperie is a former manor house rebuilt at the end of the 18th century. It is situated in open countryside, five minutes from the centre of town, and surrounded by a two-hectare park with a small lake. Nature-lovers will find peace and a warm welcome here. In the large entrance hall there is a magnificent staircase which leads to the upper floors. The bedrooms are all comfortable and tastefully furnished with antiques and regional furniture. There is a well-stocked lounge/library, where a good log fire burns in winter. Breakfast, which can include home-made apple juice and the local brioche, is served in the dining room.

How to get there *(Map 14): on D80, five minutes from the town centre, via the Route Nationale from Cholet.*

Hôtel La Barbacane★★

2, place de l'Eglise
85130 Tiffauges (Vendée)
Tel. 51.65.75.59 – Fax 51.65.71.91 – Mme Bidan

Open all year. **Rooms** 16 with telephone, bath or shower, WC and TV. **Price** single 220-285F, double 249-325F. **Meals** breakfast 27-40F. No restaurant. **Credit cards** accepted. **Pets** dogs allowed. **Facilities** swimming pool, billiards, garage. **Nearby** ruins of château of Gilles de Retz ('Blue Beard'), 18-hole golf course at Cholet.

The Barbacane is a handsome 19th-century building and has a park extending for 1 hectare behind the hotel. All the bedrooms are comfortable and have their own bathrooms. Some look out on the entrance courtyard in front of the church and some on the park. The ones on the top floor have a panoramic view of Gilles de Retz's château. In summer there is a bar service around the swimming pool and in the garden, which is planted with old cedars, magnolias, wisteria and roses. There is no restaurant but the nearest one adjoins the grounds.

How to get there *(Map 15): 20km west of Cholet via D753 towards Montaigu.*

Auberge de la Rivière★★
85770 Velluire (Vendée)
Tel. 51.52.32.15 - M. and Mme Pajot

Open all year (closed 10 Jan – 20 Feb and Tuesday in low season). **Rooms** 11 with telephone, bath, WC (6 with TV). **Price** single 320F, double 380F. **Meals** breakfast 50F, served 0800-1030; half board 315-345F, full board 395-495F (per pers., 3 days min.) **Credit cards** Visa. **Pets** dogs allowed (+30F). **Nearby** church of Notre-Dame and museum of the Vendée at Fontenay-le-Comte, Poitou marshes, 9-hole golf course at Niort. **Restaurant** service 1215-1400, 2000-2130 (closed Sunday evening and Tuesday in low season); menus 85-205F, also à la carte; specialities: feuilleté de langoustines, foie gras chaud, fish.

This hotel is in the little village of Velluire on the banks of the Vendée and is only a few kilometres from Fontenay-le-Comte. The place is very peaceful and there are various types of bedrooms. The most pleasant are Numbers 11 and 12 on the first floor, which overlook the river. Numbers 5 and 6 on the ground floor of the annexe look directly over the water. The large dining room, where Mme Pajot serves sea fish and regional specialities, has lots of natural light. This is an agreeable and unpretentious place to stay, far from tourist routes and near the Ile de Ré, famous for is salt marshes, through which run a network of canals; these have won them the nick-name Venise Verte.

How to get there *(Map 15): 45km north west of Niort via N148 towards Fontenay-le-Comte, then D938 to Nizeau and D68 to Velluire*

Auberge de Maître Pannetier★★
Place du Corps-de-Garde
85120 Vouvant (Vendée)
Tel. 51.00.80.12 - M. and Mme Guignard

Open all year (closed Sunday evening and Monday). **Rooms** 8 with telephone, bath or shower, WC and TV. **Price** single 180-250F, double 200-270F. **Meals** breakfast 26F, served from 0730; half board 250-270F, full board 300F (per pers., 3 days min.) **Credit cards** all except Amex. **Pets** dogs allowed. **Nearby** circuit of La Brière and the Guérande marshes, 18-hole La Baule golf course at Saint-Denac. **Restaurant** service 1200-1345, 1930-2100; menus 62-300F (children 38F), also à la carte; specialities: croustillant de langoustines à l'estragon, bar aux morilles, poêlée de ris de veau aux huîtres, nougat glacé sur coulis, fraises flambées sur glace vanille.

Vouvant, which is huddled in a meander of the River Mère, is one of the loveliest villages in France, and you will be quite unable to resist strolling through its streets. The hotel is on a small square not far from the church. During your stay there everything will live up to the first impression of a very friendly welcome. The bedrooms are delightful, with English style furniture in light, polished wood. The ones on the first floor are the largest and lightest but all of them are charming. Don't miss meals in the large dining room; the auberge is one of the best eating places in the region. It is decorated in country style and has a splendid fireplace. While waiting for your meal you can watch the lobsters in their tank near the kitchen.

How to get there *(Map 15): 45km north west of Niort via N148 to Fontenay-le-Comte, then D938; at Alouette take D30.*

432

Les Trois Saules★★

Saint-Groux
16230 Mansle (Charente)
Tel. 45.20.31.40 – M. Faure

Open all year. **Rooms** 10 with telephone, shower (1 with bath), WC and TV. **Price** single 170F, double 195F. **Meals** breakfast 25F, served 0800-1000; half board 170F, full board 215 F (per pers., 3 days min.) **Credit cards** Visa, Eurocard, MasterCard. **Pets** dogs allowed. **Facilities** parking. **Nearby** cathedral of St-Pierre at Angoulême, romanesque churches at St-Armand-de-Boixe, Ruffec, Braconne forest, La Rochefoucault, 9-hole l'Hirondelle golf course at Angoulême. **Restaurant** service 1215-1345, 1915-2045 (closed Sunday evening and Monday lunchtime); menus 57-155F, also à la carte; specialities: sole aux cèpes, feuilleté de Saint-Jacques au pineau, bar au beurre blanc, magret de canard aux choux.

This is a real country auberge, simple but comfortable. The bedrooms are not large and their decor is fairly plain, but all of them have showers and one has a bathroom. Regular guests meet here in summer to cycle, fish, relax or swim in the River Charente which flows at the bottom of the garden. The Faure family have owned the hotel for several generations and are the largest family in the village. They all devote themselves to the care of hotel guests with great enthusiasm and kindness and their restaurant is famous throughout the region.

How to get there (Map 23): 26km north of Angoulême via N10 to Mansle, then D361 (3km north west).

Le Logis

17610 Dompierre-sur-Charente (Charente-Maritime)
Tel. 46.91.02.05 – Fax 46.91.00.53
Mme Cocuaud

Open 1 March – 31 Oct. **Rooms** 5 with bath, shower and WC. **Price** double 420F. **Meals** breakfast 45F; half board 430F (per pers., 3 days min.) **Credit cards** not accepted. **Pets** dogs not allowed. **Nearby** Cognac museum at Cognac, distilleries visit at Matha, 18-hole golf course at Cognac. **Restaurant** table d'hôte meals on reservation 200F (wine incl.); specialities: seasonal cuisine.

This hotel is in a fine 17th-century house on a slight rise a few hundred metres from the River Charente, amid the vineyards of Cognac. All the principal rooms, which are nicely proportioned and well furnished, are open to guests. The bedrooms display the same characteristics: they are comfortable, light, airy and prettily decorated. Mme Cocuaud is a lady of character and has a sense of humour; she is a witty hostess and her meals are prepared with the produce she buys in the market every morning.

How to get there *(Map 22): 13km west of Cognac via N141, then D83 (along the banks of the Charente).*

Hôtel France et Angleterre et Champlain★★★

20, rue Rambaud
17000 La Rochelle (Charente-Maritime)
Tel. 46.41.34.66 - Fax 46.41.15.19 - Mme Jouineau

Open all year. **Rooms** 37 with telephone, bath or shower, WC, TV (28 with minibar). **Price** single 290F, double 440F, suite 550F. **Meals** breakfast 40F, served 0715-1130. No restaurant. **Credit cards** Visa, Amex, Diners. **Pets** dogs allowed (+30F). **Facilities** garage (35-48F). **Nearby** New World museum, Lafaille museum, Protestant and arts museum at La Rochelle, Ile de Ré, Esnandes, church portal and keep at Vouvant, Poitou marshes, 18-hole La Prée golf course at La Rochelle.

This 17th-century former convent hides a beautiful garden behind its walls. This is a good place for breakfast. To get to the garden you cross a large hall and some lovely reception rooms. Period woodwork, antique statues and lovely old furniture create a warm and elegant ambience. The bedrooms, reached by lift or by the splendid stone staircase, offer you the choice of a comfortable modern style or the charm and elegance of an earlier era. They are all different in decor but all are comfortable, though you will probably prefer those which overlook the garden. There is no restaurant but the hotel has a demi-pension arrangement with a nearby restaurant. The friendliness of the welcome is just one of the pleasant characteristics of this place.

How to get there (Map 22): in the centre of La Rochelle.

Le Prieuré★★
14, rue de Cornebouc
17380 Tonnay–Boutonne (Charente-Maritime)
Tel. 46.33.20.18 - M. Vernoux

Open 5 Jan – 23 Dec. **Rooms** 18 with telephone, bath or shower, WC and TV. **Price** single 250F, double 295-450F. **Meals** breakfast 45F, served 0730-1000; half board 600-740F (per pers., 3 days min.) **Credit cards** Visa. **Pets** dogs allowed. **Facilities** parking. **Nearby** the house of Pierre Loti, naval museum and royal ropeyard at Rochefort, Brouage, island of Aix (depart from Pointe de la Fumée), Moeze, 9-hole Oléron golf course at Rochefort. **Restaurant** service 1930-2130; menu 140F, also à la carte; specialities: mignon de veau fourré au foie gras, pieds paquets braisés, duo de lotte et Saint-Jacques aux petits légumes, terrine aux trois chocolats, nougat glacé.

The building is in a typically Charentais style with a solid, stone-built appearance. This is very much a family house, the small lounges have an informal atmosphere with their fireplace, cosy corners, bookshelves and potted plants. In the dining room the floor, the furniture and the doorways are all in different kinds of wood. Pictures in muted colours fit in nicely with the tranquil atmosphere. The comfortable bedrooms have recently been refurbished and the bathrooms are brand new. There are two more rooms in a small annexe in the middle of the garden. You will enjoy the cooking.

How to get there (*Map 22*): *21km east of Rochefort via N137. If on A10, exit at Saint-Jean-d'Angely.*

Résidence de Rohan★★★

Parc des Fées
17640 Vaux-sur-Mer (Charente-Maritime)
Tel. 46.39.00.75 - Fax 46.38.29.99 - M. and Mme Seguin

Open Easter – 15 Nov. **Rooms** 41 with telephone, bath or shower, WC and TV. **Price** single and double 300-650F. **Meals** breakfast 45F, served 0730-1300. No restaurant. **Credit cards** Eurocard, MasterCard, Amex, Visa. **Pets** dogs allowed. **Facilities** tennis (+50F), parking. **Nearby** lighthouse at Cordouan, La Rochelle, Sablonceaux abbey, Talmont-sur-Gironde, 18-hole Côte de la Beauté golf course at Royan.

This pretty little family house is in a little wood which runs behind the beach at Nauzan. The pink and white 19th-century building has green lawns sloping gently down to the beach, with chaises longues scattered among the pines. Inside, the decoration is quite different from what you might expect to find in a seaside house. The velvet-covered armchairs in the lounge, the mahogany furniture in Charles X style in the bar, the carpets and rugs all create a rather opulent ambience. All the bedrooms are well furnished but those in the annexe are more spacious; some of them open out onto the garden where you can have your breakfast if you wish.

How to get there *(Map 22): 3km north west of Royan via D25, which follows the coast in the direction of Saint-Palais-sur-Mer.*

Au Marais★★★

46-48, quai Louis-Tardy
79510 Coulon (Deux-Sèvres)
Tel. 49.35.90.43 - Fax 49.35.81.98 - M. and Mme Nerrière

Open 15 March – 15 Nov. **Rooms** 11 with telephone, bath, WC and TV. **Price** double 360F. **Meals** breakfast 50F, served 0730-1000; half board 380F (per pers.) **Credit cards** Visa. **Pets** dogs allowed (+25F). **Nearby** Poitou marshes, museums and church of Notre-Dame at Niort, 18-hole golf course at Maziéres-en-Gatine. **Restaurant** service 1200-1330, 1930-2130 (closed Sunday evening and Monday); menu 165F, also à la carte. Cooking with market produce.

The Poitou marshes surround the hotel, which is on the River Sèvre in the district of Niort. The landing for the boats which tour the canals is a short walk away. The hotel is in traditional Poitou style and has been completely restored without losing any of its character. The carefully chosen furniture is in local style. The bedrooms are pleasant and have well designed bathrooms. The restaurant is separate from the hotel and this ensures a calm and tranquil atmosphere for resident guests. The pastel decor does not quite fit in with the character of the place but the food, which features fresh market produce, is excellent and original. Note that at weekends the lowest price menu is not available. You will find a cordial and kind welcome here.

How to get there *(Map 15): 10km west of Niort via D9 and D1 (beside the Sèvre niortaise).*

Château d'Olbreuse★★

79210 Mauzé-sur-le-Mignon (Deux-Sèvres)
Tel. 49.04.85.74 – M. Arrive

Open March – end Jan (closed Sunday evening and Monday in low season). **Rooms** 11 with telephone, bath or shower and WC. **Price** single and double 185-350F. **Meals** breakfast 35F, served 0800-1000; half board 245F, full board 350F (per pers., 3 days min.) **Credit cards** Visa **Pets** dogs allowed. **Facilities** parking. **Nearby** Maillezais abbey, Fontenay-le-Comte, Poitou marshes, 18-hole golf course at La Rochelle. **Restaurant** service 1200-1400, 1930-2100; menus 88-200F, also à la carte; specialities: ris de veau braisés au pineau, nougat glacé à l'angélique de Niort.

Who would guess that Eleanor d'Olbreuse, later Duchess of Brunswick, from whom all the European royal families are descended, was born in this elegant little château of the Vendée. The interior of the château is pleasant but plain. The dining room and lounge are in a rustic style and have impressive fireplaces. The elegant, old-fashioned bedrooms are on the first floor and look out on the countryside or on the inner courtyard of the château. The cordial welcome and the excellent cooking are typical of traditional French hospitality. This is an ideal base for exploring the Venise Verte of the marshes which lie close by.

How to get there (Map 22) 40km east of La Rochelle via N11.

Le Logis Saint–Martin★★★

Chemin de Pissot
79400 Saint-Maixent-l'Ecole (Deux-Sèvres)
Tel. 49.05.58.68 – Fax 49.76.19.93 – Mme Verdier

Open 1 March – 15 Nov. **Rooms** 10 with telephone, bath or shower, WC and TV. **Price** single 300F, double 380F, suite 450F. **Meals** breakfast 45F, served 0730-0930; half board 375F, full board 475F (per pers., 3 days min.) **Credit cards** Amex, Visa, MasterCard. **Pets** dogs allowed (+40F). **Facilities** parking. **Nearby** Local history museum, arts museum, church of Notre-Dame at Niort, church at Melle, 18-hole golf course at Mazières-en-Gatine. **Restaurant** service 1230-1400, 1930-2130; menus 98-160F, also à la carte; specialities: lumas à l'ail doux, andouille du val de Sèvres, Saint-Jacques au riesling, cheesecake à la façon de Sylvie.

This big 17th-century stone house, cool in hot weather and warm in winter, is a charming place for a weekend. From here you can walk along the River Sèvre which flows past the hotel and through the landscape described by René Bazin in 'L'Eglise Verte', or you can enjoy the local architecture (the region is rich in Romanesque art and buildings). The comfortable bedrooms look out on the river and are all light and airy. The cooking is good and you will get a very warm welcome.

How to get there (Map 15): 24km north east of Niort via N11.

Le Roumanin★★

Chemin des Plèches
04550 Esparron-de-Verdon (Alpes-de-Haute-Provence)
Tel. 92.77.15.91 - Mme Tellier

Open 15 March – 1 Oct and for All Saints. **Rooms** 10 with telephone, bath, shower, WC (1 with TV). **Price** double 260-270F. **Meals** breakfast 35F, served 0800-1000; half board 235-265F. **Credit cards** not accepted. **Pets** dogs not allowed. **Facilities** swimming pool, parking. **Nearby** Gorges du Verdon, lakes route, 18-hole golf course at Pierrevert. **Restaurant** service 2000, on reservation only; Provençal cooking.

Here is a nice simple hotel for lovers of nature and beautiful landscapes. It was built recently and has a marvellous view of the turquoise waters of Lake Esparon. Because of the many 'ins' and 'outs' of its architecture, one feels as though one is in a private house. The interior of the building is uncluttered, almost austere; not a bad thing in very sunny regions. The white walls, old furniture and blue Provençal fabrics are delightful. The bedrooms are in the same simple style but are very comfortable and well cared for. Each has a private terrace. Six overlook the delightful garden of aromatic plants which slopes down to the swimming pool, and in the distance are the lake and the mountains. The other four do not have a view but are cooler. In any of them you will enjoy perfect peace. You will also appreciate Mme Tellier's Provençal cooking along with her courtesy and kindness. One could not hope for a more pleasant place at such reasonable prices.

How to get there *(Map 34): 60km north east of Aix-en-Provence via A51, exit Gréoux-les-Bains, then D952 to Gréoux-les-Bains and D82 (1km from the village).*

Auberge Charembeau★★

Route de Niozelles
04300 Forcalquier (Alpes–de–Haute–Provence)
Tel. 92.75.05.69 - M. Berger

Open 1 Feb – 30 Nov. **Rooms** 12 with telephone, bath or shower and WC. **Price** single 235F, double 305F. Rooms with kitchenette 1350-2100F per week. **Meals** breakfast 37F, served 0800-0930. No restaurant. **Credit cards** accepted. **Pets** dogs allowed (+20F). **Facilities** swimming pool, tennis (+60F), mountain bikes, parking. **Nearby** Lure mountain, Salagon priory, Ganagobie priory, château de Sauvan, Saint-Michel-l'Observatoire.

This little hotel in the middle of the lovely country-side of the Forcalquier region is run by a friendly couple who have given the old restored house a nice family atmosphere. The bedrooms, all of which look out over the surrounding countryside, are simple and in good taste. Some of them have cooking facilities, which is useful for families who want the freedom of self-catering. In front of the house is a terrace which is perfect for those who want nothing more than to laze about enjoying the Provençal landscape.

How to get there *(Map 34): 39km south of Sisteron via N85 (or A51, exit La Brillane), then D12 towards Forcalquier. It's 4km from Forcalquier via N100 towards Niozelles.*

Auberge du Clos Sorel★★★

Les Molanès
04400 Pra-Loup (Alpes-de-Haute-Provence)
Tel. 92.84.10.74 – Mme Mercier

Open 15 Dec – 15 April and 20 June – 10 Sept. **Rooms** 8 with telephone, bath, WC and TV. **Price** single 400F, double 520-600F. **Meals** breakfast 44F, served 0800-1030; half board +180F (per pers., 3 days min.) **Credit cards** Visa, Amex. **Pets** dogs allowed (+35F). **Facilities** swimming pool, tennis (+40F). **Nearby** ski-ing from hotel, Colmars, route de la Bonette. **Restaurant** service 1230-1430; menu 105F, also à la carte; specialities: morilles, ravioles, gigots.

Clos Sorel is a hamlet which time truly seems to have passed by, although it is on the ski slopes of Pra-Loup. Well located on a hillside, an old farmhouse has been converted into the Auberge du Clos Sorel. The building has lovely stone walls and an entranceway built of logs, and blends in perfectly with the surrounding chalets. Inside, original features such as beams, an impressive fireplace and sloping ceilings have been retained, and these combine with the polished furniture to create the kind of warm and cosy atmosphere one looks forward to coming back to after a long day spent skiing or walking. In the evening, dinner is served by candlelight in what used to be the main room of the farmhouse. The tables are pretty and the cuisine is refined. In summer, a swimming-pool and tennis courts add to the many attractions of the inn. A relaxed and informal atmosphere prevails.

How to get there (Map 34): 70km south west of Gap via D900B and D900 to Barcelonnette, then D902 and D109 to Pra-Loup.

Auberge de Reillanne**

04110 Reillanne (Alpes–de–Haute–Provence)
Tel. 92.76.45.95
M. Bellaiche

Open all year. **Rooms** 7 with telephone, bath, WC and minibar. **Price** single 200F, double 300F. **Meals** breakfast 40F; half board 300F (per pers., 2 days min.) **Credit cards** Visa. **Pets** dogs not allowed. **Facilities** parking. **Nearby** Manosque, priories of Salagon and Ganagobie, château de Sauvan. **Restaurant** service 1900-2100 (closed Wednesday except for residents); menus 115-140F; specialities: piccata de fois gras aux navets confits, soliman d'agneau et la menthe et au miel, home-smoked fish and duck breast.

Located in a part of the Luberon which has remained unspoiled, this hotel is surrounded by greenery. The few bedrooms are large, plainly furnished, but warm and comfortable, the emphasis being on natural materials: light-coloured wood or cane, unbleached wool and flowery fabrics. All the bedrooms have pleasant views and lovely bathrooms with terracotta tiling. There is no charge to use the minibars in the rooms: guests decide how much they want to pay for the drinks; obviously trust is the key-word here. Maurice Bellaiche chose the hotel business because he enjoys it, and has created a peaceful and; above all friendly atmosphere. He does the cooking himself, and his good seasonal cuisine is based on fresh local produce, with a touch of exoticism. You will find it all the more delectable for the charming dining-room where meals are served. This is a pleasant address, both engaging and unpretentious.

How to get there *(Map 34): 15km north west of Manosque towards Apt, then N100 and D214 towards Reillanne.*

Le Pyjama★★★

04400 Super-Sauze (Alpes-de-Haute-Provence)
Tel. 92.81.12.00 - Fax 92.81.03.16
Mme Merle

Open 15 Dec – 12 April and 1 July to 30 Aug. **Rooms** 10 with telephone, bathroom, WC, TV, minibar. **Price** single 250-310F, double 300-420F, suite 450-550F. **Meals** breakfast 39F. No restaurant. **Credit cards** accepted. **Pets** dogs allowed. **Nearby** ski-ing from the hotel, village of Colmars, Beauvezer, gorges of Saint-Pierre, Guillaumes via the col des Champs, route de la Bonette.

Having spent twenty years running another hotel in the resort, Geneviève Merle (ski champion Carole Merle's mother), has recently had this small hotel built, using materials and designs which blend perfectly with the surroundings. Eight of the ten bedrooms face south, their terraces overlooking a field of larch trees. They are tastefully decorated, with very pleasant bathrooms. M. Merle owns an antique shop nearby, and it has provided the hotel furniture. Four rooms have a mezzanine which can accommodate two extra people. In the annexe there are four self-contained flatlets complete with kitchen areas, very convenient for families. The hotel doesn't have its own restaurant, but there are many in the resort, or higher up. This is an extremely comfortable establishment, at the foot of the slopes, offering a friendly welcome and an informal atmosphere.

How to get there *(Map 34): 79km south east of Gap via D900B and D900 towards Barcelonnette, then D9 and D209 to Super-Sauze.*

Auberge du Choucas***

Monêtier-les-Bains
05220 Serre-Chevalier (Hautes-Alpes)
Tel. 92.24.42.73 - Fax 92.24.51.60 - Mme Sánchez-Ventura

Open 18 Dec – 2 Nov (closed Monday and Tuesday in low season). **Rooms** 8 and 4 suites with telephone, bath, WC and TV. **Price** single 590-690F, double 590-740F, suite 1050-1250F. **Meals** breakfast 62F, served 0745-1000; half board 485-595F, 605-735F (per pers., 3 days min.) **Credit cards** Eurocard, MasterCard, Visa. **Pets** dogs allowed (+60F). **Nearby** ski lifts (500m), valley of la Vallouise, valley of la Clarée, 9-hole Montgenèvre golf course (23km). **Restaurant** service from 1230 and 1930; menus and à la carte; gastronomic specialities.

Monêtier-les-Bains is an old Alpine village perched at an altitude of 1560m, making it the highest of Serre-Chevalier. Gourmets will be especially enchanted by what they find at the Auberge du Choucas: home-made preserves and crispy bread rolls at breakfast, and talented chef Yves Gattechaut's exquisite sauces enhancing refined dishes, rounded off by delicious desserts. The bedrooms are cosy and comfortably furnished with a small lounge area in front of the picture windows looking out onto the mountains. And if you are interested in myths and legends, your hostess can tell you all the local stories.

How to get there (Map 27): 14km north west of Briançon via N91.

Mas de la Pagane

15, avenue du Mas-Ensoleillé
06600 Antibes (Alpes-Maritimes)
Tel. 93.33.33.78 - Fax 93.74.55.37 - Mme Ott

Open all year. **Rooms** 5 with telephone, bath, shower, WC, TV and minibar. **Price** single and double 550F. **Meals** breakfast 35F. **Credit cards** Amex, Eurocard, Visa. **Pets** dogs allowed. **Facilities** parking. **Nearby** Picasso museum at Antibes, Cap d'Antibes, Villa Thuret, chapel of La Garoupe, Fernand Léger museum at Biot, 18-hole Opio golf course at Valbonne. **Restaurant** service 1200-1430, 2000-2230 (closed Sunday evening); menu 130F, also à la carte; specialities: poisson à l'apicius, beignets de cervelle sauce safran, poivron braisé et fondant d'aubergine.

This is the kind of address one likes to find in the Provence that has charmed so many artists. Close to the yacht harbour, this old house is tucked away from the rest of the town in beautiful grounds. Inside, contemporary works of art, lovely fabrics and antique furniture have been combined with consummate skill. In the bedrooms, the decor is very elegant, with impeccable bathrooms (in room 1, the bathroom has retained its turn-of-the-century furnishings). The cuisine is far from second-best: it is light, innovative... in short, delectable. In summer, meals can be served on the flowery terrace. The bar opens out into the garden, and provides the perfect setting for an evening drink against a background of music: there are jazz concerts on Friday evenings. (Needless to say, it is well soundproofed). You've guessed it, it's a friendly place.

How to get there (Map 35): take Avenue du Mas-Ensoleillé at crossroads at entrance to Antibes, then signs for hotel.

447

Hôtel de Paris★★★

34, boulevard d'Alsace
06400 Cannes (Alpes–Maritimes)
Tel. 93.38.30.89 - Fax 93.39.04.61 - M. Lazzari

Open 20 Jan – 10 Nov. **Rooms** 45 and 5 suites, with telephone, bath or shower, WC and TV. **Price** single 500-650F double 550-750F, suite 900-1600F. **Meals** breakfast 50F, served 0700-1100. No restaurant. **Credit cards** Amex, Diners, Visa. **Pets** dogs not allowed. **Facilities** parking (80F). **Nearby** massif du Tanneron, Auribeau-sur-Siagne, Mougins, Vallauris, îles de Lérins, 27-hole Cannes golf course at Mandelieu.

This hotel is in a large white house near the motorway. Its facade is decorated with columns and pediments in typical turn of the century Côte d'Azur style. Although the hotel is in the centre of Cannes it has a garden (a bit noisy) with palms and cypresses around a very pleasant swimming pool. The interior is very smart. The bedrooms are decorated with prints. The suites are luxurious and have a private sitting room. All the rooms are air conditioned and soundproofed and some have a balcony on which you can have breakfast. A good place to stay right in the centre of Cannes.

How to get there *(Map 34): in the town centre.*

La Bergerie★★★

Castillon
06500 Menton (Alpes–Maritimes)
Tel. 93.04.00.39 – M. Ballairé

Open 1 April – 30 Sept. **Rooms** 14 with bath and WC. **Price** double 350-400F. **Meals** breakfast 38F, served 0800-1100; half board 300-320F, full board 390-430F (per pers.) **Credit cards** not accepted. **Pets** dogs allowed. **Nearby** Jean Cocteau museum at Menton, villages of Gorbio, Sainte-Agnès, l'Annonciade and Castellar, valley of la Roya, 18-hole Monte Carlo golf course at La Turbie. **Restaurant** service 1200-1400, 1930-2130; menus 95-150F; specialities: coq au vin, brochettes Bergerie, petite salé.

This is primarily a very large restaurant furnished with cane chairs and tables and with a beautiful view over the village and the sea. On the first floor there is a lounge reserved for hotel clients which opens out onto a terrace. The bedrooms have an individual and intimate charm and the bathrooms are excellent. You will find various styles of old furniture wherever you go in this delightful house and good carpets on all the floors. All around you are lovely views of the valley.

How to get there *(Map 35): 12km north of Menton via D2566 towards Sospel.*

Auberge du Soleil★

Quartier Porta-Savel
06390 Coaraze (Alpes-Maritimes)
Tel. 93.79.08.11 - Fax 93.79.31.73 - M. and Mme Jacquet

Open 15 March – 15 Nov. **Rooms** 8 and 2 suites in annexe with telephone, bath or shower, WC, TV on request. **Price** single 290-380F, double 310-460F, suite 390-900F. **Meals** breakfast 40F, served 0800-1200; half board 320-390F, (per pers., 3 days min.) **Credit cards** Eurocard, MasterCard, Amex, Visa. **Pets** dogs allowed (+35F). **Facilities** heated swimming pool, boules, table tennis. **Nearby** Mercantour reserve, valley of the Merveilles, Turini forest, villages of Roure and Roubion, 18-hole Opio golf course at Valbonne. **Restaurant** service 1200-1400, 1930-2100; menu 125F, also à la carte; specialities: tourte maison, gibelotte de lapin, caille aux raisins.

This hotel is only half an hour from Nice and not far from the magnificent nature reserve of Mercantour. It is splendidly situated in a medieval village 640 metres up on a rocky outcrop. The maze of narrow village streets ensures total peace and calm: you may need to call on the hotel to help with your luggage up the steep slopes. You will find an informal, almost bohemian atmosphere in the hotel quite different from that of a traditional establishment, but it is all in elegant good taste. There is a summer lounge situated in a cool vaulted cellar and an attractive dining room which extends out over a covered terrace with panoramic views of the valley. The cooking is simple and good. The garden slopes down in steps to the swimming pool and orchard, where you can pick the fruit without feeling guilty.

How to get there *(Map 35): 2km north of Nice via A8 exit Nice-Est, then voie rapide towards Drap-Sospel. At the Pointe des Contes, left towards Contes-Coaraze.*

Le Manoir de l'Etang★★★

66, allée du Manoir
06250 Mougins (Alpes-Maritimes)
Tel. 93.90.01.07 - Fax 92.92.20.70 - Mme Gridaine-Labro

Open all year (except Nov and Feb). **Rooms** 15 with telephone, bath or shower, WC (10 with TV and minibar). **Price** double 500-850F, suite 1200F. **Meals** breakfast 50F, served 0800-1100. **Credit cards** Amex, Eurocard, Visa. **Pets** dogs allowed. **Facilities** swimming pool, parking. **Nearby** Cannes, massif du Tanneron, Auribeau-sur-Siagne, Vallauris, 27-hole Cannes golf course at Mandelieu. **Restaurant** service 1200-1400, 2000-2200 (closed Sunday evening and Tuesday in low season); menus 145-190F, also à la carte; specialities: raviolis d'agneau à la crème de romarin, filet de veau et son rognon à la graine de moutarde, nougat glacé maison.

This superb 19th-century house, surrounded by cypresses and oleander, overlooks a lake in an undulating 7-hectare park. On the ground floor there is a warmly decorated lounge with terracotta-tiled floor, piano and cane furniture, and an airy dining room overlooking the pool framed by olive trees. Beyond the pool there are extensive views over the Provençal landscape. The comfortable bedrooms are brightened by cheerful materials with flower and fruit patterns. You will enjoy the tranquil atmosphere and the good humour of the owners, who will give you a real family welcome. A delightful and charming place to stay.

How to get there *(Map 34): 7km north of Cannes via N85.*

Le Mas Candille★★★
Boulevard Rebuffel
06250 Mougins (Alpes-Maritimes)
Tel. 93.90.00.85 - Fax 92.92.85.56 - M. Amzallag

Open all year. **Rooms** 23 with telephone, bath or shower, WC, TV and minibar. **Price** single and double 800-950F, suite 1500-1700F. **Meals** breakfast 65F, served 0715-1100. **Credit cards** accepted. **Pets** dogs allowed. **Facilities** swimming pool, tennis, parking. **Nearby** Cannes, massif du Tanneron, Auribeau-sur-Siagne, Vallauris, 27-hole Cannes golf course at Madelieu. **Restaurant** service 1200-1500, 1930-2200, closed 3-30 November; menus 135-215F also à la carte; specialities: mille feuille ris de veau, foie gras poêlé au pinot des charentes, tournedos de lotte sur tagliatelles safranées.

This is a beautiful 18th-century Provençal house which has been turned into a luxury hotel. You will find much of the old atmosphere but, inevitably, a bit of authentic character has been traded for superlative comfort. The ground floor opens out onto a superb terrace shaded by scented pines and cypresses and looking out over a green landscape and the foothills of the Alpes-Maritimes. You will eat some delicious meals here. The bedrooms have been completely refurbished and decorated in a blend of light colours. They are slightly impersonal in character but they all have either a wonderful view or a private terrace. This is a quiet place and you will be received cordially.

How to get there (Map 34): 7km north of Cannes via N85.

Hôtel La Pérouse★★★★

11, quai Rauba-Capeu
06300 Nice (Alpes-Maritimes)
Tel. 93.62.34.63 - Fax 93.62.59.41 - M. Mercadal

Open all year. **Rooms** 65 with telephone, bath or shower, WC, TV and minibar. **Price** single 340-1150F, double 565-1150F, suite 1400-1920F. **Meals** breakfast 75F, served 0630-1100. **Credit cards** accepted. **Pets** dogs allowed. **Facilities** swimming pool, sauna, jacuzzi, solarium. **Nearby** Turini forest, valley of La Tinée (Roure, Roubron), valley of La Vésubie, villages of Utelle, Belvédère, le Boréon, Venanson, 18-hole Opio golf course at Valbonne, 18-hole Bastide-du-Roy golf course at Biot. **Restaurant** service 1200-1500, 1930-2200, closed 15 Sept – 15 May; à la carte; specialities: grills in the hotel gardens.

L a Pérouse is in a large Mediterranean–style mansion at the foot of the château that dominates old Nice and the Baie des Anges. It is surrounded by aloes and lemon trees and to reach it you have to take one of the two lifts from the quayside. The bedrooms are spacious and quiet, and prices vary according to whether you have a view of the garden or the sea. Some of them have a terrace with deck chairs. In summer you might be tempted to spend a good deal of time at the hotel in order to take advantage of the barbecue, swimming pool and solarium.

How to get there *(Map 35): in the town centre.*

Auberge de la Madone***

06440 Peillon (Alpes–Maritimes)
Tel. 93.79.91.17
Famille Millo

Open all year except 20 Oct – 20 Dec and 7 Jan – 24 Jan (closed Wednesday). **Rooms** 20 with telephone, bath, shower and WC. **Price** double 400-780F, suite 850-1100F. **Meals** breakfast 50F, served 0800-1000; half board 420-700F. **Credit cards** Visa, Eurocard, MasterCard. **Pets** dogs not allowed. **Facilities** tennis, parking. **Nearby** Nice, valleys of La Tinée and La Vésubie, 18-hole Mont-Agel golf course. **Restaurant** service 1230-1400, 1930-2030; menus 130-250F, also à la carte; specialities: bouillabaisse froide, carré d'agneau aux petits légumes fondants.

The Auberge is a good place for those with a taste for adventure. All around it are deep ravines and rocky summits which you would hardly suspect existed only twenty minutes from Nice. From the hotel's sunny terraces you will have all the time in the world to look out on Peillon, one of the more spectacular villages in the Niçois hinterland, perched on a steep crag and with superb views all round. You can explore it on foot, up the steep stairways which lead up to the Chapel of the Pénitents Blancs. The hotel has an attractive decor with all the refinements for a comfortable stay. The excellent regional cooking is reasonably priced and encourages visitors who prefer the tranquillity of Peillon to the tourist frenzy of the Nice coast.

How to get there (Map 35): 19km north of Nice via D2204 towards L'Escarène, then D21 towards Peillon. On the left as you enter the village.

Hôtel Les Deux Frères★★

Place des Deux-Frères
Roquebrune Village, 06100 Cap-Martin (Alpes-Maritimes)
Tel. 93.28.99.00 - Fax 93.28.99.10 - M. Inthout

Open 7 Dec – 30 Oct (closed Thursday). **Rooms** 10 with telephone, bath or shower, WC and TV. **Price** single 350F, double 420F. **Meals** breakfast 35F. **Credit cards** Amex, MasterCard, Visa. **Pets** dogs allowed (+35F). **Nearby** Rue Moncolet at Roquebrune, La Turbie church, footpath to Cap Martin, 18-hole Monte Carlo golf course at La Turbie. **Restaurant** service 1200-1400, 1930-2200; à la carte; specialities: fish, duck, foie gras.

The two brothers of the hotel name are the two rocks that gave their name to the village of Roquebrune. The place called after them is on one of the best sites in the medieval village, protected by its Carolingian castle, and was chosen for the school built here in 1854. This was just in front of the Café de la Grotte and overlooked the bay of Monte Carlo. The school was eventually closed and for fifteen years it was abandoned until a Dutch architect decided to restore this house with its green shutters. He turned the classrooms into pretty white-walled bedrooms, and the courtyard into a restaurant. Around the great fireplace he installed comfortable leather covered settees and created a place that most guests find it difficult to tear themselves away from in the evenings. The decor is delightful, there are always plenty of flowers about and you will receive a warm welcome.

How to get there *(Map 35): 5km west of Menton via A8 or N98.*

Auberge du Colombier★★★

06330 Roquefort-les-Pins (Alpes–Maritimes)
Tel. 93.77.10.27 - Fax 93.77.07.03 - M. Wolff

Open all year. **Rooms** 20 with telephone, bath, shower, WC and TV **Price** single 200-350F, double 350-550F, suite 680F. **Meals** breakfast 50F; half board +170F, full board +340F. **Credit cards** accepted. **Pets** dogs allowed (+40F). **Facilities** swimming pool, tennis (+40F), parking. **Nearby** Nice, Grasse, gorges of Le Loup and Gourdon, 18-hole Opio golf course at Valbonne. **Restaurant** service 1200-1430, 1900-2200 (closed Tuesday in low season); menus 140-180F, also à la carte; specialities: salade gourmande de caille tiède au foie gras, chariot de pâtisseries maison.

This old stagecoach stop on the route from Nice to Grasse (once a two-day journey) still makes a good overnight halt or a pleasant base from which to explore the many attractions of the French Riviera. The auberge was modernised in 1980 but preserves its old charm. Today it has a good swimming pool, a tennis court and some more recently built bedrooms, in which, however some of the atmosphere has been lost. You will find a pleasant welcome here and a restaurant which is renowned for its cuisine and its 'specialités maison'.

How to get there *(Map 34): 25km west of Nice via A8, exit Villeneuve-Loubet, then D2085 towards Grasse.*

Hôtel Brise Marine★★★

58, avenue Jean-Mermoz
06230 Saint-Jean-Cap-Ferrat (Alpes-Maritimes)
Tel. 93.76.04.36 - Fax 93.76.11.49 - M. Maîtrehenry

Open 1 Feb – 30 Oct. **Rooms** 16 with telephone, bath or shower, WC and TV. **Price** double 600-655F. **Meals** breakfast 55F, served 0800-1000. No restaurant. **Credit cards** Access, Eurocard, MasterCard, Visa. **Pets** dogs allowed. **Nearby** St Pierre chapel (Cocteau) at Villefranche, Villa Ephrussi-de-Rothschild at Saint-Jean-Cap-Ferrat, Villa Kerylos at Beaulieu, 18-hole La Bastide-du-Roy golf course at Biot.

Among the luxurious villas, palaces and residences of the nobility in Saint-Jean-Cap-Ferrat there is a little Italian house built in the 19th century. This is now the Hôtel Brise Marine, and it still has a delightful garden with flowers, palm trees, espaliers, stone balustrades, fountains and terraces. The owner has personally looked after the hotel and its sixteen elegant and comfortable little bedrooms for forty-five years. All of them look out on the gardens of an inaccessible château and the surrounding sea. You will get a really friendly welcome here as well as excellent breakfasts.

How to get there (Map 35): 15km east of Nice via N98.

Hôtel Le Hameau★★★

528, route de La Colle
06570 Saint-Paul-de-Vence (Alpes-Maritimes)
Tel. 93.32.80.24 - Fax 93.32.55.75 - M. Huvelin

Open 15 Feb – 15 Nov and 22 Dec – 8 Jan. **Rooms** 14 and 3 apartments with telephone, bath or shower, WC and minibar. **Price** single 320F, double 360-500F, suite 620F. **Meals** breakfast 45F, served 0800-1000. No restaurant. **Credit cards** accepted except Diners. **Pets** dogs allowed. **Facilities** swimming pool, parking. **Nearby** chapel of Le Rosaire (Matisse), perfume museum, Carzou museum at Vence, Maeght Foundation, church of Saint-Charles-Borromée at Saint-Paul-de-Vence, les Clues de Haute-Provence, 18-hole Opio golf course at Valbonne.

You approach this white 1920s house, which looks over the valley and the village of Saint-Paul-de-Vence, up a path bordered by lemon trees in a flowering garden. The hotel is terraced and arcaded and almost hidden by honeysuckle, fig trees and climbing vines. The bedrooms are large and prettily decorated, the furniture is traditional Provençal. Numbers 1, 2 and 3 have a loggia and an impressive view of Saint Paul. The old iridescent green tiles of some of the bathrooms are superb. In the adjoining 18th-century farmhouse there are other smaller attic rooms but they all have a lovely view. The friendly welcome you will find here will explain why so many guests return.

How to get there *(Map 34): 20km west of Nice via A8, exit Cagnes-sur-Mer, then D7 towards Vence via La Colle-sur-Loup; it's 1km before Saint-Paul-de-Vence.*

Hôtel Golf Opio–Valbonne★★★

Route de Roquefort-les-Pins
06560 Valbonne (Alpes-Maritimes)
Tel. 93.40.21.05 - Fax 93.40.22.50 - M. Takasu

Open all year (closed 20 Nov – 20 Dec). **Rooms** 32 with telephone, bath, WC, TV and minibar. **Price** single 360-680F, double 470-800F. **Meals** breakfast 40F, served 0700-1030. **Credit card**s accepted except Diners. **Pets** dogs allowed (+30F). **Facilities** swimming pool, tennis, golf practice, putting green, golf lessons, parking. **Nearby** Cannes, Picasso museum at Antibes, Fernand Léger museum at Biot, 18-hole Opio golf course at Valbonne. **Restaurant** service 1200-1400, 1930-2200; menus from 150F, also à la carte; Provençal cooking.

Occupying an old château and its farmhouse, this hotel is a place specially for golf enthusiasts – it is surrounded by all the facilities they need. The rooms have all been refurbished in an individual style, and according to whether they are in the château or the farmhouse they are either elegant or rustic in decor. The rooms in the farmhouse are spacious but the ones in the château are even larger. The ambience is chic but relaxed and you receive a very cordial welcome. You will enjoy the Provençal food in the restaurant. If you fancy arriving by helicopter there is no problem; the hotel has a heliport.

How to get there *(Map 34): 23km north of Cannes via A8, Antibes exit, then D103 and D3.*

Auberge des Seigneurs et du Lion d'Or★★
Place du Frêne
06140 Vence (Alpes-Maritimes)
Tel. 93.58.04.24 - Fax 93.24.08.01 - M. and Mme Rodi

Open 15 Dec – 15 Nov. **Rooms** 10 with telephone, shower, WC and TV. **Price** single 270F, double 290-310F. **Meals** breakfast 48F, served 0730-1030. **Credit cards** accepted. **Pets** dogs allowed. **Nearby** chapel of Le Rosaire (Matisse), perfume museum, Carzou museum at Vence, Maeght Foundation, church of St-Charles-Borromée at Saint-Paul-de-Vence, les Clues de Haute Provence, 18-hole Opio golf course at Valbonne. **Restaurant** service from 1230 and 1930; menus 190-210F, also à la carte; specialities: carré d'agneau à la broche, tian vençois.

This is a very lovely, almost timeless auberge. Some parts of it date from the 14th century and some from the 17th. In its day it has welcomed many famous guests such as Francis I and, more recently, Renoir, Modigliani, Dufy and Soutine. M. Rodi knows the exact dates of their visits and will enjoy telling you about them. The hotel is situated in a wing of the Château des Villeneuve de Vence, which is mostly occupied by the Carzou museum. It is on the square where the ash tree planted by Francis I flourishes still. The reception rooms contain an eclectic collection of objects (a 16th-century washstand, an olive oil press, modern lithographs, etc) all of which have a history. The bedrooms are large, furnished plainly but appropriately for the building, and there is always a basket of fruit and some flowers awaiting every guest. The most attractive rooms look out on the square, the quietest over the rooftops. The whole place is full of character and very welcoming.

How to get there *(Map 34): 10km north of Cagnes-sur-Mer via D36.*

Hôtel Welcome★★★

1, quai Courbet
06230 Villefranche-sur-Mer (Alpes-Maritimes)
Tel. 93.76.76.93 - Fax 93.01.88.81 - M. and Mme Galbois

Open 20 Dec – 20 Nov. **Rooms** 32 with air-conditioning, telephone, bath or shower,
WC (29 with TV, 30 with minibar). **Price** single 350-650F, double 350-900F. **Meals**
breakfast 50-95F, served 0700-1030; half board 375-590F (per pers.) **Credit cards**
accepted. **Pets** dogs allowed (+25F). **Nearby** the Lower Corniche, St-Jean-Cap-Ferrat
(Villa Ephrussi de Rothschild), Beaulieu (Villa Kerylos), 18-hole Opio golf course at
Valbonne. **Restaurant** service 1230-1400, 1930-2400; menus 180-250F, also à la
carte; specialities: loup grillé, bouillabaisse traditionnelle, filet de saint-pierre à
l'oseille, carré d'agneau rôti au beurre de romarin.

On the quayside of the old port of Villefranche you will find
colourful fishing boats, a chapel decorated by Jean Cocteau
and a hotel (in the pedestrian precinct) built on the site of a 17th-
century monastery. The hotel is modern with plenty of balconies
belonging to large, comfortable, sunny rooms, all of them air-
conditioned. The balconies have sun loungers and small tables on
which you can spread out your breakfast. On the top storey the
rooms are in a nautical style with copper fittings and exotic woods.
They are smaller than the other rooms but rather inviting.

How to get there *(Map 35): 6km from Nice via N559.*

Villa Gallici★★★★

Avenue de la Violette
13100 Aix-en-Provence (Bouches-du-Rhône)
Tel. 42.23.29.23 - Fax 42.96.30.45 - M. Dez

Open all year. **Rooms** 17 with telephone, bath, WC and TV. **Price** single 600-1300F, double 700-1400F, suite 1300-1700F. **Meals** breakfast 80F. **Credit cards** accepted. **Pets** dogs not allowed. **Facilities** swimming pool, parking. **Nearby** Place d'Albertas, Hôtel de Ville, St Sauveur Cathedral (burning bush triptych by N. Froment) at Aix-en-Provence, Roquefavour aqueduct, 18-hole Club des Milles golf course. **Restaurant** Le Clos de la Violette, menus 175-290F; specialities: filets de rouget aux croutons, râble de lapereau en pébrade, millefeuille de chocolat blanc aux framboises.

When he came back to France Gil Dez would not rest until he had found a bastide to exercise his talents as an interior decorator and create the top-class 'hôtel de charme' that Aix-en-Provence was lacking. The result is remarkable. The villa has been decorated with exquisite style, and designed like a home rather than a hotel. The bedrooms are all spacious and comfortable, and individually decorated. 'Toile de Jouy' and gingham have been associated in one of them, while another boasts a flowery cotton canopied bed side by side with boldly striped fabrics... In each room styles, colours and materials have been subtly and successfully combined. In the immaculate bathrooms earthenware tiles, Carrara marble and glossy white wood panelling create an impression of extreme refinement. Breakfast beneath the plane-trees on the terrace is a delight. The cuisine served in Le Clos de la Violette, the restaurant just next door to the hotel, is probably the best you can find in Aix and its close surroundings. This is a truly charming place.

How to get there (Map 33): *near the archbishop's palace.*

Le Prieuré★★

Route de Sisteron
13100 Aix-en-Provence (Bouches-du-Rhône)
Tel. 42.21.05.23 - M. and Mme Le Hir

Open all year. **Rooms** 23 with telephone (21 with bath, WC, minibar). **Price** single and double 170-390F. **Meals** breakfast 35F, served 0700-1000; no restaurant. **Credit cards** accepted. **Pets** dogs not allowed. **Facilities** parking. **Nearby** Place d'Albertas, Hôtel de Ville, St Sauveur Cathedral (triptych of the burning bush by N. Froment) at Aix-en-Provence, Roquefavour aqueduct, 18-hole Club des Milles golf course, 18-hole Fauveau golf course.

Just at the entrance to Aix on the route des Alpes you will find the old Archbishop's Priory charmingly converted into a romantic little hotel. The bedrooms are very cosy with lovely fabrics and period-style furniture. All of them look out over the splendid garden of the Pavillon Lenfort, which was designed in the 17th century by Le Nôtre. There is no access to it from the hotel but the garden gives the hotel rooms a charming view and tranquillity – and those are worth having. Breakfast is served in your room or, on fine days, on the terrace among the hydrangeas. This is a very pleasant, well-kept place, and you will be well received with great cordiality.

How to get there *(Map 33): 2km north of Aix-en-Provence on the Sisteron road.*

Hôtel Cardinal★★

24, rue Cardinale
13100 Aix-en-Provence (Bouches-du-Rhône)
Tel. 42.38.32.30 - Fax 42.26.39.05 - Mme Bonifaci

Open all year. **Rooms** 30 with telephone, bath, WC and TV. **Price** single 200-260F, double 250-290F, suite 320-390F. **Meals** breakfast 27F, served 0700-1030. No restaurant. **Credit cards** accepted. **Pets** dogs allowed. **Nearby** Place d'Albertas, Hôtel de Ville, St Sauveur Cathedral (burning bush triptych by N. Froment) at Aix-en-Provence, Roquefavour aqueduct, 18-hole Club des Milles golf course, 18-hole Fauveau golf course.

A short walk from the Place Mirabeau, in one of the little streets of the historic centre of the town you will find the 17th-century building that houses the hotel. The old furniture, some in regional style, gives the interior the old fashioned charm of a provincial hotel. The bedrooms are spacious, comfortable and welcoming. Some of them have a sofa-bed which means you can accommodate a third person, and an eating area. You will be well looked after and the prices for a long stay will please you.

How to get there *(Map 33): in the centre of the town.*

Hôtel des Quatre–Dauphins★★

54, rue Roux-Alphéran
13100 Aix-en-Provence (Bouches-du-Rhône)
Tel. 42.38.16.39 - Fax 42.38.60.19- MM. Darricau and Juster

Open all year. **Rooms** 12 with telephone, bath or shower, WC, TV and minibar. **Price** single 250-280F, double 320-360F, suite 450-480F (3 pers.) **Meals** breakfast 35F, served 0700-1000. No restaurant. **Credit cards** Visa. **Pets** dogs allowed. **Nearby** Place d'Albertas, Hôtel de Ville, St Sauveur Cathedral (burning bush triptych by N. Froment) at Aix-en-Provence, Roquefavour aqueduct, 18-hole Club des Milles golf course, 18-hole Fauveau golf course.

This three-storey family house in a quiet side street near the famous Place des Quatre Dauphins in Aix has recently been converted into a hotel. On the ground floor there is a small reception area and a lounge which also serves as a breakfast room. The bedrooms are on the upper floors. The decor is in the Provençal style, with pretty fabrics which go well with the painted wooden furniture. The rooms are not very large and the furnishings are simple but they provide the essential needs. The bathrooms are well equipped. The whole place is furnished with good taste and has considerable charm.

How to get there (Map 33): in the centre of the town.

Mas de la Bertrande***

Chemin de la Plaine
Beaurecueil 13100 Aix-en-Provence (Bouches-du-Rhône)
Tel. 42.66.90.09 - Fax 42.66.82.01 - M. and Mme Bertrand

Open 15 March – 15 Feb (closed Sunday evening and Monday in low season). **Rooms** 10 with telephone, bath, WC, TV and minibar. **Price** single 320F, double 320-520F. **Meals** breakfast 50F, served until 1100; half board 560F (obligatory 15 June-15 Sept). **Credit cards** Visa, Amex, Diners. **Pets** dogs allowed (+35F). **Facilities** swimming pool, parking. **Nearby** Place d'Albertas, Hôtel de Ville, St Sauveur Cathedral (burning bush triptych by N. Froment) at Aix-en-Provence, Roquefavour aqueduct, 18-hole Club des Milles golf course, 18-hole Fauveau golf course. **Restaurant** service 1200-1400, 2000-2200; menus 100-190F, also à la carte; specialities: cassolette de moules, sole farcie à la truite de mer, râble de lapin à l'estragon, fraises au poivre vert.

La Bertrande is 10km from Aix-en-Provence at the foot of Cézanne's much loved Mont Saint Victoire. The old farm has been completely rebuilt but the setting and the friendly welcome you will receive are pure Provençal. The lounge and dining room both have terraces which are delightful in summer. The cooking is light and simple and very good. The two bedrooms in the main building are the largest but the others have private terraces looking on to the garden; be warned, however, that they can get rather warm in very hot weather. The swimming pool, surrounded by lawns and cypresses, is a boon in this inland location where it can get very hot.

How to get there *(Map 33): 10km east of Aix-en-Provence via D17, then D46 to Beaurecueil, then D58 and follow signs.*

Hôtel d'Arlatan***

26, rue du Sauvage
13200 Arles (Bouches-du-Rhône)
Tel. 90.93.56.66 - Fax 90.49.68.45 - M. Desjardin

Open all year. **Rooms** 41 with air-conditioning, telephone, bath, WC, TV and minibar.
Price double 455-680F, suite 750-1300F. **Meals** breakfast 50F, served 0700-1100.
No restaurant. **Credit cards** accepted. **Pets** dogs allowed. **Facilities** parking (+50F).
Nearby Saint Trophime church, les Aliscamps, Réattu museum at Arles, abbey of
Montmajour, the Camargue, 18-hole Servanes golf course at Mouriès.

This hotel, like Arles itself, is almost a museum of the past and
contains traces of many different eras in its building. It was
built on the site of the basilica and baths of Constantine and is a
patchwork of architectural styles. This is a very unusual hotel,
owned for three generations by the same family, who have not
only refurbished it but have also preserved its ancient fabric. It
would take a whole book to describe the Arlatan bedrooms. In
suite 43 there are fragments of a 4th-century wall and 17th-century
wooden beams. In suite 41 is a monumental 17th-century fireplace.
We recommend that you ask for the recently refurbished
bedrooms, among them rooms 23 and 27 which have a view of
the Rhone, or 34, one of the least expensive which has beautiful
stone walls, or, or course, one of the large or small suites. Whichever
you choose you will love this charming hotel hidden away in its
little street facing the gardens.

How to get there *(Map 33): in the centre of the town, signposted.*

Grand Hôtel Nord–Pinus★★★★

Place du Forum
13200 Arles (Bouches-du-Rhône)
Tel. 90.93.44.44 – Fax 90.93.34.00 – Mme Igou

Open 1 March – 31 Dec. **Rooms** 22 with telephone, bath, WC, TV and minibar. **Price** single 550-700F, double 700-850F, suite 1500F. **Meals** breakfast 65F, served 0700-1100. **Credit cards** accepted. **Pets** dogs allowed. **Nearby** Saint-Trophime church, les Aliscamps, Réattu Museum at Arles, abbey of Montmajour, the Camargue, 18-hole Servanes golf course at Mouriès. **Restaurant** service 1200-1400, 1930-2200; menus 120-180F, also à la carte; Provençal cooking.

Picasso, Cocteau, Dominguez are just some of the famous names in the visitors book of this oddly named establishment. The hotel was run for some time by Germaine, a chanteuse, and Nello, a famous clown, both of whom were well known characters in Arles. When they died the hotel lost its soul. It has returned under the care of Anne Igou, whose love for the place has brought back the magic and atmosphere with a skilful restoration which combines sensitivity and good taste. The bedrooms are large, with pretty furniture and Provençal fabrics, and the bathrooms have every facility. It is worth remembering to ask for suite 10 or the bedrooms looking on to the courtyard. These are recommended for people who are concerned about the noise levels of Arles in summer. This is a really charming place.

How to get there (*Map 33*): *in the town centre.*

Hôtel Castel–Mouisson★★

Quartier Castel Mouisson
13570 Barbentane (Bouches–du–Rhône)
Tel. 90.95.51.17 - Mme Mourgue

Open 15 March – 15 Oct. **Rooms** 17 with telephone, bath and WC. **Price** double 250-280F, suite 360F. **Meals** breakfast 30F, served 0800-1030. No restaurant. **Credit cards** not accepted. **Pets** dogs not allowed. **Facilities** swimming pool, tennis, parking. **Nearby** Barbentane, Avignon, Villeneuve-lès-Avignon, abbey of St-Michel-de-Frigolet, 18-hole golf course at Châteaublanc-les-Plans.

This peaceful and reasonably priced hotel is at the foot of the Montagnette not far from Avignon. It was built fourteen years ago in the style of a Provençal farmhouse and is surrounded by tranquil countryside. There are cypresses and fruit trees growing beneath the grey cliffs of the Montagnette, which overlooks the valley. The bedrooms are simple but reasonably comfortable. Breakfast is available but there is no restaurant. However, there are plenty of good eating places in the towns and villages around. In hot weather you can cool off in the swimming pool.

How to get there *(Map 33): 8km south west of Avignon via N570, then D35 towards Tarascon along the Rhône.*

Hôtel Le Benvengudo***

13520 Les Baux-de-Provence (Bouches-du-Rhône)
Tel. 90.54.32.54 - Fax 90.54.42.58
M. Rossi

Open 1 Feb – 15 Nov. **Rooms** 20 with telephone, bath, WC and TV. **Price** double 460-590F, suite 630-840F. **Meals** breakfast 52F, served 0815-1015; half board 495-560F (per pers., 3 days min.) **Credit cards** Amex, MasterCard, Visa. **Pets** dogs allowed (+50F). **Facilities** swimming pool, tennis, parking. **Nearby** contemporary art museum in the Hôtel des Porcelets at Les Baux, Queen Jeanne's pavilion, Alphonse Daudet's windmill at Fontvieille, the Val d'enfer, 9-hole golf course at Les Baux, 18-hole Servanes golf course at Mouriès. **Restaurant** service 1930-2100 (closed Sunday); menu 220F; specialities: velouté de crabes, assiette du pêcheur au safran, magret de canard aux baies roses.

The jagged outline of the Alpilles recalls some of the highest mountain ranges in the world, and their white rocks and dry vegetation give this part of Provence a look of Greece. The Benvengudo hides at the foot of this little range of mountains. The hotel was built twenty-one years ago but has the air of always having been there. The bedrooms, some of which are air-conditioned, are very comfortable; each one has its individual style and some have small private terraces. There is a rustic touch to the lounge and dining room. In summer you can dine out of doors by the swimming pool under the olive trees.

How to get there *(Map 33): 20km west of Cavaillon via A7, Cavaillon exit, then D99 to Saint-Rémy and D5.*

Le Mas d'Aigret★★★

13520 Les Baux-de-Provence (Bouches-du-Rhône)
Tel. 90.54.33.54 - Fax 90.54.41.37
M. Phillips

Open 25 Feb – 5 Jan. **Rooms** 15 with telephone, bath, WC, TV and minibar. **Price** double 450-850F, suite 850F. **Meals** breakfast 65F, served 0800-1000; half board 570-745F (per pers.) **Credit cards** accepted. **Pets** dogs allowed (+40F). **Facilities** swimming pool, parking. **Nearby** contemporary art museum in the Hôtel des Porcelets at Les Baux, Queen Jeanne's pavilion, the Val d'enfer, Alphonse Daudet's windmill at Fontvieille, 9-hole golf course at Les Baux, 18-hole Servanes golf course at Mouriès. **Restaurant** service 1215-1330, 1915-2100 (closed Wednesday lunchtime); menus 130-350F, also à la carte; specialities: lasagnes de langoustines au miel de romarin, rognons d'agneau rôtis au muscat et foie gras, tarte au chocolat noir.

This old farm, built in 1730 and recently restored, stands in an old cave dwelling. All the bedrooms have their own terrace and TV with three satellite channels. Room 16 and Apartment 15, which are a little to one side, are the most attractive. There is a vaulted lounge and library with large tables. The dining room with its stone walls is built into the rock and so are the lounge bar and music room. The furniture is a pleasant blend of old and new with Provençal fabrics. The restaurant has very good food at very affordable prices. The hotel can arrange special green fees if you want to play golf. A charming place for a holiday.

How to get there *(Map 33): 20km west of Cavaillon via A7, Cavaillon exit, then D99 to Saint-Rémy and D5.*

Le Clos des Arômes★★

10, rue Paul-Mouton – Rue Agostini
13260 Cassis (Bouches-du-Rhône)
Tel. 42.01.71.84 – Mme Grinda

Open all year. **Rooms** 8 with telephone, bath or shower, WC and TV. **Price** double 260-420F. **Meals** breakfast 40F, served 0800-1000. **Credit cards** Amex, MasterCard, Eurocard, Visa. **Pets** dogs allowed (+30F). **Facilities** parking (+45F). **Nearby** the Calanques: Port-Miou, Port-Pin and Envau, 18-hole La Salette golf course at Marseille. **Restaurant** service 1200-1400, 1930-2230; menus 95-120F, also à la carte; Provençal cooking.

Though situated in a little street in the village, this 'dolls house' hotel is surrounded by a garden that is a riot of blue and white with lavender, peonies, arum lilies and marguerites. In fine weather this makes a fragrant setting for breakfast and for dinners of light and delicious Provençal dishes. Indoors the ambience is just as delightful, with lavender blue painted furniture, flowered tablecloths and a large fireplace. The bedrooms, with blue and yellow Provençal fabrics, all look out on the garden. The hotel is very quiet though in the middle of the village and only a few metres from the old port. You will get a warm and friendly welcome from Mme Grinda, the owner.

How to get there *(Map 33): 23km east of Marseille via A50 towards Toulon, Cassis exit.*

Hôtel Les Roches Blanches★★★

Route de Port-Miou
13260 Cassis (Bouches-du-Rhône)
Tel. 42.01.09.30 - Fax 42.01.94.23 - M. Dellacase

Open Feb – beg. Nov. **Rooms** 29 with telephone, bath or shower, WC, TV (15 with minibar). **Price** single 380F, double 380-800F, suite 900-1500F. **Meals** breakfast 65F, served 0700-1200; half board 425-925F (per per., 2 days min.) **Credit cards** Diners, Eurocard, MasterCard, Visa. **Pets** dogs allowed (+35F). **Facilities** swimming pool, parking. **Nearby** the Calanques: Port-Miou, Port-Pin and Envau, 18-hole La Salette golf course at Marseille. **Restaurant** service 1230-1400, 1930-2100; menus 170-220F, also à la carte; specialities: seafood, bouillabaisse.

L es Roches Blanches was built as a private house in 1855 and turned into a hotel in 1930. Built on rocks close to the calanques of Cassis, it combines all the attractions of a seaside hotel with those of an old-fashioned house. The terraced garden leads down to a private beach and the spacious dining room has windows looking out to sea. The bedrooms have just been completely refurbished but their elegance has not been sacrificed to modern convenience. Some of them have terraces surrounded by pines and with views either out to sea or over the port and Cap Canaille. The owners of the hotel believe in preserving the character of the original house and have kept some of the pretty 1930s furniture as well as the great wrought-iron Art Deco staircase. They have also kept the rather nice mosaic tables in the garden, where there is also an unusual swimming pool with a view of the sea below.

How to get there *(Map 33): 23km east of Marseille via A50 towards Toulon, Cassis exit.*

473

Auberge Provençale★★★

Place de la Mairie
13810 Eygalières (Bouches-du-Rhône)
Tel. 90.95.91.00 - M. Pezevil

Open all year (closed Wednesday). **Rooms** 5 with telephone, bath or shower and WC. **Price** double 200-480F. **Meals** breakfast 40F, served 0830-1030; half board 330-630F (per pers., 2 days min.) **Credit cards** Visa, MasterCard. **Pets** dogs allowed (+30F). **Facilities** parking. **Nearby** Les Baux, St-Rémy-de-Provence, Fontvieille, 18-hole Servanes golf course at Mouriès. **Restaurant** service 1230-1330, 1930-2130; menus 120-190F, also à la carte; specialities: Saint-Jacques aux pâtes fraîches, plateau de hors d'oeuvre, marmite du pêcheur au safran.

The auberge is in the centre of a wonderful village of the Alpilles which has been miraculously preserved unchanged. Formerly a restaurant in a 18th-century post house, it has recently become a small five-room hotel. The three most comfortable bedrooms (our favourites are numbers 4 and 5) look out over a tree shaded courtyard. The other two are smaller and overlook the Place de la Mairie. The owner is also the chef. During fine weather meals are served on the terrace – otherwise they are served in the restaurant, which has a handsome fireplace. The cooking is traditional and includes specialities from various regions. There is grilled fish, magret of duck and turbot à la crème. You will receive a cordial welcome but what a pity there is no lounge.

How to get there *(Map 33): 13km south of Cavaillon via A7, Cavaillon exit, then D99 and D74a.*

Mas dou Pastré

Quartier Saint-Sixte
13810 Eygalières (Bouches-du-Rhône)
Tel. 90.95.92.61 - M. and Mme Roumanille

Open all year. **Rooms** 8 with telephone, bath or shower, WC, TV (3 with minibar).
Price double 290-450F. **Meals** breakfast 40F, served 0830-1030. No restaurant.
Credit cards accepted. **Pets** dogs not allowed. **Facilities** swimming pool, parking.
Nearby Les Baux, St Rémy-de-Provence, Fontvieille, 18-hole Servanes golf course at
Mouriès.

Madame Roumanille, who has just renovated this old
farmhouse as she would have done her own home, is a
friendly and efficient hostess. Throughout the house, the ceilings
and walls are decked out in the colours of Provence, and there is
a wealth of antique furniture, paintings, engravings, prints, bunches
of dried flowers and local curios... enough to make you feel at
home, or better than that. The evocatively-named bedrooms are
all different: their decor owes much to carefully chosen features,
and to the owners' boundless imagination in adding a touch of
exuberance and humour. You can also sleep in an authentic,
elaborately carved wooden caravan, really old but equipped with
air-conditioning and every modern comfort. Breakfast is delicious
(there are always fresh fruit juices) whether you have it outside or
in the charming dining-room, and the crockery varies depending
on where you are sitting. This is an excellent and very Provençal
address, set amidst olive-trees and cypresses.

How to get there *(Map 33): 13km south of Cavaillon via A7, Cavaillon
exit, then D99 and D74a.*

Le Relais de la Magdelaine★★★★
Route d'Aix-en-Provence
13420 Gémenos (Bouches-du-Rhône)
Tel. 42.32.20.16 - Fax 42.32.02.26 - M. and Mme Marignane

Open 15 March – 15 Jan. **Rooms** 24 with telephone, bath or shower, WC and TV. **Price** single 395-420F, double 420-700F, suite 900F. **Meals** breakfast 65F, served from 0715; half board 590F, full board 800F (per pers., 3 days min.) **Credit cards** Visa, MasterCard. **Pets** dogs allowed (+30F) but not in the swimming pool. **Facilities** swimming pool, parking. **Nearby** Marseille, Aix-en-Provence, Cassis and the Calanques, 18-hole La Salette golf course at Marseille. **Restaurant** service 1200-1400, 2000-2130; menu 240F, also à la carte; specialities: galettes de grenouilles à la provençale, pavé de canard au miel de lavande, griottes au chocolat sauce pistache.

To find this beautiful 18th-century country house, covered in ivy and roses, you leave a rather boring highway, drive along an avenue of century-old plane trees and cross a French formal garden designed by Le Nôtre. Here you will find M. and Mme Marignane, who have been welcoming a distinguished international clientele for thirty years. Their dedication and good taste in creating a very special holiday hotel is evident in the bedrooms. These have lovely old furniture and are superb; those that look out on the terrace are the largest. Their son looks after the cooking, which is a refined version of Provençal food. The garden and swimming pool are very pleasant and you will be delighted by the cordial welcome.

How to get there (Map 33): 23km from Marseille via A50 towards Toulon, Aubagne-Est or Aubagne-Sud exit, then D2 to Gémenos.

New Hôtel Bompard★★★

2, rue des Flots-Bleus
13007 Marseille (Bouches-du-Rhône)
Tel. 91.52.10.93 – Fax 91.31.02.14 – M. Antoun

Open all year. **Rooms** 46 with telephone, bath, WC, TV and minibar. **Price** single 395F, double 450F. **Meals** breakfast 48F, served 0700-1100. No restaurant. **Credit cards** accepted. **Pets** dogs allowed. **Facilities** parking. **Nearby** Vieille Charité, art museum, Cantini museum at Marseille; Cassis and the Calanques: Port-Miou, Port Pin and Envau; Aix-en-Provence, 18-hole La Salette golf course at Marseille.

The Hotel Bompard, which is situated on the Corniche which runs around the Bay of Marseille, has the unusual advantage of having a large garden though it is in the city. The bedrooms, most of which have a large balcony which looks out over the acacias and palm trees in the grounds, are charming. They are furnished in a modern, practical style and offer plenty of comfort. The most quiet and pleasant rooms are those in the main building, which has recently been refurbished and air-conditioned. The tranquillity and the cordial welcome at the Hotel Bompard make it a good place to stay, but as it is ten minutes from the centre of the city you will need a car or taxi to get to and fro. You can hire a car at the hotel.

How to get there *(Map 33): on the J F Kennedy corniche, follow signs from Le Ruhl restaurant.*

Hôtel de Servanes★★

13890 Mouriès (Bouches-du-Rhône)
Tel. 90.47.50.03 - Fax 90.47.56.77
M. Revoil

Open 15 Jan – 15 Dec. **Rooms** 22 with telephone (20 with bath, 11 with WC, 16 with TV). **Price** 220-450F. **Meals** breakfast 35F, served 0700-1000; half board 220-350F, full board 330-450F (per pers., 3 days min.) **Credit cards** Visa, Eurocard. **Pets** dogs allowed. **Facilities** swimming pool, parking. **Nearby** Les Baux, Saint-Rémy-de-Provence, Fontvieille, 18-hole Servanes golf course at Mouriès. **Restaurant** service 1200-1430, 1900-2130; menus 90-140F, also à la carte; Provençal cooking.

This dream holiday haven is reached by a gravel road bordered by cypress and olive trees. The beautiful, 200-hectare, Provençal estate, which has been owned by the same family for five generations, has been planted with lovely Mediterranean trees. You will find a charming old-fashioned ambience here. The large sitting rooms contain antique furniture and paintings and engravings collected, perhaps, by an ancestor who served in the diplomatic service in the Far East. The effect might be a bit dismal in winter. The bedrooms have a certain charm and some of them are elegant and stylish, for example numbers 1 and 3. Some others, with simpler decor but still with old furniture, have the advantage of terraces looking out on the swimming pool. You will eat very well in the dining room situated in the old vaulted kitchens. The atmosphere of the hotel is very pleasant and convivial and the Servanes golf course is next door.

How to get there (Map 33): 14km west of Salon-de-Provence via N113 then D5 towards Les-Baux-de-Provence.

Le Berger des Abeilles★★

13670 Saint-Andiol (Bouches-du-Rhône)
Tel. 90.95.01.91 - Fax 90.95.48.26
Mme Grenier

Open 1 Jan – 25 Feb, 4 March – 30 Sept, 25 Nov – 31 Dec (closed Monday except public holidays). **Rooms** 6 with telephone, bath or shower, WC and TV. **Price** double 320F. **Meals** breakfast 45F, served 0730-1000; half board 330F (per pers., 3 days min.) **Credit cards** Visa, Amex. **Pets** dogs allowed. **Facilities** parking. **Nearby** Les Baux, Saint-Rémy-de-Provence, Avignon. **Restaurant** service 1230-1400, 2000-2130; menus 140-260F, also à la carte; specialities: salade de caille confite à l'huile d'olive sur galette d'épeautre, daube de joues d'agneau aux épices, mousse au miel de lavande et vieux marc de Provence.

Le Berger des Abeilles is as welcoming as a hotel could possibly be. There are only six bedrooms and the owners can thus provide a personal style of service. All the rooms are perfectly comfortable, but you should choose, if available, 'Alexia' or 'Caroline' (the rooms are named after the women in the family and those two are our favourites). A few items of period furniture set the trend for the cheerful, intimate decor. Mme Grenier does the cooking herself and her cuisine has an excellent reputation. Dinner is served in a fine rustic-style dining-room or outside in the shade of a gigantic plane-tree. The noise of traffic on the main road, muffled by luxuriant vegetation, can hardly be heard in the hotel garden, and not at all indoors (thanks to those thick walls...) A good stopping-place!

How to get there (Map 33): 13km south of Avignon via N7 (2km from Saint-Andiol).

Hostellerie de Cacharel***

Route de Cacharel
13460 Les Saintes-Maries-de-la-Mer (Bouches-du-Rhône)
Tel. 90.97.95.44 - Faxs 90.97.87.97 - M. Colomb de Daunant

Open all year. **Rooms** 11 with telephone, bath or shower and WC. **Price** single and double 500F. **Meals** breakfast 45F, served 0800-1030. **Credit cards** MasterCard, Eurocard, Visa. **Pets** dogs allowed. **Facilities** swimming pool, horse trekking, parking. **Nearby** church of Saintes-Maries-de-la-Mer, gipsy pilgrimage (24 and 25 May), sea wall (20km), Arles, 18-hole Servanes golf course at Mouriès. **Restaurant** snacks available.

The hostellerie is an old farmhouse on the borders of the Camargue, a land of nature reserves, placid lakes and white horses. The bedrooms are furnished charmingly and look out either on a flower-filled inner courtyard or on the lakes, and salt marshes. As the hotel is part of the farm estate guests can walk or ride all over the property. There is no restaurant but you can get snacks if you want them. You will receive a good welcome at this tranquil and genuine Camargue house in what is rather a popular tourist region.

How to get there *(Map 33): 38km south west of Arles. 4km north of Saintes-Maries-de-la-Mer by D85a, called the Route de Cacharel.*

Mas du Clarousset★★★

Route de Cacharel
13460 Les Saintes-Maries-de-la-Mer (Bouches-du-Rhône)
Tel. 90.97.81.66 - Fax 90.97.88.59 - Mme Eyssette

Open all year. **Rooms** 10 with telephone, bath, WC, TV and minibar. **Price** single 730F, double 750F. **Meals** breakfast 50F, served 0700-1100; half board 675F, full board 910F (per person). **Credit cards** accepted. **Pets** dogs allowed (+50F). **Facilities** swimming pool (+55F), gipsy evenings (on request), parking. **Nearby** church of Saintes-Maries-de-la-Mer, gipsy pilgrimage (24 and 25 May), sea wall (30km), Arles, 18-hole Servanes golf course at Mouriès. **Restaurant** service 1200-1400, 2000-2200 (closed Monday and Tuesday lunchtime); menus 250-350F, also à la carte; specialities: sufrigi aux croûtons, terrine de canard sauvage, loup en croûte.

Mas du Clarousset is a good place to absorb the spirit of Provence. Here, Henriette gives a special welcome to lovers of the Camargue and likes to introduce them to the local way of life with gypsy evenings, walks on little known beaches and a midnight Christmas mass to which everyone rides on horseback. This very pleasant place has 10 pretty and comfortable bedrooms in an annexe, all with private terraces and views over the Carmargue. Each room has a separate private entrance and there is room for your car by the door. After a day's excursion in the area you can relax and cool off in the swimming pool in the garden. You will also appreciate the good traditional Provençal food that Henriette serves in the restaurant.

How to get there *(Map 33): 38km south west of Arles via D570, then D85a (7km from Saintes-Maries).*

Lou Mas du Juge★★★

Quartier Pin Tourcat
13460 Saintes–Maries–de–la–Mer (Bouches–du–Rhône)
Tel. 66.73.51.45 – Fax 66.73.51.42 – M. and Mme Granier

Open all year. **Rooms** 7 with bath or shower and WC (4 with TV). **Price** single 350F, double 400F, suite 400-600F. **Meals** breakfast 30F. **Credit cards** not accepted. **Pets** dogs not allowed. **Facilities** parking. **Nearby** church of Saintes-Maries-de-la-Mer, gipsy pilgrimage 24 and 25 May, sea wall (30km), Arles, 18-hole Servanes golf course at Mouriès. **Restaurant** service 1200-1300, 2000-2100; menus 300-350F; specialities: anchoïades, terrine maison, salade frisée à l'aïl avec fromage frais de brebis, sandre et turbot grillés.

As you drive through the Camargue you will see a giant bottle at the side of the road; this tells you that you are on the right road and that the farm hotel Lou Mas du Juge is not far off. Here you can feel the true spirit of the Camargue and enjoy the meals and parties put on by your convivial host. The large farm has several bedrooms, all of them pleasant, spacious and furnished with old furniture. Each one has a large bathroom and a good view of the Camargue countryside. There is what some might consider a slight snag, namely that the place is very much sought after for receptions, but don't feel put out by the celebrations as the proprietors are very good at creating a friendly atmosphere among all their guests.

How to get there *(Map 33): 38km south west of Arles via D540, then D85, the route du Bac du Sauvage.*

Château des Alpilles★★★★

Ancienne route des Baux
13210 Saint-Rémy-de-Provence (Bouches-du-Rhône)
Tel. 90.92.03.33 - Fax 90.92.45.17 - Mmes Bon

Open 15 March – 15 Nov, 20 Dec – 4 Jan. **Rooms** 19 with telephone, bath, WC, TV, minibar (some air-conditioned). **Price** single 760-810F, double 860-980F, suite 1150-1460F. **Meals** breakfast 65F, served 0730-1200. **Credit cards** accepted. **Pets** dogs admitted (+40F). **Facilities** swimming pool, tennis, sauna, parking. **Nearby** Frédéric Mistral museum at Maillane, Eygalières, Les Baux, Avignon, Arles, 9-hole golf course at Les Baux, 18-hole Servanes golf course at Mouriès. Light meals on reservation, 150-200F.

The château was built at the beginning of the 19th century by one of the oldest families of Arles and became the meeting place of politicians and writers staying in the region. It still has the feeling of a holiday château where one comes to pass the summer. The lounge, the bar and the dining room, richly decorated with plasterwork and mirrors, are all very pleasant rooms and open out on to the garden. The bedrooms have period furniture, are all comfortable, and have large bathrooms with full facilities. The great park, in which there is a swimming pool and tennis court, is planted with old trees and rare species. This is a traditional hotel that has adapted well to modern tastes.

How to get there (Map 33): 14km west of Cavaillon via A7, exit Cavaillon, then D99; it's 1km from St-Rémy-de-Provence.

Le Mas des Carassins***

1, chemin Gaulois
13210 Saint-Rémy-de-Provence (Bouches-du-Rhône)
Tel. 90.92.15.48 - M. and Mme Ripert

Open 15 March – 15 Nov. **Rooms** 10 with telephone, bath and WC. **Price** single 325-475F, double 355-495F. **Meals** breakfast 43F, served 0800-0930. No restaurant. **Credit cards** Visa, Eurocard, MasterCard. **Pets** dogs not allowed. **Facilities** parking. **Nearby** Frédéric Mistral museum at Maillane, Eygalières, Les Baux, Avignon, Arles, 9-hole golf course at Les Baux, 18-hole Servanes golf course at Mouriès.

This old 19th-century farm is now a small family hotel with ten rooms. It is situated a little outside the centre of St Rémy-de-Provence in a small, quiet though not especially attractive street. When in its pretty garden however you can imagine yourself in the middle of the country. The bedrooms are all different. In 'Magnaneraie', for example, there is a rustic ambience with stone walls, while 'Jasse' is the only room with a terrace. There is a pretty dining room and a small, pleasant lounge with cane furniture. No restaurant, but if you are staying in the hotel the helpful Mme Ripert will prepare a snack for you.

How to get there *(Map 33): 14km west of Cavaillon by A7, exit Cavaillon by A7, then D99.*

Logis du Guetteur★★★

Place du Château - 83460 Les Arcs-sur-Argens (Var)
Tel. 94.73.30.82 - Fax 94.73.39.95
M. Callegari

Open all year (closed 15 Jan – 15 Feb). **Rooms** 10 with telephone, bath or shower, WC, TV and minibar. **Price** double 450F. **Meals** breakfast 45F, served 0800-1030, half board 430F, full board 550F (per pers., 2 days min.) **Credit cards** Amex, Visa, Diners, Eurocard. **Pets** dogs allowed (+30F). **Facilities** swimming pool, parking. **Nearby** Sainte-Rosaline chapel (4km from Arcs), château d'Entrecasteaux, abbey of Le Thoronet, Seillans, Simon Segal museum at Aups. **Restaurant** service 1200 and 1915; menus 130-330F, also à la carte; specialities; saumon fourré à l'écrevisse, Saint Jacques au beurre de muscat, pigeon de ferme aux truffes, ris de veau aux oranges, bourride.

The old 11th-century Château du Villeneuve in which the Logis is situated was restored in 1970, and its medieval appearance with rough stone walls has been preserved. In your comfortable, pleasantly furnished bedroom you won't need to worry about enemies scaling the castle walls but you will be able to enjoy the panoramic views. Relax and let the charm of the place take over. The dining room, which is in the old cellars, has a covered terrace where you will eat looking out over the superb view, with the belltower and rooftops below you. There is a swimming pool, the food is good and the welcome cordial.

How to get there *(Map 34): 12km south of Draguignan via N555 and D555; in the medieval village.*

Hostellerie Bérard***
Rue Gabriel-Péri
83740 La Cadière d'Azur (Var)
Tel. 94.90.11.43 - Fax 94.90.01.94 - M. and Mme Bérard

Open all year. **Rooms** 40 with telephone, bath or shower, WC, minibar (suites have TV). **Price** single 320-390F, double 517-595F, suite 750-900F. **Meals** breakfast 65F, served 0730-0930. **Credit cards** Amex, Visa, Eurocard, MasterCard. **Pets** dogs allowed (+40F). **Facilities** swimming pool, games room, tennis, parking. **Nearby** Sanary exotic garden, Bandol, village of Le Castellet, 18-hole La Salette golf course at Marseille. **Restaurant** service 1230-1330, 1930-2130 (closed Sunday evening and Monday in low season); menus 160-350F, also à la carte; specialities: petite soupe crémeuse de moules au pistil de safran, croustillant de loup à la sauce corail.

You ought to arrive in this pretty village on market day (Thursday), when everyone gathers on the terrace of the café. You will enjoy the festive atmosphere but don't worry about being disturbed by it for the hotel has a quiet garden behind its medieval walls. The bedrooms in the former convent are large, cool in summer, decorated in varied tones of brown and with beautiful bathrooms with Salernes tiles. The same tiles are found in the 'bastide' rooms which are more traditional, but also more colouful with their pretty Provençal curtains and bedcovers. All of them are comfortable and well furnished. You will have a choice of views: the rooftops, the garden, the ramparts, the village itself or the countryside with the medieval village of Castellet in the distance. You will be charmed by Danièle Bérard's friendly and helpful welcome and enjoy the cooking, which has an excellent reputation.

How to get there (Map 34): 24km north of Bandol via D559 and D266.

Auberge du Puits Jaubert★
Route du Lac de Fondurane
83440 Callian (Var)
Tel. 94.76.44.48 – M. Fillatreau

Open 15 Dec – 15 Nov (closed Tuesday). **Rooms** 8 with bath or shower and WC. **Price** double 250-300F. **Meals** breakfast 35F, served 0800-1100; half board 300F, full board 420F (per pers., 3 days min.) **Credit cards** Eurocard, Visa. **Pets** dogs allowed. **Facilities** parking. **Nearby** Saint-Cassien lake, massif du Tanneron, chapel of Notre-Dame-de-Peygros, Auribeau-sur-Siagne, 18-hole golf course at Valescure. **Restaurant** service 1200-1330, 2000-2130; menus 180 and 240F, also à la carte; specialities: feuilleté d'escalopes de saumon, tournedos au thym.

To the west of Cannes lies the massif of Tanneron, the land of mimosa, and it is in this beautiful area, in the middle of the countryside, that you will find the Auberge du Puits Jaubert. Converted from a 15th-century farm, it lies at the end of a track winding along the banks of Lake Saint-Cassien. It is a lovely dry stone building roofed in round Genoese tiles. The same lovely stonework is found in the large dining room where a collection of old farming implements adds to the country atmosphere. In summer it is a real pleasure to dine under the foliage of the verandah or in the shade of the plane trees. The cooking is good, and the bedrooms simple but not lacking in comfort. They have just been completely renovated and prettily decorated in pastel colours. The service can be a bit variable.

How to get there *(Map 34): 33km from Fréjus via A8, exit Les Adrets-de-l'Estérel, then D37 towards Montauroux and D56; follow signs.*

Hostellerie Lou Calen★★★

1, cours Gambetta
83850 Cotignac (Var)
Tel. 94.04.60.40 – Fax 94.04.76.64 – M. and Mme Mendes

Open 15 March – 31 Dec. **Rooms** 16 with telephone and bath (3 with shower, 15 with WC, 12 with TV). **Price** double 260-580F. **Meals** breakfast 45F, served 0730-1030; half board 620-920F, full board 880-1200F (2 pers.) **Credit cards** Amex, Diners, Visa, MasterCard. **Pets** dogs allowed (+40F). **Facilities** swimming pool, parking. **Nearby** abbey of Le Thoronet , château d'Entrecasteaux, Verdon gorges, Ste-Croix lake, 18-hole Barbaroux golf course at Brignoles. **Restaurant** service 1200-1430, 1730-2130 (closed Wednesday in low season); menus 120-235F, also à la carte; specialities: foie gras maison.

All around Cotignac there are cliffs topped by Saracen towers. The village itself, with its squares shaded by plane trees, its pavement cafés and moss–covered fountain, is an ideal place for enjoying the life of a Provençal village. The hotel is at the entrance to the village, near the old wash house; it is in the centre of things but surrounded by countryside and has a garden hidden behind its façade. The dining room extends into a garden terrace with the swimming pool below. The bedrooms are in various styles, sizes and prices but they are all charming and comfortable. Some have a loggia, others have fire–places where fires are lit in the autumn. However, the sound proofing in some of the rooms is not good.

How to get there *(Map 34): 24km north of Brignoles via A8, Brignoles exit, then D562 towards Carcès and D13 towards Cotignac.*

Moulin de la Camandoule***
Chemin Notre-Dame-des-Cyprès
83440 Fayence (Var)
Tel. 94.76.00.84 – Fax 94.76.10.40 – M. and Mme Rilla

Open all year. **Rooms** 11 with telephone, bath, shower, WC and TV. **Price** single 250-450F, double 450-625F, suite 675F. **Meals** breakfast 45F, served 0800-1000; half board 445-555F (obligatory 15 March-31 Oct.) **Credit cards** Eurocard, Access, Visa. **Pets** dogs allowed (+40F). **Facilities** swimming pool, parking. **Nearby** Seillans, Bargème, Ste-Roseline chapel (4km from Arcs), château d'Entrecasteaux, abbey of Le Thoronet, 18-hole golf course at Roquebruune-sur-Argens. **Restaurant** service 1230-1500, 2000-2200 (closed Tuesday); menus 185-260F, also à la carte.

This old olive oil mill has been well preserved and today belongs to an English couple who run it like an old-fashioned English guest house. You will get a warm, friendly welcome and all the services and comforts of a good hotel. The interior decoration is in excellent taste. The bedrooms are furnished in an attractive Provençal style, but the attention to detail is a bit uneven. In the unusual lounge the old machinery of the oil press has been cleverly incorporated into the decor. Around the hotel are large grounds through which the River Camandre flows. A look at the menus on the walls of the swimming pool bar will tell you about the attention given to the cooking. Mme Rilla, who worked for many years in England on radio and TV food programmes, has made La Camandoule a good destination for travellers who like to eat well.

How to get there (Map 34): 31km north of Fréjus via D4, then D19.

La Grillade au feu de bois★★

Flassans-sur-Issole
83340 Le Luc (Var)
Tel. 94.69.71.20 - Fax 94.59.66.11 - Mme Babb

Open all year. **Rooms** 16 with telephone, bath or shower, WC and TV. **Price** single and double 400-550F, suite 900F. **Meals** breakfast 40F, served 0800-1030. **Credit cards** accepted. **Pets** dogs allowed. **Facilities** heated swimming pool, parking. **Nearby** abbey of La Celle, La Loube mountain, 18-hole Barbaroux golf course at Brignoles. **Restaurant** service 1200-1345, 1930-2100; menu 180F, also à la carte; traditional Provençal cooking.

The owner of this well restored 18th-century farmhouse has been here since the hotel opened. The vaulted dining room with its white walls is very welcoming and opens out onto a terrace shaded by fine trees, the oldest of which is a 100 year old mulberry. The bedrooms are superb, large and comfortable. If you wish you can have a room in one of the bungalows in the grounds, which are quiet and peaceful. Though the N7 highway is only 500m away you will not hear any noise from it. The cooking is excellent and, as you might expect, there are many very good things from the grill.

How to get there *(Map 34): 13km east of Brignoles via N7.*

La Vieille Bastide

83780 Flayosc (Var)
Tel. 94.70.40.57 – Fax 94.84.61.23 – M. Guidi

Open all year (closed Monday). **Rooms** 7 with telephone, bath, WC, TV and minibar.
Price double 255-315F. **Meals** breakfast 30F, served 0730-1000; half board 240-305F, full board +80F. **Credit cards** accepted. **Pets** dogs allowed (+30F). **Facilities** swimming pool, parking. **Nearby** Seillans, Bargème, Ste-Roseline chapel (4km from Arcs), château d'Entrecasteaux, abbey of Le Thoronet, Simon Segal museum à Aups. **Restaurant** service 1230 and 1930; menus 98-230F, also à la carte; Provençal cooking.

This hotel is in an old *bastide* which has been rebuilt, extended and generally improved. The bedrooms are comfortable, many of them with cheerful pink wallpaper and pastel fabrics. The view from them varies, some of them look out on the garden and others on the swimming pool, and their prices (all very reasonable) vary accordingly. In the lounge there is a large sofa and two armchairs by the fireplace where a wood fire burns in winter. Adjoining it is a spacious dining room. You can also dine or have your breakfast on the shaded terrace looking out on the countryside with its olive and cypress trees. You will receive a very friendly welcome.

How to get there (Map 34): *7km west of Draguignan via D557 through Salernes.*

Auberge du Vieux Fox★★

Place de l'Eglise
83670 Fox-Amphoux (Var)
Tel. 94.80.71.69 – Fax 94.80.78.38 – M. Martha

Open 15 Jan – 15 Dec (closed Tuesday and Wednesday lunchtime in low season).
Rooms 8 with telephone, bath or shower, WC (2 with TV). **Price** single 135F, double
260-350F. **Meals** breakfast 35F, served 0830-1000; half board 525-630F, full board
700-800F (per 2 pers., 3 days min.) **Credit cards** Amex, MasterCard, Visa. **Pets** dogs
allowed (+35F). **Facilities** parking. **Nearby** abbeys of Le Thoronet and La Celle,
Verdon lake and gorges, 18-hole Barbaroux golf course at Brignoles. **Restaurant**
service 1230 and 1915; menus 115-245F, also à la carte; specialities: agneau de
Haute-Provence, galette du berger.

The old village of Fox–Amphoux, perched on its wooded crag,
was first a Roman camp and then became a headquarters of
Knights Templars. The hotel is in the old presbytery adjoining the
church in the centre of the village. The interior will instantly charm
you: there is a delightful dining room with prettily laid tables
alongside lovely old furniture. In summer you can also have your
breakfast on the enchanting little terrace in the shade of a large fig
tree. The bedrooms and bathrooms have been renovated this year.
They are comfortable and look out on the massifs of Sainte-Victoire
and Sainte-Beaume. In addition to the comfort and charm of this
place you can count on good food and reasonable prices. It is a
good idea to take demi-pension during your stay.

*How to get there (Map 34): 32km north of Brignoles via A8, exit Saint-
Maximin-la-Sainte-Baume, then D560 to Tavernes, D71 and D32.*

La Boulangerie***

Route de Collobrières
83310 Grimaud (Var)
Tel. 94 43.23.16 - Fax 94.43.38.27 - Mme Piget

Open 1 April – 10 Oct. **Rooms** 11 with telephone, bath, WC (2 with TV, 1 with minibar).
Price single 560F, double 660-690F, suite 780-1320F. **Meals** breakfast 50F, served
0745-1100. **Credit cards** Amex, Visa. **Pets** dogs allowed (+60F). **Facilities**
swimming pool, tennis, table tennis (100F), parking. **Nearby** la Garde-Freinet,
ridgeway to the Notre-Dame-des-Anges hermitage, Collobrières, Carthusian
monastery of La Verne, Saint-Tropez, 9-hole Beauvallon golf course at Sainte-
Maxime. **Restaurant** reserved for hotel guests, service 1200-1330; à la carte;
specialities: aïoli de poissons, poulet fermier aux truffes.

This place has nothing to do with bakeries as its name would
suggest, but it has a very different atmosphere from a traditional
hotel. Its ambience is more like a holiday house in the interior of
Provence, far away from the crowds, in a tranquil place in the
Massif des Maures. Everything conspires to produce this
impression: the terrace where you can have your meals, or the
dining room, which is part of the lounge. There is a happy
informality that makes you feel instantly at ease. The bedrooms
have the same homely atmosphere and are more like guest rooms
in a friend's house than hotel bedrooms.

How to get there *(Map 34): 10km west of Saint-Tropez via D14; 1km
from the village.*

Le Verger

Route de Collobrières
83310 Grimaud (Var)
Tel. 94.43.25.93 – Fax 94.43.33.92 – Mme Zachary

Open March – Nov. **Rooms** 9 with telephone, bath or shower, WC, TV, (3 with air-conditioning). **Price** double 550-800F. **Meals** breakfast 60F, served 0830-1130. **Credit cards** Eurocard, Visa. **Pets** dogs allowed. **Facilities** swimming pool, parking. **Nearby** la Garde-Freinet, ridgeway to the Notre-Dame-des-Anges hermitage, Collobrières, Carthusian monastery of La Verne, Saint-Tropez, 9-hole Beauvallon golf course at Sainte-Maxime. **Restaurant** service 1200-1430, 1930-2330; à la carte; specialities: fleurs de courgettes sauce mousseline, médaillon de lotte au curry, carré d'agneau au miel, feuilleté de saumon au basilic, bourride.

This pretty house looks more like a private dwelling than a traditional hotel. The bedrooms have French windows which open on to a terrace or a lawn with fruit trees. The decor has been planned with care: the style is Provençal, with good quality fabrics, and the bathrooms are handsome and have every facility. You will find your bed turned down every evening, and bouquets of flowers which will add a pleasant touch of the countryside to your room. Every day the restaurant is filled with loyal followers of M. Zachary who remember him when he was chef at the Bigorneaux in Saint Tropez, and there will be other new enthusiasts who know about his good cooking. M. Zachary gets his aromatic herbs and vegetables from the kitchen garden. You will be welcomed in a very friendly way.

How to get there *(Map 34): 9km west of St-Tropez. From A8, exit Le Luc, then D558 towards St-Tropez; before Grimaud, D14 towards Collobrières and follow signs.*

494

Le Manoir★★★

Ile de Port-Cros
83400 Hyères (Var)
Tel. 94.05.90.52 - Fax 94.05.90.89 - M. Buffet

Open 1 May – 1 Oct. **Rooms** 24 with telephone, bath or shower and WC. **Price** double with half board 675-900F, with full board 800-1050F (per pers., 3 days min.) **Meals** breakfast 55F, served 0745-1000. **Credit cards** Visa, Diners. **Pets** dogs not allowed. **Nearby** nature trails in the Port-Cros national park, Porquerolles. **Restaurant** service 1300 and 2000; menus 250-300F also à la carte; specialities: bourride provençale, baron d'agneau à la broche, fricassée de gambas au whisky.

The eucalyptus, the palm trees, the white walls of the Manoir with columns at the entrance evoke a nostalgic and exotic daydream of days gone by. The island of Pont-Cros is a nature reserve and no vehicles are allowed. The hotel was opened just after the war in this private house and it still preserves a family atmosphere, blending conviviality with elegance. There is a large lounge and several small ones which card players frequent towards the end of the summer season. The bedrooms are cool and charming and some of them have little loggias; from Room 8 you can see the sea through the trees. You will enjoy the tranquility of the 12 hectares of parkland around the hotel.

How to get there *(Map 34): ferry connection from Le Lavandou and Cavalaire (tel. 94.71.01.02); from Hyères-La Tour Fondue (tel. 94.58.21.81). Cars not allowed on the island. Airport Toulon-Hyères.*

Les Glycines★★★

Place d'Armes - Ile de Porquerolles
83400 Hyères (Var)
Tel. 94.58.30.36 - Fax 94.58.35.22 - M. Fanara

Open 10 April – 15 Oct. **Rooms** 17 with air-conditioning, telephone, bath or shower, WC and TV. **Price** double 800-1200F. **Meals** breakfast 50F, served 0800-1000; half board 650-850F (per pers.) **Credit cards** Visa. **Pets** dogs not allowed. **Nearby** bike rides along island paths, beaches, boat hire, Port-Cros. **Restaurant** service 1930-2230: menus, also à la carte; specialities: loups grillés, petits farcis de Provence, sardines au gros sel, agneau à l'ail doux.

The hotel has been completely refurbished and is situated on the main square of the village, but as there are no cars on the island it is very peaceful. Set back in its garden, which has a century-old fig tree, the hotel with its whitewashed walls and blue shutters still has the peaceful atmosphere of Provençal houses of yesteryear. The bedrooms, all comfortable and air conditioned, open on to the garden or the square, and have a pleasant atmosphere with pastel tinted walls, Provençal fabrics and ceramic floor-tiles. The bathrooms are also elegant and have every facility. The meals include Mediterranean specialities and are served in the cool shady garden on tables with brightly patterned tablecloths.

How to get there *(Map 34): ferry connection from Hyères or La Tour Fondue (tel. 94.58.21.81) or boat-taxi from l'Oustau (tel. 94.58.30.13) at any time. Cars not allowed on the island. Airport Toulon-Hyères (7km).*

Mas des Brugassières★★

Plan-de-la-Tour
83120 Sainte-Maxime (Var)
Tel. 94.43.72.42 - Fax 94.43.00.20 - M. and Mme Geffine

Open 15 March – 31 Oct and Christmas holiday. **Rooms** 14 with telephone, bath or shower and WC. **Price** double 420-550F. **Meals** breakfast 38F, served 0830-1000. No restaurant, but snacks by the pool at lunchtime. **Credit cards** Eurocard, Mastercard, Visa. **Pets** dogs allowed (+60F). **Facilities** swimming pool, tennis, parking. **Nearby** massif des Maures, 9-hole Beauvallon golf course at Sainte-Maxime.

This house lies in the heart of the Massif des Maures by a quiet road; and if you dream of spending a few days by a swimming pool in the peace of these wooded mountains behind St Tropez, this is the place. The white-walled bedrooms are light and airy and open out on to the swimming pool or small private terraces. Breakfasts are copious but the hotel does not have a restaurant. On certain days, however, there are buffet meals and barbecues available by the pool.

How to get there *(Map 34): 15km north west of Sainte-Maxime via D25 and D74; 1km from the village.*

La Maurette

83520 Roquebrune-sur-Argens (Var)
Tel. 94.45.46.81
M. and Mme Rapin

Open 15 March – 25 Oct. **Rooms** 9 with bath or shower and WC. **Price** double 320-370F. **Meals** breakfast 35F, served 0800-1000. **Credit cards** Eurocard, MasterCard, Visa. **Pets** dogs not allowed. **Facilities** swimming pool, parking. **Nearby** Roquebrune, Fréjus cathedral, massif de l'Estérel, 18-hole golf course at Roquebrune. **Restaurant** service 1930 (closed Wednesday and Sunday); menu 100F; Provençal family cooking.

Monsieur Rapin may well owe his vocation as a hotelier to a grandfather who owned a hotel in Cannes. But is 'hotelier' the right word in his case? For, rather than a hotel, La Maurette is a guest house. It is the kind of place where you will almost feel you have been invited... And anyway, would a hotel really choose such a secluded location, well away from crowds? Facing the rock of Roquebrune and the first hills of the Massif des Maures, this could be the setting for a monastery. Behind the hotel there is the Estérel, the Mediterranean and the valley. The bedrooms are bright, cheerful, and very comfortable; carefully chosen furniture, curios and paintings give them great character. The table d'hôte meals are delicious: good home-cooked local dishes, gratins, meats roasted in a woodburning oven, and desserts. Facilities include a decent-size swimming-pool, and your hosts are warm and friendly. Who could ask for more?

How to get there *(Map 34): 10km west of Fréjus via N7 and D7; 2km from the village on the hill (follow signs); from A8, Le Muy exit.*

Hôtel Le Pré de la Mer★★★
Route des Salins
83990 Saint-Tropez (Var)
Tel. 94.97.12.23 - Fax 94.97.43.91 - Mme Blum

Open Easter – 30 Sept. **Rooms** 3 and 9 studios (with kitchenette) with telephone, bath, shower, WC, TV and minibar. **Price** single and double 475-600F, studios 600-800F. **Meals** breakfast 50F, served 0830-1200. No restaurant.**Credit cards** Visa. **Pets** dogs allowed (+50F). **Facilities** parking. **Nearby** l'Annonciade museum at St-Tropez, la Garde-Freinet, ridgeway to Notre-Dame-des-Anges hermitage, Collobrières, Carthusian monastery of La Verne, 9-hole Beauvallon golf course at Sainte-Maxime.

This is a low-roofed white house built in St Tropez–Mexican style. The bedrooms are large and comfortable, cooled by powerful fans. Some of them have a kitchen (to help you forget the prices of the restaurants in Saint-Tropez...) and all have a private terrace with white wooden table and chairs, perfect for breakfast and possibly other meals. The terraces lead out into a pleasant garden where lemon and pomegranate trees and oleanders bloom. But to get into this peaceful haven just minutes from Saint-Tropez you will have to appeal to Joséphine Blum, the owner, who likes to choose her clientele.

How to get there (Map 34): 3km east of Saint-Tropez on the Salins road.

Le Ferme d'Augustin***

Plage de Tahiti
83350 Ramatuelle (Var)
Tel. 94.97.23.83 – Fax 94.97.40.30 – Mme Vallet

Open 25 March – 15 Oct. **Rooms** 34 with telephone, bath (4 with shower), WC, TV and minibar. **Price** double 580-1600F, suite 1800F. **Meals** breakfast 80F, served 0600-1400. No restaurant. **Credit cards** Visa, Eurocard, Amex. **Pets** dogs allowed (+70F). **Facilities** swimming pool, parking. **Nearby** l'Annonciade museum at St-Tropez, la Garde-Freinet, ridgeway to the Notre-Dame-des-Anges hermitage, Collobrières, Carthusian monastery of La Verne, 9-hole Beauvallon golf course at Ste-Maxime.

This used to be the family's farmhouse and has now been completely renovated. Before entering the house itself you will be captivated by the pine woods and the garden full of wisteria, bougainvillea, rambling roses and the great parasol-shaped mulberry trees. In the lounges, antique country style furniture is tastefully combined with modern sofas. The bedrooms have pretty bathrooms with wall tiles from Salernes. They all overlook the garden and have a balcony or a terrace commanding sea views. The hotel occupies a truly enviable position, just metres away from Tahiti beach. If you want to stay on the beach all day, packed lunches are available; the bar also serves light meals until midday.

How to get there (Map 34): 5km from St-Tropez on the Tahiti beach road.

La Ferme d'Hermès**

Route de l'Escalet - Val de Pons
83350 Ramatuelle (Var)
Tel. 94.79.27.80 - Fax 94.79.26.86 - Mme Verrier

Open 1 April – 31 Oct. **Rooms** 9 with telephone, bath or shower, WC, TV, minibar and kitchenette. **Price** double 600-900F, suite 850-1100F. **Meals** breakfast 70F, served 0900-1200. No restaurant. **Credit cards** MasterCard, Visa. **Pets** dogs allowed (+50F). **Facilities** swimming pool, parking. **Nearby** l'Annonciade museum at St. Tropez, la Garde-Freinet, ridgeway to the Notre-Dame-des-Anges hermitage, Collobrières, Carthusian monastery of La Verne, 9-hole Beauvallon golf course at Sainte-Maxime.

A dirt track winding through vineyards, a fragrant garden full of rosemary and olive-trees, a pink-coloured house: this is the place in the Midi you have always dreamed of. Mme Verrier is an attentive hostess, and there are many thoughtful details: a cosy fireplace, home-made cakes and jam at breakfast, bunches of flowers everywhere. The bedrooms are delightful and some of them have a small terrace leading straight out into the vineyards. All of them have a kitchenette, just the thing for those who don't want do the rounds of the restaurants in Saint-Tropez every day.

How to get there (Map34): 2km south of Ramatuelle on the l'Escalet road.

La Figuière★★★

Route de Tahiti
83350 Ramatuelle (Var)
Tel. 94.97.18.21 - Fax 94.97.68.48 - M. Béraud and Mme Chaix

Open 9 April – 10 Oct. **Rooms** 45 with air-conditioning, telephone, bath (3 with shower), WC, (31 with TV, 42 with minibar). **Price** double 500-900F, suite 1300-1400F. **Meals** breakfast 60F, served 0800-1100. **Credit cards** Visa. **Pets** dogs allowed (+60F). **Facilities** swimming pool, tennis (80F), parking. **Nearby** l'Annonciade museum at St-Tropez, La Garde-Freinet, ridgeway to the Notre-Dame-des-Anges hermitage, Collobrières, Carthusian monastery of La Verne, Saint-Tropez, 9-hole Beauvallon golf course at Sainte-Maxime. **Restaurant** service 1200-1500, 2000-2300; à la carte; specialities: grills.

Opening the shutters in the morning to a vista of sunny vineyards is a rare pleasure. It is one of the many charms of this hotel set in the countryside a few kilometres from Saint-Tropez. La Figuière is composed of five small typical Provençal buildings in a garden full of fig trees. The bedrooms are quiet and screened from each other; some open on to the vineyards, others on to a pleasant terrace. Grills are served at lunchtime by the swimming pool encircled by lavender, and there is a tennis court behind the hotel.

How to get there *(Map 34): 2.5km south of Saint-Tropez on the Tahiti beach road.*

Hôtel des Deux Rocs★★★

Place Font d'Amont
83440 Seillans (Var)
Tel. 94.76.87.32 - Fax 94.76.88.08 - Mme Hirsch

Open 1 April – 11 Oct. **Rooms** 15 with telephone, bath or shower, WC and minibar. **Price** double 240-500F. **Meals** breakfast 40F, served 0800-1000; half board 290-420F, full board 390-520F (per pers., 3 days min.) **Credit cards** Eurocard, MasterCard, Visa. **Pets** dogs allowed. **Nearby** chapel of St-André at Comps-sur-Artuby, Fayence, les Arcs and the Ste-Roseline chapel, château d'Entrecasteaux, abbey of Le Thoronet, 18-hole golf course at Roquebrune-sur-Argens. **Restaurant** service 1200-1400, 1930-2100(closed Tuesday and Thursday lunchtime); menus 135-210F, also à la carte; specialities: crotin de chavignol en croûte, filet de loup à la crème de basilic, feuilleté aux pommes.

Standing at the top of the splendid village of Seillans, close to the city walls and the old castle, the Hôtel des Deux Rocs is a large Provençal style building with rows of windows similar to some Italian houses. Variety is the keynote of the decor, which is exquisite. You will feel at home and relaxed in the small lounge with a fireplace. The bedrooms are all individually designed: period furniture, wall fabrics, curtains, everything down to the bathroom towels gives a personal touch to each one of them. Breakfast can be served at tables set up in the pleasant little square, and home-made jams are just one among many thoughtful details which make a stay here memorable. You will love this hotel and prices are very reasonable.

How to get there *(Map 34): 34km north of Fréjus via A8, Les Adrets exit, then D562 towards Fayence and D19.*

Les Bastidières

2371, avenue de la Résistance
Cap Brun - 83100 Toulon (Var)
Tel. 94.36.14.73 - Fax 94.42.49.75 - M. and Mme Lagriffoul

Open all year. **Rooms** 5 with telephone, bath, WC, TV and minibar. **Price** double 550-650F. **Meals** breakfast 60F, served 0800-1100. No restaurant. **Credit cards** not accepted. **Pets** dogs allowed (+50F). **Facilities** swimming pool, parking. **Nearby** Mont Faron (cable car), Ollioules, Ollioules gorges and Evenos, villages of Le Castellet and La Cadière-d'Azur, Cap Sicié.

This fine Provençal house occupies a most enviable position in the exclusive Cap Brun neighbourhood on the heights of Toulon. Set amidst greenery and yet close to the sea, its gardens combine Provençal plants with more exotic species. A great 17th-century gateway opens on to an old white stone drive surrounded by a large lawn, palm trees and aged pines, and terracotta urns overflowing with geraniums. The bedrooms are spacious, comfortable and tastefully decorated in Provençal style, with beamed ceilings and period furniture. Those at the back of the house are the quietest. Each one has a terrace surrounded by plants and flowers. The bathrooms are big and fully equipped. The swimming pool is big too, and has Mediterranean flowers and exotic plants all around.

How to get there *(Map 34): 81km south east of Aix-en-Provence via A8, Toulon exit. Cap Brun is the residential area east of Toulon, towards Le Pradet.*

Auberge Saint-Pierre★★★

Quartier Saint-Pierre
83690 Tourtour (Var)
Tel. 94.70.57.17 - Mme Marcellin

Open 1 April – 15 Oct. **Rooms** 18 with telephone, bath or shower and WC. **Price** double 430-520F. **Meals** breakfast 50F, served 0800-1100; half board 500F, full board 650F (per pers., 3 days min.) **Credit cards** not accepted. **Pets** dogs allowed (+30F). **Facilities** swimming pool, tennis, sauna (80F), riding, bikes, archery, table tennis, parking. **Nearby** caves of Villecroze, chapel of St-André at Comps-sur-Artuby, Bargème, Simon Segal museum at Aups. **Restaurant** service 1200-1300, 2000-2030 (closed Wednesday); menus 170-220F; specialities: brouillade aux truffes, pigeonneau aux nouilles, jambonnette d'agneau à la broche, lapereau farci sauce sariette.

The Auberge is a 16th-century 'bastide'. Its secluded position in the middle of the countryside and the greenery around make it just the place to relax. In the sitting room country furniture is arranged around the fireplace and there is a collection of prehistoric objects, which were found on the property, on display. The dining room; decorated in Provençal style, was once the courtyard of the house. The bedrooms are comfortable. The Marcellin family's warm welcome, and the good Provençal cooking, make a stay here a delightful prospect.

How to get there *(Map 34): 19km west of Draguignan via A8, Le Muy exit; 3km from Tourtour.*

Château de Trigance★★★
83840 Trigance (Var)
Tel. 94.76.91.18 – Fax 94.47.58.99
M. Thomas

Open 20 March – 7 Nov. **Rooms** 10 with telephone, bath, WC and TV. **Price** double 480-680F, suite 800F. **Meals** breakfast 58F, served 0730-1000; half board 520-690F (per pers.) **Credit cards** Amex, Eurocard, Diners, Visa. **Pets** dogs allowed. **Facilities** parking. **Nearby** Verdon canyon, ridgeway from La-Palud-sur-Verdon, Moustiers-Sainte-Marie, 9-hole château de Toulane golf course at La Martie. **Restaurant** service 1200-1400, 1930-2100 (closed Wednesday lunchtime in low season); menus 190-320F, also à la carte; specialities: tian de saumon au sabayon de muscat, tournedos de pintade aux pignons, pissaladière de lotte au beurre de citron.

Originally a fortress built in the 9th century by the monks of the abbey of Saint-Victor, the château de Trigance became a castle, belonging to the Counts of Provence, two hundred years later. It is a massive stone building occupying an impregnable position at the top of a hill. The lounge, dining-room and bar area, with vaulted ceilings, occupy one of the wings. The bedrooms surround the huge and magnificent terrace, thus ensuring more peace and privacy. They are extremely comfortable: the decoration is sober (in keeping with the character of the building) and shows taste and flair, enhanced by personal touches. The restaurant serves excellent local specialities. Drinks can be served on the terrace facing breathtaking scenery. In summer plays are performed on the esplanade by the ramparts. The owners extend a warm welcome.

How to get there *(Map 34): 44km north of Draguignan via D995 towards Verdon gorges, at Comps-sur-Artuby D995, then D90.*

Hôtel de la Mirande★★★★

Place de la Mirande
84000 Avignon (Vaucluse)
Tel. 90.85.93.93 - Fax 90.86.26.85 - M. Stein

Open all year. **Rooms** 19 with telephone, bath, shower, WC, TV and minibar. **Price** double 1300-1900F, suite 2600F. **Meals** breakfast 95F, served until 1130. **Credit cards** accepted. **Pets** dogs allowed (+80F). **Facilities** parking (+75F). **Nearby** palace of the Popes, Notre-Dame des Doms, Campana collection at the Petit-Palais, Calvet museum, Villeneuve-Lès-Avignon, 18-hole Châteaublanc golf course. **Restaurant** service 1900-2145; menus 200-420F, also à la carte; specialities: filet rouget barbet dans son croustillant Provençal, terrine de roquefort au rivesaltes et noix.

This marvellous hotel in Avignon, which was recently opened, is the work of architect Gilles Grégoire and interior decorator François-Joseph Grap. The inner courtyard has been turned into a delightful conservatory, where the wicker armchairs in delicate caramel colours set the tone. Off this there is a stunning sequence of rooms richly decorated with fine antiques, Provençal style fabrics, flowery cambrics, and chintzes. The bedrooms are spacious, elegant and comfortable, and all have a sitting room or ante-room. The ones on the first floor are bigger than those on the mezzanine and second floor. This exquisite and luxurious establishment should pave the way for a new generation of hotels.

How to get there *(Map 33): in the town centre, at the foot of the Palais des Papes.*

L'Anastasy

Ile de la Barthelasse
84000 Avignon (Vaucluse)
Tel. 90.85.55.94 - Fax 90.82.94.49 - Mme Manguin

Open all year. **Rooms** 4 with bath or shower. **Price** single and double 300-350F. **Meals** breakfast incl. **Credit** cards not accepted. **Pets** dogs allowed. **Facilities** swimming pool, parking. **Nearby** palace of the Popes, Notre-Dame des Doms, campana collection at the Petit-palais, Calvet museum, Villeneuve-lès-Avignon, 18-hole Châteaublanc golf course. **Restaurant** service 1300 and 2030; menu 100F; Provençal and Italian cooking.

L'Anastasy used to be a farm, typical of the area surrounding Avignon, where animals and harvests were the sole concern. Now the barns and stables have been converted to make a large family house where friends and guests can be welcomed. On the ground floor there is now a spacious lounge and kitchen–dining-room which is the very heart of the house, for the warm and friendly hostess, Olga Manguin, enjoys nothing more than cooking for her guests, and the Provençal and Italian specialities she excels at are delicious. The bedrooms are pretty, but do not all have en suite bathrooms. If you can do without, you will enjoy all the attractions of the house, and of the terrace leading into the garden planted with lavender and rosemary, hollyhocks and acanthus. You can be sure to find a convivial atmosphere, and there will be no invasion of your privacy, but it would be a pity not to join in the rhythm of life here. That way, you could meet Olga's friends, including journalists, directors, stage designers and actors who wouldn't dream of staying anywhere else during the Avignon Festival.

How to get there *(Map 33): 6km north of Avignon; from Avignon head for Villeneuve-lès-Avignon over the Daladier bridge.*

Les Géraniums*

Place de la Croix
Le Barroux - 84330 Caromb (Vaucluse)
Tel. 90.62.41.08 - Fax 90.62.56.48 - M. and Mme Roux

Open all year (closed Wednesday in low season). **Rooms** 22 with telephone, bath or shower and WC. **Price** single and double 200-240F. **Meals** breakfast 30F, served 0800-1000; half board 220-240F, full board 310-330F (per pers., 3 days min.) **Credit cards** Amex, Diners, Visa. **Pets** dogs allowed (+30F). **Facilities** parking. **Nearby** château de Barroux, pharmacy museum at the Hôtel-Dieu in Carpentras, Mazan Gallo-Roman cemetery, dentelles de Montmirail, 9-hole Le Grand Avignon golf course. **Restaurant** service 1215-1330, 1915-2100; menus 80-250F, also à la carte; specialities: omelette aux truffes, lapin à la sarriette, chevreau au romarin, terrine maison aux pruneaux.

Le Barroux is a village set high on a hill between the Ventoux and the jagged peaks of Montmirail, commanding stunning views of the whole Avignon area. The place has a charm of its own, and this small hotel provides pleasantly comfortable accommodation. It also houses that typical French institution, the "café de la place", thus offering first-hand insight into local village life. The bedrooms are simple but pleasant and have recently been improved. The nicest ones are those with a small terrace. The menu features good local dishes based on fresh products, and is likely to include game in the season. Meals can be served on the terrace or in the lofty dining room.

How to get there *(Map 33): 9km from Carpentras via D938; between Carpentras and Malaucène.*

Château de Rocher–La Belle Ecluse

42, rue Emile Lachaux
84500 Bollène (Vaucluse)
Tel. 90.40.09.09 - Fax 90.40.09.30 - M. Carloni

Open all year. **Rooms** 18 with telephone, bath or shower, WC and TV. **Price** single and double 220-360F. **Meals** breakfast 45F, served 0730-1030; half board 240-360F, full board 320-440F (per pers., 3 days min.) **Credit cards** accepted. **Pets** dogs allowed (+30F). **Facilities** parking. **Nearby** arc de triomphe and ancient theatre at Orange, Henri Fabre museum at Sérignan, 9-hole Grand Avignon golf course. **Restaurant** service 1200 and 1900; menus 110-300F; also à la carte; specialities: huîtres au champagne, ris d'agneau à la provençale.

A fine country house built in 1828, the Château has been converted into a hotel. It is set in the middle of a lovely 4-hectare park containing both domestic and wild animals and a large garden. The bedrooms are big, comfortable and light and have been recently refurbished by the new owners. They now all have fully-equipped bathrooms. The most attractive is room 6, with a terrace overlooking the garden, and the most amusing is room 8, in the former chapel, which has stained glass windows. The gourmet cuisine can be served outside on the terrace, in summer, or in the "Richelieu" dining-room, which has a painted wooden ceiling, a beautiful carved stone chimney and above it a portrait of the Cardinal.

How to get there *(Map 33): 25km from Orange via A9, Bollène exit, towards town centre then towards Gap, Nyons road.*

Château de Saint-Ariès

Route de Saint Ariès
84500 Bollène (Vaucluse)
Tel. 90.40.09.17 – Fax 90.30.45.62 – M. de Loye

Open 2 March – 2 Jan. **Rooms** 5 with bath, shower and WC. **Price** double 580-710F, suite 910-1010F. **Meals** half board rates on request. **Credit cards** Visa, Eurocard. **Pets** dogs allowed on request. **Facilities** swimm. **Nearby** arc de triomphe and ancient theatre at Orange, Henri Fabre museum at Sérignan, 9-hole Grand Avignon golf course. **Restaurant** table d'hôtes menu 230F; specialities: caillettes à la provençale, estouffade de bœuf, blancs de vollaille sauce au curry, chèvres chauds en salade.

The Château de Saint-Ariès looks like a Tuscan villa lost in the Provençal countryside. It was because she had fallen in love with those Italian gems that one of Michel de Loÿe's ancestors decided, some time around 1820, to have the present house built in place of the then existing château. Tucked away in 20 hectares of parkland, it is hidden from view, and as soon as you walk through the door, you will be surprised and delighted with the beauty around you. The lounge, dining-room, library, bedrooms and 1930s bathrooms have all been recently refurbished and decorated with lavish amounts of care and attention. Michel de Loÿe wants his guest to feel as if they were being welcomed into a friend's home, so the house is scattered with family portraits and furniture, Souleïado fabrics, books and curios. The conviviality of his table d'hôte dinners also contributes in no small way to that impression. Breakfast is excellent, and in summer is served on the terrace facing the fine landscaped grounds. This is a very lovely place.

How to get there *(Map 33): 25km from Orange via A9, Bollène exit, Saint Ariès road.*

Hostellerie du Prieuré★★★
84480 Bonnieux (Vaucluse)
Tel. 90.75.80.78
Mme Keller

Open Feb – end Oct. **Rooms** 10 with telephone, bath, WC and TV. **Price** single 350F, double 470-520F. **Meals** breakfast 40F, served 0800-1100. **Credit cards** Visa, Eurocard, MasterCard. **Pets** dogs allowed (+suppl.) **Facilities** parking. **Nearby** northern Luberon (Saignon, Saint-Symphorien priory, Lacoste, Ménerbes, Oppède-le-Vieux, Maubec, Robion), 18-hole Saumane golf course. **Restaurant** service 1200-1330, 1800-2100 (closed Tuesday and Wednesday lunchtime, Tuesday, Wednesday, Thursday lunchtime in July, August and September); menu 145-200F; specialities: cassolette de ris d'agneau à l'orange, rognon de veau au genièvre, crépinette de langoustine.

L'Hostellerie du Prieuré is in the village, but the main reception rooms and bedrooms face the garden and the valley. The interior decoration is very comfortable and elegant, creating an atmosphere that is both intimate and opulent. The bedrooms are delightful; all different, but No 9 has a terrace with a view of the valley. In summer there is a bar and restaurant service in the garden. There is no carte, but you can find a good choice of specialities on the two menus. The welcome and service are a little aloof.

How to get there *(Map 33): 27km east of Cavaillon via D2 and N100 towards Apt, then D36.*

Hostellerie de Crillon-le-Brave★★★★
Place de l'église
84410 Crillon-le-Brave (Vaucluse)
Tel. 90.65.61.61 - Fax 90.65.62.86 - M. Chittick

Open 1 April – 2 Jan. **Rooms** 22 with telephone, bath or shower, WC (TV on request). **Price** single and double 750-1150F, suite 1250-1450F. **Meals** breakfast 75F, served 0730-1100; half board +250F, full board +420F (per pers., 3 days min.) **Credit cards** accepted except Diners. **Pets** dogs allowed (+60F). **Facilities** swimming pool, garage. **Nearby** Bédoin, dentelles de Montmirail, chapel of Le Grozeau, château du Barroux, pharmacy museum at Hôtel-Dieu in Carpentras, 9-hole Grand Avignon golf course. **Restaurant** service 1200-1400, 1930-2130; menus 210-340F, also à la carte.

A few olive groves separate Mont Ventoux from the small village of Crillon-le-Brave, which sits at the top of a hill. Just next to the church stands this fine hotel: formerly a large family house, its bedrooms are still named after the people who once lived there. The building still has its worn flagstone floors and is tastefully decorated with terracotta objects and Provençal antiques found at nearby Isle-sur-la-Sorgue. The bedrooms are extremely comfortable and cosy, and their yellow-ochre walls evoke the Midi sun. The two lounges contain shelf-loads of old books, comfy sofas and windows looking over the rooftops of the village. A terraced garden, with pretty wrought iron furniture in its many shady corners, leads down from a waterlily pond to the swimming-pool.

How to get there (Map 33): 15km north of Carpentras via D974 and D138.

513

Hostellerie La Manescale

Route de Faucon
Les Essareaux - 84340 Entrechaux (Vaucluse)
Tel. 90.46.03.80 - Fax 90.46.03.89 - Mme Warland

Open Easter – Oct. **Rooms** 6 with telephone, bath or shower, WC, TV and minibar. **Price** double 315-525F, suite 735F. **Meals** breakfast 55F, served 0830-1000; half board 380-590F (per pers., 2 days min). **Credit cards** Amex, Diners, Eurocard, Visa. **Pets** dogs allowed (+60F). **Facilities** swimming pool, parking. **Nearby** cathedral of Notre-Dame-de-Nazareth at Vaison-la-Romaine, dentelles de Montmirail, Séguret, 9-hole Grand Avignon golf course. **Restaurant** for guests only; service at 1945 (closed Monday evening); menu 170F; specialities: cooking with fresh local produce.

Formerly a farmhouse and now carefully rebuilt and restored, this pleasant hostellerie stands among vineyards and olive trees between Drôme and Vaucluse, facing Mont Ventoux. The bedrooms are luxuriously equipped and tastefully decorated, providing every thoughtful detail. Some of them (the 'Provence' room, for instance) are small suites. The pleasure of a good breakfast on the terrace is enhanced by the magical scenery: a peaceful valley, crowned by the Ventoux, displaying a subtle and ever-changing palette of colours and light. Hotel facilities also include a superb swimming pool. This is a place one would like to keep to oneself, but enthusiastic readers' letters have made sharing the secret a pleasure.

How to get there *(Map 33): 8km east of Vaison-la-Romaine via D205. From A7, take Bollène exit.*

Les Florets★★

Route des Dentelles
84190 Gigondas (Vaucluse)
Tel. 90.65.85.01 - Fax 90.65.83.80 – Mme Bernard

Open March – Dec (closed Wednesday). **Rooms** 13 with telephone, bath or shower and WC. **Price** double 340-375F. **Meals** breakfast 40F, served 0800-1000; half board 720F, full board 980F (2 pers., 3 days min.) **Credit cards** accepted. **Pets** dogs allowed (+40F). **Facilities** parking. **Nearby** chapel of Notre-Dame-d'Aubune, Séguret, dentelles de Montmirail, cathedral and Roman bridge at Vaison-la-Romaine, 9-hole Grand Avignon golf course. **Restaurant** service 1200-1400, 1930-2100; menus 90-200F, also à la carte; specialities: pieds et paquets maison, aïolade du comtat, lapin au miel et citron.

Les Florets occupies an enviable position in the middle of the countryside, below the peaks of Montmirail and in the heart of the Gigondas vineyards. This is a simple country hotel, traditional in style, with a pleasant family atmosphere. The jagged peaks ('dentelles') above can be viewed from the terrace, where a vine provides welcome shade. As the hotel is 400 metres up it tends to be a bit cooler than down below in the plain. The bedrooms are simple and unpretentious, but comfortable enough (bathrooms have hip baths) and they look out on to the trees. We recommend rooms 14, 16 and 19 and the new and very charming bedrooms in the annexe. In the restaurant, regional specialities are set off by Gigondas wines. The owner will be glad to show you around his cellar and have you sample his own production.

How to get there *(Map 33): 25km east of Orange via D975 towards Vaison-la-Romaine, then D8 and D80; it's on the Route des Dentelles de Montmirail.*

Hôtel La Gacholle★★★
Route de Murs
84220 Gordes (Vaucluse)
Tel. 90.72.01.36 – Fax 90.72.01.81 – M. Roux

Open 1 March – 15 Nov. **Rooms** 12 with telephone, bath, WC, TV and minibar. **Price** double 480-520F. **Meals** breakfast 49F, served 0730-1000; half board 425F, full board 540F (per pers.) **Credit cards** Eurocard, MasterCard, Visa. **Pets** dogs allowed (+25F). **Facilities** heated swimming pool, tennis, parking. **Nearby** les Bories, Sénanque abbey, Roussillon, l'Isle-sur-la-Sorgue, Fontaine de Vaucluse, 9-hole Saumane golf course. **Restaurant** service 1215-1415, 1930-2115; menus 150-260F, also à la carte; specialities: compote de lapereau à la farigoule et sariette, noisettes d'agneau à la gousse d'ail, gratin de fruits rouges sauce abricot.

Gordes, like Apt, Bonnieux and Roussillon, is ideally situated for exploring the Luberon. This stone–walled hotel lies about 1km from the village, which rises in terraces on one of the promontories of the Vaucluse. Inside, the rustic Provençal character of the building has been emphasised. The bedrooms are nicely decorated, well equipped, and have breathtaking views. (Rooms 1, 2 and 3 also have small private terraces and access to the garden). The terrace and the swimming pool command stunning panoramic views of the valley of the river Coulon, the Luberon mountains and the hills towards Aix. This is an excellent place for a weekend.

How to get there *(Map 33): 25km north east of Cavaillon via D2 then D15; in the village.*

Ferme de la Huppe

Route D 156
Les Pourquiers - 84220 Gordes (Vaucluse)
Tel. 90.72.12.25 - Fax 90.72.01.83 - Mme Konings

Open 1 April – 7 Nov. **Rooms** 6 with telephone, bath, shower, WC, TV and minibar.
Price single 400F, double 500F. **Meals** breakfast 25F, served 0800-1000. **Credit
cards** Eurocard, MasterCard, Visa. **Pets** dogs not allowed. **Facilities** swimming pool,
parking. **Nearby** les Bories, Sénanque abbey, Roussillon, l'Isle-sur-la-Sorgue,
Fontaine de Vaucluse, 9-hole Saumane golf course. **Restaurant** service 1200-1330,
1930-2100; menus 140-190F, also à la carte; seasonal cooking.

The small road winding across the Luberon plain gradually turns
into a track. This beautifully restored old farmhouse stands in
an extremely quiet and secluded setting, and the hoopoe – 'huppe'
– which gives its name to the place still nests in an old tree-trunk
nearby. Everything revolves around the fig tree, the olive trees and
the well in the middle of a small inner courtyard. It gives access to
the six delightful bedrooms named after the ancient parts of the
building, for example 'la cuisine' (the kitchen), 'l'écurie' (the stable)
or 'la cuve' (the vat). Their terracotta floors, thick walls and typically
small windows ensure both privacy and coolness, and there are also
ancient features and elegant fabrics. All have every comfort. A
covered patio adjoining the dining room looks onto a fine
swimming pool screened by flowers and lavender. Young chef
Gérald Konings' inspired efforts in the kitchen are gaining him a
fast-growing reputation in a region which sets very high culinary
standards. Excellent service and reasonable prices.

How to get there *(Map 33): 25km north east of Cavaillon via D2 then
D15; it's in the village.*

Hôtel Les Romarins★★★

Route de Sénanque
84220 Gordes (Vaucluse)
Tel. 90.72.12.13 - Fax 90.72.13.13 - Mme Charles

Open 15 Feb – 15 Jan. **Rooms** 10 with telephone, bath or shower, WC, TV (8 with minibar). **Price** single 380F, double 380-650F. **Meals** breakfast 45F, served 0800-1100. No restaurant. **Credit cards** Eurocard, Amex, Visa. **Pets** dogs allowed (+35F). **Facilities** swimming pool, parking. **Nearby** les Bories, Sénanque abbey, Roussillon, l'Isle-sur-la-Sorgue, Fontaine de Vaucluse, 9-hole Saumane golf course.

This 200-year-old house has just been fully refurbished and turned into a hotel; it is the only establishment in Gordes commanding a view of the old houses of the village. That is a fine asset indeed if, as we do, you delight in that breathtaking assemblage of ancient walls, terraced gardens and cypresses. Most of the bedrooms have this view, but make sure when booking. They are neat and comfortable simply and elegantly decorated in either Directoire or contemporary style. Breakfast – with the view of Gordes – is delicious and can be served in a small, bright dining-room, or outside in the shade of an ancient mulberry tree. There aren't many bedrooms, so the atmosphere is friendly and informal (all the more so with a talking pet parrot on the staff!). The bird, however, is not in sole charge, and M. and Mme Charles extend an urbane and congenial welcome.

How to get there *(Map 33): 25km north east of Cavaillon via D2 then D15; it's in the village.*

Domaine Le Moulin Blanc★★★★

Chemin du Moulin
Les Beaumettes - 84220 Gordes (Vaucluse)
Tel. 90.72.34.50 - Fax 90.72.25.41 - Mme Diez

Open all year. **Rooms** 18 with telephone, bath, WC, TV and minibar. **Price** single and double 450-960F, suite 880-1200F. **Meals** breakfast 65F, served 0700-1100; half board 460-700F, full board 660-900F (per pers., 2 days min.) **Credit cards** accepted. **Pets** dogs allowed. **Facilities** swimming pool, tennis, parking. **Nearby** les Bories, Sénanque abbey, Roussillon, Isle-sur-la-Sorgue, Fontaine de Vaucluse, 9-hole Saumane golf course. **Restaurant** service 1200-1400, 1900-2200; menus 195-385, also à la carte; specialities: foie gras frais de canard, salade de langoustines aux artichauts, petite brandade de rouget et ses filets grillés, noisette d'agneau et purée d'olives, special lobster menu.

Formerly a staging post, then a flour mill, the Moulin Blanc has been restored to the highest standards. The bedrooms are magnificent. The ones opening into the garden are quieter than those overlooking the road. A superb vaulted hall houses a dining room and lounge. The grounds, planted with pine-trees and cypresses, are as attractive as the house. The restaurant serves good food using fresh local produce. Ideally located between Gordes, Roussillon and Bonnieux, the Moulin Blanc stands at the very heart of historic Provence.

How to get there *(Map 33): 20km north east of Cavaillon via D2 and N100 towards Apt.*

Le Mas des Grès★★

Route d'Apt
84800 Lagnes (Vaucluse)
Tel. 90.20.32.85 - Fax 90.20.21.45 - M. and Mme Hermitte

Open 1 March – 31 Nov. **Rooms** 12 with telephone, bath, WC (6 with TV). **Price** double 300-550F, suite 950F. **Meals** breakfast 50F, served 0800-1100. **Credit cards** Eurocard, MasterCard, Visa. **Pets** dogs not allowed. **Facilities** swimming pool, parking. **Nearby** Isle-sur-la-Sorgue, Fontaine de Vaucluse, Gordes, les Bories, Sénanque abbey, 9-hole Saumane golf course. **Restaurant** for guests only; service 2000-2200; menu 115F; Provençal cooking.

A delightful place, full of joie de vivre and even a touch of eccentricity. The owner, an interior decorator from Savoy, jokes about the "rustico–Byzantine" style, but the decoration has in fact been very tastefully handled. The lounge and the bedrooms are elegantly simple; as charming as the guest room you would expect to find in a friend's house. Room 8 can accommodate a whole family, and room 6 is perfect for children. The restaurant, for guests only, serves decent food which can be enjoyed beneath a vine. M. Hermitte's warm and friendly approach makes dinner a special pleasure. Meals are available on a half-board basis. Set among orchards, the Mas des Grès is a truly precious address, a bit like your own home in the Luberon.

How to get there (Map 33): 5km south east of Isle-sur-la-Sorgue via N100 and D99.

Mas des Capelans

84580 Oppède (Vaucluse)
Tel. 90.76.99.04 – Fax 90.76.90.29
M. and Mme Poiri

Open 15 Feb – 15 Nov (closed Sunday). **Rooms** 8 with telephone, bath, WC (4 with TV). **Price** double 400-800F, suite 600-900F. **Meals** breakfast 50F, served 0830-1030; half board 350-500F (per pers., 3 days min.) **Credit cards** accepted. **Pets** dogs allowed (+70F). **Facilities** heated swimming pool, billiards, parking. **Nearby** the north of Luberon (Ménerbes, Lacoste, Bonnieux, St-Symphorien priory, Buoux, Saignon, Apt), 9-hole Saumane golf course. **Restaurant** service at 2000; table d'hôte menu 160F; specialities: lapereau au romarin, navarin aux petits légumes, pintade aux cerises, fameux desserts de Jacqueline.

The Mas des Capelans once belonged to the monks of the abbey of Sénanque, who used the building to breed silkworms. The eight guest bedrooms are large and very comfortable, and have been carefully decorated. Each one is named after the view it commands: Roussillon, Gordes, or simply after the vineyard it overlooks, like some of the ground-floor rooms (which have private entrances). The pine furniture and continental quilts on the beds are quite unusual in this area, and the decor tends towards the Swiss chalet style. The Mas has pleasant surroundings, and dinner in the courtyard beneath the mulberry-trees and acacias is one of the highlights of a stay.

How to get there (Map 33): 10km east of Cavaillon via D2, towards Apt, then D29 towards Maubec and D178. From A7, take Cavaillon exit.

Hôtel Arène★★★
Place de Langes
84100 Orange (Vaucluse)
Tel. 90.34.10.95 - Fax 90.34.91.62 - M. and Mme Coutel

Open 15 Dec – 31 Oct. **Rooms** 30 with telephone, bath or shower, WC, minibar (22 with TV). **Price** single and double 310-410F. **Meals** breakfast 40F, served 0700-1200. No restaurant. **Credit cards** accepted. **Pets** dogs allowed. **Facilities** parking. **Nearby** ancient theatre and arc de triomphe at Orange, Mornas, Henri Fabre museum at Sérignan, 9-hole Grand Avignon golf course.

Ideally situated close to the Roman theatre, in a small pedestrianized square shaded by hundred-year old plane trees, the 'Arène' is the most sought-after hotel in town. M. and Mme Coutel devote lavish amounts of care to their guests' well-being, and are constantly refurbishing and embellishing the house. The bedrooms, all different, are comfortable and cheerful, though some are a little dark. There is no restaurant, but there is a pleasant lounge with a large fireplace and period furniture. This is a very popular place and it is necessary to book well ahead, especially during the festival.

How to get there *(Map 33): in the old town centre.*

Mas des Aigras

Chemin des Aigras
84100 Orange (Vaucluse)
Tel. 90.34.81.01 – Fax 90.34.05.66 – M. and Mme Pernelle

Open all year. **Rooms** 11 with telephone, bath or shower, WC and TV. **Price** single 320F, double 320-390F. **Meals** breakfast 40F, no restaurant. **Credit cards** accepted. **Pets** dogs allowed. **Facilities** swimming pool, parking. **Nearby** ancient theatre and arc de triomphe at Orange, Mornas, Henri Fabre museum at Sérignan, 9-hole Grand Avignon golf course.

With a limited number of rooms and a beautiful garden with swimming pool, this hotel has all the appeal of a private house. Beyond some vineyards lies the road to Orange, which is but minutes away. The bedrooms are pleasant and extremely comfortable. Although it lacks diversity, the olive-wood furniture creates a warm atmosphere. Breakfast is served in an elegant dining-room leading out into the garden. Hotel facilities also include a tennis court, so a stay in the Mas des Aigras provides the opportunity to relax or to exercise. Dinner is not served at the Mas, but your hosts will be glad to provide information about the restaurants in the area.

How to get there *(Map 33): in the north of the town.*

Hôtel L'Hermitage★★

Route de Carpentras
84210 Pernes-les-Fontaines (Vaucluse)
Tel. 90.66.51.41 - Fax 90.61.36.41 - Mme Oury

Open all year. **Rooms** 20 with telephone, bath, WC and TV. **Price** single 260-350F, double 270-340F. **Meals** breakfast 35F, served 0730-1100; half board 265-290F (per pers., 3 days min.) **Credit cards** Diners, Eurocard, Visa. **Pets** dogs allowed (+30F). **Facilities** swimming pool, parking. **Nearby** Venasque church, Gallo-Roman cemetery at Mazan, Carpentras, 9-hole Grand Avignon golf course. **Restaurant** (1km away) service 1200-1400, 1900-2200; menus 100-210F, also à la carte; specialities: petite marmite du pécheur, filets de rascasse à l'arlésienne, noisettes d'agneau Provençales.

Conveniently close to the many local places of interest, L'Hermitage is a fine country house set in 2 hectares of grounds. The Provençal-style furniture and many personal objects to be found around the house add to its charm. The bedrooms are very well kept; those on the top floor command beautiful views of the Ventoux, rooms 6, 7 and 14 have a large terrace, and rooms 8 and 10 a small balcony. The wisteria shading the terrace, the tall plane-trees and the terracotta urns full of flowers are but a few of the appealing features of the gardens. You can take meals on a half-board basis in a restaurant 1km away which belongs to the same family.

How to get there (Map 33): 4km south of Carpentras via D938.

Auberge de Cassagne****

450, allée de Cassagne - 84130 Le Pontet (Vaucluse)
Tel. 90.31.04.18 - Fax 90.32.25.09
MM. Gallon and Boucher

Open all year. **Rooms** 21 and 3 apartments with telephone, bath or shower, WC, TV and minibar. **Price** single 420-490F, double 490-1280F, suite 1280-1780F. **Meals** breakfast 75F, served 0730-1030; half board 740-1135F, full board 920-1315F (per pers.) **Credit cards** accepted. **Pets** dogs allowed (+40F). **Facilities** tennis (+50F), parking (+20F). **Nearby** palace of the Popes, Campana collection at the Petit Palais and Calvet museum at Avignon, Villeneuve-lès-Avignon, 9-hole Grand Avignon golf course, 18-hole Châteaublanc golf course at Avignon. **Restaurant** service 1200-1330, 1930-2130; menus 210-440F, also à la carte; specialities: terrine Provençale au coeur de foie gras, filets de rouget au citron vert, émincé d'agneau et côtelettes de lapereau panées aux petits légumes farcis.

The Auberge de Cassagne is run by Jean-Michel and Françoise Gallon in this old Provençal house. In summer you can enjoy, in the magnificent flower-filled garden, the renowned cooking of the young chef Philippe Boucher, who trained under Georges Blanc and Bocuse. The very fine cellar has been entrusted to André Trestour. The bedrooms – pleasantly decorated and furnished in Provençal style – are comfortable, though rather small. Some are located in the main building and others around the very lovely swimming pool.

How to get there *(Map 33): 5km east of Avignon via A7, Avignon-Nord exit, then 5 mins. and left on small road before the lights.*

Mas de Garrigon★★★

Route de St-Saturnin
84220 Roussillon (Vaucluse)
Tel. 90.05.63.22 - Fax 90.05.70.01 - Mme Rech-Druart

Open all year. **Rooms** 9 with telephone, bath, shower, WC, TV and minibar. **Price** single 680F, double 700F, suite 890F. **Meals** breakfast 65F, served 0730-1030; half board 700-900F, full board 850-1050F (per pers.) **Credit cards** Amex, Diners, Visa. **Pets** dogs allowed (+65F). **Facilities** swimming-pool, riding, parking. **Nearby** Gordes, les Bories, Sénanque abbey, Isle-sur-la-Sorgue, Luberon, 9-hole Saumane golf course. **Restaurant** service 1200-1500, 2000-2130 (closed Sunday evening and Monday); menus 165-320F, also à la carte; specialities: pavé de loup aux truffes et son jus, pigeonneau au miel et à l'épautre du Ventoux, daube à l'ancienne.

This old farmhouse has character and is typically Provençal in style. It lies at the foot of the Luberon and is a pleasant place to stay at any time of year. The swimming-pool, with deck-chairs around, encourages guests to relax in the sun, and lunch can be served there. The lounge has a magnificent fireplace and is perfect for listening to classical music or reading a book chosen from the well-stocked bookshelves. The bedrooms are tastefully furnished and all have their own terrace facing south and looking out on the Luberon. The menu depends on what's available that day in the market, and the cooking is refined and good. The Mas is ideally situated for touring Provence, as all the principal places of interest are within a 100km radius.

How to get there *(Map 33): 48km east of Avignon via N100 towards Apt, then D2 towards Gordes and D102.*

Auberge du Presbytère

Place de la Fontaine
Saignon - 84400 Apt (Vaucluse)
Tel. 90.74.11.50 - Mme Bernardi

Open all year (closed Wednesday). **Rooms** 10 with bath or shower (5 with WC). **Price** double 170-300F. **Meals** breakfast 35F, served 0830-1000. **Credit cards** Amex, Visa. **Pets** dogs allowed (+30F). **Nearby** Saignon church, Luberon, Buoux, St-Symphorien priory, Bonnieux, Lacoste, Ménerbes, Oppède, Maubec, Robion, 9-hole Saumane golf course. **Restaurant** service 1230-1400, 2000-2230; menu 135F; Provençal cooking.

W hen M. and Mme Bernardi left Saint-Tropez their intention was to open a small guest house. Chance, however, decided otherwise, but that initial idea has not been altogether discarded, for guests are welcomed like friends. The Auberge du Presbytère is made up of three village houses joined together, making for an entertaining variety of floor levels. The decoration is that of a country house, with period furniture and Pierre Frey and Souleïado Provençal-style fabrics. The bedrooms (not all of which yet have en suite bathrooms) are charming and have lovely curtains made by Mme Bernardi herself. The restaurant offers a daily menu featuring delicious traditional and local dishes. A charming and friendly place to stay in the heart of the Luberon.

How to get there (Map 33): 6km south east of Apt; in the village.

Hostellerie Le Beffroi★★★
Rue de l'Evêché
84110 Vaison-la-Romaine (Vaucluse)
Tel. 90.36.04.71 - Fax 90.36.24.78 - M. Christiansen

Open mid March – end Nov. **Rooms** 22 with telephone, bath or shower, minibar (16 with TV, 18 with WC). **Price** single 170F, double 280-595F, suite 595-685F. **Meals** breakfast 44F, served 0730-0945; half board 359-516F, full board 514-671F (per pers., 3 days min.) **Credit cards** accepted. **Pets** dogs allowed (+30F). **Facilities** minigolf, games, table tennis, parking. **Nearby** arc de triomphe and ancient theatre at Orange, Mornas, Henri Fabre museum at Sérignan. **Restaurant** service 1200-1345, 1915-2130 (closed Monday, Tuesday and Friday lunchtime); menu 185F, also à la carte ; specialities: salade de queues de langoustines aux truffes d'été, pavé de loup en croûte d'épices de Provence, pigeon du comtat à l'orange et au miel, crème brûlée aux herbes folles.

This hotel is located high up in the medieval part of Vaison, and consists of several private houses joined together. The buildings' character has been preserved and there are tiled floors, polished panelling, spiral staircases and fine antiques, paintings and curios. The bedrooms are all different and antique lovers will be especially taken by the quality of the period furniture. The lounges are also pleasantly furnished and have open fireplaces. A superb terrace garden gives lovely views over the rooftops of the town.

How to get there (Map 33): 30km north east of Orange via D975; at the top of the town.

Auberge de la Fontaine

Place de la Fontaine
84210 Venasque (Vaucluse)
Tel. 90.66.02.96 – Fax 90.66.13.14 – M. and Mme Soehlke

Open all year. **Rooms** 5 suites with air-conditioning, telephone, bath, WC, TV and minibar. **Price** suite 700F. **Meals** breakfast 50F. **Credit cards** Visa, MasterCard, Eurocard. **Pets** dogs allowed. **Facilities** parking. **Nearby** Venasque church, Gallo-Roman cemetery at Mazan, Pernes-les-Fontaines, Carpentras, 9-hole Grand Avignon golf course. **Restaurant** service every evening 2000-2200 and Sunday 1200-1400; (closed Wednesday and from mid-Nov to mid-Dec); menu 200F, also à la carte; specialities: assiette du pêcheur, choucroute au foie gras, gibier frais en saison, pigeonneau aux airelles.

The Auberge de la Fontaine is a fine old village house which Ingrid and Christian Soehlke have completely restructured inside, creating an amusing maze of mezzanines, terraces and flights of steps. They want their hotel to seem more like a friend's house, where guests can feel free and relaxed – and it would be difficult not to feel at ease: each suite (there are five) includes a bedroom and a sitting room with a fireplace, tastefully decorated and furnished in very Provençal style and equipped with direct-dial phone, television, cassette and CD player. Each one has a secluded terrace and a kitchenette, but the charming dining-room and the Soehlkes' tasty food are well worth a try.

How to get there (Map 33): 11km south of Carpentras via D9.

Auberge Les Bichonnières★★

Route de Savigneux
01330 Ambérieux-en-Dombes (Ain)
Tel. 74.00.82.07 – Fax 74.00.89.61 – M. Sauvage

Open all year (closed Sunday evening and Monday in low season). **Rooms** 10 with telephone, bath or shower and WC. **Price** single 210F, double 230-300F. **Meals** breakfast 35F, served 0800-1000; half board 230F (per pers., 3 days min.) **Credit cards** Amex, Eurocard, Visa. **Pets** dogs allowed. **Facilities** parking. **Nearby** Trévoux, bird reserve at Villard-les-Dombes, Montluel, Pérouges, 18-hole Le Clou golf course at Villard-les-Dombes. **Restaurant** service 1215-1400, 1930-2100; menus 110-233F, also à la carte; specialities: grenouilles fraîches, volaille de Bresse.

Not far north of Lyon, this roadside (yet quiet) inn is an old farmhouse which has been restored but still retains its rustic character – not a fake, kitsch version of rustic, as is too often the case, but the genuine article with all its charm. A flowery courtyard where meals can be enjoyed in the shade of large white parasols brings to mind Italian pavement cafés. The bedrooms are comfortable and their pleasant decor is in keeping with the rural character of the building. This hotel provides a good stopping place just before Lyon and an ideal base for exploring the picturesque Dombe area dotted with lakes. Chef Marc Sauvage trained with Fernand Point and prepares regional specialities using fresh local produce.

How to get there (Map 26): 30km north of Lyon via A6, Villefranche exit, then D904 towards Bourg-en-Bresse, then Villard-les-Dombes.

Auberge des Chasseurs★★★

Naz–Dessus – 01170 Echenevex (Ain)
Tel. 50.41.54.07 – Fax 50.41.90.61
M. Lamy

Open 10 March – 15 Dec. **Rooms** 15 with telephone, bath or shower, WC and TV.
Price single 350-500F, double 400-600F. **Meals** breakfast 50F, served 0800-1000;
half board 480F (per pers.) **Credit cards** accepted. **Pets** dogs allowed (+40F).
Facilities swimming pool, tennis, parking. **Nearby** le Pailly and col de la Faucille,
château de Fernet-Voltaire, 9-hole Maison Blanche golf course at Echenevex.
Restaurant service 1200-1330, 1900-2130; menus 175-280F, also à la carte;
specialities: filet de daurade grillée au fenouil, grenouilles sautées fines herbes.

Standing on the slopes of the Jura, amidst fields and woods, and
yet conveniently close to Geneva (just 15 minutes away), the
Auberge des Chasseurs is an old farmhouse which has been very
well restored. In the entrance hall, a very pretty wooden staircase
leads up to the bedrooms, which are fully equipped and individually
decorated. A pleasant and cosy lounge for reading or watching
television is also on the first floor. The hotel has a lovely garden
and a shady terrace from which Mont Blanc can be seen on a clear
day. In the restaurant the service is very attentive and your hosts
will gladly help you choose from the delicious fish specialities on
the menu (among them an excellent *turbot à la rhubarbe*). The young
owner, who has a passion for photography (hence the beautiful
Cartier-Bresson views in the hotel), is a friendly and helpful host.

How to get there *(Map 20): 17km north west of Genève via D984 towards
St-Genis-Pouilly, then D978c towards Echenevex; at Chevry head for Naz-
Dessus.*

Hostellerie du Vieux Pérouges★★★★

Place du Tilleul – 01800 Pérouges (Ain)
Tel. 74.61.00.88 – Fax 74.34.77.90 – M. Thibaut

Open all year except Jan (closed Wednesday and Thursday lunchtime in low season).
Rooms 28 with telephone, bath, shower, WC (4 with TV). **Price** single 390-700F,
double 450-900F, suite 980F. **Meals** breakfast 60F, served 0800-1200. **Credit cards**
MasterCard, Eurocard, Visa. **Pets** dogs allowed. **Facilities** parking. **Nearby** Trévoux,
bird reserve at Villard-les-Dombes, Montluel, 18-hole Le Clou golf course at Villard-
les-Dombes. **Restaurant** service 1200-1400, 1900-2100; menus 170-390F, also à
la carte; specialities: filet de carpe farci à l'ancienne, volaille de Bresse, panaché
pérougien, galette de l'hostellerie.

The hotel lies among the narrow streets of the medieval part of
the town. The bedrooms in the 'Pavilion of the three seasons'
are charming; not unexpectedly, 'Spring' is bright and fresh. The
annexe has a lot of old-fashioned charm. The bedrooms in it
overlook the garden and the countryside. Room 2 has warm
colours and antique furniture, and although it faces the street it is
very attractive. The bedrooms in the main building are more
expensive and take you back through time: stone stairways, stained-
glass windows and four-poster beds combine to create a medieval
effect – whether seigneurial, as in the 'Noble' bedroom, or more
modest, as in the 'Remparts' bedroom, each one takes you back
to the Pérouges of the Middle Ages. The same atmosphere is found
in the restaurant, where local specialities are served by staff in
traditional dress. The antique furniture is exceptional.

How to get there *(Map 26): 35km north east of Lyon via A42, Pérouges
exit.*

532

Hôtel de la Santoline

07460 Beaulieu (Ardèche)
Tel. 75.39.01.91 – Fax 75.39.38.79 – M. and Mme Espenel

Open March – 15 Nov. **Rooms** 6 with telephone, bath, WC, minibar (some with air-conditioning). **Price** double 270-360F, suite 490F. **Meals** breakfast 35F, served 0800-1000; half board 290-410F, full board 375-495F, (per pers., 3 days min.) **Credit cards** Diners, Visa. **Pets** dogs allowed (+30F). **Facilities** swimming pool, parking. **Nearby** La Cocalière cave, bois de Païolive, corniche du Vivarais from Les Vans to la Bastide-Puylaurent, 6-hole Rouvet golf course. **Restaurant** service 1930-2130 (closed lunchtime Nov-April); menus 135-240F, also à la carte; specialities: blinis au saumon et aux épinards, assiette d'agneau, pieds et paquets.

Standing right in the middle of Provençal Ardèche, la Santoline is a converted stone hunting lodge. It is a haven of peace and commands views as far as the Cévennes. A fine vaulted cellar has been turned into a dining-room, and the simple decor of the bedrooms, which all have pretty bathrooms, is perfectly in tune with the unadorned style of the building. Our favourites are Room 5 and especially Room 4 at the top of the house, under the eaves; both have a marvellous outlook and are equipped with air conditioning. The swimming pool is much appreciated in summer, as is the pleasant flowery terrace where breakfast and dinner can be served. Pierre and Marie-Danièle Espenel, who did all the restoration work themselves, are friendly hosts, and prices are very reasonable considering the quality of this small hotel.

How to get there *(Map 32): 84km north of Nîmes via N106 to Alès, then D904 and D104 to La Croisée de Jalès, then D225.*

Château d'Urbilhac***

07270 Lamastre (Ardèche)
Tel. 75.06.42.11 – Fax 75.06.52.75
M. and Mme Xompero

Open 1 May – 5 Oct. **Rooms** 13 with telephone, bath or shower and WC. **Price** single 450F, double 500-650F. **Meals** breakfast 65F, served 0800-1100; half board 500-575F (per pers.) **Credit cards** accepted. **Pets** dogs allowed (+35F). **Facilities** heated swimming pool, tennis, parking. **Nearby** Tournon, Vivarais steam train between Tournon and Lamastre, 9-hole golf course at Chambon-sur-Lignon. **Restaurant** service 1230 and 1930 (closed lunchtime except weekends); menu 200-280F; specialities: soupe de moules ananou, papillote de truite farcie au foie gras, griottes rôties au sucre roux.

The Château d'Urbilhac, built in the last century in Renaissance style, over the cellars of a 16th–century fortified house, is set in 60 hectares of parkland. A weekend here is like a dream of 19th-century living, without a false note, for the Château could be a museum of the furniture of that age. The emphasis here is on character and authenticity and a vivid period atmosphere prevails throughout. Whether in the bedrooms, the sitting rooms or dining-room, there are velvet and damask perfectly in harmony with the tapestries. Engravings, paintings, mirrors, chandeliers, even the elegant china, take one a century back in time – but without sacrificing any modern comforts. A peaceful setting and a warm welcome are other noteworthy features of the *vie de Château* awaiting you in this hotel at reasonable prices.

How to get there (Map 26): 36km west of Valence via D533.

Grangeon

07800 Saint-Cierge-la-Serre (Ardèche)
Tel. 75.65.73.86 - Mme Valette

Open 1 April – All Saints. **Rooms** 7 of which 4 with bath, 2 with shower, 2 with WC.
Price double 270-350F. **Meals** breakfast 35F, served 0800-0900; half board 270F
(per person, 2 days min.) **Credit cards** not accepted. **Pets** small dogs allowed.
Facilities parking. **Nearby** Valence museum, villages and châteaux of the Ardèche,
18-hole Valence golf course at St-Didier-de-Charpey. **Restaurant** service 1930 on
reservation; menu 150F; specialities: agneau au miel, papillotes de lapin à l'aneth
et au pastis.

Grangeon is the ideal place for those seeking a peaceful retreat
and for nature lovers. It has an estate of 63 hectares of parkland
and forests, 4km away from the nearest village, and is reached by
a small road winding through hills and woods . The house itself
was built at the beginning of the 18th century and has seven
bedrooms. The decoration combines wood and stone to create a
warm country atmosphere. All kinds of vegetables grow in Mme
Valette's lovely terraced garden, and as she bakes her own bread
and keeps sheep she is almost self-sufficient. Set in the heart of the
Ardèche region and yet only 15km from the motorway, Grangeon
provides an opportunity to bury yourself in the countryside.

How to get there *(Map 26): 35km south of Valence via A7, Loriol exit,*
then N104 towards Privas; at Les Fonts-du-Pouzin D265 towards Saint-
Cierge-la-Serre (follow signs).

Manoir de la Roseraie★★★

26230 Grignan (Drôme)
Tel. 75.46.58.15 – Fax 75.46.91.55
M. and Mme Alberts

Open all year except 6-31 Jan and 15-20 Nov (closed Monday in low season). **Rooms** 15 with telephone, bath or shower, WC and TV. **Price** single and double 600-1000F, suite 1500F. **Meals** breakfast 75F, served 0800-1030; half board 540-740F (per pers., 3 days min.) **Credit cards** accepted. **Pets** dogs accepted (+50F). **Facilities** swimming pool, tennis, sauna, parking. **Nearby** château and museum of Mme de Sévigné at Grignan, Poët-Laval, Dieulefit, 9-hole Valaurie golf course. **Restaurant** service 1200-1330, 2000-2115; menus 200-240F; specialities: filet de veau sous croûte thym, filet de sole à la graine de moutarde, foie gras maison.

In this fine private mansion built in 1850 by the mayor of Grignan, Michèle Alberts and her husband have tastefully refurbished and decorated the bedrooms and the suite. Those on the ground and first floors are very big, with high ceilings, and are bright and comfortable, while the ones on the second floor have more cosy dimensions. They have colourful and sometimes unusual bathrooms (the 'Baccara' room, for instance, has a circular bath). The elegant salmon pink dining room looks out on the extensive grounds which are another noteworthy feature of the Manoir. Limes, cedars and bougainvillea are among a wide range of trees and plants (including 350 rose bushes). The swimming pool does not spoil the design of the garden. Meals and the breakfast buffet are served on the large terrace in summer. Very friendly hosts.

How to get there *(Map 33): 90km north of Avignon via A7, Montélimar-Sud exit, then N7 and D133.*

Hôtel Bellier★★

Avenue de Provence
26420 La Chapelle-en-Vercors (Drôme)
Tel. 75.48.20.03 – Fax 75.48.25.31 – Mme Bellier

Open 18 June – 25 Sept. **Rooms** 12 with telephone, bath or shower, WC and TV. **Price** single 150-180F, double 360-440F. **Meals** breakfast 40F, served 0800-1130; half board 330-370F, full board 450-490F (per pers., 3 days min.) **Credit cards** Amex, Eurocard, Diners, Visa. **Pets** dogs allowed. **Facilities** swimming pool, parking. **Nearby** Pont-en-Royans, route des Petits et Grands Goulets, la Luire cave, 9-hole golf course at Corrençon-en-Vercors. **Restaurant** service 1230-1345, 1930-2115; menus 90-210F, also à la carte; specialities: truite Bellier, poulet aux écrevisses, pintadeau au genièvre, ballottine de caneton aux pistaches et foie gras.

This hotel is built in chalet style and stands in a raised position on the edge of the village. Its terrace and flower-filled garden have a lovely view of the fields and mountains around. It is a mountain hotel and the interior is Alpine in design. The bedrooms are quiet and comfortable. In the restaurant, the menu is both refined and varied, and meals can be served outside. There is a swimming pool. You will get a friendly welcome.

How to get there *(Map 26): 63km east of Valence. 62km south west of Grenoble via D531 to Villard-de-Lans, then D103.*

Domaine du Colombier***
Route de Donzère
Malataverne – 26780 Montélimar (Drôme)
Tel. 75.90.86.86 – Fax 75.90.79.40 – M. and Mme Barette

Open all year. **Rooms** 20 and 5 suites with telephone, bath, WC and TV. **Price** single 380-580F, double 450-860F, suite 860-1200F. **Meals** breakfast 65F, served 0730-1100. **Credit cards** accepted. **Pets** dogs allowed (+45F). **Facilities** swimming pool, bowling alley, bicycles, parking. **Nearby** Poët-Laval, Nyons, château and museum of Mme de Sévigné at Grignan, villages of the Drôme between Montélimar and Orange. **Restaurant** service 1215-1415, 1915-2130 (closed Monday lunchtime in low season); menus 180-220F, also à la carte; specialities: omelette aux truffes et foie gras, pot-au-feu de mer aux ravioles de Royan, noix de ris de veau au champagne.

Formerly a 14th-century abbey, the Domaine du Colombier maintains its tradition of hospitality to travellers to this day, as it is now a pleasant hotel conveniently located on the road south. Although only minutes off the motorway it seems to be in the middle of the countryside. When you walk through the door be prepared to find a lot of furniture and fabrics piled up in the entrance hall, for it is also a shop. The bedrooms are bright, colourful and comfortably fitted. Three of them even have a small mezzanine. In the garden, the swimming pool surrounded by loungers is a place to relax. The lavender-blue furniture in the dining-room is Provençal in style, and dinner – or an evening drink – can also be served in the patio.

How to get there (Map 33): 9km south of Montélimar via N7 and D144a (2km after Malataverne).

Le Capitelle★★

Rue du Rempart
26270 Mirmande (Drôme)
Tel. 75.63.02.72 - Fax 75.63.02.50 - Mme Boucher

Open 15 Jan – 15 Nov (closed Tuesday and Wednesday lunchtime). **Rooms** 10 with telephone, bath or shower (7 with WC). **Price** double 230-430F. **Meals** breakfast 42F, served 0730-0930; half board 307-407F. **Credit cards** Diners, Visa. **Pets** dogs allowed (+33F). **Facilities** garage (+50F). **Nearby** Mirmande church, Pöet-Laval, Nyons, 18-hole Valdaine golf course. **Restaurant** service 1200-1400, 1900-2100; menu 150-210F, also à la carte; specialities: brouillade aux truffes du Tricastin, demi pigeon farci au foie gras de canard, tulipe de fruits rouges, nougat glacé.

La Capitelle is a tall Renaissance building with mullioned windows. The lounge and dining-room have vaulted ceilings and handsome stone fireplaces. Items of period furniture combine well with more simple contemporary fittings to create an elegant and yet warm atmosphere. A sober and sure taste is also in evidence in the bedrooms, which are all different. The hotel stands in the centre of Mirmande, a listed village, and has no garden, but its leafy setting provides peace and quiet. In the restaurant, a friendly and attentive chef prepares excellent gourmet cuisine and regional specialities.

How to get there *(Map 26): 17km north of Montélimar via N7, then D57 (it's at the entrance to Mirmande).*

Auberge du Vieux Village★★

Route de Gap
Aubres – 26110 Nyons (Drôme)
Tel. 75.26.12.89 – Fax 75.26.38.10 – Mme Colombe

Open all year. **Rooms** 23 with telephone, bath, shower, WC, TV (13 with minibar).
Price single and double 300-780F, suite 1100F. **Meals** breakfast 52F, served 0800-
1030; half board 360-657F, full board 440-737F. **Credit cards** Visa, Amex, Diners.
Pets dogs allowed. **Facilities** heated swimming pool, health centre, sauna and
sunbed (60F), parking. **Nearby** château and museum of Mme de Sévigné at Grignan,
Drôme villages (La Garde-Adhémar, Clansayes, Saint-Paul-Trois-Châteaux, Saint-
Restitut, Suze-la-Rousse, Montségur-sur-Lauzon, Saint-Turquoit, Visan).
Restaurant service 1200-1400, 1930-2100 (closed Wednesday lunchtime in low
season); menus 80-178F, also à la carte; specialities: agneau au miel, poulet fermier
à l'estragon, selle d'agneau aux champignons, gratins de légumes.

This hotel is built on a high point where a castle once stood, so
it has exceptional views over the village and the whole valley.
The Auberge has a terrace with loungers where the panorama can
be enjoyed to the full. The bedrooms are subdued in style,
comfortable and quiet. They are all equipped with colour television
and have wonderful views. The dining-room (where smoking is
forbidden) has period furniture (including a fine clock) and large
picture windows.

*How to get there (Map 33): 55km south east of Montélimar via A7,
Montélimar-Sud exit, then D133, D141, D538 and D94 towards Gap.
It's 7km from Nyons.*

Auberge des 4 Saisons***

Place de l'Eglise
26130 Saint-Restitut (Drôme)
Tel. 75.04.71.88 – Fax 75.04.70.88 – M. Fritsch

Open all year except Jan. **Rooms** 10 with telephone, bath or shower, WC (5 with TV). **Price** single 270-340F, double 350-450F. **Meals** breakfast 40-45F, served 0800-1000; half board 300-360F (per pers., 7 days min.) **Credit card** Amex, Diners, MasterCard, Visa. **Pets** dogs allowed. **Nearby** château and museum of Mme de Sévigné at Grignan, Drôme villages (La Garde-Adhémar, Clansayes, Saint-Paul-Trois-Châteaux, Saint-Restitut, Suze-la-Rousse, Montségur-sur-Lauzon, Saint Turquoit, Visan. **Restaurant** 'Restaurant des 36 Soupières', service 1230-1330, 1930-2130 (closed Saturday lunchtime); à la carte; specialities: feuilleté d'escargots à la sauce roquefort, carré d'agneau aux herbes.

Several ancient stone houses covered in creeper have been converted to accommodate the Auberge des 4 Saisons and, next to it, the very good Restaurant des 36 Soupières. Set in the medieval part of the village, they give on to the small square where the church stands. The bedrooms are all comfortable and quiet; they are furnished with antiques and everything is well matched and neat. Some are like small apartments, and in one of them a closet has been made into a child's bedroom.

How to get there (Map 33): 9km north of Bollène via D160 (it's in the village).

Château de Passières★★

38930 Chichilianne (Isère)
Tel. 76.34.45.48 – Fax 76.34.46.25
M. Perli

Open 1 Feb. – 1 Nov (closed Sunday evening and Monday in low season). **Rooms** 23 with telephone, bath, shower (20 with WC). **Price** single 280F, double 280-420F. **Meals** breakfast 35F, served 0730-0930; half board 310F, full board on request (per pers., 3 days min.) **Credit cards** Visa. **Pets** dogs allowed. **Facilities** swimming pool, tennis, sauna, parking. **Nearby** Mont Aiguille, Vercors plateau. **Restaurant** service 1215-1330, 1915-2100 (closed Monday in low season and from Nov to Jan); menus 95-200F, also à la carte; specialities: fricassée de cèpes et escargots, escalope de saumon du miel de pissenlit.

The hotel occupies a truly exceptional position at the foot of the Mont Aiguille, an extraordinary rock which dominates the entire area. This 15th-century castle has been skilfully restored by Yvon Perli and has 23 bedrooms. Three of them are magnificent, with superb panelling, and surround you with all the trappings of the lord of the manor. The other ones offer every modern comfort at reasonable prices. The dining-room is spacious and sunny, and the menu features traditional but inventive cuisine which can also be enjoyed on the terrace. The lounge has a romantic air, with cosy settees and a wealth of curios as well as a collection of portraits on the walls. Outside, there is a pleasant swimming pool with lovely scenery all round. The Château de Passières is definitely the place to stay in this little-known region.

How to get there *(Map 26): 50km south of Grenoble via N75 towards Sisteron until Clelles, then D7 and D7b.*

Domaine de Clairefontaine**

38121 Chonas-L'Amballan (Isère)
Tel. 74.58.81.52 – Fax 74.58.80.93
Mme Girardon

Open 1 Feb – 20 Dec. **Rooms** 14 and 2 apartments with telephone (13 with bath and WC), TV on request. **Price** single and double 260-350F, suite 360-700F. **Meals** breakfast 40F, served 0730-0900. **Credit cards** Eurocard, MasterCard, Visa. **Pets** dogs allowed. **Facilities** tennis, parking. **Nearby** St-Pierre church and lapidary museum at Vienne, wine tasting. **Restaurant** service 1200-1400, 1900-2130 (closed Sunday evening and Monday lunchtime); menus 120-350F, also à la carte; specialities: l'œuf du domaine brouillé au caviar, profiterolles de truite à la fondue de légumes, foie gras chaud.

Clairefontaine is a family business run by Mme Girardon and her two sons, who will soon be taking over altogether and are responsible for the excellent food served there. One of them is in charge of the morning croissants, pastries, and other desserts, while the other supervises everything else in the kitchen. Enjoyment of the food is enhanced by the beautiful view from the dining room across the grounds, where peacocks parade on the lawns beneath age-old trees. The bedrooms differ greatly in style and furnishings and will appeal to all tastes and pockets. In the main building the high-ceilinged rooms with creaking floors and period furniture have a distinctive country house atmosphere (room 3 is probably the finest, but they all have charm), and those in the annexe have every modern comfort.

How to get there *(Map 26): 12km south of Vienne via A7, Vienne exit, then N7 or N86 and D7 towards Le Péage-en-Roussillon.*

Chalet Mounier★★

38860 Les Deux-Alpes (Isère)
Tel. 76.80.56.90 - Fax 76.79.65.51 - M. and Mme Mounier

Open 27 June – 10 Sept and 15 Dec – 3 May. **Rooms** 48 with telephone, bath or shower, TV (44 with WC). **Price** single 250-450F, double 280-690F. **Meals** breakfast incl., served 0730-0930; half board 275-490F, full board 345-560F (per pers., 3 days min.) **Credit cards** Visa. **Pets** dogs allowed. **Facilities** heated swimming pool, sauna, health centre, garage (+35F). **Nearby** ski lifts (100m), village of Venosc, Bézardé valley. **Restaurant** service 1230-1400, 1930-2100; menus 115-250F, also à la carte.

This chalet was originally a mountain refuge and farm but since 1933 has grown into a large and modern hotel, though without losing its character. The welcoming entrance hall immediately establishes the atmosphere of the hotel. You will be charmed by the decor of the lounge and the restaurant, whose large windows open onto the garden and the swimming pool and onto the snow-clad slopes in winter. The bedrooms are all comfortable and all have balconies with unrestricted views of the mountains. Robert Mounier the chef prides himself on his 'gourmand' cuisine, which is excellent and perfectly served. There is also a newly opened small restaurant which goes in for haute cuisine menus. Although the hotel is on one of the main streets of the village, it is reasonably quiet and the atmosphere is very friendly.

How to get there (Map 27): 74km south east of Grenoble via N85 to Vizille, then N91 to Chambon through Bourg-d'Oisans, then D213 to Les Deux-Alpes.

Château de la Commanderie***

17, avenue d'Echirolles
Eybens- 38320 Grenoble (Isère)
Tel. 76.25.34.58 - Fax 76.24.07.31 - M. de Beaumont

Open all year. **Rooms** 25 with telephone, bath or shower, WC, TV and minibar. **Price** single 365-580F, double 400-580F. **Meals** breakfast 50F, served 0700-1000; half board 370-490F (per pers., 3 days min.) **Credit cards** Amex, Visa, Diners. **Pets** dogs allowed (+50F). **Facilities** swimming pool, parking. **Nearby** Grenoble museum, massifs of Vercors, Chartreuse and Oisans, 18-hole Bresson-Eybens golf course. **Restaurant** service 1200-1400, 1930-2145 (closed Saturday and Sunday lunchtime); menu 170F, also à la carte.

Formerly a hospice of the knights of Malta, the Château de la Commanderie is ideally located just 5km from the centre of Grenoble and half an hour from the ski slopes. A large, lovely walled garden planted with centuries-old trees gives it an air of space and tranquillity rare in a town hotel. The bedrooms combine modern comforts and facilities with period furniture, old engravings and carefully chosen fabrics. Breakfast is a substantial affair served on the terrace in summer, or in vast 17th-century rooms decorated with Aubusson tapestries and family portraits. Good food is served in the restaurant, and a friendly, family atmosphere prevails.

How to get there (Map 26): 4km south east of Grenoble via the bypass (south). 500m from Eybens.

Le Lièvre Amoureux★★★

38840 Saint-Lattier (Isère)
Tel. 76.64.50.67 – Fax 76.64.31.21
M. Poreda

Open 15 Feb – 15 Dec (closed Sunday evening and Monday in low season). **Rooms** 14 with telephone, of which 12 with bath, 5 with TV. **Price** double 320-420F, suite 380F. **Meals** breakfast 45F, served 0730-1030. **Credit cards** Amex, Visa, Diners. **Pets** dogs allowed (+40F). **Facilities** swimming pool, parking. **Nearby** Saint-Bernard college at Romans, palais du facteur Cheval, Saint-Antoine abbey. **Restaurant** menus 165-195F, also à la carte; specialities: game, hare on the spit.

This comfortable and welcoming small hotel is in the countryside facing the foothills of the Vercors, to the east of Valence. The bedrooms are in different buildings; those by the swimming pool are large enough to allow a sitting area in each of them. Though modern, they are full of charm and their large windows open onto a private terrace. In the distance, a plantation of walnut trees reminds one of the local speciality. The other bedrooms, in a small turn-of-the-century house, are also faultless and have a lovely old fashioned atmosphere. One slight drawback is that they are within earshot of the railway line, so visitors who like total silence should opt for the modern bedrooms by the pool.

How to get there *(Map 26): 15km north of Romans via N92.*

Hostellerie du Bois Prieur

Domaine de Granjean-Galafray
42360 Cottance (Loire)
Tel. 77.28.06.69 - Fax 77.28.00.55 - M. and Mme Bonnard

Open 1 April – 1 Nov. **Rooms** 4 and 1 suite with telephone, bath, shower, WC and TV. **Price** double 350-450F, suite 590F. **Meals** breakfast 35F, served 0800-1000; half board 345-465F. **Credit cards** Eurocard, MasterCard, Visa. **Pets** dogs allowed (+50F). **Facilities** swimming pool, tennis, riding, mountain bikes, parking. **Nearby** Gallo-Roman museum at Feurs, Pommiers, Montbrison college, château de la Bastie-d'Urfé, 18-hole Forez golf course at Montrond-les-Bains. **Restaurant** service at 2000; traditional cooking, home made pâtisseries.

Set among the hills of the Charolais area, this old farmhouse has recently been restored to the highest standards. The bedrooms have obviously been decorated with guests' comfort in mind. They have wood panelling, painted furniture, colourful fabrics and continental quilts: in other words they are irresistibly cosy and charming. The largest room is wonderful, particularly in winter. In an adjacent building, a fine central fireplace separates the dining-room from a small lounge with a piano. The whole effect is warm and intimate, with antique furniture and carpets, and guests feel as if they are being welcomed into someone's home, rather than staying in a hotel. The hotel serves table d'hôte meals (for guests only) and the home-cooked food is excellent: in summer, meals are served outside. There are many shady corners in the garden where one can sit and relax. The welcome is warm and friendly.

How to get there *(Map 25): 53km north of St-Etienne via A72, Feurs exit, then N89 to Feurs, then D107.*

Hôtel des Artistes★★★

8, rue Gaspard-André
69002 Lyon (Rhône)
Tel. 78.42.04.88 – Fax 78.42.93.76 – Mme Durand

Open all year. **Rooms** 45 with telephone, bath or shower, WC, TV (36 with minibar). **Price** single 310-380F, double 340-410F. **Meals** breakfast 45F, served 0700-1130. No restaurant. **Credit cards** Amex, Diners, Visa. **Pets** dogs allowed (+30F). **Nearby** Hôtel de Ville, art museum at Lyon, Yzeron, Mont d'Or lyonnais, Trévoux, Pérouges, 18-hole Lyon Verger golf course, 9-hole Lyon Chassieux golf course.

The Hôtel des Artistes (a favourite haunt of artists, as its name and many autographs indicate) is in that old quarter of Lyon which lies between the embankments of the Rhône and Saône, close to the Place Bellecour and the Célestins theatre. The bedrooms are decorated with very simple, modern furniture, and the soft colours of the decor differ from one to another. They are all comfortably equipped, with television and good soundproofing, and some have air conditioning. Breakfast is very good, and there is a friendly atmosphere. Special weekend rates are sometimes available.

How to get there *(Map 26): in the town centre near Place des Célestins.*

La Sivolière★★★

Quartier des Chenus
73120 Courchevel (Savoie)
Tel. 70.08.08.33 - Fax 79.08.15.73 - Mme Cattelin

Open 1 Dec – 1 May. **Rooms** 30 with telephone, bath, WC and TV. **Price** double 725-1670F. **Meals** breakfast 75F, served at any time. **Credit cards** Visa. **Pets** dogs not allowed. **Facilities** sauna, jacuzzi. **Nearby** ski-ing, cable car to la Saulire, 9-hole Courchevel golf course, 18-hole Méribel golf course. **Restaurant** service 1200-1430, 1900-2300; menus 120-250F; specialities: Savoyard dishes, côte de bœuf à la cheminée.

Lying sheltered by trees at the foot of the ski pistes, this is Courchevel's 'hôtel de charme'. Although quiet and tranquil it is within walking distance of the life of the village centre. The hotel's friendly atmosphere reflects the personality of Mme Cattelin, who looks after her guests personally and has spent twenty years creating what some would call a little paradise. Everything in the chalet is in good taste: the decoration, the food, the welcome. Its success is due to the many little touches such as pot pourris, fresh flowers and pretty tablecloths, the delicious plats du jour and the tasty home-made tarts. The same care and attention to detail is found in the ski room and living rooms. This is the kind of place that visitors tend to keep secret in order to prevent popularity spoiling the spirit of the place.

How to get there *(Map 27): 50km south east of Albertville via N90 to Moûtiers, then D915 and D91.*

La Tour de Pacoret★★

Montailleur
73460 Grésy-sur-Isère (Savoie)
Tel. 79.37.91.59 - Fax 79.37.93.84 - M. Chardonnet

Open mid April – 1 Nov. **Rooms** 10 with telephone, bath or shower, WC and TV. **Price** single 275F, double 410F. **Meals** breakfast 40F, served 0800-1000; half board 295-350F, full board 360-410F (per pers., 3 days min.) **Credit cards** Visa. **Pets** small dogs allowed (+30F). **Facilities** parking. **Nearby** Conflans, fort du Mont, château de Miolans, 27-hole Giez-Faverges golf course. **Restaurant** service 1200-1330, 1930-2100; menus 100-190F, also à la carte; specialities: délice de Savoie, home-smoked salmon.

This beautiful 14th-century watchtower, standing in the middle of the countryside, at the top of a hill and at the foot of the Alps, has been transformed into an intimate and elegant hotel. A cheerful lounge devoted to reading and music, a dining-room with chalet-style panelling, and carefully chosen watercolours and drawings make a harmonious ensemble. The bedrooms are individually decorated, with well-chosen furnishings and fully-equipped bathrooms. The terrace gardens command splendid views of the snow-capped Alps and of the Isère valley down below, and meals and drinks can be served there in the shade of the wisteria or garden umbrellas. The kitchen garden supplies fresh produce for the table. You will be warmly welcomed by extremely friendly hosts.

How to get there *(Map 27): 19km south west of Albertville via N90 towards Montmélian until Pont-de-Grésy, then D222 and D201 towards Montailleur.*

Adray-Télébar★★

73550 Méribel-les-Allues (Savoie)
Tel. 79.08.60.26 – Fax 79.08.53.85
M. Bonnet

Open 20 Dec – 24 April. **Rooms** 26 with telephone, bath or shower (24 with WC).
Price single 380-450F, double 450-680F. **Meals** breakfast 60F, served 0800-1100;
half board 450-650F, full board 500-700F (per pers., 3 days min.) **Credit cards** not
accepted. **Pets** dogs allowed. **Nearby** ski-ing, mountain excursions. **Restaurant**
service 1200-1600, 2000-2200; menu 195F, also à la carte; specialities: escalope
à la crème, steak au poivre, tarte aux myrtilles.

This pretty chalet is only a few metres from the chairlift and the
ski pistes but is well situated above the valley and with
spectacular views of pinewoods and mountains. You reach it via
Meribel 1600, where you will have to leave you car; the hotel staff
meet you and take you to the chalet. The Adray is unrivalled at
Meribel, and at lunchtime the large sunny terrace is invaded by
skiers. The atmosphere is cheerful, the home cooking excellent.
The bedrooms are plain but welcoming, with rustic furniture
creating a comfortable atmosphere. You will find a friendly
welcome and good service here; just the place for making the most
of the mountains and ski amenities without paying the higher prices
of hotels in the village centre.

How to get there *(Map 27): 44km south of Albertville via N90 and D95,*
then D90.

Le Yéti★★

73553 Méribel-les-Allues (Savoie)
Tel. 79.00.51.15
M. and Mme Saint Ghilhem

Open 20 Dec – 20 April. **Rooms** 28 with telephone, bath, WC and TV. **Price** half board 750-950F (per pers.), 1500F in February. **Credit cards** not accepted. **Pets** dogs allowed. **Nearby** ski-ing, mountain excursions, swimming pool. **Restaurant** service 1200-1400, 1930-2100; menu 180F, also à la carte; specialities: rôtisserie, raclette, fondue.

This hotel, just opened, is situated on the eastern slopes of the resort and right by the centre of the ski pistes. It has superb views. Sophie and Frédéric Saint Guilhem, who are both mountain guides, have put a lot of enthusiasm into creating the interior ambience, and it shows: the walls are clad in rough wood, polished by hand, and the furnishings are attractive: kilims on the floor and comfortable armchairs by the bar and in front of the fireplace. The bedrooms are really comfortable, furnished in the style one expects in a mountain chalet. The panoramic restaurant has a south facing terrace and below it there is a small swimming pool for summer visitors. Frédéric is always at hand to advise you on mountain walks and climbs or to listen to your adventures on your return.

How to get there (Map 27): 44km south of Albertville via N90 and D95, then D90.

Les Châtaigniers

Rue Maurice-Franck
73110 La Rochette (Savoie)
Tel. 79.25.50.21 - Fax 79.25.79.97 - Mme Rey

Open all year (closed Wednesday in low season). **Rooms** 5 and 1 apartment with telephone, bath, WC (2 with TV). **Price** single and double 420-650F, suite 720-920F. **Meals** breakfast 55-90F, served 0730-1000; half board from 415F (2 pers.) **Credit cards** Amex, Visa, Diners. **Pets** dogs not allowed. **Facilities** swimming pool, parking. **Nearby** Saint-Pierre-de-Chartreuse, Charmant Som, belvédère des Sangles, la Grande Chartreuse convent, 9-hole Uriage golf course at Grenoble. **Restaurant** service 1200-1330, 1930-2200; menus 98-175F, also à la carte; specialities: foie gras mi-cuit au torchon, poissons.

O nce a family house, Les Châtaigniers is surrounded by valleys and mountains. Whether in the elegant lounge (which has a grand piano), in the beautiful dining-room, or in one of the large, comfortably-fitted bedrooms, you will feel absolutely at ease. The success of both the decor and the ambience is down to your two remarkable hosts. Philippe Roman is a chef and a poet and, having trained with several renowned chefs, now offers either traditional meals or poetic dinners; Madame Rey is a charming hostess with impeccable taste who speaks several languages. The atmosphere is lively and light-hearted, and you will certainly want to stay on.

How to get there (Map 27): 30km north of Grenoble via A41, Pontcharra exit, then D925; at La Rochette towards Arvillard and Val Pelouse.

La Savoyarde★★★
73150 Val-d'Isère (Savoie)
Tel. 79.06.01.55 - Fax 79.41.11.29
M. Marie

Open 1 Dec – 5 May. **Rooms** 46 with telephone, bath, WC, TV (3 with minibar). **Price** single 735F, double 875F, suite 1100F. **Meals** breakfast 55F; full board 825F (per pers., 3 days min.) **Credit cards** accepted. **Pets** dogs allowed (+80F). **Facilities** sauna, jacuzzi, solarium, massage, parking. **Nearby** ski-ing, Col de l'Iseran. **Restaurant** service 1930-2230; menu 195F, also à la carte.

This, the 'classic' hotel of Val d'Isère, is in the heart of the 'espace Killy' in the old village. It has been owned by the same family for four generations, each of which has added something to the character of the place as well as to its comfort. The bedrooms of the hotel, which has been recently refurbished, are plain but in good taste. Some of them have exposed beams which fit in well with the pine furniture and patchwork bedcovers, others have pleasant balconies with unrestricted views of the ski pistes and the Manchet valley. All of them have good bathrooms. The dining room is very convivial and lively at dinner, and the cooking is of high quality. A hotel cherished by a loyal clientele.

How to get there (Map 27): 85km south east of Albertville via N90 to Bourg-Saint-Maurice, then D902 to Val-d'Isère.

Hôtel La Savoyarde★★★

28, route des Moussoux
74400 Chamonix (Haute-Savoie)
Tel. 50-53.00.77 – Fax 50.55.86.82 – Mme Janin

Open 15 Dec – 13 Nov. **Rooms** 14 with telephone, bath, WC and TV. **Price** double 480-600F. **Meals** breakfast 46F, served from 0700. No restaurant. **Credit cards** Amex, Visa, MasterCard. **Pets** dogs allowed. **Facilities** garage (+40F), parking. **Nearby** ski-ing, mountain excursions, 18-hole Praz golf course (3km).

This hotel at the foot of the Brévent is surely one of the best situated hotels in Chamonix. It overlooks the village and has a superb view of the Aiguille du Midi. Refurbished in the last two years, this charming place is in a style which evokes both an English country cottage and an Alpine chalet. There are two adjoining buildings, both well cared for and, in summer, surrounded by flowers. A pleasing flight of steps lead into the attractive entrance hall which sets the tone of the house: painted ceilings, white walls and a cosy atmosphere. The owners have resisted the temptation to go in for a pseudo-rustic decor in search of an intimate and comfortable style. The bedrooms are light and airy and have furniture which has been specially designed for the hotel. All of them have balconies or terraces and only two of them are at the back of the hotel. Among our favourites are 5, which has a large balcony, and 14 with its exposed beams. One drawback: in the bedrooms near the stairs, early morning skiers can sometimes wake guests who are less enthusiastic early risers. A very valuable address in Chamonix.

How to get there *(Map 27): 67km north east of Albertville via N212 to Saint-Gervais, then N205. By A40, Le Fayet exit.*

Hôtel du Jeu de Paume★★★★

705, route du Château – Le Lavancher
74400 Chamonix (Haute-Savoie)
Tel. 50.54.03.76 – Fax 50.54.10.75 – Mmes Prache and Blanc

Open 15 Dec – 15 Nov. **Rooms** 24 with telephone, bath, shower, WC, TV and minibar. **Price** single 750-880F, double 950-1050F, suite 1200-1320F. **Meals** breakfast 70F, served 0730-1030; half board 640-725F (per pers., 5 days min.) **Credit cards** accepted. **Pets** dogs allowed (+50F). **Facilities** swimming pool, tennis, sauna, parking. **Nearby** ski-ing at Argentières (Les Grands Montets, 10km), and at Chamonix (7km), 18-hole Praz golf course (9km). **Restaurant** service 1200-1430, 1930-2130; menu 310F, also à la carte.

Elyane and Guy Prache, who own the elegant Hôtel du Jeu de Paume in the heart of the Ile Saint-Louis in Paris, have just opened this delightful chalet hotel at Lavancher, 7km from Chamonix, on the edge of a pine wood and overlooking the Argentière valley. The hotel is luxurious, refined and very comfortable; it's the chalet 're-invented', with wood playing a major role in the decor. The bedrooms all have every comfort, are furnished with good taste, and nearly all of them have balconies. There is the same comfortable cosiness in the bar and lounges. Throughout the hotel there are pieces of furniture, mirrors and paintings bought by the owners in moments of enthusiasm at antique shops. The cooking is good and traditional and you will receive a good welcome here. In winter the hotel car will take you to the departure points for the ski pistes.

How to get there *(Map 27): 67km north east of Albertville via N212. By A40, Le Fayet exit.*

Au Cœur des Prés★★★

74920 Combloux (Haute-Savoie)
Tel. 50.93.36.55 – Fax 50.58.69.14
M. Paget

Open 20 Dec – 15 April and 1 June – 25 Sept. **Rooms** 34 with telephone, bath, WC and TV. **Price** single 280-300F, double 380-420F. **Meals** breakfast 38F, served from 0730; half board 360-410F, full board 415F (per pers.) **Credit cards** Visa. **Pets** dogs allowed. **Facilities** tennis, sauna, jacuzzi, garage (25F), parking. **Nearby** ski lifts (1km) – Megève, Chamonix, 18-hole Mont d'Arbois golf course at Megève. **Restaurant** service 1230-1400, 1930-2030; menu 130-180F, also à la carte.

This hotel has the advantage not only of a superb view of Mont Blanc and the Aravis chain, but also of being surrounded by a large meadow which isolates it from neighbouring traffic and noise. The majority of the bedrooms looking out towards Mont Blanc have balconies and are comfortable, though their decor is a little impersonal. The ones in the third floor attics have more character. The lounge offers accommodating armchairs and a big fireplace, and the dining room is charming too: it has a tiled floor, exposed beams, pink tablecloths and a panoramic view. The hotel has been awarded prizes by the commune for its summer flower display and is ideal for those who like peace and tranquillity amid impressive scenery.

How to get there *(Map 27): 36km north east of Albertville via N212 to Combloux through Megève. By A40, Le Fayet exit.*

Les Roches Fleuries★★★

74700 Cordon (Haute-Savoie)
Tel. 50.58.06.71 – Fax 50.47.82.30
M. Picot

Open 20 Dec – 15 April, 1 May – 25 Sept. **Rooms** 28 with telephone, bath, WC and TV. **Price** double 500-600F, suite 700-900F. **Meals** breakfast 50F, served 0730-1000; half board 380-470F (per pers., 3 days min.) **Credit cards** Amex, Visa, Diners. **Pets** dogs allowed (+35F). **Facilities** heated swimming pool, health centre (50F), parking. **Nearby** ski lifts (700m) – Megève, Chamonix, 18-hole Mont d'Arbois golf course at Megève. **Restaurant** service 1230-1400, 1930-2130; menus 130-265F also à la carte; specialities: piccata de lapereau au beaufort, feuillantine de perches du lac aux épinards.

Cordon lies between Combloux and Sallanches on the threshold of Mont Blanc and is a delightful village all year round. In summer the chalets nestle among cherry and walnut trees, in winter there are sensational views of the Aiguilles de Chamonix and the Aravis mountains. The bedrooms are prettily furnished and most of them have terraces on which you can enjoy the view, the peace and the sun. Like the bedrooms, the lounge and dining room are furnished in a comfortable rustic style. In winter the blaze in the fireplace creates a warm and cosy ambience. The cooking is good, the welcome attentive and friendly.

How to get there *(Map 27): 43km north east of Albertville via N212 to Sallanches, then D113. By A40, Le Fayet exit.*

Marceau Hôtel★★★

115, chemin de la Chappelière
74210 Doussard (Haute-Savoie)
Tel. 50.44.30.11 - Fax 50.44.39.44 - M. and Mme Sallaz

Open 1 Feb – 1 Oct (closed Sunday evening and Wednesday in low season). **Rooms** 16 with telephone, bath or shower, WC (14 with TV). **Price** double 450F, suite 660F. **Meals** breakfast 50F, served 0730-1000; half board 450-735F, full board 480-810F (per pers., 3 days min.) **Credit cards** Amex, Diners, Eurocard, Visa. **Pets** dogs allowed (+50F). **Facilities** tennis, parking. **Nearby** lake of Annecy, le Semnoz by the ridgeway, gorges of Le Fier, 18-hole Annecy golf course at Talloires. **Restaurant** service 1230-1400, 1930-2100; menus 130-330F, also à la carte; specialities: longe de veau Marceau, féra du lac au chignin, blanquette de homard.

In one of the most touristic areas of France a peaceful haven well off the beaten track is a most welcome thing. Set in the middle of the countryside, overlooking lake and valley, this elegantly comfortable hotel is precisely that... and much more. In the dining-room, subtle shades of pink blend perfectly with the colours of the wood, and large windows open on to beautiful surroundings. There is an attractive lounge for watching television or reading by the fireside. In summer, both view and sunshine can be enjoyed on a delightful terrace next to the kitchen garden. The bedrooms are tastefully decorated, with carefully chosen furniture. There are fresh flowers are everywhere. You will find a very friendly welcome.

How to get there *(Map 27): 20km south of Annecy via N508 towards Albertville.*

Chalet-Hôtel Crychar★★★

74260 Les Gets (Haute-Savoie)
Tel. 50.75.80.50 – Fax 50.79.83.12
Mme Bouchet

Open 15 Dec – 15 April, 20 June – 15 Sept. **Rooms** 12 with telephone, bath, WC and TV. **Price** double 360-525F, suite 630-750F. **Meals** breakfast 42.50F. No restaurant. **Credit cards** accepted. **Pets** dogs not allowed. **Facilities** sauna (60F), solarium, garage (+40F), parking. **Nearby** ski-ing, Séous, Morzine, Avoriaz.

In the middle of the pistes in winter (yet only 100 metres from the centre of the village) and surrounded by green alpine meadows in summer, this modern hotel feels like a traditional mountain chalet because it has a restricted number of rooms. The bedrooms are light, airy, well decorated and of a good standard, with balconies and bathrooms. The hotel is well provided with leisure amenities including table tennis, a swimming pool, an authentic Finnish sauna and various kinds of exercise equipment. The lack of a restaurant makes for peace and quiet in the hotel and there are plenty of eating places close by.

How to get there *(Map 27): 86km north east of Annecy via A41, then A40 Cluses exit, then D902 to Les Gets via Taninges.*

Chalet-Hôtel Peter Pan★

74310 Les Houches (Haute-Savoie)
Tel. 50.54.40.63 - M. and Mme Bochatay

Open 20 Dec – 30 April, 1 June – 30 Sept. **Rooms** 13 with bath or shower (2 with WC). **Price** double 180-255F. **Meals** breakfast 32F, served 0800-1000; half board 190-215F, full board 222-248F (per pers., 3 days min.) **Credit cards** not accepted. **Pets** dogs allowed. **Facilities** parking. **Nearby** ski lifts (1km), 18-hole Praz golf course at Chamonix (7km). **Restaurant** service 1230 and 1930; menus 85-125F, also à la carte; specialities: saumon frais à l'oseille, braserades, tarte tatin, nougat glacé.

Michel Bochatay and his wife have been in this beautiful converted 18th-century farm for seventeen years. It is on high ground near Houches and has a superb view of the valley of Chamonix. In this delightful place the owners have created an original and welcoming ambience, with high quality food at reasonable prices. The two chalets are entirely constructed of wood and are real pieces of history. Meals are served by candlelight on prettily set little wooden tables bright with posies of flowers. The bedrooms vary in size and style. Rooms 1 and 2 are spacious (2 is the only one with a bathroom) and Room 6 in the attic is more intimate and looks out on the valley. The rooms in the annexe are smaller and four of them only have a washbasin. Nevertheless, thanks to the tranquillity, the charming ambience and the warm welcome the Peter Pan is a great success.

How to get there *(Map 27): 59km north east of Albertville via N212, then N205. By A40, Le Fayet exit. 7km west of Chamonix.*

Hôtel de la Croix Fry★★

Manigod - 74230 Thônes (Haute-Savoie)
Tel. 50.44.90.16 - Fax 50.44.94.87
Mme Guelpa-Veyrat

Open 15 June – 15 Sept, 15 Dec – 15 April. **Rooms** 12 with telephone, bath, WC and minibar. **Price** double 600-1000F, suite 1000F. **Meals** breakfast 48F, served 0800-1000; half board 480-600, full board 530-650F (per pers., 3 days min.) **Credit cards** accepted. **Pets** dogs allowed (+25F). **Facilities** swimming pool, tennis, parking. **Nearby** Manigod valley, village of Chinaillon, gorges of Le Fier, Annecy, 18-hole Annecy golf course at Talloires. **Restaurant** service 1230-1330, 1930-2030; menus 160-300F, also à la carte; regional cooking.

This is the kind of hotel one would like to find more often in the French Alps to avoid having to go to five-star establishments. It is comfortable and cosy and its bedrooms – all named after mountain flowers – have had much care lavished on them over the years: beamed ceilings and old furniture create a snug chalet atmosphere. The ones facing the valley have breathtaking views and are very sunny. All have either a balcony, a terrace or a mezzanine to make up for the tiny bathrooms. The former stables, converted into a bar with seats covered in sheepskin, lead into the dining-room, which faces the massif de la Tournette. This is a good address in summer or winter, and you are strongly advised to book well in advance, for the hotel has a large and faithful following.

How to get there *(Map 27): 27km east of Annecy via D909 to Thônes, then D12 and D16 to Manigod.*

Le Coin du Feu***

Route de Rochebrune
74120 Megève (Haute-Savoie)
Tel. 50.21.04.94 – Fax 50.21.20.15 – M. and Mme Sibuet

Open 20 Dec – 5 April and 20 July - 31 Aug. **Rooms** 23 with telephone, bath, WC and TV. **Price** single 500-600F, double 450-620F. **Meals** breakfast 35F; half board 650-800F. **Credit cards** Visa, Amex. **Pets** dogs allowed. **Nearby** ski lifts (200m), 18-hole Mont d'Arbois golf course. **Restaurant** service 1930-2230; menu 250F, also à la carte; specialities: regional cooking and fish from the lake.

This hotel has long been known as the most appealing place to stay in Megève for those who like tradition. Its success lies in its handsome pine furniture, its oak panelling, the flowered fabrics and above all its welcoming fireside. Its restaurant, the Saint-Nicholas, attracts Megève regulars who come here for its simple but delicious home cooking or the traditional raclettes and fondues. The bedrooms are cheerful and pretty and you will get a very friendly welcome.

How to get there *(Map 27): 34km north east of Albertville via N212. By A40, Le Fayet exit.*

Le Fer à Cheval★★★
36, route du Crêt-d'Arbois
74120 Megève (Haute-Savoie)
Tel. 50.21.30.39 - Fax 50.93.07.60 - M. Sibuet

Open 20 Dec – Easter and 1 July – 10 Aug. **Rooms** 41 with telephone, bath, WC, TV (35 with minibar). **Price** double with half board 605-805F (per pers.) **Meals** breakfast 40F, served 0745-1130. **Credit cards** Visa, Amex. **Pets** dogs allowed (+45F). **Facilities** swimming pool, sauna, jacuzzi, health centre, parking. **Nearby** ski lifts (500m), 18-hole Mont d'Arbois golf course. **Restaurant** service 1930-2130; à la carte.

This is one of the most charming hotels in Megève. Everything about it is a success. The chalet has been very well refurbished and its beams and panelling create a warm and comfortable setting for the patinated and polished antique furniture and the variety of fabrics and objets d'art. We can't recommend any particular bedroom – they are all delightful and any variation in price is only due to size. In winter meals are served by the fireplace in the dining room, in summer by the swimming pool. Guests receive a warm welcome.

How to get there *(Map 27): 34km north east of Albertville via N212. By A40, Le Fayet exit.*

La Bergerie★★★

Rue de Téléphérique- 74110 Morzine (Haute-Savoie)
Tel. 50.79.13.69 - Telex 309 066F - Fax 50.75.95.71
Mme Marullaz

Open 19 Dec – 20 April. **Rooms** 27 rooms, studios or apartments with telephone, bath, WC, TV (21 with minibar). **Price** room 260-330F, studio 400-680F, apartment 580-900F. **Meals** breakfast 50F, served 0700-1100. No restaurant. **Credit cards** Visa, Eurocard, MasterCard. **Pets** dogs allowed. **Facilities** swimming pool, sauna, solarium, health centre, games room, parking, garage. **Nearby** ski lifts (50m) – Avoriaz, Evian, 9-hole Morzine golf course, 18-hole Royal Hôtel golf course, Evian.

This is the favourite hotel of the residents of Morzine, although it has changed in style. Now it has studios and apartments as well as individual bedrooms, all sharing the hotel's services. The Mourgues armchairs and the orange and yellow check fabrics on the Knoll-style chairs in the lounge make for a delightful 1970s style. The best bedrooms are those facing south which look out over the garden and swimming pool. There is no restaurant but light snacks are provided on request.

How to get there *(Map 27): 93km north east of Annecy via A41 and A40, Cluses exit, then D902.*

Chalet Rémy★

74170 Saint-Gervais (Haute-Savoie)
Tel. 50.93.11.85 – Mme Didier

Open all year. **Rooms** 19 with basin and 1 apartment with bathroom. **Price** double 200F, suite 750F (8 pers.) **Meals** breakfast 30F, served 0800-1000; half board and full board 260-320F (per pers., 3 days min.) **Credit cards** Eurocard, MasterCard, Visa. **Pets** dogs allowed. **Nearby** ski lift (300m), Mont-d'Arbois golf course at Megève (15km). **Restaurant** service 1200-1400, 1700-2100; menu 85F, also à la carte; family cooking.

This hotel is an old 18th-century farm which through the centuries has managed to keep all its old woodwork: panels, ceilings, mouldings, and the staircase leading to the superb gallery serving the bedrooms, all create a lovely harmony of dark red wood tones. The dining room is set out with small tables lit by candles, and the home cooking is of a high standard. The mistress of the hotel is an enthusiast of classical music, which accompanies meals. It is the simplicity of the bedrooms that is their charm, and though short of bathroom facilities they are absolute jewels of their type, with walls, floors and ceilings all of wood. The Chalet Remy has another advantage: set apart from Saint-Gervais and reached by a winding road, it is surrounded by pine woods and meadows and faces the impressive mass of Mont Blanc.

How to get there (Map 27): 50km north east of Albertville via N212 and D909 to Robinson and Le Bettex. By A40, Le Fayet exit.

Hôtel Beau Site★★★

74290 Talloires (Haute-Savoie)
Tel. 50.60.71.04 – Fax 50.60.79.22 – M. Conan

Open 14 May – 11 Oct. **Rooms** 29 with telephone, bath or shower, WC, TV (10 with minibar). **Price** single 280-300F, double 400-720F, suite 850-900F. **Meals** breakfast 50F, served 0730-1030; half board 380-560F, full board 420-600F (per pers., 2 days min.) **Credit cards** Amex, Diners, MasterCard, Eurocard, Visa. **Pets** dogs allowed. **Facilities** tennis (60F), private beach, parking. **Nearby** Ermitage St-Germain, château de Menthon-St-Bernard, Thorens and Montrottier, Annecy, 18-hole Annecy golf course at Talloires. **Restaurant** service 1230-1400, 1930-2115; menus 150-250F, also à la carte; specialities: fish from the lake.

With grounds reaching right down to the banks of the lake of Annecy, the Hôtel Beau Site reminds one of hotels on the Italian lakes. It is not, however, an old grand hotel but a family house converted into a hotel at the end of the 19th century, and has retained many of the features which make for gracious living: a vast and sunny dining-room–cum-verandah decorated with old plates; a delightfully cosy lounge with period furniture; and lawns well provided with deck chairs to relax in... The bedrooms have been completely refurbished (the ones in the annexe are just as nice as those in the main building), have a terrace and many look out on the lake. Some of them are decorated with antiques, others are more modern, and some have a mezzanine. The food is excellent. The hotel is specially noted for its warm and friendly welcome.

How to get there (Map 27): 13km from Annecy via A41, Annecy exit. At Annecy, take east bank of lake towards Thônes until Veyrier, then Talloires.

INDEX

A

B

C

574

NOTES

NOTES

1993-1994

GUIDE TO

B&Bs

OF CHARACTER AND CHARM

IN FRANCE

● 382 ADDRESSES ● WITH ROAD MAPS ●

RIVAGES